THE 50 GREATEST PLAYERS IN DETROIT TIGERS HISTORY

Robert W. Cohen

TAYLOR TRADE
Lanham • Boulder • New York • London

Published by Taylor Trade Publishing
An imprint of The Rowman & Littlefield Publishing Group, Inc.
4501 Forbes Boulevard, Suite 200, Lanham, Maryland 20706
www.rowman.com

Unit A, Whitacre Mews, 26-34 Stannary Street, London SE11 4AB

Distributed by NATIONAL BOOK NETWORK

British Library Cataloguing in Publication Information Available

Library of Congress Cataloging-in-Publication Data

Cohen, Robert W.
  The 50 greatest players in Detroit Tigers history / Robert W. Cohen. — 1st Edition.
    pages cm
  "Distributed by NATIONAL BOOK NETWORK"—T.p. verso.
  Includes bibliographical references and index.
  ISBN 978-1-63076-099-1 (paperback : alk. paper) — ISBN 978-1-63076-100-4 (e-book) 1. Detroit Tigers (Baseball team)—Biography. 2. Baseball players—Rating of—United States. I. Title. II. Title: The fifty greatest players in Detroit Tigers history.
  GV875.D6C64 2015
  796.357'640977434—dc23
                                                                            2015020112

∞™ The paper used in this publication meets the minimum requirements of American National Standard for Information Sciences—Permanence of Paper for Printed Library Materials, ANSI/NISO Z39.48-1992.

Printed in the United States of America

This book is dedicated to the members of the 1968 world champion Detroit Tigers, who emerged victorious in one of the most exciting World Series I witnessed as a youngster.

Contents

Acknowledgments

I would like to express my gratitude to the grandchildren of Leslie Jones, who, through the Trustees of the Boston Public Library, Print Department, supplied many of the photos included in this book.

I also wish to thank Jeffrey Marren of LegendaryAuctions.com, Richard Albersheim of Albersheimsstore.com, Kate of RMYauctions.com, Steve of CollectAuctions.com, Mearsonlineauctions.com, Mainlineautographs.com, Denny McLain, Keith Allison, Jerry Reuss, Charles Thurmond, T. Scott Brandon, James Hering, Jack Webster, and Adam Okurowski, each of whom generously contributed to the photographic content of this work.

Introduction

THE TIGER LEGACY

Originally founded in 1894 as a member of the Western League, the American League's minor league predecessor, the Detroit Tigers spent their first two seasons playing at Boulevard Park, situated on East Lafayette (then called Champlain Street), between Helen and East Grand Boulevard, near Belle Isle. In 1896, they moved into newly constructed Bennett Park, built by team owner George Vanderbeck at the corner of Michigan and Trumbull Avenues. The Tigers subsequently became one of the American League's eight charter franchises in 1901, when the junior circuit raised itself to major league status by raiding the more established National League of many of its best players.

Although various legends persist as to how the Tigers originally acquired their nickname, including one involving the orange stripes they wore on their black stockings, Richard Bak presented the most commonly accepted theory in his 1998 book, *A Place for Summer: A Narrative History of Tiger Stadium*. In his work, Bak explains that the moniker originated from the Detroit Light Guard military unit (also known as "The Tigers"), a group that played a significant role in certain Civil War battles, and in the 1898 Spanish-American War. Initially referred to in the news as both the "Wolverines" and the "Tigers," the Detroit franchise sought and received formal permission from the Light Guard to use its trademark when it entered the major leagues in 1901. It has continued to bear that nickname ever since.

The Tigers experienced little in the way of success over the course of their first six American League seasons, posting a winning record just twice, while also finishing as high as third in the standings on just two occasions. However, with the emergence of 20-year-old Ty Cobb as the game's greatest player in 1907, the Tigers compiled a record of 92–58 under new manager Hughie Jennings, capturing in the process the first of their three consecutive A.L. pennants. Unfortunately, they subsequently managed to post just a tie in Game One of the World Series against the Chicago Cubs, en route to losing the Fall Classic in five games. Detroit and Chicago once again represented their respective leagues in the World Series the following year, with the Cubs again needing only five games to dispose of their A.L. counterparts. Although the Tigers fared somewhat better against the Pirates in the 1909 Fall Classic, they once again came up short, eventually falling to Pittsburgh in seven games. Ty Cobb and fellow outfielder Sam Crawford paced the Tigers' offense during their three-year reign as A.L. champions, while "Wild" Bill Donovan, George Mullin, and Ed Killian anchored Detroit's pitching staff.

After failing to finish atop the A.L. standings in each of the next two seasons, the Tigers moved into Navin Field in 1912. Named after owner Frank Navin, who purchased the team from William Yawkey following the conclusion of the 1907 campaign, Navin Field was built on the same location as Bennett Park. Although plumbing fixture manufacturer Walter Briggs, Sr., who assumed ownership of the club after Navin passed away during the 1935 season, expanded the ballpark in 1938 and renamed it Briggs Stadium, the Tigers continued to play their home games on the same piece of land. In fact, even after broadcast media owners Fred Knorr and John Fetzger took over control of the franchise in 1956 and renamed the ballpark Tiger Stadium in 1961, the Tigers remained at the same locale. They continued to call Tiger Stadium home until Mike Ilitch, who acquired the club eight years earlier, opened Comerica Park in 2000.

Meanwhile, the Tigers remained competitive on the field throughout most of the second decade of the twentieth century, finishing second and third in the A.L. standings two times each, with their strongest showing during that period coming in 1915, when they posted 100 victories. Sam Crawford and Bobby Veach combined with the incomparable Ty Cobb during that time to give Detroit one of the greatest outfields in baseball history. Unfortunately for the Tigers, though, they had very little in the way of pitching in most of those years, preventing them from returning to the World Series. A similar trend developed during the 1920s, even after Cobb became the team's player/manager in 1921. Outfielder Harry Heilmann evolved into one of the game's great hitters, capturing four batting titles, including leading the league with a mark of .403 in 1923. But, with a pitching staff that typically allowed the opposition nearly as many runs as they scored, the Tigers failed to seriously contend for the A.L. pennant at any point during the decade.

Led by slugging first baseman Hank Greenberg, brilliant all-around second sacker Charlie Gehringer, and an improved pitching staff that included Tommy Bridges and Schoolboy Rowe, the Tigers once again rose to prominence during the 1930s, capturing back-to-back pennants in 1934 and 1935. After losing the 1934 World Series to the St. Louis Cardinals in seven games, the Tigers won their first world championship the following year, defeating the Chicago Cubs in the Fall Classic in six games. The Tigers finished second to the Yankees in two of the next four years, as New York reeled off an unprecedented four consecutive world championships. The Bengals finally earned a return trip to the World Series in 1940 by edging out the Indians and Yankees in a close three-team pennant race. However, they came up just a bit short in the Fall Classic, losing to the Cincinnati Reds in seven games.

The retirement of Gehringer and the loss of Greenberg to military service during World War II caused the Tigers to struggle somewhat the next few seasons. But, buoyed by the mid-season return of Greenberg and the extraordinary pitching of two-time A.L. MVP Hal Newhouser in 1945, they returned to the top of the league standings, after which they once again defeated the Cubs in the World Series, this time in seven games.

The Tigers continued to contend for the A.L. flag under managers Steve O'Neill and Red Rolfe from 1946 to 1950, finishing second in the league three times and posting a winning record in each of those five seasons. However, they subsequently entered into their next period of mediocrity, winning more games than they lost in only 3 of the next 10 seasons. Nevertheless, several standout performers graced the Detroit roster during that time, including Hall of Fame third baseman George Kell, 1959 A.L. batting champion Harvey Kuenn, pitchers Jim Bunning and Frank Lary, and Tiger legend Al Kaline.

The Tigers once again emerged as contenders during the 1960s, posting a winning record all but once from 1961 to 1967, including a 101-victory showing in the first of those campaigns. They captured their first pennant in 23 years in 1968, with A.L. MVP and Cy Young Award winner Denny McLain's 31 wins leading the way. The Tigers subsequently mounted a memorable comeback in the World Series, overcoming a three-games-to-one deficit to the St. Louis Cardinals by sweeping the last three contests, with Mickey Lolich earning World Series MVP honors by throwing three complete-game victories. Other outstanding performers on the Tiger clubs of that period included first baseman Norm Cash, outfielder Willie Horton, and catcher Bill Freehan.

Although the Tigers earned a postseason berth in 1972 by capturing the
A.L. East title, they failed to make it back to the World Series until 1984,
when they easily advanced to the playoffs by posting a team-record 104 victories during the regular season. After sweeping the Kansas City Royals in
three straight games in the American League Championship Series (ALCS),
they routed the overmatched San Diego Padres in the Fall Classic, disposing
of them in five games. Detroit's powerful world championship squad included sluggers Kirk Gibson and Lance Parrish, exceptional middle infielders Lou Whitaker and Alan Trammell, and standout pitchers Jack Morris
and Dan Petry. Somewhat surprisingly, the Tigers have yet to win another
world championship since their dominating 1984 performance. Although
they have since advanced to the ALCS five more times (1987, 2006, and
2011–2013), they have made it back to the World Series just twice, losing
to the St. Louis Cardinals in five games in 2006, and being swept by the
San Francisco Giants in four straight games in 2012. Yet, with outstanding
players such as Miguel Cabrera, Justin Verlander, Victor Martinez, David
Price, and Ian Kinsler currently manning their roster, it appears to be only
a matter of time before the Tigers once again hoist the World Series trophy.
Their next world championship will be their fifth. Meanwhile, the Tigers'
11 pennants give them the fourth-highest total in A.L. history, behind only
the New York Yankees, the Philadelphia/Oakland Athletics, and the Boston
Red Sox.

In addition to the level of success the Tigers have reached as a team over
the years, a significant number of players have attained notable individual
honors while playing in Detroit. The Tigers boast 12 MVP winners, placing
them third in the American League, behind only the Yankees and Athletics.
They also have featured five Cy Young Award winners, two Triple Crown
winners (Ty Cobb in 1909 and Miguel Cabrera in 2012), two pitching Triple Crown winners (Hal Newhouser in 1945 and Justin Verlander in 2011),
12 home run champions, and 26 batting champions—more than any other
major league team. Meanwhile, 16 members of the Baseball Hall of Fame
spent at least one full season playing for the Tigers, 9 of whom had most of
their finest seasons in Detroit.

FACTORS USED TO DETERMINE RANKINGS

It should come as no surprise that selecting the 50 greatest players ever to
perform for a team with the rich history of the Detroit Tigers presented
a difficult and daunting task. Even after I narrowed the field down to a
mere 50 men, I found myself faced with the challenge of ranking the elite

players that remained. Certainly, the names of Ty Cobb, Al Kaline, Hank Greenberg, Charlie Gehringer, Miguel Cabrera, and Justin Verlander would appear at, or near, the top of virtually everyone's list, but the order might vary somewhat from one person to the next. Several other outstanding performers have gained general recognition through the years as being among the greatest players ever to wear a Tiger uniform. Hal Newhouser, Alan Trammell, Lou Whitaker, and Jack Morris head the list of other Tiger icons. But, how does one differentiate between the all-around brilliance of Al Kaline and the offensive dominance of Ty Cobb; or the pitching greatness of Justin Verlander and the extraordinary hitting ability of Miguel Cabrera? After initially deciding which players to include on my list, I then needed to determine what criteria I should use to formulate my final rankings.

The first thing I decided to examine was the level of dominance a player attained during his time in Detroit. How often did he lead the American League in some major offensive or pitching statistical category? How did he fare in the annual MVP and/or Cy Young voting? How many times did he make the All-Star team?

I also needed to weigh the level of statistical compilation a player achieved while wearing a Tigers uniform. Where does a batter rank in team annals in the major offensive categories? How high on the all-time list of Tiger hurlers does a pitcher rank in wins, ERA, complete games, innings pitched, shutouts, and saves? Of course, I also needed to consider the era in which the player performed when evaluating his overall numbers. For example, modern-day starting pitchers such as Justin Verlander and Max Scherzer are not likely to throw nearly as many complete games or shutouts as Hal Newhouser, who anchored Detroit's starting rotation during the 1940s. And Miguel Cabrera, who has spent the past seven years in Detroit, is likely to average many more home runs per season than someone like Sam Crawford, who played for the Tigers during the first two decades of the twentieth century.

Other important factors I needed to consider were the overall contributions a player made to the success of the team, the degree to which he improved the fortunes of the ball club during his time in Detroit, the manner in which he impacted the team, both on and off the field, and the degree to which he added to the Tiger legacy of winning. While the number of pennants the Tigers won during a particular player's years with the ball club certainly entered into the equation, I chose not to deny a top performer his rightful place on the list if his years in Detroit happened to coincide with a lack of overall success by the team. As a result, the names of players such as Cecil Fielder and Bobby Higginson will appear in these rankings.

One other thing I should mention is that I only considered a player's performance while he played for the Tigers when formulating my rankings. That being the case, the names of exceptional players, such as Goose Goslin and Rocky Colavito, both of whom had most of their best years while playing for other teams, may appear lower on this list than one might expect.

Having established the guidelines to be used throughout this book, we are ready to take a look at the 50 greatest players in Tigers history, starting with number 1 and working our way down to number 50.

Ty Cobb

Courtesy of the Library of Congress, Bain Collection

Al Kaline and Charlie Gehringer were tremendous all-around players, and Hank Greenberg and Harry Heilmann both rank among the greatest right-handed hitters in baseball history. Nevertheless, the level of dominance that Ty Cobb displayed over the course of his 22 seasons with the Tigers made him the only possible choice for the top spot in these rankings. The holder of 90 major league records when he retired at the conclusion of the 1928 campaign, Cobb dominated his era as no other player ever has, with the exception of Babe Ruth. Cobb led the American League in a major statistical category an astounding 74 times while playing for the Tigers, topping the junior circuit in batting average a record 11 times over a 13-year stretch. The owner of Major League Baseball's highest career batting average (.366 or .367, depending on the source), Cobb also ranks second all-time in hits (4,191), triples (295), and runs scored (2,246), fourth in doubles (724) and stolen bases (892), fifth in total bases (5,854), eighth in runs batted in (1,938), and ninth in on-base percentage (.433). The "Georgia Peach," as he came to be known, also stole home a major league record 54 times over the course of his career.

Yet, in spite of his extraordinary list of accomplishments, Cobb has been vilified through the years for the animosity he often displayed toward others and the warlike mentality he brought with him to the field each day. Tormented by personal demons that once drove him into a sanitarium, Cobb played the game of baseball with an anger and contentiousness never manifested by any other player in the history of the sport. His sense of purpose and will to excel made him the greatest player of his era. However, his combativeness and surly disposition also made him the most hated man in baseball for more than two decades.

Born in the small rural community of Narrows, Georgia, on December 18, 1886, Tyrus Raymond Cobb attended Franklin County High School in nearby Royston, and he simultaneously spent his first few years in organized baseball playing for the Royston Rompers, the semipro Royston Reds, and the Augusta Tourists of the South Atlantic League. After being sold to Detroit for $750 on August 24, 1905, the 18-year-old outfielder made his major league debut with the Tigers six days later, just three weeks after his mother, Amanda Chitwood Cobb, shot and killed his father, William Herschel Cobb, in an apparent case of mistaken identity. Cobb's mother claimed at her subsequent murder trial that she heard strange noises emanating from the porch of her private home while sitting home alone late one evening. Rushing to the window, she shot the intruder once in the stomach and again in the face. The victim of the shooting turned out to be Cobb's father, who, it later surfaced, intended to surprise his wife, since he suspected her of infidelity. Cobb later attributed his ferocious style of play to the death of his domineering father, who told his son when he first elected to make baseball his chosen profession, "Don't come home a failure!" Cobb explained his actions on the ball field by saying, "I did it for my father. He never got to see me play . . . but I knew he was watching me, and I never let him down."

Cobb struggled in his first year with the Tigers, batting just .240 over the season's final month. However, he began to assert himself during his sophomore campaign of 1906, compiling a batting average of .316 over the first four months of the season, before finally succumbing to the enormous pressures that permanently affected his persona. With the weight of his father's death and the subsequent murder trial of his mother already exacting a major toll on his psyche as the season progressed, the 19-year-old found his mettle being further tested by the brutal hazing he received at the hands of his Detroit teammates, who resented his arrogance and boastful nature. Cobb believed himself to be the most talented player in the game, and he let everyone else around him know exactly how he felt. He also considered anyone who disagreed with him to be his adversary, be it opponent or teammate. Feeling that they needed to put the pugnacious youngster in his place, Cobb's Tigers teammates took every possible opportunity to abuse him mentally and physically, even assigning one of the tougher members of the club the task of "roughing him up" occasionally to keep him in line. No longer able to cope with the daily stress, Cobb had to spend the final six weeks of the season in a sanitarium. He later recalled that the treatment he received from his teammates during the early stages of his career turned him into "a snarling wildcat."

Further elaborating on the warlike attitude he brought with him to the baseball diamond, Cobb said, "Baseball is a red-blooded sport for red-blooded men. It's no pink tea, and mollycoddles had better stay out. It's a struggle for supremacy, a survival of the fittest." He added, "I had to fight all my life to survive. They were all against me, but I beat the bastards and left them in the ditch."

Meanwhile, in discussing the reputation he developed over the years for being a "dirty" player, Cobb stated, "The base paths belonged to me, the runner. The rules gave me the right. I always went into a bag full speed, feet first. I had sharp spikes on my shoes. If the baseman stood where he had no business being and got hurt, that was his fault." He further defended himself by telling Fred Lieb in *Baseball as I Have Known It*, "I may have been fierce, but never low or underhanded."

Even though they resented their young teammate, the other members of the Tigers benefited greatly from the passion with which Cobb played the game when he returned to the team in 1907. Displaying an aggressive style of play that the *Detroit Free Press* once described as "daring to the point of dementia," Cobb captured the first of three consecutive batting titles, leading the league with a mark of .350. He also topped the circuit with 119 RBIs, 212 hits, 53 stolen bases, and a .468 slugging percentage, in leading Detroit to the first of three straight A.L. pennants. Although Cobb's numbers slipped somewhat the following year, he still managed to lead the league in eight different offensive categories, including batting average (.324), RBIs (108), triples (20), and slugging percentage (.475). Cobb subsequently posted the best numbers of his young career in 1909, topping the circuit in virtually every major statistical category, including home runs (9), RBIs (107), batting average (.377), hits (216), runs scored (116), stolen bases (76), on-base percentage (.431), and slugging percentage (.517), en route to capturing the Triple Crown.

The only blemishes on Cobb's record during those three seasons ended up being Detroit's three World Series losses and the Georgia Peach's personal failures in the Fall Classic. Cobb batted a combined .262 in his only three World Series appearances, with no home runs, 9 RBIs, and just 7 runs scored.

Cobb's image also suffered as a result of his involvement in several unfortunate incidents that displayed the anger he carried inside. One such incident occurred in spring training in 1907. Well-known for his racial intolerance, Cobb complained to a black groundskeeper about the condition of the Tigers' field in Augusta, Georgia. Not satisfied with the response he received, Cobb physically attacked the terrified man and subsequently began choking the man's wife when she attempted to intervene.

Another horrific episode took place on May 15, 1912, at Hilltop Park in Manhattan, during a game between Cobb's Tigers and the New York Highlanders. Angered by a heckling fan who had been shouting insults to him from the stands the entire game, Cobb finally lost control of his temper when the fan called him a "half-nigger." After vaulting the fence, Cobb began stomping and kicking the fan with his spikes. When fans in the immediate vicinity began yelling that the man lacked the ability to defend himself since he had no hands, Cobb replied, "I don't care if he doesn't have any feet," and kept kicking him until park police eventually pulled him away.

Still, in spite of his many transgressions, Cobb remained baseball's greatest player. After finishing a close second in the 1910 batting race to Cleveland second baseman Napoleon Lajoie with a mark of .383, Cobb led the league in hitting in each of the next five seasons, compiling averages of .420, .409, .390, .368, and .369, respectively. He also topped the circuit in hits, on-base percentage, and slugging percentage three times each during that period, and he led the league in runs scored and stolen bases twice each, with his 96 thefts in 1915 remaining a single-season record for another 47 years. Cobb won the inaugural A.L. MVP trophy in 1911, when he batted a career-high .420 and also topped the circuit in nine other offensive categories, including RBIs (127), runs scored (147), hits (248), triples (24), doubles (47), and stolen bases (83).

Cobb continued to post extraordinary numbers throughout the remainder of the decade, winning three more batting titles, and never hitting any lower than .371. After injuries limited him to only 112 games and a batting average of "just" .334 in 1920, Cobb resumed his onslaught on A.L. pitching the following year—his first as Detroit's player/manager—by hitting a career-high 12 home runs, driving in 101 runs, scoring 124 times, and challenging teammate Harry Heilmann for the A.L. batting title with a mark of .389. Cobb again finished second in the batting race in 1922, this time placing runner-up to George Sisler's .420 with a mark of .401. Cobb continued to serve the Tigers as player/manager until 1926, when he resigned his post amid allegations made by former pitcher Dutch Leonard that Cobb conspired with Tris Speaker to fix a game played between the Tigers and Indians in 1919. After initially retiring as a player, Cobb resurfaced with the Athletics in 1927 and spent his final two years playing under Connie Mack in Philadelphia. He retired for good at the conclusion of the 1928 campaign with the highest lifetime batting average in history (.367), and with more runs batted in (1,938), runs scored (2,246), hits (4,191), stolen bases (892), and total bases (5,854) than any other player. Cobb's amazing list of accomplishments prompted the members of the Baseball Writers Association of America (BBWAA) to name him on 222 of the 226 ballots they cast in the inaugural Baseball Hall of Fame election held in 1936—more than any of the other four initial inductees, Babe Ruth, Honus Wagner, Christy Mathewson, and Walter Johnson.

Shirley Povich, longtime sports columnist and reporter for the *Washington Post*, expressed the sentiments held by many writers of his day when he stated emphatically during a 1990s television interview, "If Babe Ruth isn't the greatest baseball player who ever lived, then Ty Cobb is, by far!"

Ruth himself once praised his bitter rival for his playing ability when he said, "Cobb is a prick. But he sure can hit. God Almighty, that man can hit!"

Hall of Fame outfielder Tris Speaker, who competed against both Ruth and Cobb, had this to say: "The Babe was a great ballplayer, sure, but Cobb was even greater. Babe could knock your brains out, but Cobb would drive you crazy."

Casey Stengel paid Cobb the ultimate tribute, saying, "I never saw anyone like Ty Cobb; no one even close to him. He was the greatest all-time ballplayer. That guy was superhuman, amazing."

Courtesy of the National Photo Company, Library of Congress

George Sisler, as a member of the St. Louis Browns, spent most of his career playing against Cobb. The Hall of Fame first baseman said, "The greatness of Ty Cobb was something that had to be seen, and to see him was to remember him forever."

Yet, in spite of his greatness as a ballplayer, Cobb was disliked by virtually everyone in the sport. When Cleveland's Napoleon Lajoie edged out Cobb for the A.L. batting title on the final day of the 1910 season, Tiger outfielder Sam Crawford displayed the disdain he felt toward his teammate by sending Lajoie a congratulatory telegram.

Nevertheless, Crawford, who played alongside Cobb in the Detroit outfield for 13 seasons, expressed his admiration for his former teammate as a player when he stated years later, "He (Cobb) didn't out-hit and he didn't out-run them; he out-thought them."

Crawford provided further insight into his longtime teammate's psyche when he suggested, "He [Cobb] was still fighting the Civil War, and as far as he was concerned, we were all damn Yankees. But who knows, if he hadn't had that terrible persecution complex, he never would have been about the best ballplayer who ever lived."

Cobb said later in life that he regretted some of his earlier actions and that he knew he made some mistakes. Suggesting that he likely would do some things differently if he had the chance to live his life again, he said wistfully, "I would have had more friends."

Ty Cobb passed away at the age of 74 on July 17, 1961, after losing a long battle with cancer. About 150 friends and relatives attended a brief funeral service held for him in Cornelia, Georgia. Only three former players attended the ceremony—Ray Schalk, Mickey Cochrane, and Nap Rucker, each of whom the wealthy Cobb assisted financially after their careers in baseball ended.

TIGERS CAREER HIGHLIGHTS

Best Season

There are so many great seasons from which to choose, with Cobb's 1909, 1911, 1912, 1915, and 1917 campaigns heading the list. Cobb won the Triple Crown in the first of those years, making it an extremely strong contender. In addition to leading the league with 9 home runs, 107 RBIs, and a .377 batting average, he topped the circuit with 116 runs scored, 216 hits, 76 stolen bases, 296 total bases, a .431 on-base percentage, and a .517 slugging percentage. However, Cobb posted equally impressive numbers in 1912, when he knocked in 83 runs, scored 120 times, amassed 23 triples, 61 steals, and 323 total bases, and led the league with 226 hits, a .409 batting average, a .584 slugging percentage, and a 1.040 OPS.

He had another extraordinary season in 1915, following up an injury-marred 1914 campaign by driving in 99 runs and topping the junior circuit with 144 runs scored, 208 hits, a career-high 96 stolen bases, and a .369 batting average, .486 on-base percentage, and .973 OPS. Cobb again compiled exceptional numbers in 1917, when he knocked in 102 runs, scored 107 times, and led the league with 225 hits, 24 triples, 44 doubles, 55 stolen bases, 335 total bases, a .383 batting average, a .444 on-base percentage, and a .570 slugging percentage.

Nevertheless, the feeling here is that Cobb had his greatest season in 1911, when he established career highs in most offensive categories. In addition to finishing second in the league with 8 home runs and a .467 on-base percentage, he topped the circuit with 127 RBIs, 147 runs scored, 248 hits, 24 triples, 47 doubles, 83 steals, 367 total bases, a .420 batting average, a .621 slugging percentage, and a 1.088 OPS. Cobb also did a solid job in the field, leading all A.L. outfielders with 376 putouts—the second-highest total of his career.

Memorable Moments/Greatest Performances

A terror on the base paths, Cobb accomplished the rare feat of stealing second, third, and home in the same inning a total of five times during his career.

In a game against the New York Highlanders on May 12, 1911, Cobb put on display for all to see his unusual combination of skill and cunning, turning in one of his finest all-around performances. After earlier scoring all the way from first base on a single to right field, he scored another run from second base on a wild pitch. Cobb later tied the contest with a two-run double in the seventh inning. He then watched as the New York catcher and infielders argued the call at second base. Realizing that no one on the Highlanders had remembered to call time-out, Cobb strolled unobserved to third base, after which he casually walked toward home plate as if to get a better view of the argument. He then broke into a run and slid into home plate for the eventual winning run.

Cobb turned in another brilliant performance on July 19, 1912, when he collected 7 hits in a doubleheader split with the Philadelphia Athletics. The 7 safeties gave him a major league record 14 hits over the course of consecutive doubleheaders. He concluded the month with an amazing 68 hits, establishing in the process another major league mark.

Cobb had the most productive day of his career on May 5, 1925, when the 38-year-old outfielder elected to drive home a point by eschewing for the moment his usual scientific approach to hitting. Well-known for his split-handed grip that sacrificed power for bat control, Cobb told reporters before a contest against the St. Louis Browns that he intended to swing for the fences that day in order to prove that home run hitters such as Babe Ruth possessed no special skill. Sliding his hands down to the knob of the bat, Cobb proceeded to go 6-for-6, with 3 home runs, 5 RBIs, and 4 runs scored, in leading the Tigers to a 14–8 win over St. Louis. His 16 total bases established a new A.L. record. He followed that up the very next day by hitting 2 more homers and driving in another 6 runs during an 11–4 Tiger victory. Cobb then went back to his normal style of hitting, concluding the campaign with 12 home runs and a .378 batting average.

Yet Cobb experienced his greatest thrill in baseball much earlier in his career, revealing to famous sportswriter Grantland Rice during a 1930 interview, "The biggest thrill I ever got came in a game against the Athletics in 1907 (on September 30). . . . The Athletics had us beaten, with Rube Waddell pitching. They were two runs ahead (8–6) in the ninth inning when I happened to hit a home run that tied the score. This game went 17 innings to a tie (9–9), and a few days later, we clinched our first pennant. You can understand what it meant for a 20-year-old country boy to hit a home run off the great Rube, in a pennant-winning game, with two outs in the ninth."

NOTABLE ACHIEVEMENTS

- Batted over .300 in 21 of 22 seasons with Tigers, surpassing the .350 mark 15 times and batting over .400 three times (1911, 1912, 1922).
- Knocked in more than 100 runs seven times.
- Scored more than 100 runs 10 times, surpassing 140 runs scored twice (1911, 1915).
- Topped 200 hits nine times, reaching 220 on three occasions.
- Finished in double digits in triples 17 times, surpassing 20 three-baggers on four occasions.
- Surpassed 30 doubles 14 times, topping 40 two-baggers on four occasions.
- Stole more than 50 bases nine times, surpassing 75 steals on three occasions.
- Walked more than 100 times once (118 in 1915).
- Struck out as many as 50 times in a season just once entire career (55 in 1907).
- Compiled on-base percentage in excess of .400 18 straight times (1909–1926), surpassing .450 on 10 occasions.
- Posted slugging percentage in excess of .500 on 13 occasions, topping .600 once (.621 in 1911).
- Compiled an OPS in excess of 1.000 eight times.
- Led the American League in batting average 11 times; on-base percentage seven times; slugging percentage eight times; OPS ten times; hits eight times; total bases six times; stolen bases six times; runs scored five times; RBIs four times; triples four times; doubles three times; and home runs once.
- Led A.L. outfielders in assists twice; putouts once; fielding percentage once; and double plays turned four times.
- Led A.L. center fielders in assists once.
- Major League Baseball's all-time leader in career batting average (.367) and defensive games as outfielder (2,934).
- Ranks among Major League Baseball's all-time leaders in runs scored (2nd); hits (2nd); triples (2nd); doubles (4th); total bases (5th); stolen

bases (4th); RBIs (8th); career on-base percentage (9th); games played (5th); at-bats (5th); outfield assists (2nd); double plays turned as out-fielder (2nd); and outfield putouts (5th).

- Holds Tigers career records for highest batting average (.368) and on-base percentage (.434); and most RBIs (1,805), runs scored (2,088), hits (3,900), triples (284), doubles (665), total bases (5,466), stolen bases (869), plate appearances (12,117), and at-bats (10,591).
- Ranks among Tiger career leaders in walks (4th), slugging percentage (4th), OPS (3rd), and games played (2nd).
- Holds Tiger single-season records for highest batting average (.420), most runs scored (147), most hits (248), and most stolen bases (96).
- Holds major league record for most hits in one month (68 in July 1912).
- Hit 3 home runs in one game on May 5, 1925.
- One of only two major league players to accumulate 4,000 career hits (Pete Rose).
- One of only two major league players to bat over .400 as many as three times (Rogers Hornsby).
- 1909 A.L. Triple Crown winner.
- 1911 A.L. MVP winner.
- Member of Major League Baseball's All-Century Team.
- Third on *The Sporting News* 1999 list of Baseball's 100 Greatest Players.
- Three-time A.L. champion (1907–1909).
- Elected to Baseball Hall of Fame by members of BBWAA in 1936.

2

Hank Greenberg

Courtesy of LegendaryAuctions.com

H ad he not spent much of his career competing against arguably the two greatest first basemen in baseball history in Lou Gehrig and Jimmie Foxx, Hank Greenberg likely would be better remembered today for having been one of the most prolific sluggers in baseball history. Further diminishing Greenberg's legacy is the fact that he spent almost five full peak seasons serving his country during World War II. He also missed most of another season with a broken arm. Yet, even though Greenberg played the equivalent of only nine and a half seasons in the major leagues, he made a huge impact during his relatively brief career, leaving a lasting impression on all those who saw him perform. Joe DiMaggio once said of Greenberg, "He was one of the truly great hitters, and when I first saw him bat, he made my eyes pop out." Greenberg's potent bat also caused the eyes of many an opposing pitcher to widen, as he went on to hit 331 home runs, drive in 1,276 runs, win two A.L. MVP awards, and lead the Tigers to four pennants and two world championships.

Born to Romanian-born Orthodox Jewish immigrant parents in New York City's Greenwich Village on January 1, 1911, Henry Benjamin Greenberg moved with his family to the Bronx at age 7. Hampered by flat feet and a lack of coordination as a youngster, Greenberg worked diligently to overcome his physical deficiencies. After graduating from James Monroe High School in the Bronx, he attended New York University on an athletic scholarship for one semester before choosing to leave school to pursue a career in baseball.

Standing 6'4", weighing 220 pounds, and possessing great physical strength, Greenberg seemed to have all the physical tools needed to succeed at the major league level. Yet he remained unsure of himself, especially early in his career, when he viewed his size and lack of grace as major obstacles to his success. Greenberg's high school baseball coach explained years later, "Hank was so big for his age and so awkward that he became painfully self-conscious. The fear of being made to look foolish drove him to practice constantly and, as a result, to overcome his handicaps."

Greenberg's hard work eventually paid off, with the Giants, Yankees, and Senators all courting him before he finally elected to sign with the Tigers in January 1930. The big first baseman spent the next three years in Detroit's minor league farm system, excelling at Raleigh, North Carolina, in 1930, Evansville in the Illinois-Indiana-Iowa League in 1931, and Beaumont in the Texas League in 1932. It was at Beaumont that Greenberg received his first dose of anti-Semitism.

At one point during the season, Greenberg's teammate Jo-Jo White began circling him slowly, staring at him intently all the while. When Greenberg asked White to explain his actions, his teammate replied that he was merely curious, since he had never seen a Jew before. Greenberg later revealed, "I let him keep looking for a while, and then I said, 'See anything interesting?'" Looking for horns and finding none, White responded, "You're just like everyone else."

The 22-year-old Greenberg joined Detroit in 1933, displaying right from the start his abilities as a hitter by knocking in 87 runs and batting

.301 in 117 games with the Tigers. Although he remained a bit clumsy in the field, he worked extremely hard on his defense, eventually turning himself into an above-average defensive first baseman.

Greenberg had his breakout year in 1934, helping the Tigers win 101 games and the A.L. pennant by hitting 26 home runs, driving in 139 runs, scoring 118 others, batting .339, accumulating 201 hits, and topping the circuit with 63 doubles, en route to earning a sixth-place finish in the league MVP voting. Although Detroit lost the World Series to St. Louis in seven games, Greenberg acquitted himself well, batting .321, collecting 9 hits, homering once, and knocking in 7 runs.

Even though Greenberg's religion, and the ridicule he had to endure as a result, sparked a considerable amount of controversy from the time he first joined the Tigers, it became a public issue for the first time when he announced late in 1934 that he planned to sit out games the Tigers had scheduled for Rosh Hashanah (the Jewish New Year) and Yom Kippur (the Day of Atonement). With their team in the middle of a pennant race, Tiger fans grumbled, "Rosh Hashanah comes every year, but the Tigers haven't won the pennant since 1909." Finally, after putting a great deal of thought into the matter, Greenberg decided to play on Rosh Hashanah. However, he elected not to play on Yom Kippur, the holiest of all Jewish holidays. After the first baseman hit 2 home runs during Detroit's 2–1 pennant-clinching victory played on the Jewish New Year, the *Detroit Free Press* ran the Hebrew lettering for "Happy New Year" across its front page the following day. Meanwhile, columnist and poet Edgar A. Guest wrote a poem entitled "Speaking of Greenberg," which ended with the lines, "We shall miss him on the infield and shall miss him at the bat / But he's true to his religion—and I honor him for that."

In truth, Greenberg did not consider himself to be a particularly religious man. However, as the first true Jewish star in professional sports, he considered it his duty to set a good example for his people, and to be a positive role model for the Jewish youth of America. Long after his playing career ended, Greenberg revealed, "When I was playing, I used to resent being singled out as a Jewish ballplayer. I wanted to be known as a great ballplayer, period. I'm not sure why or when I changed, because I'm still not a particularly religious person. Lately, though, I find myself wanting to be remembered not only as a great ballplayer, but even more as a great Jewish ballplayer."

Greenberg subsequently established himself as one of baseball's elite players in 1935, when he led the Tigers to their second consecutive pennant by finishing among the league leaders with a .328 batting average, 121 runs scored, 203 hits, 16 triples, 46 doubles, and a .628 slugging percentage, while topping the circuit with 36 home runs, 170 runs batted in, and 389 total bases. His outstanding performance earned him A.L. MVP honors.

The Tigers then captured their first world championship, defeating the Chicago Cubs in six games in the World Series, although they did so without the help of Greenberg for the final four contests after he badly injured his wrist in Game Two. Even before hurting himself, though, Greenberg derived little pleasure from the Fall Classic since he had to endure an endless stream of taunts from the Chicago bench. Constantly reminding Greenberg of his Jewish heritage, the Cubs players hurled ethnic slurs at him when he stood in the field and whenever he stepped into the batter's box. As the slugger stood at home plate on one particular occasion waiting for the opposing pitcher to deliver his pitch, one Chicago player yelled, "Throw him a pork-chop . . . he can't hit that!" The abuse finally became so distasteful that home plate umpire George Moriarty stopped the game and instructed the Cubs to tone down their remarks.

Unfortunately, Chicago's shabby treatment of Greenberg did not prove to be an isolated incident, especially early in his career. Anti-Semitism ran rampant throughout the United States at the time, with Detroit being one of the nation's least-tolerant places. Henry Ford, one of the city's leading citizens, harbored deep resentment toward people of the Jewish faith, having published during the 1920s *The International Jew*, a work that blamed a Jewish conspiracy for both communism and a capitalistic plot designed to destroy Christian civilization. Meanwhile, Father Coughlin expressed pro-Nazi sentiments and regularly denounced Jews and blacks during his weekly radio shows that aired throughout the city.

Things being as they were at that time, Greenberg often had to endure verbal abuse from fans and opposing players alike. Although not the first Jewish man to play in the major leagues, he was one of a select few who elected not to conceal his heritage by changing his name. Furthermore, Greenberg soon established himself as the first truly great Jewish player to don a big-league uniform. As a result, he became a symbol of success for many Jewish Americans, as much as he became a target of abuse for those people who resented him merely because of his faith. Although Greenberg usually chose to ignore the many derisive comments people directed toward him, he sometimes elected to retaliate when his adversary pushed him too far.

One such incident took place during a game against the Chicago White Sox. With Greenberg holding on Chicago base runner Joe Kuhel at first base, the White Sox first baseman attempted to spike his counterpart as he slid back to the bag on an attempted pickoff. Greenberg responded by slapping Kuhel, prompting others to intervene before the confrontation escalated. However, Greenberg followed the White Sox players into their clubhouse at the conclusion of the game and proceeded to berate Kuhel in front of the entire team. Not one member of the White Sox moved a muscle as the hulking Greenberg continued to convey his anger to Kuhel, who sat quietly throughout the entire diatribe. Detroit pitcher Eldon Auker, who followed his teammate into the Chicago clubhouse and observed the entire episode, later suggested that the Chicago player's submissive attitude during the reproach "was probably a good thing because Hank was real tough."

Following Detroit's World Series victory in 1935, Greenberg reinjured his wrist in an early-season collision in 1936, forcing him to miss all but 12 games. He returned the following year, though, to have one of his finest seasons. In addition to hitting 40 home runs, batting .337, scoring 137 runs, and amassing 49 doubles and 200 hits, Greenberg knocked in 183 runs, falling just 1 RBI short of tying Lou Gehrig's A.L. record. His extraordinarily productive campaign earned him a third-place finish in the A.L. MVP balloting.

Greenberg again placed third in the MVP voting in 1938, when he batted .315, drove in 146 runs, led the league with 144 runs scored, and topped the circuit with 58 home runs, to finish 2 homers shy of Babe Ruth's then single-season mark of 60. Although Greenberg continued to reject the notion years later, some of his Tigers teammates believed that opposing pitchers refused to pitch to the slugger during the season's final days because they didn't want a Jewish player to break the Babe's record.

Greenberg had another very solid year in 1939, hitting 33 home runs, knocking in 112 runs, scoring 112 times, and batting .312. He then became the first player to win the MVP award at two different positions in 1940, after he moved to left field prior to the start of the season to make room at first base for young slugger Rudy York. Greenberg ended up leading the Tigers to the pennant by batting .340, scoring 129 runs, and topping the circuit with 41 home runs, 150 RBIs, 50 doubles, and a .670 slugging percentage. Although the Tigers subsequently lost the World Series to the Reds in seven games, Greenberg batted .357, with 10 hits, 1 home run, 6 runs batted in, and 5 runs scored.

Greenberg's strong anti-Nazi sentiments prompted him to become the first major league player to enlist in the U.S. military at the beginning of World War II. Initially drafted in 1940, Greenberg spent all but the first 19 games of the 1941 campaign serving his country, before being honorably discharged on December 5, 1941, after the U.S. Congress elected to

Courtesy of Boston Public Library, Leslie Jones Collection

release men aged 28 years and older from service. However, Greenberg elected to reenlist immediately when the Japanese bombed Pearl Harbor just two days later. After graduating from Officer Candidate School, he was commissioned as a first lieutenant in the U.S. Army Air Forces. Greenberg eventually served overseas in the China-Burma-India Theater, scouting locations for B-29 bomber bases. He remained on active duty until he was finally discharged four and a half years later, in mid-1945.

Greenberg showed little rust when he returned to the Tigers, homering in his first game back, driving in 60 runs in only 78 games, and clinching the pennant for Detroit with a grand slam home run in the final game of the season. He then hit 2 home runs and knocked in 7 runs against the Cubs in the World Series, leading the Tigers to a seven-game victory.

Greenberg spent only one more year in Detroit, leading the American League with 44 home runs and 127 RBIs in 1946, before being traded to Pittsburgh at the end of the season, where he spent his final year mentoring future Hall of Famer Ralph Kiner. Greenberg later said, "Ralph had a natural home run swing. All he needed was somebody to teach him the value of hard work and self-discipline. Early in the morning on off-days, every chance we got, we worked on hitting." Kiner went on to hit 51 home runs for the Pirates that year, and he later gave Greenberg much of the credit for the success he experienced during his Hall of Fame career.

Greenberg retired at the end of the 1947 campaign to take a front-office position with the Cleveland Indians. He ended his career with 331 home runs, 1,276 RBIs, 1,051 runs scored, 1,628 hits, 379 doubles, a .313 batting average, a .412 on-base percentage, and a .605 slugging percentage. Greenberg hit 306 homers, knocked in 1,202 runs, scored 980 times, collected 1,528 hits, amassed 366 doubles, batted .319, compiled a .412 on-base percentage, and posted a .616 slugging percentage while playing for the Tigers. In addition to batting well over .300 each year, he averaged 39 home runs, 150 RBIs, and 127 runs scored in the 6 full seasons he played between 1934 and 1940.

After serving as Cleveland's farm director in 1948 and 1949, Greenberg became the team's general manager in 1950. A shrewd judge of talent, he subsequently helped build the Indians team that put an end to New York's five-year reign as A.L. champions in 1954 by winning 111 games. From Cleveland, Greenberg moved on to the Chicago White Sox as part-owner and vice president. During his time in Chicago, Greenberg gained induction into the Baseball Hall of Fame, elected by the members of the BBWAA in 1956. He retired from baseball in 1963 and subsequently became a successful investment banker. Greenberg remained a physically strong and imposing figure until he developed cancer during the 1980s. He finally lost his battle with the dreaded disease on September 4, 1986, passing away in Beverly Hills, California, at the age of 75.

Long after his passing, Hank Greenberg continues to be largely overlooked when conversations arise concerning the all-time greats. But the men who saw him play are well aware of the potent bat he wielded.

Ted Williams, who saw quite a bit of Greenberg his first few years in Boston, later ranked the big first baseman as the 11th greatest hitter in baseball history in his 1995 book entitled *Ted Williams' Hit List*. Williams described Greenberg in his work as "one of the most intelligent guys I ever met in baseball. . . . Pitchers knew that you didn't give him too much of the same thing, because he'd lay for it and he'd hit it."

The Splendid Splinter went on to say, "My most vivid memory of Greenberg was that he'd hit a ball to the outfield and you'd think that you had it, and it would go back, back, back into the upper deck. A lot of times Greenberg would hit a fly ball to me in Detroit and my first reaction was, 'Oh, I'll get that,' and damn it, it goes deep into the seats. He didn't look like he'd smacked it that hard. It just had that little under-carry. . . . Greenberg had the loftiest ball in the majors. Yes, he was a great hitter!"

Goose Goslin, Charlie Gehringer, and Hank Greenberg. Courtesy of Boston Public Library, Leslie Jones Collection

Williams added, "Hank Greenberg could do it all. He hit the ball a ton, crushed it like few have ever done. Unfortunately, his career was one of the casualties of the war. Nevertheless, the impact he made in just 1,394 games is nothing short of amazing."

TIGERS CAREER HIGHLIGHTS

Best Season

Although Greenberg failed to capture A.L. MVP honors in either 1937 or 1938, he performed magnificently both years. After hitting 40 home runs, driving in a league-leading 183 runs, scoring 137 times, amassing 200 hits, 14 triples, 49 doubles, and a career-high 397 total bases, batting .337, and compiling a 1.105 OPS in the first of those campaigns, he topped the circuit with 58 homers, 144 runs scored, and 119 walks the following year, while also knocking in 146 runs, batting .315, and posting a career-best 1.122 OPS. However, Greenberg was equally productive in his two MVP seasons of 1935 and 1940. En route to earning MVP honors for the first time, he led the league with 36 home runs, 170 RBIs, and 389 total bases, scored 121 runs, accumulated 203 hits, 16 triples, and 46 doubles, batted .328, and compiled an OPS of 1.039.

When Greenberg won his second MVP trophy in 1940, he topped the circuit with 41 homers, 150 RBIs, 50 doubles, 384 total bases, a .670 slugging percentage, and a 1.103 OPS. He also placed among the league leaders with 129 runs scored, 195 hits, a .340 batting average, and a .433 on-base percentage. In addition to leading the league in a career-best six offensive categories, Greenberg moved to left field to accommodate the slugging Rudy York at first base—a gesture that helped the Tigers capture the A.L. pennant. Furthermore, Greenberg carried the Tigers on his back down the stretch, hitting 15 home runs during the month of September, to help them overcome a four-game deficit in the standings. All things considered, 1940 would have to be considered Greenberg's finest all-around season.

Memorable Moments/Greatest Performances

Greenberg displayed his awesome power at the plate on September 19, 1937, when he became the first player to hit a home run into the center-field bleachers at Yankee Stadium, delivering a blow that traveled about 500 feet.

A tremendous clutch hitter throughout his career, Greenberg batted .318, hit 5 home runs, and knocked in 22 runs in the 23 World Series games in which he appeared. He hit two of his biggest homers on September 10, 1934, when, after electing to play on Rosh Hashanah, he gave the Tigers all the runs they needed to clinch the A.L. pennant with a 2–1 victory over the Red Sox.

Nevertheless, Greenberg hit the most memorable home run of his career more than a decade later, on the final day of the 1945 regular season, when he sent the Tigers to the World Series by blasting a game-winning, ninth-inning grand slam against St. Louis that turned a 3–2 deficit into 6–3 victory. Reflecting back on the moment years later, Greenberg said, "Standing at the plate, my fear was that it would go foul, but it did not, and we won the game when we set down the Browns in the bottom of the ninth. There were hardly any people in the stands when I hit the homer, and not many newspapermen either. But it was no big deal; my teammates gave me a big welcome. The best part of that homer was hearing how the (second-place) Washington Senators players responded: 'Goddam, that dirty Jew bastard, he beat us again.'"

NOTABLE ACHIEVEMENTS

- Hit more than 30 home runs six times, surpassing 40 homers four times and 50 homers once.
- Knocked in more than 100 runs seven times, topping 150 RBIs on three occasions.
- Scored more than 100 runs six times, surpassing 120 runs scored on four occasions.
- Batted over .300 nine times, topping the .320-mark on five occasions.
- Topped 200 hits three times.
- Finished in double digits in triples twice.
- Surpassed 40 doubles five times, topping 50 two-baggers twice and 60 two-baggers once.
- Drew more than 100 walks twice.
- Compiled on-base percentage in excess of .400 nine times.
- Posted slugging percentage in excess of .600 eight times.
- Compiled an OPS in excess of 1.000 seven times.
- Led the American League in home runs four times; RBIs four times; runs scored once; doubles twice; total bases twice; walks once; slugging percentage once; and OPS once.
- Led A.L. first basemen in putouts twice; assists twice; and fielding percentage once.
- Led A.L. left fielders in putouts once and assists once.
- Ranks among Major League Baseball's all-time leaders in slugging percentage (6th) and OPS (6th).
- Holds Tigers career records for highest slugging percentage (.616) and highest OPS (1.028).
- Ranks among Tigers career leaders in home runs (3rd); RBIs (6th); batting average (10th); on-base percentage (3rd); runs scored (10th); doubles (8th); triples (9th); total bases (9th); and walks (10th).
- Holds Tiger single-season records for most home runs (58); most RBIs (183); most doubles (63); most extra-base hits (103); most total bases (397); and highest slugging percentage (.683).
- Two-time A.L. MVP (1935, 1940).
- First player to win MVP at two different positions.
- Two-time *Sporting News* All-Star selection (1935, 1940).
- Four-time A.L. All-Star (1937–1940).

- Number 37 on *The Sporting News* 1999 list of Baseball's 100 Greatest Players.
- Four-time A.L. champion (1934, 1935, 1940, 1945).
- Two-time world champion (1935, 1945).
- Elected to Baseball Hall of Fame by members of BBWAA in 1956.

3

Charlie Gehringer

Courtesy of LegendaryAuctions.com

One of the very best players ever to man the position of second base, Charlie Gehringer proved to be Major League Baseball's premier second sacker for virtually all of the 1930s. A superb all-around player who excelled at every aspect of the game, Gehringer led the American League in numerous statistical categories over the course of his career, including batting average, runs scored, hits, triples, doubles, stolen bases, putouts, and assists. Gehringer helped lead the Tigers to three pennants and one world championship, won an MVP award, and represented the American League at second base in each of the first six All-Star games, doing so in such an understated and consistent manner that he eventually came to be known as "The Mechanical Man."

Born in Fowlerville, Michigan, on May 11, 1903, Charles Leonard Gehringer grew up on a farm just outside the city of his birth. After attending Fowlerville High School, from which he graduated in 1922, Gehringer enrolled at the University of Michigan, 30 miles from the family farm. While starring in baseball, football, and basketball at Michigan, Gehringer continued to play for the Fowlerville town team in his spare time. He elected to leave college following his freshman year after being discovered by Detroit left fielder Bobby Veach, who subsequently brought the 20-year-old second baseman down to the Tigers training facility for a tryout. Gehringer so impressed Detroit player/manager Ty Cobb that the legendary Tigers star urged club owner Frank Navin to sign him to a contract on the spot. Cobb was later quoted as saying, "I knew Charlie would hit, and I was so anxious to sign him that I didn't even take the time to change out of my uniform before rushing him into the front office to sign a contract."

Gehringer spent virtually all of 1924 and 1925 in the minor leagues, making only brief appearances with the Tigers at the end of both seasons. However, shortly after earning a spot on the major league roster at the start of the 1926 campaign, he established himself as the club's starting second baseman, a position he held for the next 16 years. Gehringer had a solid rookie campaign, batting .277, scoring 62 runs, and finishing second in the league with 17 triples. He gradually evolved into the league's top second baseman over the course of the next two seasons, excelling both at the bat and in the field. After batting .317, scoring 110 runs, stealing 17 bases, and leading all A.L. second basemen with 438 assists and 84 double plays in 1927, he earned an eighth-place finish in the 1928 MVP voting by batting .320, scoring 108 runs, collecting 193 hits, and topping all players at his position with 507 assists.

Gehringer developed into one of the American League's finest all-around players in 1929, when he established new career highs with 13 home runs, 106 runs batted in, and a .339 batting average, topped the circuit with 131 runs scored, 215 hits, 19 triples, 45 doubles, and 27 stolen bases, and led all players at his position with 404 putouts and a .975 fielding percentage.

Gehringer continued to perform at an extremely high level the next four seasons, batting well over .300 and scoring in excess of 100 runs three times each, and surpassing 100 RBIs and 200 hits twice each. After finishing among the league leaders with 144 runs scored, 47 doubles, and 19 stolen bases in 1930, he placed near the top of the league rankings with 42 doubles and a .325 batting average in 1933. In fact, over the nine-year stretch that began in 1932 and ended in 1940, Gehringer put together streaks of eight consecutive seasons in which he batted well over .300, seven straight seasons in which he scored well in excess of 100 runs, and five consecutive years in which he knocked in more than 100 runs and amassed more than 200 hits. The Mechanical Man performed so consistently that he really earned that nickname, with his quiet demeanor and propensity for compiling exceptional numbers without drawing attention to himself once prompting former Tigers teammate and manager Mickey Cochrane to say of him, "He says hello on Opening Day and goodbye on Closing Day, and in between all he does is hit .350."

New York Yankees Hall of Fame left-hander Lefty Gomez also expressed his admiration for the level of consistency Gehringer reached by suggesting, "You can wind him up in the spring and he'll hit .320 with 40 doubles."

An extremely quiet and unassuming man, Gehringer rarely displayed his emotions on the field, prompting Ty Cobb to once note, "He'd [Gehringer] say hello at the start of spring training and goodbye at the end of the season, and the rest of the time he let his bat and glove do all the talking for him."

Acknowledging his quiet demeanor, Gehringer said, "I wasn't a rabble rouser. I wasn't a big noisemaker in the infield, which a lot of managers think you've got to be or you're not showing. But I don't think it contributes much."

The left-handed-hitting Gehringer also developed a reputation during the early 1930s as one of the most difficult hitters in baseball to strike out, fanning a total of only 93 times between 1930 and 1933, including just 17 times in 699 total plate appearances in 1930. Detroit manager Del Baker suggested, "Let Gehringer come to bat each time two strikes down to the pitcher, and he wouldn't bat more than 15 points under his season's average."

And, as for Gehringer's defense, no one fielded his position more smoothly or more effortlessly. He had quick hands and rarely lost a ball he got his glove on, leading all league second basemen in fielding percentage and assists seven times each, and topping the circuit in putouts on three separate occasions. Baseball authority H. G. Salsinger once wrote: "He [Gehringer] lacks showmanship, but he has polish that no other second baseman, with the exception of the great Napoleon Lajoie, ever had. He has so well-schooled himself in the technique of his position that he makes the most difficult plays look easy."

Courtesy of RMYauctions.com

After being joined by Hank Greenberg on the right side of the Tigers infield the previous season, Gehringer helped lead Detroit to the A.L. pennant in 1934 by topping the circuit with 134 runs scored and 214 hits, while also placing among the leaders with 127 RBIs, 50 doubles, and a .356 batting average, en route to earning a second-place finish in the league MVP voting. Although the Tigers subsequently lost the World Series to the Cardinals in seven games, Gehringer batted .379, with 11 hits and 5 runs scored.

The Tigers repeated as A.L. champions in 1935, with their second baseman having another fabulous year. In addition to hitting 19 home runs and driving in 108 runs, Gehringer finished among the league leaders with 123 runs scored, 201 hits, and a .330 batting average. He placed sixth in the league MVP balloting, with teammate Greenberg winning the award. Detroit then defeated the Chicago Cubs in six games in the World Series, Gehringer starring once again by batting .375 and driving in 4 runs.

The New York Yankees subsequently began a four-year run as league champions in 1936, finishing 19 and a half games in front of the second-place Tigers. Nevertheless, Gehringer had one of his finest seasons, driving in 116 runs, scoring 144 others, batting .354, compiling 227 hits, leading the league with 60 doubles, and striking out a career-low 13 times in 731 total plate appearances. His outstanding performance earned him a fourth-place finish in the league MVP voting.

Although the Tigers again finished a distant second to the Yankees in 1937, Gehringer earned league MVP honors by knocking in 96 runs, scoring 133 times, amassing 40 doubles and 209 hits, and topping the circuit with a .371 batting average. By winning his first batting title at the age of 34, Gehringer became the oldest player to lead his league in that particular category for the very first time.

Gehringer had another big year in 1938, batting .306, driving in 107 runs, scoring 133 times, and establishing new career highs with 20 home runs and 113 walks. He also had solid seasons in 1939 and 1940, before his skills finally began to diminish the following year. After batting a career-low .220 in 1941, Gehringer lost his starting second base job the following season, spending most of his time coming off the Detroit bench as a pinch hitter. He retired at the conclusion of the 1942 campaign with a career batting average of .320, 1,427 RBIs, 1,774 runs scored, 2,839 hits, 184 home runs, 181 stolen bases, 146 triples, 574 doubles, a .404 on-base percentage, and a .480 slugging percentage. With the exception of home runs and slugging percentage, he ranks among the Tigers' all-time leaders in each of those categories. Meanwhile, Gehringer trails only Eddie Collins in runs scored and Napoleon Lajoie in doubles among major league second basemen. In addition to winning the MVP trophy in 1937, Gehringer finished in the top 10 in the balloting seven other times.

After retiring from baseball, Gehringer enlisted in the U.S. Navy, where he served for three years before being released in 1945. He briefly considered making a comeback at age 41, later stating, "I came out of the service in such good shape that I felt I could've played a few years." However, he eventually chose to go into business selling fabrics to automobile manufacturers instead.

After being elected to the Hall of Fame by the members of the BBWAA in 1949, Gehringer served three years as Detroit's general manager, before taking over as the team's vice president in the mid-1950s. He eventually went back to his fabric-selling business, continuing with the company until 1974, when he sold his interest in the firm. Gehringer also served as a member of the Baseball Hall of Fame Veterans Committee from 1953 to 1990. He passed away on January 21, 1993, in Bloomfield Hills, Michigan, at age 89 from complications due to a stroke he suffered the previous month. Twenty-five years earlier, though, a special committee of baseball writers voted Gehringer the game's greatest living second baseman as part of baseball's centennial celebration in 1969. Legendary Negro Leagues pitching star Satchel Paige, who faced Gehringer several times on barnstorming tours, was one who concurred with the results of that election, once identifying the Tiger second baseman as the best major league hitter he ever faced.

CAREER HIGHLIGHTS

Best Season

Gehringer earned A.L. MVP honors in 1937, when he won his only batting title by posting a career-high mark of .371. He also knocked in 96 runs, scored 133 times, amassed 209 hits and 40 doubles, and compiled an OPS of .978. However, Gehringer actually compiled better overall numbers the previous year, when he earned a fourth-place finish in the MVP voting by driving in 116 runs, batting .354, and establishing career highs with 144 runs scored, 227 hits, 60 doubles, 356 total bases, and a .987 OPS. He also performed brilliantly in 1930 and 1934, batting .330 in the first of those years, while also hitting 16 homers, knocking in 98 runs, scoring 144 times, collecting 201 hits, 15 triples, and 47 doubles, and compiling a .938 OPS. Gehringer helped lead the Tigers to the A.L. pennant four years later by batting .356, driving in a career-high 127 runs, amassing 50 doubles, posting a .967 OPS, and topping the circuit with 134 runs scored and 214 hits.

Although a strong case could certainly be made for any of those years, I ultimately decided to go with Gehringer's 1929 campaign. Even though he compiled slightly better overall numbers in at least one or two other seasons, Gehringer displayed the degree to which he excelled in all facets of the game over the course of that 1929 campaign by knocking in 106 runs, batting .339, accumulating 337 total bases, compiling an OPS of .936, and leading the American League with 131 runs scored, 215 hits, 45 doubles, and a career-best 19 triples and 27 stolen bases. He also led all A.L. second basemen in putouts and fielding percentage and finished second in assists.

Memorable Moments/Greatest Performances

A tremendous postseason performer for the Tigers, Gehringer played brilliantly in both the 1934 and 1935 Fall Classics, posting batting averages of .379 and .375, and scoring 9 runs in 13 total games.

Gehringer had one of his greatest days at the plate on May 27, 1939, when he hit for the cycle in a 12–5 win over the St. Louis Browns. The Tiger second baseman finished the game 4-for-5, with 5 RBIs and 2 runs scored.

Gehringer had another big game 10 years earlier, on August 5, 1929, when he accomplished the rare feat of collecting 3 triples in one game. However, he played perhaps his finest all-around game just nine days later, on August 14, 1929, when he showed his appreciation to the fans who were in attendance to honor him on Charlie Gehringer Day in Detroit by putting on a memorable performance. In addition to flawlessly handling 10 chances in the field, Gehringer went 4-for-5, with a homer, 4 runs scored, and a steal of home during a 17–13 Tigers win over the Yankees. Years later, Gehringer identified the contest as his greatest thrill in baseball, revealing in author Richard Bak's book, *Cobb Would Have Caught It: The Golden Age of Baseball in Detroit*:

> They presented me with a set of golf clubs. They were beautiful: matched Spalding irons and woods with a beautiful leather bag. They also were right-handed, and of course I'm left-handed. But I learned how to play the game right-handed, those clubs were so nice. Anyway, we played the Yankees that day and we won big. I started off with a home run. I had four hits and almost hit for the cycle, and, to top it off, I stole home. I probably had some better afternoons, but that was kind of a special day.

NOTABLE ACHIEVEMENTS

- Batted over .300 thirteen times, topping the .350-mark on three occasions.
- Scored more than 100 runs twelve times, surpassing 130 runs scored on six occasions.
- Knocked in more than 100 runs seven times, surpassing 120 RBIs once (127 in 1934).
- Hit 20 home runs once (1938).
- Surpassed 200 hits seven times.
- Finished in double digits in triples seven times, topping 15 three-baggers on four occasions.
- Topped 30 doubles ten times, 40 doubles seven times, 50 two-baggers twice, and 60 doubles once.
- Stole more than 20 bases once (27 in 1929).
- Drew more than 100 walks twice.
- Compiled on-base percentage in excess of .400 nine times, surpassing .450 on two occasions.
- Posted slugging percentage in excess of .500 seven times.

- Led the American League in batting average once; runs scored twice; hits twice; doubles twice; triples once; and stolen bases once.
- Led A.L. second basemen in fielding percentage seven times; assists seven times; putouts three times; and double plays turned four times.
- Ranks among Tigers career leaders in runs scored (2nd); RBIs (4th); hits (3rd); extra-base hits (3rd); doubles (2nd); triples (3rd); batting average (9th); walks (3rd); stolen bases (9th); on-base percentage (7th); OPS (6th); games played (4th); plate appearances (3rd); and at-bats (3rd).
- Ranks second all-time among major league second basemen in runs scored, doubles, and assists.
- 1937 A.L. MVP.
- Hit for the cycle on May 27, 1939.
- Six-time *Sporting News* All-Star selection (1933–38).
- Six-time A.L. All-Star; started first six All-Star games (1933–38) at second base for the American League.
- Number 46 on *The Sporting News* 1999 list of Baseball's 100 Greatest Players.
- Three-time A.L. champion (1934, 1935, 1940).
- 1935 world champion.
- Elected to Baseball Hall of Fame by members of BBWAA in 1949.

4

Al Kaline

Courtesy of CollectAuctions.com

Nicknamed "Mr. Tiger" because he appeared in more games with the Tigers than any other player and represented the franchise through the years with class and dignity, both on and off the field, Al Kaline was among the finest all-around players of his generation. A true "five-tool" player, Kaline possessed the ability to hit, hit with power, run, field, and throw with the best players in the game, impressing everyone who saw him perform with his vast array of skills.

Bob Scheffing, who managed Kaline in Detroit from 1961 to 1963, stated flatly, "I wouldn't trade him for Mantle OR Mays."

Another former Tigers manager, Chuck Dressen, who piloted the team from 1963 to 1966, sang the praises of his right fielder when he proclaimed, "I don't want to sound like one of those guys who manages in Chicago and says this Chicago player is the best, then manages in St. Louis and says this St. Louis player is the best. But I've been watching Kaline, and he's the best player who ever played for me. Jackie Robinson was the most exciting runner I ever had . . . and Hank Aaron was the best hitter. But, for all-around ability, I mean hitting, fielding, running, and throwing, I'll go with Al."

Both managers perhaps lacked total objectivity when making their assessments, but Baltimore Orioles Hall of Fame third baseman Brooks Robinson offered a completely unbiased opinion when he suggested, "There have been a lot of great defensive players. The fella who could do everything is Al Kaline. He was just the epitome of what a great outfielder is all about—great speed, catches the ball, and throws the ball well."

A tremendous defensive outfielder with a powerful throwing arm, Kaline earned 10 Gold Gloves over the course of his 22 seasons in Detroit, compiling during his career the eighth most assists of any right fielder in major league history. A pretty fair hitter, Mr. Tiger posted a lifetime batting average of .297, won a batting title, and hit more home runs (399) than any other player in franchise history. Kaline accomplished all he did after arriving in the big leagues at the tender age of 18, having never played a single game in the minors.

Born in Baltimore, Maryland, on December 19, 1934, Albert William Kaline grew up in a sports-minded family that included a father and two uncles who played semipro baseball. After overcoming at the age of eight a case of osteomyelitis that necessitated the removal of a segment of bone from his left foot, young Al developed into an outstanding pitcher in youth baseball, enrolling in several organized leagues each season. Kaline went on to star in baseball and basketball at Baltimore's Southern High School, where he became the first member of his family to earn a diploma. Having earned all-state honors as an outfielder all four years at Southern High, Kaline signed with the Tigers for a bonus of $35,000 following his graduation, after which he bypassed the minor leagues completely. The 18-year-old outfielder made his major league debut with the Tigers just a few days later, replacing Jim Delsing in center field during the latter stages of a 5–2 loss to the Athletics in Philadelphia on June 25, 1953. Kaline spent the remainder of the year serving mostly as a late-inning defensive replacement or pinch-runner, appearing in only 30 games, garnering just 28 official at-bats, batting .250, and hitting his first big-league home run.

Recalling years later the uneasiness he felt when he first joined the Tigers, Kaline recounted, "I didn't know who was on the team, but I saw every eye as I walked down the aisle (of the team bus). It looked like a thousand eyes were staring at me saying, 'Who is this young punk?' I just kept my eyes straight ahead."

Kaline continued, "I'll never forget that first night with the team. Going to the ballpark on the bus was the hardest 30 minutes of my life. I had to walk down that aisle between all the players. I really didn't know too much about the Tigers at that time. . . . As the days went on, I didn't mind the games. In fact, I looked forward to them. That was the easiest part of all. I couldn't wait to get to the ballpark. I'd be the first one there, and I was willing to do anything. I think that's why the veterans liked me."

Kaline established himself as Detroit's starting right fielder the following year, earning a third-place finish in the Rookie of the Year balloting by batting .276, driving in 43 runs, and leading all players at his position with 280 putouts and 16 assists. After hitting just 4 home runs in his first full season, the slender 6'1", 175-pound 19-year-old received advice from none other than Ted Williams, who instructed him to improve his wrist strength over the winter by squeezing baseballs as hard as he could.

The Splendid Splinter's counsel ended up paying huge dividends, as Kaline hit safely in 23 of his first 24 games in 1955, including driving 7 balls out of the ballpark during the season's first month. He concluded the campaign with 27 homers, 102 RBIs, 121 runs scored, and a league-leading 200 hits, 321 total bases, and .340 batting average, earning in the process his first All-Star nomination and a close second-place finish to Yogi Berra in the A.L. MVP voting. By topping the circuit with a .340 average at only 20 years of age, Kaline became the youngest batting champion in A.L. history.

Kaline drew raves from some of the American League's most respected judges of talent with his fabulous performance at such a young age. In discussing the Tigers outfielder, Yankees manager Casey Stengel said, "The kid murders you with his speed and arm. . . . He's made some catches I still don't believe. . . . I sort of hate to think what'll happen when he grows up."

Meanwhile, Ted Williams, whose advice Kaline wisely heeded at the end of the previous campaign, gushed, "There's a hitter! In my book, he's the greatest right-handed hitter in the league."

Nevertheless, Kaline ended up feeling somewhat burdened by the high expectations the gaudy numbers he produced in just his second full season placed on him, noting years later, "It put a lot of pressure on me because I was at a young age and the writers around here and throughout the league starting comparing me to Cobb. It put a lot of pressure on me."

Kaline, though, did not disappoint in 1956, once again posting huge offensive numbers. In addition to hitting 27 home runs, scoring 96 runs, and batting .314, he finished second in the league with 128 RBIs, 32 doubles, 194 hits, and 327 total bases, en route to earning a third-place finish in the A.L. MVP balloting.

Kaline continued to excel in subsequent seasons, even though the 1955 and 1956 campaigns turned out to be the finest of his career. After hitting 23 home runs, driving in 90 runs, and batting .295 in 1957, Kaline missed a significant amount of playing time in three of the next five seasons due to a series of injuries he sustained. He sat out several games in 1958 after being hit by a pitch. A fractured shoulder landed him on the DL for nearly a month in 1959, and, after getting off to a torrid start in 1962, he missed 57 games when he broke his right collarbone while making a diving, game-saving catch that sealed Detroit's 2–1 victory over New York on May 26.

Courtesy of Jack Webster

Yet, Kaline posted solid numbers in each of those five seasons, batting over .300 four times and hitting more than 20 home runs twice. He performed particularly well in 1959, 1961, and 1962, batting .327 in the first of those years, with 27 homers, 94 RBIs, and a league-leading .530 slugging percentage and a .940 OPS. In addition to finishing second in the league to teammate Norm Cash in the 1961 batting race with a mark of .324, Kaline scored 116 runs and topped the circuit with 41 doubles. Although limited to just 100 games the following year, Kaline batted .304, hit 29 home runs, and knocked in 94 runs.

Kaline had one of his finest seasons in 1963, earning a second-place finish to New York's Elston Howard in the A.L. MVP voting by hitting 27 home runs, knocking in 101 runs, batting .312, and leading all players at his position in fielding percentage for the fourth of five times. He also won the sixth of his ten Gold Gloves, and the third of his seven in succession.

Constant pain in the same (left) foot that had been affected by osteomyelitis years earlier plagued Kaline throughout much of the 1964 and 1965 campaigns, finally forcing him to wear corrective shoes. Sportswriter Milton Gross described Kaline's deformed foot, saying, "The pinky and middle finger don't touch the ground. The fourth toe is stretched. The second and third are shortened. The first and third toes overlap; the second and the fourth are beginning to overlap the big toe, which has begun to bend to the left. It is hard to believe, but for all of his career with the Tigers, while he has been called the 'perfect player,' Kaline has bordered on being a cripple."

Kaline still managed to post decent numbers in each of those seasons, before improving his offensive production in 1966 and 1967. After batting .288, driving in 88 runs, and tying his career high by hitting 29 homers in 1966, he earned his fourth top-five finish in the MVP balloting the following year by hitting 25 home runs, scoring 94 times, and finishing third in the league with a .308 batting average.

Although Kaline missed nearly two months of the 1968 campaign after being hit by a pitch that broke his arm, he returned to the Tigers lineup in time to help lead them to victory over St. Louis in the World Series by batting .379, with 2 homers and 8 RBIs. Kaline spent one more year playing right field exclusively, before splitting his time in each of the next four seasons between the outfield and first base. Even though he failed to compile as many as 500 official at-bats in any of those campaigns, Kaline remained a productive hitter, reaching the 20-homer plateau for the ninth and final time in 1969, earning his fourteenth All-Star nomination in 1971, and batting over .300 for the ninth and final time the following year. After serving the Tigers primarily as a designated hitter in 1974, Kaline elected to announce his retirement. He ended his career with 399 home runs, 1,583 runs batted in, 1,622 runs scored, 3,007 hits, 75 triples, 498 doubles, a .297 lifetime batting average, a .376 on-base percentage, and a .480 slugging percentage. In addition to hitting more home runs than any other Tigers player, he holds the franchise record for most games played (2,834). Kaline also ranks either second or third in team history in most other statistical categories. He earned a total of 10 top-ten finishes in the league MVP voting, placing in the top five in the balloting on four separate occasions.

Following his retirement, Kaline became the color commentator on Tigers telecasts, continuing in that capacity until 2002, when he assumed a position in the front office, serving the team as a special assistant to Tigers president/CEO/general manager Dave Dombrowski. His duties included working with outfielders during spring training. Prior to taking on that role, though, he became the tenth player to be inducted into the Baseball Hall of Fame in his first year of eligibility, being so honored by the members of the BBWAA in 1980.

Looking back at the success he experienced over the course of his career, Kaline said, "When I first came up to the Tigers I was scared stiff, but I had desire. Desire is something you must have to make it in the majors. I was never satisfied with being just average."

Legendary manager Billy Martin, who piloted the Tigers in three of Kaline's final four seasons, stated that the outfielder reached his ultimate goal, suggesting on one occasion, "I have always referred to Al Kaline as 'Mister Perfection.' He does it all—hitting, fielding, running, and throwing—and he does it with that extra touch of brilliance that marks him as a super ballplayer . . . Al fits in anywhere, at any position in the lineup, and any spot in the batting order."

CAREER HIGHLIGHTS

Best Season

Kaline appeared to be well on his way to having the finest season of his career in 1962, compiling a batting average of .336, with 13 home runs and 38 RBIs, through the first 35 games of the campaign. However, a broken collarbone suffered while making a game-saving catch against the Yankees on May 26 put him out of action for two months, limiting him to a total of only 100 games and 398 official at-bats. Although Kaline still finished the year with 29 home runs, 94 RBIs, a .304 batting average, and a career-high

.969 OPS, his overall numbers came up a bit short of the figures he compiled in his breakout season of 1955. Still only 20 years old by the end of the year, Kaline earned a second-place finish in the A.L. MVP voting in just his second full season by finishing in the league's top five with 27 home runs, 102 RBIs, and 8 triples, placing second with 121 runs scored, a .421 on-base percentage, a .546 slugging percentage, and a .967 OPS, and topping the circuit with 321 total bases and a career-high .340 batting average and 200 hits. He also finished second among A.L. right fielders with 14 assists, while leading all players at his position with 306 putouts.

Memorable Moments/Greatest Performances

Kaline had the biggest day of his career on April 17, 1955, when he led the Tigers to a 16–0 victory over the Kansas City Athletics by going 4-for-5, with 3 home runs, 6 RBIs, and 3 runs scored. Kaline's 2 homers in the bottom of the sixth inning made him the first Tigers player to reach the seats twice in the same frame, and the first American Leaguer to accomplish the feat since Joe DiMaggio did so for the Yankees in 1936.

Kaline had another huge game on August 4, 1956, when he homered twice, doubled, and knocked in all 5 Tiger runs, in leading his team to a 5–4 win over the Yankees at Briggs Stadium. However, Kaline turned in perhaps his most memorable performance against the St. Louis Cardinals in the 1968 World Series. Appearing in the postseason for the first time in his career after missing a third of the campaign with a broken arm, the 33-year-old outfielder led all Tiger batsmen with 11 hits, en route to posting a .379 batting average, with 2 home runs and 8 RBIs. Kaline got arguably the biggest hit of his career in Game Five, turning a 3–2 deficit into a 4–3 Tiger lead with a bases-loaded single in the bottom of the seventh inning. The Tigers went on to win the contest by a score of 5–3, then won the next two games, overcoming in the process a 3-games-to-1 deficit to St. Louis. The world championship marked Detroit's first in 23 years.

Kaline experienced one more memorable moment six years later, on September 24, 1974, when he doubled off Baltimore Orioles left-hander Dave McNally to become just the twelfth player in major league history to reach the 3,000-hit plateau. Kaline announced his intention to retire at season's end shortly after he reached the milestone, stating after he played in his last game on October 3, "I'm glad it's over. I really am. I don't think I'll miss it. I may miss spring training."

NOTABLE ACHIEVEMENTS

- Hit more than 20 home runs nine times.
- Knocked in more than 100 runs three times.
- Scored more than 100 runs twice.
- Batted over .300 nine times, topping .320 on three occasions.
- Reached the 200-hit mark once (200 in 1955).
- Finished in double digits in triples once (10 in 1956).
- Surpassed 30 doubles four times, topping 40 two-baggers once (41 in 1961).
- Compiled on-base percentage in excess of .400 four times.
- Posted slugging percentage in excess of .500 eight times.
- Led the American League in batting average once; hits once; doubles once; total bases once; slugging percentage once; and OPS once.
- Led A.L. outfielders in assists twice and fielding percentage twice.
- Led A.L. right fielders in assists three times; putouts five times; fielding percentage five times; and double plays turned twice.
- Holds Tiger career records for most home runs (399); walks (1,277); and games played (2,834).
- Ranks second all-time on Tigers in RBIs (1,583); hits (3,007); extra-base hits (972); total bases (4,852); plate appearances (11,596); and at-bats (10,116).
- Ranks third all-time on Tigers in runs scored (1,622) and doubles (498).
- Hit 3 home runs in one game on April 17, 1955.
- Finished second in A.L. MVP voting twice (1955, 1963).
- Ten-time Gold Glove winner.
- Five-time *Sporting News* All-Star selection (1955, 1962, 1963, 1966, 1967).
- Fifteen-time A.L. All-Star.
- Number 76 on *The Sporting News* 1999 list of Baseball's 100 Greatest Players.
- 1968 A.L. champion.
- 1968 world champion.
- Elected to Baseball Hall of Fame by members of BBWAA in 1980.

5

Harry Heilmann

Courtesy of RMYauctions.com

M any baseball historians tend to trivialize the offensive accomplishments of Harry Heilmann, claiming that he had his best years during the 1920s, which turned out to be a fabulous decade for hitters. Nevertheless, the fact remains that Heilmann established himself as one of the period's greatest hitters, with his .364 batting average representing the highest figure compiled by any A.L. player over the course of that 10-year stretch. Heilmann posted a batting average in excess of

.390 four times between 1921 and 1927, with his mark of .403 in 1923 making him the last A.L. player, with the exception of Ted Williams, to reach the .400 plateau. A feared slugger, Heilmann compiled a slugging percentage of .558 during the 1920s—a mark surpassed only by Babe Ruth, Lou Gehrig, and Al Simmons among A.L. batsmen. Meanwhile, he also averaged 14 home runs, 113 RBIs, 193 hits, 10 triples, and 40 doubles per season during the decade.

Born in San Francisco, California, on August 3, 1894, Harry Edwin Heilmann had to endure as a teenager the loss of his older brother, who drowned while attempting to swim to shore after his boat capsized. After starring in baseball at San Francisco's Sacred Heart Cathedral Preparatory High School, from which he graduated in 1912, Heilmann took a job as a bookkeeper for a biscuit-maker. His career path took a sudden turn, though, in 1913, when a former teammate from Sacred Heart asked him to fill in for the Hanford, California, team in the San Joaquin Valley League. Having impressed a scout at one of Hanford's games, Heilmann subsequently signed a professional contract with the Portland Beavers of the Northwest League. While at Portland, Heilmann similarly impressed circuit president and former major league manager Fielder Jones, who recommended the slugging young outfielder to Tigers owner Frank Navin.

Purchased by Detroit for $1,500, Heilmann made his major league debut with the Tigers on May 16, 1914, after which he struggled over the course of the next few months. With Ty Cobb, Sam Crawford, and Bobby Veach manning the three outfield spots for the Tigers, Heilmann saw a limited amount of playing time, appearing in only 68 games and batting just .225, with only 2 homers and 18 RBIs. Optioned to San Francisco of the Pacific Coast League at season's end, Heilmann spent the entire 1915 campaign playing all over the diamond for the Seals, earning a trip back to the majors by batting .364.

Although he also saw some action at other positions after he returned to Detroit in 1916, Heilmann split most of his time between right field and first base. Appearing in a total of 136 games for the Tigers, the right-hand-hitting Heilmann batted .282, hit 2 home runs, and knocked in 73 runs. He improved upon those numbers the following year, when he supplanted the aging Crawford as the team's regular right fielder by hitting 5 homers, driving in 86 runs, and batting .281. Heilmann appeared in only 79 games in 1918, missing half of the season after joining the U.S. Navy and serving on a submarine once the United States entered World War I. He returned to the Tigers, though, prior to the start of the 1919 campaign to post the best numbers of his young career. Shifted to first base by manager Hughie

Jennings because of his defensive shortcomings in the outfield, Heilmann started every game for the Tigers, finishing the year with 8 home runs, 93 RBIs, 15 triples, 30 doubles, and a .320 batting average. He followed that up with a solid 1920 campaign, during which he hit 9 homers, drove in 89 runs, and batted .309.

Even though Heilmann appeared to be developing into one of the American League's better hitters, he remained something of a disappointment, failing in the eyes of many to reach his full potential. Furthermore, most observers considered him to be a defensive liability, with his slowness of foot and deficiencies in the field prompting his teammates to nickname him "Slug" and "Harry, the Horse." The 6'1", 200-pound Heilmann continued to struggle with the glove even after the Tigers moved him to first base, leading all A.L. first sackers in errors in both 1919 and 1920.

However, everything began to come together for the 26-year-old Heilmann after Ty Cobb took over as Detroit's player/manager in 1921. Cobb took Heilmann under his wing, working with him extensively to improve his mechanics at the plate. Detroit's new manager instructed Heilmann to crouch more in the batter's box. He also told him to shift his weight more to his front foot, and to make better use of his wrists in order to generate more power.

Ted Williams further expounded upon the lessons Heilmann learned from Cobb in his book *Ted Williams' Hit List*, revealing that Heilmann told him personally, "When Cobb taught me how to hit inside-out, from then on I was never afraid to get two strikes on me. I could wait that much longer and still inside-out it and get the big part of the bat on the ball enough to drive it over the infielders. I didn't fear having two strikes on me after I learned that. I didn't try to pull the ball. I was aiming it through the middle, and, if I had to go inside-out a little bit to get it through the middle, to get the big part of the bat on the ball—BANG!—I could do it."

The livelier ball that the American League began using in 1920 also contributed to the success that Heilmann and the other hitters of the day experienced in subsequent seasons, since it forced outfielders to play deeper and farther apart, creating more space in the outfield for balls to drop. Having developed under Cobb's tutelage an exceptional line-drive stroke, Heilmann benefited as much as anyone, raising his batting average 85 points in 1921, to a league-leading mark of .394. He also topped the circuit with 237 hits and ranked among the leaders with 19 home runs, 139 RBIs, 114 runs scored, 14 triples, 43 doubles, 365 total bases, a .444 on-base percentage, and a .606 slugging percentage. Heilmann's .394 batting average enabled him to edge out teammate and mentor Cobb by 5 points in the batting race, subsequently causing a rift to develop between the two men. As daughter-in-law Marguerite Heilmann revealed years later, "When he beat Ty Cobb out for the batting championship, Ty didn't really talk with him again. He was kind of irrational about it and wasn't really dad's cup of tea."

Having found his stroke, Heilmann tormented A.L. pitchers the rest of the decade, batting below .340 just once over the course of the next eight seasons. Even a broken collarbone that forced him to miss 35 games in 1922 couldn't deter Heilmann, who finished the season with a .356 batting average, 92 RBIs, and a career-high 21 home runs. He followed that up by winning his second batting title in 1923, leading the league with a mark of .403. Heilmann also ranked among the leaders with 18 homers, 115 RBIs, 121 runs scored, 211 hits, 11 triples, 44 doubles, a .481 on-base percentage, and a .632 slugging percentage, earning in the process a third-place finish in the A.L. MVP balloting.

After batting .346, driving in 114 runs, scoring 107 times, and leading the league with 45 doubles in 1924, Heilmann had another great year in 1925, topping the circuit with a batting average of .393, while also finishing among the leaders with 134 RBIs, 225 hits, 40 doubles, a .457 on-base percentage, and a .569 slugging average. Meanwhile, he worked diligently throughout the period to improve his defense, eventually turning himself into a competent outfielder after being moved back to right field by Cobb in 1921. Heilmann led all A.L. outfielders with 31 assists in 1924, and he also topped all circuit right fielders in putouts in both 1924 and 1925.

Heilmann had another outstanding offensive year in 1926, batting .367 with 101 RBIs and 40 doubles, before winning his final batting title with a mark of .398 the following season. He also hit 14 homers, knocked in 120 runs, scored 106 times, collected 201 hits, and banged out a career-high 50 doubles in 1927 en route to earning a second-place finish to New York's Lou Gehrig in the MVP voting. When a reporter reminded Heilmann at the conclusion of that 1927 campaign that he had led the league in hitting every other year from 1921 to 1927, he replied, "Mr. Navin gives me contracts on a two-year basis. I always bear down real hard when a new contract is coming up."

Heilmann spent two more productive years in Detroit, finishing in double digits in home runs and driving in more than 100 runs both seasons, while compiling batting averages of .328 and .344. However, with Heilmann scheduled to turn 36 during the 1930 season, and with arthritis in both wrists affecting his hitting in 1929, the Tigers sold him to the Cincinnati Reds shortly after the conclusion of the 1929 campaign. Heilmann ended his time in Detroit with 164 home runs, 1,440 RBIs,

Courtesy of the Library of Congress, Bain Collection

1,209 runs scored, 2,499 hits, 145 triples, 497 doubles, a .342 batting average, a .410 on-base percentage, and a .518 slugging percentage. With the exception of home runs, he ranks among the Tigers' all-time leaders in each of those categories.

Despite being plagued by arthritis again in 1930, Heilmann posted solid numbers for the Reds, finishing the year with 19 homers, 91 RBIs, and a .333 batting average. After sitting out the entire 1931 campaign, Heilmann attempted a brief comeback with Cincinnati the following year. However, with the pain in his wrists proving to be too much to overcome, he announced his retirement after appearing in only 15 games. Heilmann finished his career with 183 home runs, 1,537 RBIs, 1,291 runs scored, 2,660 hits, 151 triples, 542 doubles, a .342 batting average, a .410 on-base percentage, and a .520 slugging percentage. His .342 batting average ties him with Babe Ruth for the twelfth-highest in major league history. It also represents the third-highest career mark ever posted by a right-handed batter, trailing only Rogers Hornsby's .358 and Ed Delahanty's .346.

Ted Williams, who ranked Heilmann as the seventeenth greatest hitter in baseball history in his book *Ted Williams' Hit List*, stated in this work, "I personally never saw Heilmann hit, but I talked to Joe Cronin and Eddie Collins, who had both seen Heilmann in action. They were both impressed with him. In fact, of all the old-timers I've talked to about Heilmann, every single one has sung his praises."

Hall of Fame pitcher Ted Lyons said in *Baseball Hall of Fame*, "Harry Heilmann was one of the most marvelous men I ever met in baseball, and one of the greatest right-handed hitters. He had a choppy stroke, but powerful. He was a tough man to pitch to."

Shortly after retiring as an active player, Heilmann became a member of the Tigers' radio broadcast team, serving in that capacity from 1934 to 1950. During that time, he further endeared himself to Tiger fans with his sense of humor, storytelling skills, and knowledge of the game. Heilmann's 17-year run as an announcer for the team unfortunately came to a premature end when he was stricken with lung cancer just prior to the start of the 1950 campaign. He died a little over one year later, on July 9, 1951, just two days before the All-Star game at Briggs Stadium. The game began with a moment of silence in his honor. The members of the BBWAA elected Heilmann to the Hall of Fame six months later, after failing to do so the previous year despite the efforts of Ty Cobb, who launched a campaign to get his ailing former teammate inducted prior to his death.

TIGERS CAREER HIGHLIGHTS

Best Season

Heilmann performed magnificently all four years he won the A.L. batting title, hitting over .390, driving in well over 100 runs, accumulating more than 200 hits and 40 doubles, and compiling an OPS well in excess of 1.000 each season. In addition to batting .393 in 1925, he knocked in 134 runs and amassed 225 hits. Two years later, he batted .398, drove in 120 runs, and accumulated a career-high 50 doubles. Heilmann posted arguably the best all-around numbers of his career in 1921, when, in addition to leading the league with 237 hits and a .394 batting average, he ranked among the leaders with 19 home runs, 14 triples, 43 doubles, 114 runs scored, a career-high 139 RBIs and 365 total bases, and an OPS of 1.051.

Nevertheless, it would be difficult to go against Heilmann's fabulous 1923 campaign, a season in which he established career highs in batting average (.403), on-base percentage (.481), slugging percentage (.632), OPS (1.113), and runs scored (121). In addition to finishing fourth in the American League in runs scored and placing either first or second in the circuit in each of the other four categories, Heilmann ranked in the top five in home runs (18), RBIs (115), hits (211), doubles (44), and total bases (331). He also finished second among A.L. right fielders with 277 putouts—a total that fell just one short of the career-high mark he posted two years later. All things considered, Heilmann had his greatest season in 1923.

Memorable Moments/Greatest Performances

Although not necessarily viewed as a home run hitter, Heilmann hit one of the longest homers ever recorded, on July 8, 1921, when he delivered a blast during a 4–1 loss to the Red Sox in Detroit that the *New York Tribune* subsequently reported as having traveled 610 feet. The story that appeared in the *Tribune* the following day claimed that the groundskeeper measured the distance. Heilmann's titanic blow proved to be the highlight of a 34-for-58 hitting spree he began in early July. Heilmann went on another hitting binge the following year, hitting safely in 10 consecutive trips to the plate, from June 16 to June 19, 1922.

Heilmann clinched two of his four batting titles by displaying his hitting prowess on the season's final day. The Tiger right fielder raised his 1925 average to .393 by collecting 6 hits during a season-ending doubleheader against the St. Louis Browns on October 4. In so doing, he edged out Cleveland's Tris Speaker for the batting title by 4 points. Two years later, Heilmann trailed Al Simmons by 1 point heading into the last day of the season. However, he ended up finishing 6 points ahead of Simmons in the batting race by hitting safely seven times during a doubleheader sweep of the Cleveland Indians. Heilmann concluded the campaign with a mark of .398.

Heilmann actually had some of the biggest days of his career during that 1927 season. On May 9 of that year, he led the Tigers to a 17–11 pounding of Boston by going 4-for-5, with 2 homers, 4 RBIs, and 3 runs scored. A little over two months later, on July 13, he led them to a doubleheader sweep of Washington by going 7-for-9, with a homer, 3 doubles, 7 RBIs, and 5 runs scored.

Heilmann had another huge game on July 26, 1928, when he enabled the Tigers to post a 13–10 victory in the second game of their doubleheader split with the Yankees by driving in 8 runs with a homer, triple, and single.

Yet, Tiger fans of the day appreciated Heilmann most for the heroic act he performed off the field on July 25, 1916, when he dove into the Detroit River to save the life of a drowning woman. The local press reported

Heilmann's act of bravery, resulting in a thunderous ovation for the young outfielder at the ballpark the following day.

NOTABLE ACHIEVEMENTS

- Batted over .300 eleven times, surpassing .350 six times, topping .390 on four occasions, and hitting over .400 once (.403 in 1923).
- Knocked in more than 100 runs eight times, surpassing 120 RBIs on four occasions.
- Scored more than 100 runs four times.
- Hit more than 20 home runs once (21 in 1922).
- Topped 200 hits four times.
- Finished in double digits in triples nine times, surpassing 15 three-baggers on two occasions.
- Surpassed 30 doubles ten times, 40 two-baggers seven times, and 50 doubles once.
- Compiled on-base percentage in excess of .400 eight times, topping .450 three times.
- Posted slugging percentage in excess of .500 nine times, topping .600 three times.
- Compiled OPS in excess of 1.000 five times.
- Led the American League in batting average four times, hits once, and doubles once.
- Led A.L. outfielders in assists once.
- Led A.L. right fielders in assists twice, putouts twice, and double plays turned once.
- Owns third-highest career batting average (.342) in major league history by a right-handed batter.
- Ranks among Tigers career leaders in batting average (2nd); RBIs (3rd); runs scored (7th); hits (4th); extra-base hits (4th); doubles (4th); triples (4th); total bases (4th); walks (9th); on-base percentage (5th); slugging percentage (3rd); OPS (4th); games played (8th); plate appearances (8th); and at-bats (7th).
- First player to homer in every major league ballpark in use.
- Finished in top five of A.L. MVP voting four times, placing second once (1927) and third once (1923).
- Number 54 on *The Sporting News* 1999 list of Baseball's 100 Greatest Players.
- Elected to Baseball Hall of Fame by members of BBWAA in 1952.

6

Sam Crawford

Courtesy of the Library of Congress, Harris & Ewing Collection

Playing alongside Ty Cobb in the Detroit outfield for parts of 13 seasons undoubtedly deprived Sam Crawford of much of the recognition he otherwise would have received over the course of his Hall of Fame career. Even though Crawford proved to be nearly the equal of Cobb in terms of run production during their time together, he invariably played second fiddle to the Georgia Peach because of the latter's superior all-around ability. Nevertheless, Crawford is generally considered to be one of the dead-ball era's greatest sluggers and one of the premier players of the first two decades of the twentieth century. The first player ever to lead both major leagues in home runs, Crawford amassed an all-time record 51 inside-the-park homers over the course of his career. He also is Major League Baseball's all-time leader in triples, with 309 three-baggers to his credit. A solid outfielder, Crawford helped teammate Cobb develop his fielding skills during the early stages of the latter's career, before the two men developed a mutual disdain for one another. Yet, even though Crawford and Cobb ended up spending most of their years together barely speaking to each other, they served as the central figures on the first three pennant-winning Tigers clubs, with Crawford playing Robin to Cobb's Batman.

Born in Wahoo, Nebraska, on April 18, 1880, Samuel Earl Crawford began playing baseball at an early age, eventually joining a traveling team in Wahoo that challenged local clubs to games and paid its expenses by passing around a hat. Although Crawford later developed a reputation for being articulate and well-read, he forsook his formal education after the fifth grade to work as a barber's apprentice. He continued to follow that career path until the spring of 1899, when the Chatham Reds of the Canadian League recruited him to play for their team for $65 per month. Crawford spent the first few months of the campaign with Chatham, before joining the Western League's Grand Rapids Rustlers, who subsequently sold him to the Cincinnati Reds in September 1899. The 19-year-old outfielder became the National League's youngest player when he made his major league debut with the Reds a few days later, on September 10. Appearing in 31 games with the club over the course of the final few weeks of the season, Crawford batted .307, collected 7 triples, and hit his first major league home run.

Crawford became Cincinnati's starting right fielder the following year, when he batted .260 and placed among the league leaders with 7 home runs and 15 triples. He developed into a star in his second full season, topping the senior circuit with 16 home runs, a record 12 of which were of the inside-the-park variety. Crawford also batted .330 and finished near the top of the league rankings with 104 RBIs and 16 triples. After another solid season in 1902, in which he led the National League with 22 triples and finished among the leaders with a .333 batting average and a .461 slugging percentage, Crawford elected to jump to the Tigers of the newly formed American League. Upon his arrival in Detroit, the left-hand-hitting outfielder immediately established himself as one of the junior circuit's top performers, concluding the 1903 campaign with 89 RBIs and a league-leading 25 triples, while also placing second in the batting race with a mark of .335.

Crawford subsequently suffered through a subpar 1904 season, in which he batted just .254 and knocked in only 73 runs. However, he rebounded somewhat the following year, placing among the league leaders with 6 home runs, 75 RBIs, 73 runs scored, 38 doubles, a .297 batting average, and a .430 slugging percentage. Crawford posted solid numbers again in 1906, concluding the campaign with 72 RBIs, 16 triples, and a .295 batting average, before beginning an exceptional nine-year run that saw him annually place among the league leaders in virtually every major statistical category. During that time, he continued to build on his reputation as one of the game's hardest hitters and most feared batsmen.

Fielder Jones, a contemporary of Crawford, said, "None of them can hit quite as hard as Crawford. He stands up at the plate like a brick house and he hits all the pitchers, without playing favorites."

Ed Barrow, who managed Crawford in the outfielder's first two years in Detroit, and later converted Babe Ruth into a full-time outfielder as general manager of the Yankees, once said that "there was never a better hitter than Crawford."

Meanwhile, F. C. Lane of *Baseball Magazine* wrote of the 6', 190-pound Crawford in 1916, "While we are no sculptor, we believe that if we were looking for a model for a statue of a slugger we would choose Sam Crawford for that role. . . . Sam has tremendous shoulders and great strength. That strength is so placed in his frame, and the weight so balanced, that he can get it all behind the drive when he smites a baseball."

Eschewing the "scientific" approach to hitting so popular during his playing days, Crawford adopted a less-complicated philosophy, once explaining, "My idea of batting is a thing that should be done unconsciously. If you get to studying it too much, to see just what fraction of a second you must swing to meet a curved ball, the chances are you will miss it altogether."

More than just an outstanding hitter, Crawford also excelled on the base paths and in the outfield early in his career, swiping a total of 367 bases and leading all A.L. outfielders with a .988 fielding percentage in 1905—a mark that exceeded the league average by 35 points. He also had above-average range and a strong throwing arm that enabled him to compile more than 20 assists in a season on three separate occasions.

But Crawford built his reputation primarily on his hitting, and on his ability to drive the ball farther than perhaps any other player in the game. During the dead-ball era, the measure of a player's slugging ability was not so much in the number of home runs he hit but in the number of triples he compiled. During the Tigers' three pennant-winning seasons of 1907, 1908, and 1909, Crawford amassed a total of 47 triples en route to tallying an all-time major league record 309 three-baggers over the course of his career. He also became the first player to lead each league in home runs when he topped the American league with 7 four-baggers in 1908. Despite being overshadowed by Ty Cobb throughout the Tigers' three-year reign as A.L. champions, Crawford proved to be a huge contributor to the success the team experienced during that time. Crawford, who usually batted fourth in the Detroit lineup, right after Cobb, led the league with 102 runs scored in 1907 and finished second to his teammate with a .323 batting average and a .460 slugging percentage. In addition to topping the circuit with 7 homers in 1908, Crawford placed second with 80 RBIs, 102 runs scored, 184 hits, a .311 batting average, and a .457 slugging percentage. He also finished second to Cobb in 1909 with 97 RBIs and a .452 slugging percentage.

Courtesy of the Library of Congress, Bain Collection

Although the Tigers failed to repeat as A.L. champions in any of the six remaining years during which Crawford remained a full-time player with them, the veteran outfielder had some of his greatest offensive seasons. After leading the league with 19 triples and 120 RBIs in 1910, Crawford posted the best numbers of his career the following year, when he placed among the league leaders with 115 RBIs, 109 runs scored, 217 hits, 14 triples, 36 doubles, 302 total bases, a .378 batting average, a .438 on-base percentage, and a .526 slugging percentage. He batted well over .300 in each of the next two seasons and amassed a total of 44 triples. Crawford led the league in RBIs and triples in each of his final two years as a full-time player, accumulating an all-time A.L. record 26 three-baggers in 1914, a year in which he finished second in the league MVP voting.

The 1915 season proved to be Crawford's last as a full-time player. Harry Heilmann's arrival in 1916 relegated Crawford to part-time status, prompting the Tigers to release him at the conclusion of the 1917 campaign after he posted a batting average of just .173 in 104 at-bats over the course of the season. Crawford ended his 19-year major league career just 39 hits short of the magical 3,000. In addition to his 2,961 hits and all-time record 309 triples, Crawford compiled 97 home runs, 1,525 RBIs, 1,391 runs scored, 458 doubles, 367 stolen bases, a lifetime batting average of .309, an on-base percentage of .362, and a slugging percentage of .452. In his 15 years with the Tigers, he hit 70 home runs, knocked in 1,264 runs, scored 1,115 times, accumulated 2,466 hits, 402 doubles, 249 triples, and 318 stolen bases, batted .309, compiled a .362 on-base percentage, and posted a .448 slugging percentage. Crawford continues to rank among the franchise's all-time leaders in RBIs, runs scored, hits, doubles, triples, and steals.

Following his release by the Tigers, Crawford migrated west, settling in Peco, California, and concluding his professional career with four productive seasons with the Los Angeles Angels of the Pacific Coast League (PCL). He subsequently remained active in the game, serving as head baseball coach at the University of Southern California from 1924 to 1929 and later becoming an umpire in the PCL.

Despite Crawford's many accomplishments on the playing field, he failed to gain induction to the Baseball Hall of Fame until 1957, when the members of the Veterans Committee finally elected him—40 years after he played his last game in the major leagues. It later surfaced that Ty Cobb, with whom Crawford spent much of his time feuding during their many years together as teammates, had a significant amount of influence in Crawford's induction to Cooperstown. Upon Cobb's death in July 1961, a reporter found hundreds of letters in his home responding to letters he had written to influential people extolling Crawford's Hall of Fame credentials.

Sam Crawford passed away 11 years after being elected to the Baseball Hall of Fame. He died on June 15, 1968, after suffering a stroke a few weeks earlier. Crawford was 88 years old at the time of his passing.

TIGERS CAREER HIGHLIGHTS

Best Season

Crawford earned a second-place finish to Philadelphia's Eddie Collins in the 1914 A.L. MVP voting by topping the circuit with 104 RBIs and 26 triples, and placing among the league leaders with 8 home runs, 183 hits, 281 total bases, a .314 batting average, a .388 on-base percentage, and a .483 slugging percentage. However, he posted significantly better numbers in virtually every offensive category in 1911, when, in addition to hitting 7 homers, knocking in 115 runs, accumulating 14 triples, 36 doubles, and 37 stolen bases, he established career highs with 109 runs scored, 217 hits, 302 total bases, a .378 batting average, a .438 on-base percentage, and a .526 slugging percentage. Crawford finished either second or third in the league in six different offensive categories in 1911, making it the finest all-around season of his career.

Memorable Moments/Greatest Performances

Crawford had one of his biggest days at the plate for the Tigers on August 16, 1903, helping them post a 12–8 victory over the New York Highlanders by going 5-for-6. On May 11, 1904, Crawford put an end to Cy Young's record streak of $24\frac{1}{3}$ consecutive no-hit innings (76 batters) when he delivered a one-out single in the seventh inning of a 1–0 loss to Young and the Red Sox.

Crawford put the finishing touches on the biggest comeback in major league history on June 18, 1911, when he hit a walk-off double in the bottom of the ninth to give the Tigers a 16–15 victory over the White Sox. Trailing Chicago by a score of 13–1 after $5\frac{1}{2}$ frames, the Tigers made up most of the deficit by scoring 5 runs in the eighth inning and another 3 runs in the bottom of the ninth.

Although the Tigers came up short in their three trips to the World Series between 1907 and 1909, with Crawford batting just .243 and knocking in only 8 runs in 70 official at-bats, the outfielder had a huge Game Five in the 1909 Fall Classic. Even though the Pirates ended up winning the contest by a score of 8–4, Crawford went 3-for-4, with a homer, double, stolen base, 2 RBIs, and 2 runs scored.

NOTABLE ACHIEVEMENTS

- Batted over .300 eight times, topping .320 four times and batting over .370 once (.378 in 1911).
- Knocked in more than 100 runs five times.
- Scored more than 100 runs three times.
- Surpassed 200 hits once (217 in 1911).
- Finished in double digits in triples fourteen straight times, topping 20 three-baggers on four occasions.
- Surpassed 30 doubles eight times.
- Stole more than 20 bases nine times, topping 30 steals three times and 40 thefts once.
- Compiled on-base percentage in excess of .400 once (.438 in 1911).
- Posted slugging percentage in excess of .500 once (.526 in 1911).
- Led the American League in home runs once; RBIs three times; runs scored once; triples five times; doubles once; and total bases once.
- Led A.L. outfielders in fielding percentage once and double plays turned once.
- Ranks among Tigers career leaders in RBIs (5th); runs scored (8th); triples (second); doubles (7th); hits (5th); extra-base hits (7th); total bases (6th); stolen bases (3rd); games played (6th); plate appearances (6th); and at-bats (6th).
- Holds Tigers single-season record for triples (26 in 1914).
- Holds major league record for most career triples (309).
- First player to lead each league in home runs.
- Finished second in 1914 A.L. MVP voting.
- Number 84 on *The Sporting News* 1999 list of Baseball's 100 Greatest Players.
- Three-time A.L. champion (1907–1909).
- Elected to Baseball Hall of Fame by members of Veterans Committee in 1957.

7

Miguel Cabrera

Courtesy of Keith Allison

rguably the finest all-around hitter in the game today, Miguel Cabrera has reached the level of greatness during his seven seasons in Detroit originally predicted for him when he first joined the Florida Marlins as a wide-eyed 20-year-old back in 2003. After starring for the Marlins for five years, Cabrera became a member of the Tigers in 2008, since which time he has established himself as baseball's dominant hitter, annually placing among A.L. leaders in most major statistical categories. In addition to topping the circuit in home runs once, RBIs twice, and doubles twice, he has won three batting titles and led the league in on-base percentage three times and slugging percentage twice. Cabrera's extraordinary hitting ability has earned him A.L. All-Star honors in each of the past five seasons, three Silver Sluggers, five top-five finishes in the league MVP voting, and two MVP trophies. Still only 31 years old as of this writing, Cabrera figures to add significantly to his list of accomplishments over the course of the next several years, giving him an excellent chance of ascending to an even loftier position in these rankings.

Born in Maracay, Aragua, Venezuela, on April 18, 1983, Jose Miguel Cabrera grew up in humble surroundings. Raised in a small home with one bathroom, a kitchen, and two rooms in a community of five homes where extended family lived, Cabrera shared a room with his younger sister. Spending much of his time in the company of a rowdy group of baseball-playing friends, who made fun of him because of his large head, Cabrera developed thick skin at an early age. Reflecting back at that particular time in his life, Cabrera revealed that he hid from his companions the annoyance he felt every time they called him "cabeza tren" (or "train head"), noting, "If you get mad, they call you that every day; can't show it."

Signing with the Florida Marlins as an amateur free agent before even graduating from Maracay High School, Cabrera began his professional career in 1999, at the tender age of 16. He subsequently advanced rapidly through Florida's farm system, gradually transitioning from shortstop to third base during his 3½ years in the minors. After being called up by the Marlins in June 2003, Cabrera made his major league debut a memorable one, hitting a walk-off home run in the first game he played, on June 20. He then went on to earn a fifth-place finish in the N.L. Rookie of the Year voting by hitting 12 home runs, driving in 62 runs, and batting .268 for the eventual world champions, splitting his time between left field and third base.

Playing the outfield almost exclusively in each of the next two seasons, the burly 6'4", 240-pound Cabrera struggled at times defensively, but his strong throwing arm enabled him to finish among the league's leading outfielders in assists both years. But, while Cabrera occasionally proved to be something of a liability in the field, his powerful bat more than compensated for any defensive shortcomings he may have displayed. After earning N.L. All-Star honors for the first of four straight times in 2004 by hitting 33 home runs, driving in 112 runs, scoring 101 times, and batting .294, Cabrera won his first Silver Slugger and finished fifth in the league MVP voting the following year after concluding the campaign with 33 homers, 116 RBIs, 106 runs scored, and a .323 batting average.

Cabrera's exceptional hitting at such a young age prompted several well-respected baseball people to sing his praises. Longtime hitting and first base coach Bill Robinson noted, "When he connects, it's almost like a shotgun going off, it's so loud." Hall of Famer Andre Dawson said of Cabrera, "He's got all the tools, and he's not intimidated by anything. . . . With Miguel, it's just a matter of how much he's really willing to push himself to get to the next level and be a great player." Jeff Conine, a teammate of Cabrera's in Florida, suggested, "He's a superstar in the making. He already is a phenomenal player, but he's going to be good for a long, long time." Hall of Famer Frank Robinson, who managed against Cabrera during the latter's first few years in the league, commented, "We haven't found a weakness in him yet. There are ways of getting him out, but, if you do it too often, he'll burn you."

Cabrera continued to post huge numbers for the Marlins in 2006 and 2007, averaging 30 homers, 117 RBIs, and 102 runs scored those two sea-

Courtesy of Keith Allison

sons, while compiling batting averages of .339 and .320 after moving back to third base. Yet, even as Cabrera established himself as one of the game's truly great hitters, concerns began to mount over his increased girth and perceived lack of dedication to his profession. A large man to begin with, Cabrera added a significant amount of bulk during his time in Florida, with some people in the know expressing the belief that his inability to take proper care of himself would eventually lead to his downfall. Others opined that Cabrera lacked the initiative and drive to maintain his high level of performance throughout the remainder of his career.

Fearing the worst, the Marlins decided to part ways with their best player, trading him and struggling pitcher Dontrelle Willis to the Detroit Tigers on December 4, 2007, for outfielder Cameron Maybin, catcher Mike Rabelo, and pitchers Andrew Miller, Dallas Trahern, Burke Badenhop, and Eulogio De La Cruz. Although Willis never regained the earlier form that made him a 22-game winner in 2005, the deal turned out to be a steal for the Tigers, who immediately shifted Cabrera to first base. In addition to driving in 127 runs, batting .292, and leading the American League with 37 home runs and 331 total bases in his first year in Detroit, Cabrera demonstrated his willingness to put in the time and effort to reach his full potential. He stated on one occasion, "When I do something, I don't want to be second best. That's the right way." Cabrera made an extremely favorable impression on Tigers general manager Dave Dombrowski, who called his new first baseman "an encyclopedia of pitchers." Choosing not to rely exclusively on his tremendous physical talent, Cabrera studies pitchers' hitting charts, watches them intently from the dugout, and files into his memory bank every pitch they throw to him. So impressed with Cabrera was Dombrowski that he stated, "He is part of our foundation now—a young player who can only continue to get better."

Former Chicago White Sox manager Ozzie Guillen also spoke glowingly of Cabrera, saying, "He can field. He can hit. He has a lot of power. He can hit the opposite way. He has everything you can ask of a major league player."

Cabrera had another big year for the Tigers in 2009, earning a fourth-place finish in the A.L. MVP balloting by placing among the league leaders in numerous statistical categories, including home runs (34), RBIs (103), batting average (.324), hits (198), total bases (334), and OPS (.942). He followed that up with an even better 2010 campaign, in which he finished among the league leaders with 38 homers, 111 runs scored, 45 doubles, 341 total bases, a .328 batting average, and a 1.042 OPS, and topped the circuit with 126 RBIs and a .420 on-base percentage, en route to earning his first A.L. Silver Slugger, the first of five consecutive All-Star nominations, and a second-place finish in the league MVP voting. Cabrera again compiled big numbers in 2011, concluding the campaign with 30 home runs, 105 runs batted in, 111 runs scored, 197 hits, a career-high 108 walks, and a league-leading 48 doubles, .344 batting average, and .448 on-base percentage.

Asked by the Tigers to move across the diamond to play third base prior to the start of the 2012 season in order to accommodate newly acquired free agent first baseman Prince Fielder, Cabrera worked extremely hard during spring training, staying late after games to take hundreds of ground balls. No one appreciated the sacrifice Cabrera made for the betterment of his team more than Fielder, who commented, "For a superstar to do what he did for me, they have to have confidence in their skills and be willing to work hard. I'll forever be grateful for Miguel's sacrifice."

Minnesota Twins manager Ron Gardenhire also praised Cabrera for his selflessness, saying, "They bring in Fielder, and it says a lot about a guy who's at the top to just say, 'No problem, I'll go over there.' Not everybody would do that."

Tigers manager Jim Leyland noted that Cabrera's positive attitude helped make him one of the team's most popular players, suggesting, "It [his popularity] starts with the fact that he's a great kid, but don't kid yourself—these guys are smart enough to know they're playing with one of the greatest players of all time. That's part of the equation."

Cabrera displayed no ill effects from the switch in positions in 2012, earning A.L. MVP and *Sporting News* MLB Player of the Year honors by having one of the finest offensive seasons in recent memory. In addition to winning the Triple Crown by leading the league with 44 home runs, 139 RBIs, and a .330 batting average, he topped the circuit with 377 total bases, a .606 slugging percentage, and a .999 OPS. Cabrera also placed near the top of the league rankings with 109 runs scored, 205 hits, 40 doubles, and a .393 on-base percentage. Cabrera also did a creditable job in the field, leading all A.L. third basemen with 127 putouts, while placing third in assists (243) and fielding percentage (.966). Tigers legend Al Kaline called Cabrera's extraordinary all-around performance "unbelievable" and suggested that the young slugger had "already qualified for Cooperstown himself." Meanwhile, Bob Nightengale of *USA Today Sports* called Cabrera "the greatest player in the game of baseball." Barry Bonds concurred with Nightengale, stating, "He's the best . . . by far . . . without a doubt—the absolute best."

Despite being plagued by injuries for much of the second half of the campaign, Cabrera compiled extremely similar numbers in 2013,

Courtesy of Keith Allison

finishing the year with 44 homers, 137 RBIs, 103 runs scored, and a league-leading .348 batting average, .442 on-base percentage, and .636 slugging percentage, en route to winning A.L. MVP and *Sporting News* MLB Player of the Year honors for the second straight time. Cabrera's fabulous season prompted the Tigers to sign him to an eight-year contract extension worth $248 million.

With the departure of Prince Fielder, Cabrera moved back to first base in 2014. Hampered by a badly injured ankle throughout most of the campaign, Cabrera experienced something of a decline in offensive production. Yet, he still managed to hit 25 homers, drive in 109 runs, score 101 times, place among the league leaders with 191 hits and a .313 batting average, and top the circuit with a career-high 52 doubles. Cabrera will enter the 2015 season with career totals of 390 home runs, 1,369 RBIs, 1,165 runs scored, 2,186 hits, and 464 doubles, a batting average of .320, an on-base percentage of .396, and a slugging percentage of .564. In his seven years with the Tigers, he has hit 252 homers, knocked in 846 runs, scored 716 times, amassed 1,344 hits and 281 doubles, batted .325, compiled a .402 on-base percentage, and posted a .578 slugging percentage. Cabrera currently ranks among the franchise's all-time leaders in home runs, batting average, doubles, on-base percentage, and slugging percentage.

With many outstanding seasons still presumably ahead of him, Cabrera figures to move up at least one or two notches in these rankings before his time in Detroit comes to an end. However, it must be remembered that he has experienced some off-field problems in the past that could eventually compromise his performance on the diamond. In addition to being called in for questioning on the morning of October 3, 2009, for disturbing the peace after engaging in a heated argument with his wife at their Michigan home, Cabrera was arrested in Florida on February 16, 2011, on suspicion of drunk driving and resisting arrest. In the time between those two incidents, Cabrera spent three months in an alcohol abuse treatment center to help him recover from his addiction. Let's hope that Cabrera, who is both a Catholic and a practitioner of Santeria, can remain on the straight and narrow. If so, he has an excellent chance of accomplishing some truly great things before he leaves the game.

TIGERS CAREER HIGHLIGHTS

Best Season

It could be argued that Cabrera had his best season for the Tigers in 2013, when he hit 44 home runs, knocked in 137 runs, scored 103 times, amassed 353 total bases, and led the American League with a career-high .348 batting average and 1.078 OPS. Yet, even though Cabrera compiled a significantly lower OPS of .999 the previous year, it would be impossible to ignore the fact that he became the first A.L. player since Carl Yastrzemski in 1967 to win the Triple Crown. Furthermore, though Cabrera led the league in four offensive categories in 2013, he topped the circuit in six different departments one year earlier. In addition to finishing first in the American League with 44 homers, 139 RBIs, and a .330 batting average in 2012, he led the league with a .606 slugging percentage, a .999 OPS, and a career-high 377 total bases. Cabrera also collected a career-best 205 hits in 2012 and accumulated 40 more putouts (127 to 87) and nearly 60 more assists (243 to 184) at third base than he did the following season. All things considered, Cabrera had his finest all-around season for the Tigers in 2012.

Memorable Moments/Greatest Performances

Although Cabrera went just 1-for-5 with a pair of strikeouts in his Detroit debut on March 31, 2008, he hit a solo home run in just his third plate appearance with his new team, increasing the Tigers' lead to 3–0 in a game they eventually lost to Kansas City by a score of 5–4 in 11 innings.

After the Tigers began the ensuing campaign by dropping three of four games to the Blue Jays in Toronto, Cabrera led them to a 15–2 victory over the Texas Rangers in the 2009 home opener at Comerica Park by going 3-for-5, with a homer, double, and 6 RBIs. Cabrera delivered 4 runs with one swing of the bat, hitting a fourth-inning grand slam that put the Tigers out in front by a score of 7–0.

Even though the Tigers dropped a 5–4 decision to the Oakland Athletics on May 28, 2010, Cabrera did all he could to keep his team in the contest, hitting 3 home runs and driving in all 4 Tiger runs.

Cabrera helped propel the Tigers into the playoffs in 2011 by hitting 6 home runs, knocking in 21 runs, and batting .429 during the month of September. He continued his hot hitting in October, batting .400, with 3 homers, 4 doubles, 7 RBIs, and 5 runs scored during Detroit's six-game loss to Texas in the ALCS.

Cabrera has also reached a couple of milestones during his time in Detroit. On August 15, 2012, he became the first player in Tigers history to hit 30 home runs in five straight seasons, surpassing both Hank Greenberg (1937–1940) and Cecil Fielder (1990–1993), each of whom accomplished the feat four consecutive times. Cabrera established a new mark in 2013, when he extended his streak to six straight seasons. The following year, on April 4, 2014, Cabrera hit a two-run homer against the Baltimore Orioles, collecting in the process the 2,000th hit of his career. The blast made him the ninth player in baseball history to amass 2,000 hits before turning 31 years of age, and the seventh-youngest to reach that plateau.

NOTABLE ACHIEVEMENTS

- Has hit more than 30 home runs six times, topping 40 homers twice.
- Has knocked in more than 100 runs seven times, surpassing 120 RBIs on four occasions.
- Has scored more than 100 runs five times.
- Has batted over .300 six times, surpassing .330 on three occasions.
- Has surpassed 200 hits once (205 in 2012).
- Has surpassed 30 doubles six times, reaching 40 four times and 50 once.
- Has drawn more than 100 walks once (108 in 2011).
- Has compiled an on-base percentage in excess of .400 three times.
- Has posted a slugging percentage in excess of .500 seven times, topping .600 on three occasions.

- Has compiled an OPS in excess of 1.000 on three occasions.
- Has led the American League in home runs twice; RBIs twice; batting average three times; doubles twice; total bases twice; on-base percentage three times; slugging percentage twice; and OPS twice.
- Has led A.L. first basemen in assists twice and double plays turned once.
- Has led A.L. third basemen in putouts once.
- Ranks among Tigers career leaders in home runs (5th); batting average (5th); doubles (10th); on-base percentage (9th); slugging percentage (2nd); and OPS (2nd).
- Hit 3 home runs in one game vs. Oakland on May 28, 2010.
- 2012 A.L. Triple Crown winner.
- Five-time A.L. Player of the Month.
- Three-time Silver Slugger winner (2010, 2012, 2013).
- Two-time A.L. Hank Aaron Award winner.
- Two-time *Sporting News* Major League Player of the Year (2012, 2013).
- Two-time A.L. MVP (2012, 2013).
- Five-time A.L. All-Star (2010, 2011, 2012, 2013, 2014).
- 2012 A.L. champion.

8

Justin Verlander

Courtesy of Keith Allison

The anchor of Detroit's pitching staff the last nine seasons, Justin Verlander has established himself during that time as one of the most dominant hurlers in all of baseball. Blessed with a resilient arm and an outstanding assortment of pitches, the hard-throwing right-hander has led A.L. pitchers in wins twice, ERA once, and strikeouts and innings pitched three times each, en route to earning six All-Star selections, four top-five finishes in the Cy Young voting, one Cy Young Award, and one league MVP trophy. More important, Verlander has helped transform the Tigers from one of baseball's weakest teams into perennial contenders for the A.L. pennant.

Born in Manakin Sabot, Virginia on February 20, 1983, Justin Brooks Verlander attended Goochland High School, during which time his father also sent him to the Richmond Baseball Academy. Capable of reaching 86 mph on the radar gun by his senior year at Goochland, Verlander subsequently enrolled at Old Dominion University in Norfolk, Virginia, where he spent the next three years establishing himself as the all-time strikeout leader in the Commonwealth of Virginia (Division I) history. After Verlander helped the USA win a silver medal in the 2003 Pan American Games, the Tigers selected him in the first round of the 2004 amateur draft, with the second overall pick.

Verlander spent less than one full season in Detroit's farm system before earning his first big-league call-up in July 2005. He appeared in two games for the Tigers that month, losing both his starts, before being returned to the minor leagues. Verlander's season ended shortly thereafter when he was placed on the disabled list due to tightness in his right shoulder. However, with the Tigers coming off 12 consecutive losing seasons, including five straight years in which they failed to win more than 72 games, the 23-year-old Verlander earned a regular spot in their starting rotation the following spring. Ready for the challenge of facing major league hitting, Verlander responded by compiling a record of 17–9 and an ERA of 3.63, earning in the process A.L. Rookie of the Year honors and a seventh-place finish in the Cy Young voting. With the Tigers increasing their win total from 71 to 95, Verlander also finished 15th in the league MVP balloting. Although Verlander subsequently struggled during the postseason, he received the honor of being named Detroit's starter for Game One of the World Series.

Verlander's outstanding rookie campaign prompted Tigers manager Jim Leyland to proclaim, "This guy is a real keeper. He's the real deal."

Impressed with the poise Verlander displayed on the mound his first year in the league, Rays manager Joe Madden commented, "That kid has so much potential, and he doesn't look a bit like a rookie. He has everything and can be as good as he wants."

Tigers catcher Ivan Rodriguez said of his battery-mate, "He's going to be a superstar in this game for a long time."

Detroit outfielder Craig Monroe added, "He's confident, halfway cocky, which is good. Maybe that is what gives him the edge."

Meanwhile, Cleveland Indians slugging DH/first baseman Travis Hafner noted, "He throws 99, which you see very rarely. He throws strikes, and he has a great curveball and changeup. He has a great future."

Verlander had an equally impressive sophomore season, finishing 2007 with a record of 18–6 that gave him a league-leading .750 winning percentage. He also compiled an ERA of 3.66, struck out 183 batters, and threw more than 200 innings (201⅔) for the first of eight straight times, en route to earning his first All-Star selection and a fifth-place finish in the Cy Young balloting.

Plagued by inconsistency throughout much of 2008, Verlander concluded the campaign with a record of only 11–17 and a career-high 4.84 ERA for a Tigers team that finished just 74–88. However, he rebounded the following year, earning All-Star honors and a third-place finish in the Cy Young voting by going 19–9, with a 3.45 ERA and a league-leading 269 strikeouts and 240 innings pitched. Verlander's 269 strikeouts represented the highest total compiled by a Detroit pitcher since Mickey Lolich fanned 308 batters in 1971. He followed that up by compiling a 3.37 ERA in 2010, while also placing among the league leaders with a record of 18–9, 219 strikeouts, and 224⅓ innings pitched.

Rapidly developing into a true workhorse, Verlander amazed Jim Leyland with his ability to maintain the same velocity on his fastball throughout an entire game, causing his manager to marvel on one occasion, "I've never had a starting pitcher who can throw 99 (mph) in the ninth inning."

Leyland added, "He's pretty impressive. He's worth the price of admission."

Verlander's unusual ability to "add" or "subtract" from the velocity on his fastball over the course of a game as the situation dictates has proven to be one of the things that makes him so difficult for opposing batters to face. Known to reach 100 mph on the radar gun during the latter stages of contests, Verlander has tremendous stamina and an extremely competitive nature. In discussing his approach to pitching, Verlander states, "I like to challenge hitters with a 'Here it is, hit it' mentality. It's definitely a big part of my game, especially when I get in situations where I need it. I usually save a little bit so it's there for me."

Meanwhile, in elaborating on his pitching style, Verlander says, "I'm a power guy. Good fastball; a knuckle-curve that I can throw for strikes; a changeup that sinks down and away from lefties and I can also throw for strikes."

After winning a total of 37 games the previous two seasons, Verlander reached the apex of his career in 2011, capturing the pitcher's version of the Triple Crown by leading all A.L. hurlers with a record of 24–5, a 2.40 ERA, and 250 strikeouts. He also led the league with 251 innings pitched and

Courtesy of Keith Allison

a WHIP of 0.920, en route to earning Cy Young and A.L. MVP honors. Although Verlander won seven fewer games the following year, concluding the 2012 campaign with a record of 17–8, he pitched nearly as well, earning a runner-up finish in the Cy Young voting by placing second in the league with a 2.64 ERA and a WHIP of 1.057, and topping the circuit with 239 strikeouts, 238⅓ innings pitched, and 6 complete games. He then pitched brilliantly in the playoffs, defeating Oakland twice in the ALDS and New York once in the ALCS, before faltering in his lone start against San Francisco in the World Series. Verlander's exceptional pitching over the course of the campaign prompted the Tigers to sign him to a seven-year, $180 million contract at season's end, making him the highest-paid pitcher in baseball history. The deal also includes a $22 million vesting option for 2020 if Verlander finishes in the top five in the Cy Young voting in 2019.

Hampered by discomfort in his pitching shoulder throughout much of 2013, Verlander posted relatively modest numbers, finishing the season with a record of 13–12 and an ERA of 3.46. Yet, he still managed to earn his fifth straight All-Star selection by leading all A.L. hurlers with 34 starts and placing near the top of the league rankings with 217 strikeouts and 218⅓ innings pitched. After undergoing core muscle surgery during the subsequent offseason, Verlander struggled through an uncharacteristically mediocre 2014 campaign that saw him compile a record of 15–12, with a 4.54 ERA and just 159 strikeouts.

The Tigers fully expect Verlander to regain his earlier form in 2015, something he will need to do if they have any realistic hope of returning to the World Series for the third time in 10 years. Since Verlander will not turn 32 until shortly before the 2015 season gets underway, there is no reason to believe that he does not still have several good years left in him. He enters the upcoming season with a career record of 152–89, which gives him an outstanding winning percentage of .631. He has also compiled an ERA of 3.53, struck out 1,830 batters in 1,978 innings of work, thrown 20 complete games, and posted a WHIP of 1.212. Verlander ranks among the Tigers' all-time leaders in wins, winning percentage, strikeouts, WHIP, and games started (298).

CAREER HIGHLIGHTS

Best Season

As well as Verlander pitched in 2012, he clearly had the greatest season of his career one year earlier, when he led A.L. starting pitchers in virtually every major statistical category. In addition to winning the Triple Crown by finishing first in wins (24), ERA (2.40), and strikeouts (250), he topped the circuit with a winning percentage of .828, 251 innings pitched, 34 starts, and a WHIP of 0.920. Verlander's 24 victories represented the highest total compiled by a Tigers pitcher since Mickey Lolich posted 25 wins in 1971. Meanwhile, his 0.920 WHIP remains the third-lowest figure ever compiled by a Tigers hurler, trailing only Willie Hernandez's mark of 0.900 in 1985 and Denny McLain's 1968 mark of 0.905. Verlander threw at least six innings and 100 pitches in each of his 34 starts, earning A.L. Cy Young and MVP honors with his fabulous performance. By being named league MVP, he became the first starting pitcher to be so honored since Boston's Roger Clemens accomplished the feat 25 years earlier. Verlander also received recognition as *Sporting News* A.L. Pitcher of the Year and MLB Player of the Year.

Memorable Moments/Greatest Performances

One of only two Tigers pitchers to throw as many as two no-hitters (Virgil Trucks was the other), Verlander accomplished the feat for the first time on June 12, 2007, when he defeated the Milwaukee Brewers by a score of 4–0 at Comerica Park. Verlander surrendered four walks and struck out 12 during the contest. He duplicated his earlier effort nearly four years later, on May 7, 2011, allowing just one base-runner during a 9–0 whitewashing of the Blue Jays in Toronto. Verlander took a perfect game into the eighth inning, before issuing a one-out walk to J. P. Arencibia. He then induced Edwin Encarnacion to hit into a double play, before retiring the side in order in the ensuing frame, facing the minimum number of 27 batters in the process.

Verlander has turned in a number of other brilliant performances. In his very next start after tossing his no-no against Toronto, he worked 5⅔ hitless innings before finally surrendering a two-out triple to Kansas City's Melky Cabrera in the top of the sixth inning. Verlander went on to allow just one run and two hits over eight innings, in coming away with a 3–1 victory. Just one month later, on June 14, 2011, Verlander took a no-hitter into the eighth inning before giving up a one-out single to Cleveland's Orlando Cabrera during a 4–0 win over the Indians. Verlander finished the game with a two-hit shutout, walking just one batter and striking out 12. He pitched another gem 11 days later, on June 25, allowing just 4 hits over 8 innings and striking out a career-high 14 batters during a 6–0 victory over the Arizona Diamondbacks.

Verlander nearly tossed the third no-hitter of his career on May 18, 2012, when he surrendered just one hit to Pittsburgh during a 6–0 home win over the Pirates. Verlander, who allowed only a one-out, ninth-inning single to Josh Harrison, finished the game with 12 strikeouts.

After failing to distinguish himself in any of his eight previous post-season starts, compiling an overall record of just 3–3 and an ERA in excess of 5.00, Verlander pitched magnificently in the 2012 playoffs. He got the Tigers off to an excellent start in the ALDS by striking out 11 batters and allowing just one run on three hits over seven innings, in earning a 3–1 Game One win over Oakland. Verlander returned to the mound five days later to toss a four-hit shutout in Detroit's 6–0 victory in the decisive fifth game. He fanned 11 A's batters in that contest, setting in the process a new record for the most strikeouts in an ALDS. Verlander continued his fabulous pitching in the ALCS against the Yankees, punctuating Detroit's four-game sweep of New York by throwing 8⅓ innings of three-hit ball, in leading the Tigers to a 2–1 win in Game Three. Unfortunately, Verlander subsequently struggled in his only World Series start against San Francisco, allowing five runs and six hits over four innings, in Detroit's 8–3 opening game loss.

Although the Tigers failed to return to the World Series in 2013, losing to Boston in six games in the ALCS, Verlander again pitched extraordinarily well in the postseason. Despite posting a record of just 1–1 in his three playoff starts, he allowed just one earned run and 10 hits over 23 innings of work, while striking out 31 batters. However, Detroit's offense betrayed him, failing to score a run in two of his three starts.

NOTABLE ACHIEVEMENTS

- Has surpassed 20 victories once (24 in 2011).
- Has won at least 17 games five other times.
- Has compiled an ERA under 3.00 twice.
- Has posted a winning percentage in excess of .700 twice, surpassing .800 once (.828 in 2011).
- Has struck out more than 200 batters five times.
- Has thrown more than 200 innings eight straight times.
- Has compiled a WHIP below 1.000 once (0.920 in 2011).
- Has led A.L. pitchers in wins twice; winning percentage twice; ERA once; strikeouts three times; innings pitched three times; complete games once; and WHIP once.
- Ranks among Tigers career leaders in wins (8th); winning percentage (4th); strikeouts (3rd); WHIP (10th); and games started (8th).
- Has thrown two no-hitters.
- 2011 A.L. Triple Crown winner for pitchers.
- Three-time A.L. Pitcher of the Month.
- 2006 A.L. Rookie of the Year.
- 2011 A.L. Cy Young Award winner.
- 2011 A.L. MVP.
- Two-time *Sporting News* A.L. Pitcher of the Year (2011, 2012).
- 2011 Major League Player of the Year.
- Six-time A.L. All-Star.
- Two-time A.L. champion (2006, 2012).

9

Hal Newhouser

Courtesy of LegendaryAuctions.com

Much like Lefty Grove, another overpowering left-hander who dominated A.L. batters a generation earlier, Hal Newhouser developed a reputation as a perfectionist with an explosive temper. Demanding as much from himself as he did from his teammates, Newhouser became well known for his volatile disposition, making him one of his sport's most unpopular players. Whether venting his anger on a teammate who failed to live up to his expectations or an inanimate object such as the clubhouse wall, Newhouser was given a wide berth by the men who played along-side him, since they came to accept him as a temperamental artist. After spending the first few years of his career laboring in mediocrity, Newhouser developed into the game's finest pitcher, mesmerizing opposing batters with his blazing fastball, exceptional overhand curve, and sharp-breaking slider. The only pitcher in major league history to win the MVP award in consecutive seasons, Newhouser compiled an overall record of 80–27 from 1944 to 1946, leading A.L. hurlers in wins all three years. He also topped the junior circuit in strikeouts and ERA in two of those three seasons, capturing the pitcher's version of the Triple Crown in 1945, when he finished 25–9, with a 1.81 ERA and 212 strikeouts. By the time Newhouser left the Tigers at the conclusion of the 1953 campaign, he had established himself as the premier left-hander of his time, and as one of the finest southpaws of the first half of the twentieth century.

Born to first-generation Czechoslovakian and Austrian immigrants in Detroit, Michigan on May 20, 1921, Harold Newhouser overcame several serious injuries he incurred during his formative years to become a stellar athlete. In addition to puncturing his stomach after falling off a woodpile onto a metal spike, young Hal received a nasty head wound when another boy hit him with a brick. He also developed a case of blood poisoning and received numerous foul-looking gashes from playing football. A true survivor, Newhouser helped make ends meet during the Great Depression by assuming a number of odd jobs, including selling papers, setting pins in a bowling alley, and collecting empty bottles for the penny deposits they returned.

Although Newhouser didn't begin playing organized baseball until he reached the age of 13, he displayed an early affinity for the game, listening to radio broadcasts of his hometown Tigers, who he dreamed of playing for one day. After making his maiden pitching appearance with a local American Legion team at 15 years of age, Newhouser went on to post a record of 42–3 over the course of the next three seasons, impressing everyone around him with his competitive spirit and will to excel. The success the lanky left-hander experienced as a teenager prompted the Tigers to sign him for a $500 bonus shortly after he graduated from Wilbur Wright High School in 1939. Newhouser subsequently advanced rapidly through Detroit's farm system, making brief stops at Alexandria in the Evangeline League and Beaumont in the Texas League, before joining the Tigers late in 1939. The 18-year-old left-hander made his major league debut with the club on September 29, allowing 3 runs over 5 innings, in absorbing his first loss as a big leaguer.

After making the Tigers' roster the following spring, Newhouser experienced the usual growing pains of most rookie pitchers, displaying a considerable amount of inconsistency on the mound. Concluding the 1940 campaign with a record of 9–9 and an ERA of 4.86, Newhouser frequently struggled with his control, walking 76 batters in only 133⅓ innings of work. The 19-year-old rookie also found it difficult to keep his emotions in check, often pacing the mound to regain his composure when running into trouble. Particularly demonstrative after being removed from contests by Detroit manager Del Baker, Newhouser eventually earned the nickname "Hurricane Hal" for the manner in which he threw temper tantrums in the clubhouse following such early exits. On one particular occasion, the irate youngster destroyed an entire case of Coca Cola, smashing each bottle against the locker room wall. Even in calmer times, Newhouser tended to be difficult to deal with, antagonizing teammates with his confrontational nature that prompted him to berate them if they made an error behind him or failed to give him proper run support.

Newhouser continued to experience difficulties in each of the next three seasons as well, even after many of the game's best players joined the military to serve in World War II. After posting a combined record of 17–25 in 1941 and 1942, Newhouser found himself unable to join the Army Air Force, as he had originally planned, when a congenital heart disorder known as a mitral valve prolapse caused him to be classified as unfit for duty. Yet, he still managed to finish just 8–17 in 1943, although he compiled a very respectable 3.04 ERA that earned him a spot on the A.L. All-Star team.

Inconsistency and wildness proved to be the primary causes of Newhouser's struggles over that three-year stretch, with his tendency to get behind in the count to opposing hitters contributing significantly to his inability to reach his enormous potential. Indeed, the young left-hander became so distraught over his lack of success that he seriously considered quitting baseball at the conclusion of the 1943 campaign to become a draftsman at Chrysler headquarters, where he spent the previous few off-seasons serving as an apprentice.

However, Newhouser's career took a sudden turn shortly after former catcher Steve O'Neill replaced Del Baker as Detroit's manager in 1943 and brought in veteran receiver Paul Richards to work with the Tigers' young pitchers. Having observed the manner in which Richards helped improve the performances of Dizzy Trout and Virgil Trucks in his first year in Detroit, Newhouser arrived at spring training in 1944 willing to listen to any words of advice the catcher had to offer. After informing Newhouser that he considered him to be more of a "thrower," Richards told the 22-year-old left-hander, "I'm going to make you a pitcher." Richards set about teaching Newhouser how to throw a slider, which the latter added to his existing three-pitch repertoire that featured a fastball, curveball, and change-up. More important, Richards taught Newhouser how to harness his emotions, turning him into a completely different pitcher, both on the mound and in the clubhouse.

Richards's work with Newhouser bordered on the miraculous, with the young left-hander concluding the 1944 campaign with a record of 29–9, a 2.22 ERA, 6 shutouts, 25 complete games, 312⅓ innings pitched, and a league-leading 187 strikeouts. By topping all A.L. hurlers in wins and strikeouts, and finishing second to Dizzy Trout in the other four categories, Newhouser earned league MVP honors, edging out his teammate by just four votes in the balloting. Newhouser posted extraordinary numbers again in 1945, leading the league with a record of 25–9, an ERA of 1.81, 212 strikeouts, 8 shutouts, 29 complete games, and 313⅓ innings pitched, en route to capturing the pitcher's version of the Triple Crown and winning A.L. MVP honors for the second straight year. After briefly toying with the idea of accepting a lucrative offer to jump to the rival Mexican League at season's end, Newhouser turned in another dominating performance in 1946, going 26–9, with 275 strikeouts, 6 shutouts, 29 complete games, 292⅔ innings pitched, and a league-leading 1.94 ERA. His exceptional campaign earned him a close second-place finish to Ted Williams in the A.L. MVP voting.

Having developed a reputation among his teammates as a temperamental superstar, Newhouser drew praise from the men who played alongside him. Birdie Tebbetts, who served as Newhouser's primary receiver for five years, stated, "I guess you could call him pretty mean out there. But that's all right with me. I like to catch mean guys who don't like to lose. . . . The woods are full of wonderful guys who can't win. Hal wasn't one of them."

Bobo Newsom, who spent two full seasons working alongside Newhouser as a regular member of Detroit's starting rotation, noted, "Every time he walks to that mound, you know you'll get a good-pitched game."

Meanwhile, in assessing the transformation he made in terms of his mental approach to the game, Newhouser suggested, "I didn't win because I controlled my temper. I controlled my temper because I began to win . . . there's no use getting mad when you're winning!"

In addition to displaying a new calm on the mound, Newhouser developed a more cerebral approach to his craft, becoming one of the first players to analyze his performance by studying film. After having each of his efforts

Hal Newhouser (right) with Tigers manager Del Baker.
Courtesy of Boston Public Library, Leslie Jones Collection

filmed through an expensive lens, Newhouser ran the movies at home in between starts, looking for flaws in his motion and grip.

Newhouser followed up his three magnificent seasons with a less-dominant 1947 campaign in which he finished just 17–17. However, only during the latter stages of the season did he learn that his performance throughout much of the year had been compromised by a broken right foot. Yet, in spite of his malady, Newhouser managed to lead all A.L. hurlers with 24 complete games and place among the leaders with a 2.87 ERA, 176 strikeouts, and 285 innings pitched. Healthy again in 1948, Newhouser returned to top form, even though he no longer possessed the blazing fast-ball he featured a few years earlier. Posting 20 wins for the final time in his career, Newhouser compiled a record of 21–12 and an ERA of 3.01, tossed 19 complete games, and threw 272⅓ innings.

Unfortunately, Newhouser developed shoulder problems during the latter stages of the 1948 campaign that caused him to pitch in pain throughout the remainder of his career. Still, relying mostly on guile and his tremendous heart, he managed to put together two more winning seasons before he found himself unable to ever again assume a regular spot in the starting rotation. After compiling a record of 18–11, tossing 22 complete games, and throwing 292 innings in 1949, Newhouser finished just 15–13 with a 4.34 ERA in 1950, with the latter mark representing his highest figure in nearly a decade.

Subsequently able to make a total of only 37 starts from 1951 to 1953, Newhouser posted a combined record during that time of just 15–16 before the Tigers elected to release him prior to the start of the 1954 campaign. However, with Newhouser's former teammate Hank Greenberg serving as GM in Cleveland, the Indians offered him another chance, signing him to work out of their bullpen. Newhouser thrived in his new role, winning 7 games and saving 7 others for a Cleveland club that ended up capturing the American League pennant. The 1954 season turned out to be Newhouser's last hurrah, though, since he retired after the Indians released him early the following year. Newhouser ended his career with a record of 207–150, an ERA of 3.06, 1,796 strikeouts in 2,993 innings of work, 212 complete games, 33 shutouts, and a WHIP of 1.311, compiling virtually all those numbers as a member of the Tigers. He continues to rank among Detroit's all-time leaders in wins, strikeouts, shutouts, complete games, innings pitched, and starts.

Following his playing career, Newhouser spent many years work-ing as a scout for several different teams, including the Tigers, Indians, Baltimore Orioles, and Houston Astros. He quit scouting after his last employer, Houston, selected Phil Nevin with the first overall pick of the 1992 draft, ignoring in the process his suggestion to tab Derek Jeter instead. That very same year, the members of the Veterans Committee ended years of frustration for Newhouser when they finally elected him to the Baseball Hall of Fame. Newhouser's long wait undoubtedly stemmed from the fact that he had two of his greatest seasons during World War II, prompting some people to label him as a "wartime pitcher." Nevertheless, the fact remains that Newhouser continued to dominate opposing batters after the game's best players returned from the military in 1946, earning a second-place finish in the A.L. MVP voting that year and compiling an overall record of 82–49 from 1946 to 1949. Newhouser cried when he heard the news of his election—not because he had made it, but because his 92-year-old mother was still alive to share in his joy. Newhouser spent the next few years suffering from emphysema and heart problems that ended up taking his life on November 10, 1998, nearly six months after he celebrated his 77th birthday. One year earlier, the Tigers honored him by retiring his number 16.

TIGERS CAREER HIGHLIGHTS

Best Season

With Newhouser pitching incredibly well from 1944 to 1946, any one of those three years would have made an excellent choice. In addition to leading the league with 29 wins and 187 strikeouts in the first of those campaigns, he finished second to teammate Dizzy Trout with a 2.22 ERA, 6 shutouts, 25 complete games, and 312⅓ innings pitched, en route to earning A.L. MVP honors. However, even though the left-hander posted fewer victories in each of the next two seasons, he compiled slightly better overall numbers. Newhouser again captured league MVP honors in 1945, when he won the pitcher's version of the Triple Crown by leading all A.L. hurlers with 25 wins, a 1.81 ERA, 212 strikeouts, 8 shutouts, 29 complete games, and 313⅓ innings pitched. He also finished third in the circuit with a WHIP of 1.114. Newhouser's total domination of the statistical categories for pitchers would seem to suggest that he had his greatest season in 1945. Still, he posted extremely similar numbers the following year, when he led the league with 26 wins, a 1.94 ERA, and a career-best WHIP of 1.069. Newhouser also finished second to Cleveland's Bob Feller with 29 complete games, 292⅔ innings pitched, 6 shutouts, and a career-high 275 strikeouts, earning in the process a close second-place finish to Ted Williams in the league MVP voting. When it is considered that most of the game's top players had returned to their respective teams by the start of the season, Newhouser pitched his best ball for the Tigers in 1946.

Memorable Moments/Greatest Performances

Newhouser hurled the pennant-clincher for the Tigers on September 22, 1945, leading his team to a 9–0 win over the St. Louis Browns by tossing a 4-hit shutout and going 2-for-3 at the plate, with a double, triple, and 3 RBIs. The American League's MVP subsequently helped the Tigers defeat the Chicago Cubs in the World Series by posting victories in Games Five and Seven, including going the distance and striking out 10 in the Series finale despite working on only two days' rest.

Newhouser had the honor of pitching in the first night game ever played at Briggs Stadium, allowing just 2 hits during a 4–1 win over the Philadelphia Athletics on June 15, 1948.

Newhouser engaged in a number of memorable pitching matchups with Cleveland ace Bob Feller—the American League's other top hurler of the period. Perhaps the most notable of those confrontations took place before nearly 40,000 fans at Cleveland's Memorial Stadium on September 22, 1946, when the 25–8 Newhouser took the mound against the 25–13 Feller in the first game of a Sunday afternoon doubleheader. Rapid Robert, who had defeated Newhouser in their three previous meetings that year, pitched well for the Indians, allowing the Tigers 3 runs on 8 hits, in going the distance. However, Newhouser proved to be his superior on that day, surrendering just 2 harmless singles and striking out 9 during a 3–0 Tigers win. Following the contest, which *The Sporting News* covered like a heavyweight championship fight in its next edition, the extremely competitive Feller lamented his bad luck but praised his opponent at the same time, stating, "The Tigers got eight hits off me. But four of them were bloopers which fell just over the infield. . . . What the heck, they had nothing to lose. We couldn't get a loud foul off Newhouser."

Newhouser posted another memorable win over Feller on the final day of the 1948 regular season, forcing a one-game playoff for the A.L. pennant between Cleveland and Boston by allowing just 5 hits during a 7–1 Tigers victory.

NOTABLE ACHIEVEMENTS

- Won more than 20 games four times, surpassing 25 victories on three occasions.
- Won at least 15 games three other times.
- Posted winning percentage in excess of .700 three times.
- Compiled ERA below 3.00 five times, posting mark under 2.00 twice.
- Struck out more than 200 batters twice.
- Threw more than 200 innings seven times, tossing more than 300 innings twice.
- Threw more than 20 complete games five times.
- Led A.L. pitchers in wins four times; ERA twice; strikeouts twice; complete games twice; innings pitched once; shutouts once; and WHIP once.
- Ranks among Tigers career leaders in wins (4th); strikeouts (4th); shutouts (3rd); complete games (4th); innings pitched (5th); games started (5th); and pitching appearances (7th).
- 1945 Triple Crown winner for pitchers.

- Two-time A.L. MVP (1944, 1945).
- Finished second in 1946 A.L. MVP voting.
- Two-time A.L. *Sporting News* Pitcher of the Year (1944, 1945).
- 1945 Major League Player of the Year.
- Three-time *Sporting News* All-Star selection (1944, 1945, 1946).
- Six-time A.L. All-Star.
- Two-time A.L. champion (1940, 1945).
- 1945 world champion.
- Elected to Baseball Hall of Fame by members of Veterans Committee in 1992.

10

Jack Morris

Courtesy of MainlineAutographs.com

A tenacious competitor with a combative spirit and a devastating split-fingered fastball, Jack Morris anchored Detroit's starting rotation for more than a decade, posting more victories (162) and throwing more complete games (133) than any other pitcher during the 1980s. The ace of the Tigers' pitching staff for most of his 14 seasons in Detroit, Morris surpassed 20 victories twice as a member of the team, averaging just over 17 wins from 1979 to 1988. One of the finest big-game pitchers of his era, Morris compiled a perfect 3–0 record during the 1984 postseason, in leading the Tigers to their first world championship in 16 years. The hard-throwing right-hander also earned four All-Star selections and three top-five finishes in the A.L. Cy Young balloting during his time in Detroit, which nevertheless also became noted for his numerous confrontations with manager Sparky Anderson and the local media.

Born in St. Paul, Minnesota, on May 16, 1955, John Scott Morris grew up rooting for the Minnesota Twins, for whom he dreamed of playing one day. An outstanding all-around athlete, Morris played basketball and baseball at local Highland Park High School, starring on the diamond as a third baseman and shortstop. Although the teenager's powerful right arm also enabled him to take the mound from time to time, he struggled with his control, prompting former Highland Park baseball coach Bill Lorenz to recall years later, "He could throw hard enough to knock down the backstop in high school. He just couldn't hit the backstop."

Offered a baseball scholarship by several colleges upon his graduation, Morris ultimately chose to attend Brigham Young University in Provo, Utah, later explaining his decision by stating, "I wanted to play for a baseball school where they played in good weather and good teams. The schedule (which included Arizona, Arizona State, Cal State Fullerton, and Hawaii) was phenomenal. I knew I would get exposure. That's why I went there."

After working under BYU coach and 1960 Cy Young Award winner Vernon Law for three years, Morris developed into an accomplished pitcher, prompting the Tigers to select him in the fifth round of the 1976 amateur draft, following his junior season. He made his major league debut a little over one year later, being called up by the Tigers in July 1977 to replace an injured Mark Fidrych on their pitching staff. Morris went 1–1 with a 3.74 ERA in his 6 starts through August, before also being placed on the disabled list by the Tigers after experiencing soreness in his pitching shoulder. Once again hampered by a sore arm in 1978, Morris made only 6 starts for the Tigers, compiling a record of 3–5 and an ERA of 4.33, in 28 total appearances.

Morris broke into Detroit's starting rotation the following year, quickly establishing himself as the ace of the starting rotation by going 17–7, with a 3.28 ERA that placed him fifth in the league rankings. Despite seeing his ERA jump to 4.18 in 1980, Morris again proved to be the Tigers' most effective pitcher, finishing the season with a record of 16–15, tossing 11 complete games, and leading the staff with 250 innings pitched. He subsequently pitched extremely well during the strike-shortened 1981 campaign, finishing 14–7 to lead all A.L. hurlers in victories, while also lowering his ERA to 3.05 and placing among the league leaders with 15 complete games, 198 innings pitched, and 97 strikeouts. Morris's strong performance earned him his first All-Star selection, a third-place finish in the A.L. Cy Young voting, and recognition as *Sporting News* A.L. Pitcher of the Year. Although Morris's ERA rose to 4.06 in 1982, he finished 17–16 and once again placed near the top of the league rankings in complete games (17) and innings pitched (266⅓).

During the latter stages of that 1982 campaign, Morris began experimenting with a pitch that turned him into an elite hurler. Relying previously on a repertoire that included a fastball, slider, and changeup, Morris felt the need to develop an "out" pitch, later recalling, "My slider started flattening out. I couldn't get the big break anymore. I was having some inconsistency with my slider . . . hanging a few too many. I was looking for that 'out' pitch. My fastball was still good, changeup was still good, but I was looking for that 'strike three' pitch."

After learning how to throw the forkball, or split-fingered fastball, from teammate Milt Wilcox late in 1982, Morris incorporated it into his repertoire the following year, recollecting, "In 1983 and 1984, I pretty much had it to myself in the American League. It was a total gift. It was like nobody knew it was coming. It was awesome. It was so much fun. And then everyone else started trying to learn how to pitch, and then hitters started to adjust to it. My forkball was above average. I could almost tell guys it was coming, and they still couldn't hit it. . . . When I threw it right, nobody hit it."

Armed with his new weapon, Morris reached the 20-win plateau for the first time in 1983, concluding the campaign with a record of 20–13, an ERA of 3.34, 20 complete games, and a league-leading 232 strikeouts and 293⅔ innings pitched, en route to earning a third-place finish in the Cy Young balloting for the second time in three years. He followed that up by posting a record of 19–11 for the eventual world champions in 1984, while also compiling an ERA of 3.60, striking out 148 batters, and throwing 240⅓ innings. Morris subsequently won the Babe Ruth Award as World Series MVP by defeating San Diego twice in the Fall Classic.

Yet, in spite of the success Morris experienced on the mound, he often found himself clashing with Tigers manager Sparky Anderson, who said of the pitcher in his autobiography, *They Call Me Sparky*, "He had the stubbornness of a mule and the grace of a thoroughbred. . . . Once he started a game, it took an act of Congress to get him out. Jack was a believer in always finishing what he started."

Anderson, who earlier in his managerial career earned the nickname "Captain Hook" for the swiftness with which he often removed his starting pitchers from contests, went on to reveal that Morris actually "broke blood vessels in my fingers slamming the ball in my hand" when he took him out of a game once.

Morris's competitive nature and burning desire to win left a lasting impression on longtime New York Yankees second baseman Willie Randolph, who stated, "He's one of those guys who, when they're out there on the mound looking down at you, you can see the fire burning in their eyes. You can see these guys are not going to play—they ain't bs-ing around and to boot they have great stuff to go with it. When you played Detroit and, when you faced Jack Morris, you knew you were in for a battle that day because he would try to sometimes intimidate you, but he was also going to come after you and try to embarrass you, too."

Morris's aggressive mind-set extended far beyond the playing field, with his combative nature causing him to lash out from time to time at members of the local media. In one of his more infamous moments, Morris told a female reporter who attempted to interview him in the Tigers clubhouse following a game, "I don't talk to women when I'm naked unless they're on top of me or I'm on top of them." For a brief period of time, Morris stopped talking to the press altogether, defending his actions by stating, "They've invaded my privacy. I have no time for myself or my family. From now on, I'm not talking. From now on, I know I won't be misquoted." Angered by Morris's proclamation, Tigers pitching coach Roger Craig said publicly that he should "quit acting like a baby." Meanwhile, the strained relationship that Morris shared with several of his teammates also caused him to resign as the club's player representative.

Nevertheless, winning always seems to cure all ills, and, with the Tigers capturing the world championship in 1984 and, with Morris playing a huge role in their victory, all sides eventually reached an amicable peace. Although the Tigers reached the playoffs just once more over the course of the next four seasons, they remained in contention most of those years, with Morris continuing to serve as the anchor of their pitching staff. In addition to winning a total of 70 games from 1985 to 1988, Morris threw 51 complete games, tossed at least 235 innings each season, and struck out more than 200 batters twice. He pitched his best ball during that four-year stretch in 1986, going 21–8, with a 3.27 ERA, 223 strikeouts, 15 complete games, 267 innings pitched, and a league-leading 6 shutouts.

Plagued by elbow problems for much of 1989, Morris finished just 6–14 with a 4.86 ERA, before undergoing surgery late in the year for a

Courtesy of MainlineAutographs.com

stress fracture. Returning to the Tigers the following year, he posted his
second consecutive losing record, concluding the campaign with a mark
of 15–18 and an ERA of 4.51, although he managed to throw nearly 250
innings and lead all A.L. hurlers with 36 starts and 11 complete games.

A free agent at season's end, Morris turned down a three-year, $9 mil-
lion offer from the Tigers to sign with the Minnesota Twins, who offered
him a guaranteed salary of $3 million a year, with the chance to earn more
based on incentives. The contract also stipulated that he had the option to
become a free agent after the end of each season.

Even though Morris expressed great joy over the idea of playing for his
hometown team after signing with the Twins, he later said, "I never wanted

to leave Detroit. Had Detroit taken care of me the way I felt I should have been taken care of, I never would have left."

Morris ended up spending just one year in Minnesota, returning to top form in 1991 by compiling a record of 18–12 and an ERA of 3.43, throwing 246⅔ innings, and leading the league with 35 starts. He subsequently helped the Twins capture their second world championship by going a perfect 4–0 in the postseason, including a memorable Game Seven win in the World Series in which he threw 10 shutout innings.

Morris joined the Toronto Blue Jays the following year, after which he won two more world championships. A key member of Toronto's 1992 championship ball club, Morris posted a league-leading 21 victories during the regular season, although he faltered during the playoffs and World Series, dropping all three of his postseason decisions. He played a less prominent role in Toronto's march to the World Series in 1993, winning just 7 games during the regular season, and failing to get a postseason start. Released by the Blue Jays at season's end, Morris signed with the Cleveland Indians, for whom he posted a mark of 10–6 in 1994, before being released by the club just three days before the players' strike ended the season. After failing to catch on with the Cincinnati Reds during the subsequent offseason, Morris attempted a comeback with the St. Paul Saints, an independent minor league team. However, when the Twins showed no interest in bringing him back to Minnesota, Morris chose to announce his retirement, ending his career with a record of 254–186, an ERA of 3.90, 2,478 strikeouts in 3,824 innings pitched, 175 complete games, 28 shutouts, and a WHIP of 1.296. Over parts of 14 seasons in Detroit, he posted an overall mark of 198–150, compiled an ERA of 3.73, struck out 1,980 batters in 3,042⅔ innings of work, threw 154 complete games and 24 shutouts, and posted a WHIP of 1.266.

Since retiring as an active player, Morris has remained close to the game, serving for a time as an occasional guest host on Tigers broadcasts and as a part-time coach for the Tigers during spring training. After serving as a color analyst for Toronto Blue Jays radio broadcasts on Sportsnet in 2013, Morris became a pre-game color analyst and substitute game analyst for Minnesota Twins telecasts on Fox Sports North. He also serves as a regular on-air contributor on KTWN-FM and the Twins Radio Network.

Although Morris failed to gain induction into the Baseball Hall of Fame during his initial period of eligibility, many people believe that the Veterans Committee will eventually admit him to Cooperstown. Hall of Fame manager Sparky Anderson, with whom Morris quarreled on numerous occasions, likely would give the former right-hander his vote were he still alive. Speaking of Morris in his autobiography, Anderson said, "When we absolutely had to win a game, I wanted Morris on the mound over any pitcher you'd give me. Nine out of ten times, he'd win. The other time, he'd keep you close enough for a shot at the end. . . . He's the best pitcher I ever had—and one of the toughest competitors."

TIGERS CAREER HIGHLIGHTS

Best Season

Morris arguably pitched his best ball for the Tigers in 1981, earning *Sporting News* A.L. Pitcher of the Year honors by leading the league in wins for the only time in his career as a member of the Tigers, and compiling a career-best 3.05 ERA. However, with the season being shortened to a mere 109 games by a players' strike, his 14 wins, 97 strikeouts, and 198 innings pitched fell far short of the figures he posted in some of his other finest seasons. That being the case, Morris had his two best years in 1983 and 1986, proving to be a bit more of a workhorse in the first of those campaigns by going 20–13 with a 3.34 ERA, and establishing career-best marks with 20 complete games, a 1.158 WHIP, and a league-leading 232 strikeouts and 293⅔ innings pitched. Still, Morris compiled extremely comparable numbers in 1986, when he finished 21–8, with a 3.27 ERA, 15 complete games, 223 strikeouts, 267 innings pitched, a WHIP of 1.165, and a league-leading 6 shutouts. It's an extremely close call, but the fact that Morris posted a much better winning percentage in 1986 (.724 to .606) for a team that won 5 fewer games (87 to 92) than it did three years earlier made the 1986 campaign the finest of his career.

Memorable Moments/Greatest Performances

Morris pitched his first truly dominant game as a member of the Tigers on August 21, 1980, when he allowed just 1 hit and 3 walks during a complete game 4–2 win over the Minnesota Twins. However, he topped that performance nearly four years later, throwing a no-hitter against the White Sox in a nationally televised contest played at Chicago's Comiskey Park on April 7, 1984. Morris struck out 8 and walked 6 during the 4–0 victory.

Morris pitched a number of other memorable games for the Tigers over the course of that 1984 campaign, turning in some of his finest efforts during the postseason. After getting the Tigers off to a good start in their ALCS matchup with Kansas City by working 7 strong innings in their 8–1 win in Game One, Morris defeated San Diego twice in the World Series, winning Game One by a score of 3–2, and posting a 4–2 win in Game Four. Morris went the distance in both contests, concluding the Fall Classic with a record of 2–0, a 2.00 ERA, and 13 strikeouts in 18 innings of work.

NOTABLE ACHIEVEMENTS

- Two-time 20-game winner (1983, 1986).
- Won at least 15 games seven other times, surpassing 17 victories on four of those occasions.
- Posted winning percentage in excess of .700 twice.
- Struck out more than 200 batters three times.
- Threw more than 200 innings nine times, tossing more than 250 frames on six occasions.
- Finished in double digits in complete games 10 times, throwing 20 complete games once (1983).
- Led A.L. pitchers in wins once; strikeouts once; shutouts once; complete games once; innings pitched once; games started once; putouts three times; and fielding percentage twice.
- Ranks among Tigers career leaders in: wins (5th); strikeouts (2nd); shutouts (8th); games started (2nd); innings pitched (4th); and complete games (8th).
- Won more games during 1980s (162) than any other pitcher in baseball.
- Finished in top five of A.L. Cy Young voting three times.
- August 1983 A.L. Pitcher of the Month.
- April 1984 A.L. Pitcher of the Month.
- July 1986 A.L. Pitcher of the Month.
- 1984 Babe Ruth Award winner as MVP of World Series.
- 1981 A.L. *Sporting News* Pitcher of the Year.
- 1981 *Sporting News* All-Star selection.
- Four-time A.L. All-Star (1981, 1984, 1985, 1987).
- 1984 A.L. champion.
- 1984 world champion.

11

Alan Trammell

Courtesy of MainlineAutographs.com

The greatest shortstop ever to play for the Tigers, Alan Trammell teamed up with second baseman Lou Whitaker to form the longest continuous keystone combination in major league history. In addition to holding MLB records for most seasons (19) and games (1,918) played alongside one another, Trammell and Whitaker turned more double plays than any other middle infield tandem in history. While Whitaker established himself as one of the finest leadoff hitters in franchise history during their 19 years together, Trammell emerged as the acknowledged leader of the Tigers, helping to vastly improve the ball club's fortunes. After finishing at, or near, the bottom of the A.L. East in each of the previous four seasons, the Tigers compiled a winning record 11 straight times, won two division titles, and captured one world championship with Trammell as their starting shortstop. An outstanding all-around player, Trammell excelled in all aspects of the game, proving to be one of the junior circuit's most consistent offensive performers by batting over .300 seven times, scoring more than 100 runs three times, knocking in more than 100 runs once, and stealing more than 20 bases three times. Meanwhile, Trammell's solid glove work enabled him to win Gold Glove honors on four separate occasions. By the time Trammell retired at the conclusion of the 1996 campaign, he ranked among Detroit's all-time leaders in virtually every major statistical category, having appeared in more games with the club than all but four other players.

Born in Garden Grove, California, on February 21, 1958, Alan Stuart Trammell attended San Diego's Kearny High School, where he starred in baseball and basketball. Although he received several scholarship offers to play both sports in college, Trammell elected to sign with the Tigers for $35,000 after they selected him in the second round of the 1976 amateur draft, stating years later, "Once I signed, I was committed. I wasn't going to be stopped; nothing could stop me in my mind. I was going to work and do whatever it took."

Despite initial concerns over his ability to hit major league pitching down the road, Trammell spent less than two full seasons in the minors before being called up by the Tigers late in 1977. The American League's youngest player at only 19½ years of age, Trammell appeared in 19 games over the final three weeks of the campaign, posting a batting average of just .186 in fewer than 50 trips to the plate.

Given a vote of confidence by Detroit manager Ralph Houk prior to the start of the 1978 season, Trammell ended up winning the starting shortstop job, joining fellow rookie Lou Whitaker in the middle of the Tigers infield. Speaking in glowing terms of his young duo, Houk noted, "Those two kids, they just play good every day. They're the best I've ever seen for their age. On the double plays, knowing where the ball is going to be, that's something you can't teach."

For his part, Trammell finished the season with 2 homers, 34 RBIs, 49 runs scored, a .268 batting average, and only 14 errors in the field, en route to earning a fourth-place finish in the A.L. Rookie of the Year voting. Although Trammell committed a career-high 26 errors the following year, he increased his offensive production, concluding the campaign with 6 home runs, 50 RBIs, 68 runs scored, and a .276 batting average.

Extremely slight-of-build when he first arrived in Detroit, Trammell gradually added some much-needed muscle to his 6-foot frame over the course of the next few seasons, eventually filling out to close to 180 pounds. At the same time, he maintained his quickness in the field and improved upon his performance at the plate by adding a good deal of power and developing an exceptional line-drive stroke that enabled him to drive the ball to all fields.

Trammell's hard work began to pay off in 1980, when he earned All-Star honors for the first of six times by hitting 9 homers, driving in 65 runs, scoring 107 times, and batting an even .300. He also won his first Gold Glove by reducing his error total to just 13, finishing second among A.L. shortstops in fielding percentage for the first of six straight times in the process.

Nagging injuries and inconsistent play hampered Trammell's performance in each of the next two seasons, limiting him to a batting average of .258 each year, and totals of only 11 home runs, 88 RBIs, and 118 runs scored over the course of those two campaigns. However, after adopting more of a closed stance at the plate, he rebounded in 1983 to earn A.L. Comeback Player of the Year honors by scoring 83 runs and establishing new career highs with 14 homers, 66 RBIs, 30 stolen bases, and a .319 batting average. Trammell's offensive resurgence continued in 1984, when, despite missing 23 games due to tendinitis in his shoulder, he helped lead the Tigers to a record of 104–58 and their first division title in 12 years by hitting 14 home runs, driving in 69 runs, scoring 85 times, and placing among the league leaders with 34 doubles, a .314 batting average, and a .382 on-base percentage. Trammell also won the last of his four Gold Gloves, with his outstanding all-around play earning him a ninth-place finish in the A.L. MVP balloting. He subsequently starred for the Tigers during the postseason, homering once, knocking in 3 runs, and batting .364 during their three-game sweep of Kansas City in the ALCS, before earning World Series MVP honors by hitting 2 home runs, driving in 6 runs, scoring 5 times, and batting .450 against San Diego in the Fall Classic.

Plagued by injuries throughout most of 1985, Trammell hit 13 home runs, drove in 57 runs, scored 79 times, and batted just .258. However, after undergoing surgery to repair his injured left knee and ailing right shoulder during the subsequent offseason, Trammell returned to top form in 1986, concluding the campaign with 21 homers, 75 RBIs, 107 runs scored, 25 steals, and a .277 batting average. His 20 homers and 20 thefts made him just the second Detroit player to surpass 20 in both categories in the same season (Kirk Gibson was the first). Tiger third baseman Darnell Coles expressed his admiration for Trammell by calling him the team's most important player "because of his consistency," suggesting, "He's always out there; he always knows what's going on; he's always talking. He keeps everybody going."

After Trammel spent the previous several seasons hitting primarily out of the number two spot in Detroit's lineup, the free-agent departure of power-hitting catcher Lance Parrish prompted manager Sparky Anderson to insert his shortstop into the cleanup spot in the batting order in 1987. Trammell responded with the finest offensive season of his career, earning the first of his three Silver Sluggers by hitting 28 home runs and placing among the league leaders with 105 RBIs, 109 runs scored, 205 hits, a .343 batting average, a .402 on-base percentage, and a .551 slugging percentage. Although the Tigers edged out Toronto for the division title by sweeping the Blue Jays in the final three games of the regular season, Trammell finished a close second to slugging Toronto outfielder George Bell in the MVP voting, losing out by a count of 332 points to 311.

Injuries began to significantly reduce Trammell's playing time the following season, with the star shortstop appearing in more than 140 games just once more in his career. Nevertheless, he continued to play well in most of those campaigns, whenever he found himself able to take the field. After batting .311, hitting 15 homers, driving in 69 runs, and scoring 73 times in only 128 games in 1988, Trammell suffered through an injury-marred 1989 campaign in which he batted just .243, hit only 5 homers, and knocked in just 43 runs. A return to relatively good health the following year enabled him to win his final Silver Slugger and earn his last All-Star selection by hitting 14 homers, driving in 89 runs, and batting .304. However, even though Trammell batted .329 in 112 games in 1993, he never again put up big offensive numbers, with his final six years in Detroit being marred by numerous trips to the DL. After spending most of the three previous seasons serving as a part-time player at various positions, Trammell elected to announce his retirement at the conclusion of the 1996 campaign. He ended his career with 185 home runs, 1,003 RBIs, 1,231 runs scored, 2,365 hits, 55 triples, 412 doubles, 236 stolen bases, a .285 batting average, a .352 on-base percentage, and a .415 slugging percentage. In addition to placing second in the A.L. MVP balloting in 1987, he finished in the top 10 in the voting two other times.

Following his retirement, Trammell spent one year serving as Detroit's hitting coach, before moving on to San Diego, where he spent the next three years coaching first base for the Padres. He returned to Detroit in 2003 to assume the managerial reins of a team that posted a losing record in each of the previous nine seasons. Trammell's managerial stint lasted three years, with the Tigers compiling an overall mark of just 186–300 during that time. Yet, even though Trammell failed to restore the Tigers to prominence, often being criticized in the press for his managerial strategies and "nice" demeanor, he helped re-instill a sense of pride and professionalism throughout the organization that contributed greatly to the success the Tigers subsequently experienced under manager Jim Leyland. After leaving Detroit, Trammell resurfaced one year later as bench coach of the Chicago Cubs, before later accepting a similar position in Arizona, where he continues to serve under manager and former teammate Kirk Gibson.

Over the course of his playing career, Trammell often found himself coming up short in comparisons made between himself and the other top shortstops of his time—Cal Ripken Jr., Ozzie Smith, and Robin Yount. Yet, there are those who believe he took a backseat to no one in terms of his all-around ability. Former Tigers manager Sparky Anderson wrote in his autobiography, "I don't like to go just by the numbers. I've seen some great shortstops—Dave Concepcion, Ozzie Smith, Cal Ripken, just to name a few. I'll take Trammell because of everything he can do. Smith is a wizard in the field and can do more with the glove. Ripken is stronger and hits with more power. But Trammell does everything. Trammell hits 15 homers a year, knocks in 90 runs a year, and plays around the .300 mark. In the field, he never botches a routine play."

Meanwhile, former player and Texas Rangers general manager Tom Grieve said in *Out by a Step: The 100 Best Players Not in the Baseball Hall of Fame*, "When I think of Alan Trammell, I think of a very steady player, a very dependable player—not a spectacular player; the kind of guy that makes all the routine plays. The kind of guy you would expect to be the captain of a team. The kind of guy that, if there's a man on third base and less than two outs, you know he's gonna put the ball in play somewhere and get the run in."

Grieve added, "There's not one thing on the field that he didn't do well. He was an excellent base runner; he could steal a base. He's a manager's dream, without the gaudy stats."

CAREER HIGHLIGHTS

Best Season

Trammell had easily his best season in 1987, when he established career highs in most statistical categories, including home runs (28), RBIs (105), runs scored (109), hits (205), total bases (329), batting average (.343), on-base percentage (.402), and slugging percentage (.551), en route to earning a close second-place finish in the A.L. MVP voting. Particularly effective down the stretch, Trammell fashioned an 18-game hitting streak, hit 6 homers, knocked in 17 runs, and batted .416 during the month of September, in helping the Tigers edge out Toronto for the A.L. East title by just 2 games.

Memorable Moments/Greatest Performances

Trammell had the first great day of his career on July 7, 1978, when he led the Tigers to a 12–7 trouncing of the Texas Rangers by going 5-for-6, with 2 RBIs and 2 runs scored. Nearly one year later, on June 12, 1979, Trammell stole home in a 9–2 victory over Oakland, becoming in the process the first Detroit player in six years to accomplish the feat.

Trammell got one of the most memorable hits of his career on June 21, 1988, when he capped a 6-run, ninth-inning rally against the Yankees by delivering a walk-off grand slam against New York reliever Cecilio Guante that gave the Tigers a dramatic 7–6 come-from-behind win.

However, Trammell will likely always be remembered most for his extraordinary performance during the 1984 postseason. After batting .364, homering once, and knocking in 3 runs against Kansas City in the ALCS, he went 9-for-20 (.450) against San Diego in the World Series, with 2 home runs, 6 RBIs, and 5 runs scored. Trammell all but cemented the Series win for the Tigers in Game 4, when he put them ahead 3 games to 1 by going 3-for-4, with a pair of 2-run homers, in a 4–2 Detroit victory.

Trammell also attained a measure of immortality on September 13, 1995, when he and teammate Lou Whitaker played in their 1,918th game together, eclipsing in the process the A.L. record previously held by Kansas City's George Brett and Frank White.

NOTABLE ACHIEVEMENTS

- Batted over .300 seven times, topping .320 twice.
- Hit more than 20 home runs twice.
- Knocked in more than 100 runs once (105 in 1987).
- Scored more than 100 runs three times.
- Surpassed 200 hits once (205 in 1987).
- Topped 30 doubles six times.
- Stole more than 20 bases three times, swiping 30 bags in 1983.
- Compiled on-base percentage in excess of .400 once (.402 in 1987).
- Posted slugging percentage in excess of .500 once (.551 in 1987).
- Led the American League in sacrifice hits twice.
- Led A.L. shortstops in double plays turned once.
- Ranks among Tigers career leaders in runs scored (6th); hits (7th); RBIs (10th); doubles (6th); extra-base hits (9th); total bases (7th); walks (7th); stolen bases (5th); games played (5th); plate appearances (5th); and at-bats (5th).
- Ranks seventh all-time among major league shortstops with 1,307 double plays.
- April 1984 A.L. Player of the Month.
- September 1987 A.L. Player of the Month.
- 1983 A.L. Comeback Player of the Year.
- 1984 World Series MVP.
- Finished second in 1987 A.L. MVP voting.
- Four-time Gold Glove winner.
- Three-time Silver Slugger winner.
- Three-times *Sporting News* All-Star selection (1987, 1988, 1990).
- Six-time A.L. All-Star.
- 1984 A.L. champion.
- 1984 world champion.

12

Lou Whitaker

Courtesy of MearsOnlineAuctions.com

Since Lou Whitaker spent virtually his entire career playing alongside Alan Trammell in the Tigers' infield, it seems only fitting that he now occupies an adjacent spot in these rankings. Whitaker, who played in more games at second base for the Tigers than anyone else, ranks among the franchise's all-time leaders in numerous statistical categories, including home runs (7th), RBIs (8th), runs scored (4th), hits (6th), doubles (5th), total bases (5th), and walks (2nd). An outstanding leadoff hitter with surprising power for a man his size, "Sweet Lou," as he came to be known to Tiger fans, hit more than 20 home runs four times, scored more than 100 runs twice, batted over .300 twice, and posted an on-base percentage in excess of .370 on eight separate occasions. A fine fielder, Whitaker earned three Gold Gloves, en route to compiling the sixth most assists and turning the fourth most double plays of any second baseman in major league history.

Born in Brooklyn, New York, on May 12, 1957, Louis Rodman Whitaker grew up in Martinsville, Virginia, after his mother moved the family there shortly after he celebrated his first birthday. Sadly, young Louis never knew his father, who engaged in illegal activities in New York, causing the younger Whitaker to tell *The Sporting News* in 1979, "He's never done anything for me. I don't hate him. I haven't got time to hate anybody. I just don't care to meet him. There's nothing emotionally happening between us."

Whitaker excelled in baseball while attending Martinsville High School, prompting the Tigers to select him as a third baseman in the fifth round of the 1975 amateur draft, less than one month after he turned 18 years of age. Subsequently assigned to Bristol, Detroit's minor league affiliate in the Appalachian League, Whitaker acquitted himself well, causing his confidence to grow to the point that he introduced himself to Tigers general manager Jim Campbell in 1976 spring training by saying, "I'm Lou Whitaker, and I'll be playing for you soon."

Whitaker backed up his words by winning MVP honors in the Florida State League while moving over to the other side of the diamond to play second base. Former Tigers shortstop Eddie Brinkman, who helped Whitaker make the transition to his new position, praised the young infielder by stating, "Whitaker is such a natural athlete that he took to second base right away."

After Whitaker had another fine season in 1977, this time for the Montgomery Rebels of the AA Southern League, the Tigers summoned him to the big leagues for the final three weeks of the campaign. Appearing in 11 games with the Tigers during the month of September, Whitaker collected 8 hits in 32 official trips to the plate, for a batting average of .250. Whitaker and first-year shortstop Alan Trammell made a strong impression on Tigers manager Ralph Houk the following spring, prompting the veteran skipper to award the starting middle infield jobs to the two rookies. In discussing the young tandem, Houk gushed, "It's the damnedest thing. You tell one of them something and he says, 'We can do it.' Like they're a team."

Whitaker and Trammell rewarded Houk for the faith he placed in them by performing extremely well in their first big-league season. Whitaker, in particular, showed a great deal of promise, earning A.L. Rookie of the Year honors by batting .285, driving in 58 runs, and scoring 71 times. The young second baseman's solid play made him an immediate fan favorite at Tiger Stadium, with the hometown fans displaying their fondness for him by serenading him with a chant of "Loooooooou" every time he stepped into the batter's box—a practice they continued throughout the remainder of his career. Initially surprised by the manner in which the fans greeted him, Whitaker later said, "I thought they were booing me at first." Meanwhile, Houk continued to sing his praises, responding to a question regarding whether or not he had ever seen a better young second baseman in his four decades in baseball by saying, "No. The only one I could think of was Bobby Richardson. He was a hell of a ballplayer, but not as good as Whitaker."

Despite missing more than 30 games in 1979 due to injury, Whitaker had a solid sophomore campaign, finishing the season with a .286 batting average, 75 runs scored, and a career-high 20 stolen bases. However, after being inserted into the leadoff spot in Detroit's lineup the following year by new manager Sparky Anderson, Whitaker struggled at the plate, forcing Anderson to drop him several notches in the batting order. Anderson, who initially expressed the belief that Whitaker would make an outstanding leadoff hitter because "he's got a great eye and he doesn't pull the ball," later suggested, "He's got to relax. Hitting somewhere else will give him a breather." Whitaker ended up batting just .233 and scoring only 68 runs in 1980. He followed that up with another subpar performance in 1981, concluding the strike-shortened campaign with a .263 batting average and 48 runs scored.

Working extensively with hitting coach Gates Brown throughout the 1982 season finally enabled Whitaker to mature as a hitter. Learning how to take better advantage of Tiger Stadium's short upper-deck porch in right field, the left-hand-swinging Whitaker established new career highs with 15 home runs, 65 RBIs, and 76 runs scored. He also batted .286 and amassed 8 triples, earning in the process a return to the leadoff spot in the batting order. In addition to teaching the 5'11", 165-pound Whitaker how to jerk the ball into the right-field stands, Brown helped improve his approach at the plate, with Whitaker stating, "In the past, if I got 2 or 3 hits in a game, I'd kind of let up. I'd lose my concentration at the plate if we had a team beat. I went to Gates and told him this. He told me none of the great hitters give up outs. He said, 'Get all you can get.'" Whitaker also had an exceptional year in the field, leading all A.L. second basemen with 470 assists, 120 double plays, and a .988 fielding percentage.

Whitaker continued to grow as a hitter in 1983, earning the first of his four Silver Sluggers and his first of five consecutive All-Star nominations by hitting 12 home runs, driving in 72 runs, scoring 94 times, and placing among the league leaders with 206 hits, 40 doubles, and a .320 batting average. He also won the first of his three straight Gold Gloves, earning in the process an eighth-place finish in the A.L. MVP voting. Whitaker followed that up with a solid 1984 campaign in which he hit 13 homers, knocked in 56 runs, scored 90 times, and batted .289 for the eventual world champions.

Although the Tigers failed to advance to the playoffs in either of the next two seasons, Whitaker had two of his most productive campaigns, hitting 21 home runs, driving in 73 runs, scoring 102 times, and batting .279 in 1985, and homering 20 times, knocking in 73 runs, scoring 95 times, and batting .269 the following year. Whitaker subsequently batted .265, hit 16 homers, and scored a career-high 110 runs for Detroit's 1987 A.L. East championship ball club, before missing a significant amount of playing time the following year due to torn cartilage in his knee. Returning to the Tigers' lineup healthy in 1989, Whitaker suddenly found himself batting third for a team that ended up finishing last in the A.L. East with only 59 victories. In an effort to hit for more power, Whitaker established career highs with 28 home runs and 85 RBIs, although his batting average slipped to .251.

Whitaker remained Detroit's full-time starting second baseman for another four years, compiling his best numbers during that time in 1991, when he hit 23 homers, knocked in 78 runs, scored 94 times, and batted .279. He continued to perform well for the club in a part-time role in 1994 and 1995, posting batting averages of .301 and .293, before electing to announce his retirement at the conclusion of the 1995 campaign. He ended his career with 244 home runs, 1,084 RBIs, 1,386 runs scored, 2,369 hits, 65 triples, 420 doubles, 143 stolen bases, a .276 batting average, a .363 on-base percentage, and a .426 slugging percentage, joining Rogers Hornsby and Joe Morgan as the only second basemen in baseball history, to that point, to surpass 200 homers, 1,000 RBIs, 1,000 runs scored, and 2,000 hits. In addition to ranking among the all-time leaders among second sackers in assists and double plays, he played in the fourth most games (2,308) and accumulated the 11th most putouts (4,771) of anyone who ever manned the position.

Following his retirement, Whitaker moved to Lakeland, Florida, where he eventually became an instructor for the Tigers during their spring training sessions in that same city. He continued to serve in that capacity through 2009, after which he and the Tigers parted ways by mutual agreement. Whitaker also devoted more time to his religion, concentrating heavily on missionary work for the Jehovah's Witnesses.

Five years after Whitaker retired, the 2000 edition of *The Biographical Encyclopedia of Baseball* summarized his career thusly: "Lou Whitaker enjoyed his share of individual glory. His 2,308 games as Tigers second baseman was 102 more than Hall of Famer Charlie Gehringer, who, like Whitaker, spent his entire 19-year career in Detroit. He joined Hall of Famer Joe Morgan as only the second player to log 2,000 games at second with 2,000 hits and 200 home runs. Nevertheless, Whitaker will best be remembered for teaming up with shortstop Alan Trammell for an A.L. record 1,918 games."

CAREER HIGHLIGHTS

Best Season

Even though Whitaker established career highs with 28 home runs and 85 RBIs in 1989, he had his three best seasons in 1983, 1985, and 1991. In addition to hitting more home runs (23), driving in more runs (78), and compiling a higher OPS (.881) in 1991 than he did in either of the other two campaigns, Whitaker scored 94 runs, batted .279, drew a career-high 90 walks, and committed only 4 errors in the field, en route to leading all A.L. second basemen with a career-best .994 fielding percentage. However, he also appeared in only 135 games in the field and accumulated far fewer assists (361) than he did in either 1983 (447) or 1985 (414). Whitaker posted fairly similar numbers in 1985, finishing the year with 21 homers, 73 RBIs, 102 runs scored, 80 walks, a .279 batting average, and an OPS of .819. Still, it could be argued that he had his finest all-around season in 1983, when he hit 12 home runs, drove in 72 runs, scored 94 times, stole 17 bases, compiled an OPS of .837, and established career highs with 206 hits, 40 doubles, 294 total bases, and a .320 batting average, all of which placed him among the league leaders. Appearing in all but 2 of the Tigers' 162 games over the course of the regular season, Whitaker also ranked among the junior circuit's top second basemen in putouts and assists, earning in the process the first of his three consecutive Gold Gloves. Whitaker's outstanding all-around performance earned him his only top-10 finish in the A.L. MVP voting and recognition at season's end as Tiger of the Year. All things considered, Whitaker had the best season of his career in 1983.

Memorable Moments/Greatest Performances

Whitaker made his first home run in the big leagues a memorable one, delivering a two-out, two-run shot in the bottom of the ninth inning against Seattle reliever Enrique Romo that gave the Tigers a 4–3 win over the Mariners on July 28, 1978.

On June 10, 1984, Whitaker had a huge game against the Orioles, going 3-for-4 and scoring a career-high 5 runs, in leading the Tigers to a 10–4 win in the opener of a doubleheader sweep of Baltimore. He had another big day on April 10, 1985, going 3-for-4, hitting a pair of homers, driving in 4 runs, and scoring 3 times during an 8–1 victory over the Indians. Later that year, Whitaker became the first leadoff hitter or second baseman to hit a home run over the right-field roof at Tiger Stadium. Whitaker flexed his muscles again on August 5, 1986, when he homered twice during an 11–9 win over the Indians at Tiger Stadium.

Whitaker's sweet swing proved to be the difference in the 1986 All-Star Game, when his two-run homer off Dwight Gooden in the second inning helped the Americans defeat the Nationals by a score of 3–2.

Whitaker had the most productive day of his career on May 4, 1994, when he led the Tigers to a 14–7 win over the Rangers by driving in 7 runs with a 3-run homer in the bottom of the third inning and a grand slam in the eighth.

NOTABLE ACHIEVEMENTS

- Hit more than 20 home runs four times.
- Scored more than 100 runs twice.
- Batted over .300 twice.
- Surpassed 200 hits once (206 in 1983).
- Accumulated more than 30 doubles three times, and 40 two-baggers once (1983).
- Stole 20 bases once (1979).
- Compiled on-base percentage in excess of .400 once (.412 in 1983).
- Posted slugging percentage in excess of .500 once (.518 in 1995).

- Led A.L. second basemen in fielding percentage twice; assists twice; putouts once; and double plays once.
- Holds Tigers all-time record for most double plays turned (1,527).
- Ranks among Tigers career leaders in home runs (7th); RBIs (8th); runs scored (4th); hits (6th); doubles (5th); extra-base hits (6th); total bases (5th); walks (2nd); stolen bases (10th); games played (3rd); plate appearances (4th); and at-bats (4th).
- Ranks among Major League Baseball's all-time leaders for second basemen in double plays (4th); assists (6th); putouts (11th); and games played (4th).
- 1978 A.L. Rookie of the Year.
- June 1983 A.L. Player of the Month.
- Three-time Gold Glove winner.
- Four-time Silver Slugger winner.
- Two-time *Sporting News* All-Star selection (1983, 1984).
- Five-time A.L. All-Star (1983–1987).
- 1984 A.L. champion.
- 1984 world champion.

13

Bobby Veach

Courtesy of the Library of Congress, Harris & Ewing Collection

O ne of the most underappreciated and unheralded players in Tigers history, Bobby Veach spent his 11 years in Detroit being overshadowed by Ty Cobb and, to a lesser degree, Sam Crawford and Harry Heilmann. After taking a backseat to Cobb and Crawford his first three years with the Tigers, Veach spent his final eight seasons in Detroit being overlooked in favor of Cobb and Heilmann. Nevertheless, Veach established himself during his time in Detroit as one of the most productive and dangerous hitters in all of baseball, driving in more runs and amassing more extra-base hits than any other player in the major leagues from 1915 to 1922. Over the course of those eight seasons, Veach averaged 107 RBIs, 14 triples, and 36 doubles, while also compiling a composite batting average of .318. A three-time A.L. RBI champ, Veach also excelled in the outfield, leading all left fielders in putouts six consecutive times, while annually placing among the league's top outfielders in assists and fielding percentage.

Born in St. Charles, Kentucky, on June 29, 1888, Robert Hayes Veach moved with his family to Madisonville, Kentucky, at the age of 12. Just one year after playing in his first organized baseball game at the relatively advanced age of 13, Veach quit school to join his father and two older brothers in the coal mines. He continued to work in the mines until shortly after he turned 17, when he moved to Herrin, Illinois, and began his professional career playing semipro ball in the old Eastern Illinois Trolley League. Five years later, Veach signed on as a pitcher with the Three-I League's Peoria Distillers, who farmed him out to the Kankakee, Illinois, team in the Northern Association early in 1910. After one year at Kankakee, Veach returned to Peoria, where he began playing the outfield on a regular basis for the first time in his young career. Impressed by the hitting ability Veach displayed over the course of the next two seasons, the Tigers purchased his contract late in 1912. The 24-year-old outfielder made his major league debut with the club shortly thereafter, posting a batting average of .342 and driving in 15 runs over the final month of the 1912 season.

Veach established himself as Detroit's starting left fielder early in 1913, concluding the campaign with a .269 batting average, 64 RBIs, and 22 stolen bases, and accumulating 16 outfield assists, beginning in the process a string of 10 consecutive seasons in which he threw out at least 14 opposing base runners. After posting solid numbers again in 1914, Veach developed into one of the American League's best hitters the following year, when he ranked among the league leaders with 178 hits, 247 total bases, a .313 batting average, a .390 on-base percentage, and a .434 slugging percentage, while amassing a league-leading 40 doubles and tying teammate Sam Crawford for the top spot in the circuit with 112 RBIs. Veach's ascension into stardom gave the Tigers easily the best outfield in baseball. In fact, with Cobb and Crawford also having exceptional seasons (the three Detroit outfielders ranked first, second, and third in the league in total bases and RBIs), *Baseball Magazine* published a five-page feature story on Veach during the campaign that stated, "with his advent, the Detroit outfield is one of the most powerful, if not the most powerful, ever assembled on a diamond."

Nearly a century later, noted baseball historian and statistician Bill James ranked Detroit's 1915 outfield as the greatest outfield of all time.

Veach placed among the league leaders in virtually every statistical category in each of the next two seasons, concluding the 1916 campaign with 91 RBIs, 92 runs scored, 15 triples, 33 doubles, a career-high 24 stolen bases, and a batting average of .306, before batting .319, finishing second in the league with 8 home runs, and topping the circuit with 103 RBIs in 1917. In the second of those years, he also began a string of six consecutive seasons in which he led all A.L. left fielders in putouts.

After leading the league with 78 RBIs in the war-shortened 1918 season, the left-hand-hitting Veach had one of his finest all-around seasons the following year. In addition to finishing second in the circuit to teammate Cobb with a career-high .355 batting average, Veach drove in 101 runs and led the league with 191 hits, 45 doubles, and 17 triples. He followed that up with another big year in 1920, batting .307, scoring 92 runs, and ranking among the league leaders with 11 homers, 113 RBIs, 188 hits, 39 doubles, and 15 triples.

As the dead-ball era drew to a close with the dawning of the 1920s, Veach's hitting style seemed much better suited for the free-swinging offensive period that immediately followed. Although he stood 5'11" and weighed only 165 pounds, Veach tended to swing from his heels, rarely changing his approach at the plate to adapt to game situations. Putting everything he had into each swing, Veach employed the hitting philosophy of a much larger man, choosing to hold the bat at the very end. He later explained, "Choking up has the effect of shortening the bat, and it seemed reasonable to suppose that, the shorter the bat, the more quickly you could swing to meet the ball. In theory, this was sound; but, in practice, I found it wouldn't work. Most of the really good hitters swing from the handle of the bat." Yet, in spite of the aggressive style of hitting Veach employed, he never struck out more than 44 times in a season, fanning a total of only 370 times in more than 7,500 plate appearances over the course of his career. And, as baseball writer Fed Lieb once noted, he "packed a terrific punch for his size."

Veach once again posted exceptional numbers in 1921, ranking among the league leaders with 16 home runs, 128 RBIs, 110 runs scored, 210 hits, 43 doubles, a .338 batting average, and a .529 slugging percentage. Yet, in spite of his outstanding performance, Veach did not find the 1921 campaign to be a particularly enjoyable one. After spending his first several seasons in Detroit being treated kindly by Tigers manager Hughie Jennings, Veach often found himself at odds with the team's new player/manager Ty

Cobb. The latter, who objected to Veach's easygoing manner and tendency to engage in friendly conversation with umpires and opposing players, instructed Harry Heilmann to provoke the team's left fielder by yelling insults at him throughout the season. Hoping to light a fire under Veach, whom Tigers historian Fred Lieb described in his book *The Detroit Tigers* as a "happy-go-lucky guy, not too brilliant above the ears," Cobb persuaded Heilmann, who followed Veach in the batting order, to taunt him from the on-deck circle. According to Al Stump in *Cobb: The Life and Times of the Meanest Man Who Ever Played Baseball*, Cobb told Heilmann, "I want you to make him mad . . . real mad. . . . While you're waiting, call him a yellow belly, a quitter, and a dog. . . . Take that smile off his face."

Although Veach ended up having one of the finest seasons of his career, he never forgave Heilmann, whom Cobb betrayed by failing to live up to his promise to tell Veach about the scheme at season's end. When Heilmann later tried to explain his actions to Veach, the latter reportedly snarled, "Don't come sucking around me with that phony line."

Even though he remained on bad terms with Cobb and Heilmann throughout the ensuing campaign, Veach had another big year, batting .327, scoring 96 runs, collecting 202 hits, and finishing second in the league with 126 RBIs. After holding out for more money prior to the start of the 1923 season, Veach found himself limited by injuries and the arrival of talented newcomer Heinie Manush to only 114 games and 340 total plate appearances. Yet he still managed to hit .321, before being jettisoned during the subsequent offseason by Cobb, who sold him to the last-place Red Sox for an undisclosed amount of cash. Although Veach played well for Boston in 1924, batting .295 and driving in 95 runs, the Red Sox elected to trade him to the Yankees early the following year. Veach split the 1925 campaign between the Yankees and Senators, serving as a bench player for both teams, before being released by Washington at season's end. The 37-year-old outfielder subsequently joined the American Association's Toledo Mud Hens, with whom he spent the next four seasons. He then spent one year with the Jersey City Skeeters in the International League, before announcing his retirement at the conclusion of the 1930 campaign.

Over parts of 14 major league seasons, Veach hit 64 home runs, knocked in 1,166 runs, scored 953 times, accumulated 2,063 hits, 393 doubles, 147 triples, and 195 stolen bases, batted .310, compiled a .370 on-base percentage, and posted a .442 slugging percentage. His Tigers numbers include 59 homers, 1,042 RBIs, 859 runs scored, 1,859 hits, 345 doubles, 136 triples, 189 stolen bases, a .311 batting average, a .370 on-base percentage, and a .444 slugging percentage. Veach also recorded 180 assists and 3,379 putouts from his spot in left field, placing him among Major League Baseball's all-time leaders in both categories for players who manned his position.

Following his retirement, Veach settled down in the Detroit area and eventually became sole owner of a coal company. After being hospitalized and undergoing a serious abdominal operation in 1943, Veach never returned to full health and passed away from lung cancer two years later, at the age of 57, on August 7, 1945. Survived by his wife and sons, he was entombed in the White Chapel Memorial Cemetery in Southfield, Michigan.

TIGERS CAREER HIGHLIGHTS

Best Season

Although Veach performed brilliantly for the Tigers from 1919 to 1922, he clearly had his two best seasons in 1919 and 1921. In the second of those campaigns, he batted .338, amassed 43 doubles, and established career highs with 16 home runs, 128 RBIs, 110 runs scored, 207 hits, a .529 slugging percentage, and a .917 OPS. Veach also did an exceptional job in the outfield, placing third among American League left fielders with 21 assists, while leading all players at his position with a .974 fielding percentage and a career-best 384 putouts. In 1919, Veach homered only three times but knocked in 101 runs, scored 87 times, finished second in the league with a career-high .355 batting average, topped the circuit with 191 hits, 17 triples, and 45 doubles, and posted an OPS of .916 that nearly matched the mark he compiled two years later. The sheer numbers would seem to suggest that Veach had his greatest season in 1921. However, it must be remembered that he posted those figures after the A.L. began using a livelier ball one year earlier. That being the case, Veach finished in the league's top five in only three major statistical categories—RBIs (4th), hits (5th), and doubles (3rd). On the other hand, he placed near the top of the league rankings in eight different offensive categories in 1919, topping the circuit in three, and finishing second in three others (batting average, RBIs, and total bases). Factoring everything into the equation, Veach had the best season of his career in 1919.

Memorable Moments/Greatest Performances

Veach joined teammates Ty Cobb and Ossie Vitt in collecting 5 hits apiece in a 16–4 Detroit victory over Washington on July 30, 1917. By each hitting safely five times during the contest, the three players tied a twentieth-century major league record. Veach finished the game 5-for-5, with a stolen base and 3 runs scored.

Veach flexed his muscles on September 8, 1922, leading the Tigers to an 8–3 win over the St. Louis Browns by homering twice against 23-game winner Urban Shocker. Veach went 3-for-4 during the contest, with 5 RBIs and 2 runs scored.

Veach, though, had the biggest day of his career on September 17, 1920, when he led the Tigers to a 14–13 victory over the Red Sox in 12 innings by becoming the first Detroit player to hit for the cycle. Veach finished the game with 6 hits, going 6-for-6, with 6 RBIs and 2 runs scored.

NOTABLE ACHIEVEMENTS

- Knocked in more than 100 runs six times, surpassing 120 RBIs twice.
- Finished in double digits in home runs twice.
- Scored more than 100 runs once (110 in 1921).
- Batted over .300 nine times, topping .320 five times and batting over .350 once (.355 in 1919).
- Surpassed 200 hits twice.
- Finished in double digits in triples 10 times, topping 15 three-baggers on three occasions.
- Surpassed 30 doubles seven times, topping 40 two-baggers on three occasions.
- Stole more than 20 bases five times.
- Posted slugging percentage in excess of .500 twice.
- Accumulated more than 20 outfield assists three times.
- Led the American League in RBIs three times; doubles twice; hits once; and triples once.
- Led A.L. outfielders in putouts once and assists once.
- Led A.L. left fielders in putouts six times; fielding percentage twice; assists once; and double plays turned once.
- Ranks among Tigers career leaders in RBIs (9th); hits (8th); doubles (9th); triples (5th); total bases (10th); extra-base hits (10th); and stolen bases (8th).
- Holds major league record for most double plays turned by a left fielder (39).
- Ranks among Major League Baseball's all-time leaders for left fielders in assists (3rd) and putouts (12th).
- Hit for the cycle on September 17, 1920.

14

Norm Cash

Courtesy of LegendaryAuctions.com

While the 1968 season came to be known as the "Year of the Pitcher," 1961 could just as easily be referred to as the "Year of the Hitter." With the expansion Washington Senators and Los Angeles Angels joining the ranks of A.L. teams, baseball experienced a dilution in pitching talent that enabled the game's top stars to compile some incredibly prolific offensive numbers. In the junior circuit alone, Roger Maris and Mickey Mantle combined to hit 115 home runs for the Yankees, with the former breaking Babe Ruth's long-standing single season home run record. Baltimore's Jim Gentile hit 46 homers and knocked in 141 runs, in fewer than 500 official at-bats. Harmon Killebrew homered 46 times and drove in 122 runs for the Minnesota Twins. Rocky Colavito hit 45 home runs, knocked in 140 runs, and scored 129 others for the Tigers. Yet, it could be argued that the sport's finest all-around hitter in 1961 was Colavito's teammate in Detroit, slugging first baseman Norm Cash. The left-hand-hitting Cash placed among the A.L. leaders with 41 home runs, 132 runs batted in, 119 runs scored, 124 walks, 354 total bases, and a .662 slugging percentage, while topping the circuit with 193 hits, a .361 batting average, a .487 on-base percentage, and a 1.148 OPS. Although Cash never again approached most of those extraordinary figures, he remained one of the American League's top sluggers for another decade, retiring in 1974 as the fourth leading left-handed home run hitter in league history, behind only Babe Ruth, Ted Williams, and Lou Gehrig.

Born in Justiceburg, Texas, on November 10, 1934, Norman Dalton Cash starred in both football and baseball while attending Sul Ross State University in Alpine, Texas. Drafted by the Chicago Bears as a running back in 1955, the talented youngster instead chose to sign as an amateur free agent with the Chicago White Sox the very same year. After two seasons of minor league ball, Cash spent 1957 in the military, before returning to Chicago's farm system in 1958. The 23-year-old first base-man/outfielder made his major league debut with the White Sox later that year, appearing in four games in the outfield and singling twice in 8 official trips to the plate. Cash assumed a part-time role with the team the following year, seeing a limited amount of action at first base, before being relegated to bench duty during the season's second half following the acquisition of Ted Kluszewski. In just over 100 official at-bats, Cash batted .240, hit 4 home runs, and knocked in 16 runs.

The White Sox subsequently included Cash in an eight-player deal they completed with the Cleveland Indians at season's end that brought Minnie Minoso back to Chicago. However, Cash never appeared in a single regular season game for the Indians since, in one of the more lopsided trades in baseball history, Cleveland elected to trade him to the Tigers for unknown third baseman Steve Demeter shortly before the 1960 campaign got under way. While Demeter's major league career ended shortly thereafter, Cash quickly established himself as the Tigers' starting first baseman upon his arrival in the Motor City, hitting 18 home runs, driving in 63 runs, and batting .286 in his first full major league season. The 6-foot, 190-pound Cash found Tiger Stadium's excellent hitting background very much to his liking, learning before long how to use his quick, compact swing to take full advantage of the ballpark's short right-field porch. The first baseman later became the first Detroit player to hit a ball completely out of Tiger Stadium—a feat he accomplished four times over the course of his career.

With the left-hand-hitting Cash sandwiched between right-handed sluggers Al Kaline and Rocky Colavito in the Detroit batting order, the Tigers scored the most runs in all of baseball in 1961, compiling in the process a regular season record of 101–61. Unfortunately, the New York Yankees put together an even more remarkable season, posting 109 victories, en route to finishing 8 games ahead of Detroit in the standings. Nevertheless, the numbers Cash compiled over the course of the campaign prevented him from taking a backseat to anyone in terms of total offensive production. In addition to leading the league in batting (.361), on-base percentage (.487), OPS (1.148), and hits (193), Cash finished sixth in home runs (41), fourth in RBIs (132) and runs scored (119), and second in walks (124), total bases (354), and slugging percentage (.662). His .361 batting average turned out to be the highest mark posted by any player during the decade of the 1960s. Cash's brilliant performance earned him a fourth-place finish in the league MVP voting, behind New York's Roger Maris and Mickey Mantle, and Baltimore's Jim Gentile.

Although many observers attributed the gaudy offensive numbers posted by several of the game's top players in 1961 to league expansion, which resulted in a dilution of pitching talent, Cash later admitted to using an illegal corked bat throughout the campaign, revealing that he drilled a hole in his bats, which he subsequently filled with a mixture of sawdust, cork, and glue. Yet, Cash also firmly believed that he received a significant amount of good fortune en route to compiling easily the greatest season of his career. Looking back on the 1961 season, Cash said, "It was a freak. Even at the time, I realized that. Everything I hit seemed to drop in, even when I didn't make good contact. I never thought I'd do it again."

Cash didn't come close to repeating his exceptional performance the following year, posting a batting average of just .243. His 118-point drop in batting average still represents the largest ever by a batting champion. Nevertheless, Cash knocked in 89 runs, scored 94 others, and finished among the league leaders with 39 home runs and 104 walks, compiling in the process a very respectable .382 on-base percentage.

Cash never again batted any higher than .283, reaching .270 only four more times in his 12 remaining years with the Tigers. Yet, he continued to post outstanding home run totals, surpassing 30 homers three more times, while hitting more than 20 long balls on six other occasions. Cash had two of his best years in 1966 and 1971, batting .279 in the first of those campaigns, while also hitting 32 homers, driving in 93 runs, and scoring 98 times. Five years later, he batted .283, finished second in the American League with 32 homers, and also placed among the league leaders with 91 runs batted in and a .531 slugging percentage. Cash earned a spot on the A.L. All-Star team and finished 12th in the league MVP voting both years. He also earned A.L. Comeback Player of the Year honors for the second time in 1971.

Although Cash performed less effectively for the Tigers during their 1968 world championship season, hitting 25 home runs, batting just .263, and driving in only 63 runs, he heated up during the latter stages of the campaign, posting a batting average of .332, hitting 11 homers, and knocking in 32 runs over the season's final 54 games. Cash subsequently made key contributions to Detroit's seven-game victory over St. Louis in the World Series, batting .385 during the Fall Classic, with a homer, 5 RBIs, and 5 runs scored.

A solid fielder, Cash possessed sure hands and outstanding quickness around first base, leading all A.L. players at his position in putouts, assists, and fielding percentage at various times, with his .997 fielding percentage in 1964 representing a record for Tiger first basemen. He also holds franchise records for most assists, putouts, and double plays by a first sacker, with his 1,317 assists placing him 18th on the all-time list among players at his position.

Still, "Stormin' Norman," as he came to be known around Detroit, gained most of his notoriety as a result of his home run hitting prowess. Once asked by Tigers pitcher Mickey Lolich why he never hit for a high average after 1961, Cash responded by saying, "Jim Campbell (Detroit's general manager) pays me to hit home runs. I can get hits if I want to . . . just watch tomorrow." Lolich revealed that Cash subsequently went 3-for-4 the next day.

Known for his hard-living, candor, sense of humor, and self-deprecating nature, Cash became extremely popular with his teammates, the media, and the fans of Detroit. Longtime Tigers teammate Al Kaline said, "When you mention Norm Cash, I just smile. He was just a fun guy to be around and a great teammate. He always came ready to play. People don't know this, but he often played injured, like the time he had a broken finger."

Cash exhibited his sense of humor on one particular occasion when he found himself about to be tagged out while trapped between first and second base. Stopping in his tracks, he formed a "T" with his hands to call time-out.

Cash displayed his ability to laugh at himself when he said of his 1,091 career strikeouts, "Pro-rated at 500 at-bats a year—that means that, for 2 years out of the 14 I played, I never even touched the ball."

As for his honesty, Cash said of his exceptional 1961 campaign, "I owe my success to expansion pitching, a short right-field fence, and my hollow bats."

Yet, Cash also possessed a dark side that forced him to spend much of his career battling alcoholism. Denny McLain, who spent several seasons rooming with Cash, described his roommate as "a modern medical miracle" who abused his body so mercilessly that he "should have turned it over to the Mayo Clinic." Still, even though Cash violated every curfew rule the team imposed, McLain revealed that he somehow arrived at the ballpark every day, "not only eager to play, but madder than hell if he didn't." Although McLain claimed that his roommate "could not make 9 a.m. workouts because he threw up until 10 a.m.," he also admitted that "I always felt better about everything when I looked over and saw Stormin' Norman at first base."

Cash's playing career ended abruptly on August 7, 1974, when the Tigers released him after he compiled a batting average of just .228 in his 53 games with them over the first four months of the campaign. The 39-year-old first baseman announced his retirement shortly thereafter, ending his career with 377 home runs, 1,103 runs batted in, 1,046 runs scored, 1,820 hits, 241 doubles, a .271 batting average, a .374 on-base percentage, and a .488 slugging percentage. Having compiled virtually all those numbers during his time in Detroit, Cash continues to rank among the Tigers' all-time leaders in most statistical categories.

After retiring from baseball, Cash spent two seasons playing professional softball with the Detroit Caesars. He also served as a broadcaster for ABC's baseball broadcasts in 1976, before becoming an announcer for Tigers cable broadcasts from 1981 to 1983. In between, though, he suffered a massive stroke in 1979 that eventually forced him to leave the broadcast booth when he began to slur his words. Cash made his final appearance at Tiger Stadium in 1986, returning to the ballpark he once called home to participate in the Equitable Old Timers Game. He died a few months later, on October 12, 1986, just one month shy of his 52nd birthday, when he drowned in an accident off Beaver Island in northern Lake Michigan after slipping while aboard a boat, hitting his head, and being knocked unconscious. Cash's body was discovered several hours later in 15 feet of water off Beaver Island.

TIGERS CAREER HIGHLIGHTS

Best Season

Was there ever any doubt? Cash not only established career highs in virtually every major statistical category in 1961, but his .487 on-base percentage and 1.148 OPS both remain franchise records. Meanwhile, his 41 homers, 124 bases on balls, and .662 slugging percentage continue to rank among the highest single-season marks ever recorded by a member of the team.

Memorable Moments/Greatest Performances

In 1960, Cash accomplished the rare feat of going the entire season without grounding into a single double play, becoming in the process the first A.L. player to do so since MLB began recording that statistic in 1940.

Cash homered over the right-field roof at Tiger Stadium a record four times, doing so for the first time on June 11, 1961, when he became the first Tigers player to accomplish the feat. Cash's blast came against Washington's Joe McClain during a 7–4 loss to the Senators.

Cash proved to be a thorn in the side of New York's pitching staff over the years, saving some of his finest performances for the Yankees. He turned in one such effort on September 16, 1968, when he led the Tigers to a 9–1 win over New York by going 3-for-5, with a homer, double, and 5 RBIs. Cash again belabored New York's pitching staff on July 6, 1971, when he homered twice and knocked in 6 runs during a 12–7 home win over the Yankees.

Cash got one of his biggest hits of the 1968 campaign when he delivered a three-run homer against Oakland on September 14 that helped make a winner out of Denny McLain for the 30th time. However, he saved his most memorable performance for that year's World Series, leading all Tiger hitters with a .385 batting average, while also homering once and driving in 5 runs. After homering and singling twice during an 8–1 Tigers victory over St. Louis in Game Two, Cash ignited Detroit's game-winning 3-run rally in the Series finale by singling against Bob Gibson with two men out, no one on base, and the score tied 0–0 in the top of the seventh inning. Jim Northrup followed two batters later with a two-run triple that provided the winning runs in Detroit's 4–1 Game 7 victory.

NOTABLE ACHIEVEMENTS

- Hit more than 20 home runs eleven times, topping 30 homers five times and 40 homers once (41 in 1961).
- Knocked in more than 100 runs once (132 in 1961).
- Scored more than 100 runs once (119 in 1961).
- Batted over .300 once (.361 in 1961).
- Drew more than 100 bases on balls twice.
- Compiled on-base percentage in excess of .400 twice.
- Posted slugging percentage in excess of .500 five times, topping .600 once (.662 in 1961).
- Compiled OPS in excess of 1.000 once (1.148 in 1961).
- Led the American league in batting average once; hits once; on-base percentage once; and OPS once.
- Led A.L. first basemen in assists three times; putouts once; and fielding percentage twice.
- Ranks among Tigers career leaders in: home runs (2nd); RBIs (7th); runs scored (9th); hits (9th); extra-base hits (8th); total bases (8th); walks (6th); OPS (10th); games played (7th); plate appearances (9th); and at-bats (9th).
- Holds Tigers single-season records for highest on-base percentage (.487) and OPS (1.148).
- Appeared in more games (1,912) and recorded more putouts (14,926), assists (1,303), and double plays (1,328) than any other Tigers first baseman.
- Finished fourth in 1961 A.L. MVP voting.
- Two-time *Sporting News* Comeback Player of the Year Award winner (1965, 1971).
- Two-time *Sporting News* All-Star selection (1961, 1971).
- Four-time A.L. All-Star (1961, 1966, 1971, 1972).
- 1968 A.L. champion.
- 1968 world champion.

15

George Kell

Courtesy of MearsOnlineAuctions.com

The American League's premier third baseman of the post–World War II era, George Kell excelled both at the bat and in the field for five different teams during a 15-year major league career that eventually landed him in Cooperstown. Having most of his finest seasons for the Tigers, Kell batted over .300 in each of his six years in Detroit, surpassing the .320-mark on four separate occasions and capturing the A.L. batting title in 1949 with a mark of .343. Kell also topped the junior circuit in hits and doubles two times each, establishing career highs in both categories in 1950, when he led the American League with 218 hits and 56 two-baggers. An outstanding fielder as well, Kell led all A.L. third basemen in assists four times, putouts twice, double plays twice, and fielding percentage seven times, topping all players at his position in the last category three times while playing for the Tigers.

Born in Swifton, Arkansas, on August 23, 1922, George Clyde Kell developed a love for baseball at an early age, telling the Associated Press in 1950, "I was a Cardinals fan as a kid. We used to make the trip up to St. Louis a couple of times a season. I worshipped the old Gas House Gang— Dizzy Dean, Pepper Martin, Joe Medwick, Leo Durocher." In his autobiography *Hello Everybody, I'm George Kell*, he recalled, "There was never a time in my life when I didn't think about playing baseball. I loved the game. I loved every part about it."

After graduating from high school at the age of 16, Kell enrolled at Arkansas State University, where he participated in intramural softball since the university did not have a baseball team. While attending Arkansas State he also began his professional career, signing with the Brooklyn Dodgers as an amateur free agent at only 18 years of age in 1940. Released by the Dodgers prior to the start of the 1942 campaign, Kell subsequently joined Lancaster of the Interstate League, with whom he led all of organized baseball with a .396 batting average in 1943. Taking note of the young third baseman's fabulous performance, Philadelphia A's owner/manager Connie Mack purchased his contract, calling him up to the majors shortly before the end of the season. Appearing in just one game at third base for the Athletics, Kell tripled in five trips to the plate, after which Mack told him, "You're a fine fielder, but I'm afraid you'll never hit."

Undeterred by Mack's appraisal, Kell won Philadelphia's starting third base job the following year, batting .268 in his rookie season. The 23-year-old third baseman followed that up by batting .272 and knocking in only 56 runs in almost 570 official at-bats as a sophomore. Looking back at his rather mediocre performances of 1944 and 1945, Kell later said, "What had happened, I believe, was that, because of manpower shortages in the majors (during World War II), I was brought up too soon. Those two years with the A's were formative seasons, which normally would have been spent in the minors. I just happened to ripen in 1946, that's all."

Kell did indeed ripen after being dealt to the Tigers for outfielder Barney McCosky early in 1946. Looking back 60 years later at the events that took place on May 18, 1946, Kell told reporter Bill Dow, "Mr. Mack said, 'George, come up to my suite; I need to talk with you,' and that's when he told me I was traded to the Tigers for Barney McCosky. It was such a shock and felt like a rejection, but Mr. Mack told me, 'George, you're going to be a good ballplayer, and I'm sending you to a team that will pay you the kind of money that I can't.' As it turned out, it was the greatest day in my life."

Kell quickly developed into one of the junior circuit's elite hitters after he arrived in Detroit, concluding the 1946 campaign with a .322 batting average that placed him fourth in the league rankings. He also led all league third basemen in putouts, assists, and fielding percentage for the second straight year, committing only 7 errors in 415 chances at the hot corner for an outstanding .983 fielding percentage.

Steve O'Neill, who managed the Tigers in 1946, sang the praises of his third baseman, saying, "He fields as well as any third baseman I ever saw. He's so versatile that in a pinch I'll bet he could play any position in the infield. He's got more competitive spirit in his little finger than most players have in their whole bodies."

Kell continued to mature in 1947, placing among the league leaders with a .320 batting average and 188 hits, establishing a new career high with 93 runs batted in, and topping all A.L. third basemen in assists for the third straight time, with a total of 333. His outstanding all-around performance earned him a fifth-place finish in the league MVP voting.

Although Kell posted a batting average of .304 the following season, injuries limited him to only 92 games, prompting him to say years later, "From a personal standpoint, 1948 turned out to be the worst year of my career." Kell's troubles began on May 8 when he found himself sidelined for three weeks after having his wrist broken by a pitch from New York's Vic Raschi. Nearly four months later, Kell's season ended prematurely when a drive off the bat of Joe DiMaggio fractured his jaw. Discussing the August 29 incident with an Associated Press reporter two years later, Kell said, "I must have been out on my feet. They told me afterwards that manager Steve O'Neill tried to take the ball away from me, and I wouldn't let them have it."

Kell returned to Detroit's lineup full-time in 1949, capturing the A.L. batting title on the season's final day with a 2-for-3 performance against Cleveland ace right-hander Bob Lemon. Kell's final mark of .3429 enabled him to barely edge out Ted Williams (.3427) in the batting race, thereby preventing the Boston slugger from winning his third Triple Crown. Kell also struck out only 13 times in more than 600 total plate appearances—the lowest total ever compiled by a batting champion.

Kell later recalled that Williams gracefully approached him the first time the Tigers faced the Red Sox the following year, saying to him, "You won the batting title, so I'm coming to your dugout." The two men went on to become good friends, growing closer after Kell joined Williams in Boston two years later.

Kell had another outstanding season in 1950, finishing a close second in the batting race with a mark of .340. He also established career highs with 101 runs batted in, 114 runs scored, and a league-leading 218 hits and 56 doubles, en route to earning a fourth-place finish in the A.L. MVP voting.

Discussing his philosophy toward hitting that prevented him from using the same batting stance twice in a game unless he experienced success in his earlier at-bats, Kell said, "Never let yourself get fooled by the same pitcher on the same pitch on the same day."

Kell's approach at the plate and short, compact right-handed swing enabled him to strike out a total of only 287 times in more than 7,500 total plate appearances over the course of his career. Although he rarely hit home runs, totaling only 78 long balls in his 15 seasons and never hitting more than 12 in any single campaign, he had good gap power, accumulating more than 30 doubles on five separate occasions. Kell so impressed fellow Hall of Fame infielder Lou Boudreau, who also managed the Indians during his playing days, that the former player/manager said when he introduced Kell at the latter's Arkansas Hall of Fame induction ceremony in 1964, "I'll put him with Ted Williams and Joe DiMaggio when you need to get the run home."

After Kell batted .319 and led the American League with 191 hits and 36 doubles in 1951, the Tigers elected to include him in a nine-player trade they completed with the Boston Red Sox early the following year that netted them veteran shortstop Johnny Pesky and slugging first baseman Walt Dropo, among others. When informing Kell of the deal, Tigers general manager Charlie Gehringer told him that he truly had no desire to part with the third baseman. However, he felt that he needed to do something to shake up the team, and the Red Sox refused to accept any offer that didn't include Kell, who later recalled, "I sure didn't want to leave Detroit, but the only thing that made it better was going to Boston because that's the other great baseball town in the American League."

Kell spent two seasons in Boston, batting over .300 each year, before being dealt to the Chicago White Sox early in 1954. He remained in Chicago for two years, before spending most of his final two seasons with the Baltimore Orioles serving as mentor to a young Brooks Robinson. Kell retired at the conclusion of the 1957 campaign with 78 home runs, 870 RBIs, 881 runs scored, 2,054 hits, 50 triples, 385 doubles, a batting average of .306, a .367 on-base percentage, and a .414 slugging percentage. In addition to batting over .300 on nine separate occasions, he knocked in more than 90 runs twice and scored more than 90 runs three times. Kell finished in the top five in the American League in batting seven times, doubles six times, and hits three times. He appeared in 10 All-Star games and placed in the top 10 in the league MVP voting three times, earning five of his All-Star selections and his three most representative finishes in the MVP balloting as a member of the Tigers. During his years in Detroit, Kell hit 25 homers, knocked in 414 runs, scored 503 times, amassed 1,075 hits, 35 triples, and 210 doubles, batted .325, compiled a .391 on-base percentage, and posted a .433 slugging percentage.

After failing to gain admittance to Cooperstown during his initial period of eligibility, Kell was elected to the Hall of Fame by the members of the Veterans Committee in 1983. Kell, who developed a reputation during his playing career as someone who didn't swear and rarely criticized umpires, displayed his humility during his Hall of Fame induction speech when he said, "I have always said that George Kell has taken more from this great game of baseball than he can ever give back. And now I know, I am deeper in debt than ever before."

Following his retirement as a player, Kell worked as a play-by-play announcer for the Orioles (1957), CBS television (1958), NBC radio (1962), and the Tigers (1959–1963 on radio, and 1965–1996 on television). From 1975 until his retirement from broadcasting, Kell teamed up with Al Kaline on Tigers telecasts, with his mellifluous Arkansas accent becoming a welcome and familiar sound to generations of Tigers fans.

Legendary Tigers broadcaster Ernie Harwell, who worked with Kell on both TV and radio, said of his former broadcast partner, "He had a very laid-back style. He was easygoing and an expert on the game. He brought the field to the booth because he played and played well. He had a conversational style that people took to."

Despite a career that took him far from home, Kell never lost his close ties to his native Arkansas, purchasing a General Motors dealership there in 1963 that he eventually passed on to his son in 1990. He also served on the Arkansas State Highway Commission from 1973 to 1983. Kell eventually retired to his small hometown of Swifton, where he experienced a devastating house fire in 2001 that took from him most of his baseball memorabilia. He was later involved in a 2004 car accident that left him seriously injured. Two years later, he returned to Detroit to throw out the first pitch before Game Four of the 2006 ALCS between the Tigers and Oakland Athletics. Greeted by a standing ovation by the fans at Comerica Park, who greatly appreciated his return to the Motor City, Kell subsequently expressed his appreciation by stating, "I'm overwhelmed. I didn't expect all of this. The standing ovation sounded like Joe DiMaggio was on the field. It was a little bit more than I expected."

George Kell passed away 2½ years later, dying in his sleep at age 86 on March 24, 2009. Following his passing, National Baseball Hall of Fame and Museum researcher Craig Muder noted, "Third base remains baseball's enigmatic position, the only one in which fielding prowess stands on equal ground with hitting skill. It is the rarest of combinations and one that has sent just 11 former Major Leaguers to the Baseball Hall of Fame—the fewest of any position. George Kell, one of those 11, died Tuesday at the age of 86. During his playing days, his skills with the lumber and the leather produced one of baseball's most consistent players of the mid-20th century."

TIGERS CAREER HIGHLIGHTS

Best Season

Kell is perhaps best remembered for edging out Ted Williams for the A.L. batting title on the final day of the 1949 regular season. However, while his league-leading mark of .343 represented the highest batting average of his career, Kell actually compiled better overall numbers the following season. After hitting only 3 home runs, knocking in just 59 runs, scoring 97 times, and collecting 179 hits, 9 triples, and 38 doubles in 1949, Kell concluded the 1950 campaign with 8 homers, 101 RBIs, 114 runs scored, a .340 batting average, and a league-leading 218 hits and 56 doubles. In addition to finishing a close second in the batting race, Kell posted an OPS of .886 that nearly matched the mark of .892 he compiled one year earlier. Meanwhile, his 56 doubles represent the third-highest total in franchise history. Kell's 8 home runs also made him the only player from 1950 to 1985 (Tommy Herr) to drive in 100 runs without reaching double figures in homers.

Memorable Moments/Greatest Performances

Kell had a number of exceptional days at the plate for the Tigers, with one of those coming on September 20, 1946, when he went 6-for-7, with 3 RBIs and 4 runs scored, during a 15–1 win at Cleveland.

Kell had another huge day on June 2, 1950, when he hit for the cycle in the second game of a doubleheader sweep of the Philadelphia Athletics. After going 1-for-4 in Detroit's 8–2 opening game win, Kell collected 4 hits in 7 trips to the plate during the Tiger's 16–5 win in the nightcap, driving in 3 runs and scoring twice in the process.

However, Kell experienced his greatest moment on the final day of the 1949 regular season, when he went 2-for-3 against Cleveland to edge out Ted Williams for the A.L. batting title by the slimmest of margins, .3429 to .3427. Fifty years later, Kell shared his memories of the day with Gene Guidi of the *Detroit Free Press*, telling the reporter: "I went into the game trailing Ted Williams by a couple of points and didn't think I had a chance because I figured Ted was good for a couple of hits that day. Bob Lemon was pitching for Cleveland against us and he was always tough, but I got a double and single my first two at-bats."

Kell also recalled that Bob Feller came out of the bullpen to face him later in the game, telling Guidi, "He [Feller] walked me in the fifth inning and then got me out in the seventh." After learning later in the contest that Williams had gone hitless in his game against the Yankees, Tigers manager Red Rolfe presented Kell with the option of protecting his lead over the Splendid Splinter in the batting race by allowing himself to be pinch-hit for in the ninth inning. However, Kell rejected the notion, telling Guidi, "I remembered Ted Williams not sitting out the last day of the [1941] season after he was already at .400, and I wasn't about to back into a batting title against him." However, Kell never had an opportunity to step to the plate again since Eddie Lake grounded into a double play to end the game, leaving Kell standing in the on-deck circle. Sharing his feelings at that particular moment, Kell revealed, "I celebrated by throwing my bats in the air. It was quite a feeling."

NOTABLE ACHIEVEMENTS

- Batted over .300 six times, topping .320 four times and batting over .340 twice.
- Knocked in more than 100 runs once.
- Scored more than 100 runs once.
- Surpassed 200 hits once (218 in 1950).
- Topped 30 doubles three times, accumulating more than 50 two-baggers once (56 in 1950).
- Compiled on-base percentage in excess of .400 twice.
- Led the American League in batting average once; hits twice; and doubles twice.

- Led A.L. third basemen in assists three times; putouts once; fielding percentage three times; and double plays turned twice.
- Ranks among Tigers career leaders in batting average (6th).
- Holds major league record for fewest strikeouts by a batting champion (13 in 1949).
- Hit for cycle on June 2, 1950.
- Finished in top five of A.L. MVP voting twice.
- Six-time *Sporting News* All-Star selection.
- Five-time A.L. All-Star.
- Elected to Baseball Hall of Fame by members of Veterans Committee in 1983.

16

Cecil Fielder

Courtesy of Jerry Reuss

One of baseball's most prolific sluggers for much of the 1990s, Cecil Fielder hit more home runs than anyone else in the game while playing for the Tigers from 1990 to 1995. The massive first baseman also knocked in more runs than any other player between 1990 and 1993, leading the major leagues in RBIs in three of those four seasons. Fielder became just the second major league player in 25 years to hit as many as 50 home runs in a single season in 1990, when he made a triumphant return to the

United States after spending the previous year in Japan. Fielder also topped the junior circuit in runs batted in for the first of three straight times that season, beginning an extraordinarily successful four-year run during which he averaged 40 homers and 127 RBIs. Just two years earlier, though, no one could possibly have imagined that Fielder would be the toast of Detroit.

Born in Los Angeles, California, on September 21, 1963, Cecil Grant Fielder attended Nogales High School in nearby La Puente, where he earned all-state honors in baseball, football, and basketball. After graduating from Nogales, Fielder turned down an offer to sign with the Baltimore Orioles, who selected him in the 31st round of the 1981 amateur baseball draft. Enrolling instead at the University of Nevada, Las Vegas, Fielder spent the next year furthering his education, while simultaneously improving his draft status by clouting home runs off collegiate pitching. The Kansas City Royals subsequently selected him in the fourth round of the 1982 draft, signing him shortly thereafter to a minor league contract. Fielder spent just one year in Kansas City's farm system, before the Royals dealt him to the Toronto Blue Jays in February 1983 for journeyman outfielder Leon Roberts.

Fielder spent most of the next four seasons advancing through Toronto's minor league system, although he made brief appearances with the Blue Jays in both 1985 and 1986. Splitting his time between first and third base, while also seeing some action at the DH spot, Fielder totaled 8 home runs and 29 RBIs in slightly over 150 official at-bats over the course of those two seasons. After earning a spot on Toronto's roster in 1987, Fielder saw his playing time increase somewhat, spending most of the next two seasons serving the Blue Jays primarily as a right-handed designated hitter and backup first baseman. Nevertheless, he found himself languishing on the Toronto bench much of the time, hitting 23 homers and driving in 55 runs, in fewer than 400 total plate appearances from 1987 to 1988.

Seeking an opportunity to play every day, the 25-year-old Fielder accepted an offer to join the Hanshin Tigers at the conclusion of the 1988 campaign. In addition to receiving a one-year contract worth more than $1 million from the Japanese team (Toronto paid him $125,000 in 1988), Fielder acquired the services of a chauffeur and a full-time interpreter. The change in scenery did wonders for Fielder, who, serving as a full-time player for the first time in years, hit 38 home runs in 1989.

Taking note of Fielder's outstanding performance in Japan, the Detroit Tigers facilitated his return to the United States by offering him a two-year contract in January 1990. After earning the team's starting first base job in spring training by impressing everyone with his prodigious power, Fielder continued his extraordinary slugging during the regular season, becoming just the fourth player in A.L. history to homer three times in one game twice in the same year. The powerful first baseman punctuated his exceptional campaign by hitting 2 home runs on the final day of the regular season, becoming in the process the first major league player to reach the 50-homer plateau since George Foster hit 52 round-trippers for Cincinnati in 1977. Fielder's 51 home runs also made him the first American Leaguer to reach that milestone since Roger Maris and Mickey Mantle both turned the trick for the Yankees in 1961. In addition to his exceptional home run total, Fielder scored 104 runs, batted .277, and led the American League with 132 runs batted in, 339 total bases, and a .592 slugging percentage, en route to earning a close second-place finish to Oakland's Rickey Henderson in the league MVP balloting. On the flip side, he also led the major leagues with 182 strikeouts, the fifth highest total compiled by any player in baseball history at the time.

Fielder's lofty home run and strikeout totals turned out to be a rather common occurrence for him. Although he never again quite reached his 1990 figures in either category, he continued to post huge numbers in both departments in subsequent seasons. Standing 6'3" and listed conservatively at 250 pounds, Fielder grew increasingly large during his time in Detroit, using his considerable girth, massive arms, and powerful legs to uncoil a ferocious swing that routinely generated both tape-measure home runs and inordinately high strikeout totals. Fielder eventually became the first Tigers player to hit a ball completely over the left field roof at Tiger Stadium, and, also, the first player ever to hit a ball over the outfield bleachers at Milwaukee's County Stadium. Meanwhile, he struck out well over 100 times in each of the next six seasons, fanning 151 times in both 1991 and 1992. Fielder also developed a reputation for being somewhat of a liability in the field, possessing neither the range nor the quickness needed to cover a significant amount of ground at first base.

Fielder had another huge offensive year in 1991, leading the American League with 44 home runs and 133 runs batted in. By doing so, he earned another second-place finish in the league MVP voting, this time finishing runner-up to Baltimore's Cal Ripken, Jr. Fielder followed that up by hitting 35 homers and knocking in a major-league-leading 124 runs in 1992, even though his batting average slipped to just .244. By leading the majors in RBIs for the third straight time, Fielder became the first player to do so since Babe Ruth accomplished the feat from 1919 to 1921.

As Fielder's tenure in Detroit lengthened, he grew increasingly popular with Tigers fans, who nicknamed him "Big Daddy" for his big smile, peaceful temperament, prodigious home runs, and massive physical stature. Fielder's weight also continued to increase over time, as he drew closer and closer to the 300-pound mark in subsequent seasons. However, as Fielder's waist continued to expand, his offensive production gradually diminished. Nevertheless, he remained one of baseball's top sluggers, annually hitting more than 30 home runs and driving in close to 100 runs for noncontending Tiger teams.

With Fielder seeing more and more action at the DH spot and Tony Clark waiting in the wings to assume the role of starting first baseman, the Tigers traded Big Daddy to the Yankees on July 31, 1996, for Ruben Sierra. Serving New York as a designated hitter and backup for Tino Martinez at first base the final two months of the campaign, Fielder helped the Yankees capture the A.L. East title by hitting 13 home runs and knocking in 37 runs, in only 53 games. Combined with the totals he compiled for the Tigers earlier in the year, those figures gave Fielder 39 homers and 117 RBIs for the season. He then helped the Yankees win the world championship by hitting 3 home runs and knocking in 12 runs during the postseason, compiling a .364 batting average against Texas in the ALDS, before posting a mark of .391 against Atlanta in the World Series.

Fielder remained in New York the following year, platooning at the DH spot against left-handed pitching. Granted free agency at season's end, he subsequently signed with the Anaheim Angels, with whom he spent the first four months of 1998, before being released in early August. Fielder joined the Cleveland Indians shortly thereafter, ending his career with them after batting just .143 in his 14 games with the club. Over the course of 13 big-league seasons, Fielder hit 319 home runs, knocked in 1,008 runs, scored 744 times, collected 1,313 hits and 200 doubles, batted .255, compiled a .345 on-base percentage, and posted a .482 slugging percentage. In his six-plus years with the Tigers, he hit 245 homers, drove in 758 runs, scored 558 runs, amassed 947 hits and 141 doubles, batted .258, compiled a .351 on-base percentage, and posted a .498 slugging percentage.

Following his playing career, Fielder encountered various financial and legal problems. After negotiating his son Prince's first professional contract, he angered the younger Fielder by insisting that he share in his son's good fortune by being rewarded a portion of his salary. The two men remained estranged for several years, but they eventually reconciled their differences. During their period of estrangement, Prince hit 50 home runs for the Brewers, making the two Fielders the only father/son duo in major league history to reach the milestone. The elder Fielder eventually got his professional life back in order, managing the South Coast League's Charlotte County Redfish in 2007, before piloting the Atlantic City Surf of the Canadian-American Association of Professional Baseball in 2008. On March

25, 2011, Fielder was named to the advisory board of the Torrington Titans of the Futures Collegiate Baseball League (FCBL). In his role with the club, Fielder assists in player development and community outreach programs.

TIGERS CAREER HIGHLIGHTS

Best Season

Fielder had a big year for the Tigers in 1991, when he led the majors with 44 home runs and 133 RBIs, scored 102 runs, batted .261, and compiled an OPS of .860. However, he performed even better the previous season, making his return to the United States an extremely successful one by leading both leagues with 51 homers, 132 RBIs, and a .592 slugging percentage. Fielder also established career highs with 104 runs scored, a .969 OPS, and a league-leading 339 total bases.

Memorable Moments/Greatest Performances

Fielder hit a number of tape-measure home runs for the Tigers, delivering one of his most notable blows during a 6–4 win over the Brewers on September 14, 1991. Facing Milwaukee starter Dan Plesac in the top of the fourth inning of a scoreless tie, Fielder hit a ball that traveled 502 feet, completely out of Milwaukee's County Stadium. The ball, which landed in the back of a passing truck, is believed to be the first one to ever leave that ballpark. Fielder hit another memorable home run during a July 3, 1993, 11–5 home loss to the Texas Rangers, when he joined Harmon Killebrew and Frank Howard as the only players ever to drive a ball onto the left-field roof at Tiger Stadium.

Fielder is also the only Tigers player to hit 3 home runs in a game on three separate occasions. He accomplished the feat for the first time on May 6, 1990, when he homered once off David Wells and twice off Jimmy Key in an 11–7 loss to the Blue Jays in Toronto. Fielder finished the game 4-for-5, with 5 RBIs and 3 runs scored. Exactly one month later, on June 6, Fielder duplicated his earlier effort, homering 3 times and driving in 5 runs, in leading the Tigers to a 6–4 win over the Indians at Cleveland Stadium. Fielder accomplished the feat for the third and final time on April 16, 1996, when he once again homered 3 times and knocked in 5 runs, this time in a 13–8 win over the Blue Jays in Toronto.

Yet, Fielder experienced perhaps his most memorable moment on the final day of the 1990 regular season, when he became the first A.L. player in nearly 30 years to reach the 50-homer plateau by hitting 2 round-trippers and driving in 5 runs during a 10–3 victory over the Yankees at Yankee Stadium.

NOTABLE ACHIEVEMENTS

- Hit more than 25 home runs seven times, topping 30 homers five times, 40 homers twice and 50 homers once (51 in 1990).
- Knocked in more than 100 runs four times, surpassing 120 RBIs on three occasions.
- Scored more than 100 runs twice.
- Compiled slugging percentage in excess of .500 three times.
- Led the American League in home runs twice; RBIs three times; total bases once; and slugging percentage once.
- Led A.L. first basemen in assists once and double plays once.
- Ranks among Tigers career leaders in home runs (6th) and slugging percentage (10th).
- Hit 3 home runs in one game three times.
- One of only two players to lead major leagues in RBIs three straight years.
- Finished second in A.L. MVP voting twice (1990, 1991).
- Two-time Silver Slugger winner (1990, 1991).
- Two-time *Sporting News* All-Star selection (1990, 1991).
- Three-time A.L. All-Star (1990, 1991, 1993).

17

Rudy York

Courtesy of Boston Public Library, Leslie Jones Collection

A powerful right-handed batter who struggled in the field at times and developed a reputation for setting hotel rooms on fire by falling asleep with burning cigarettes in his hand, Rudy York spent nine years in Detroit, establishing himself during that time as one of the top sluggers in all of baseball. A seven-time A.L. All-Star, York hit more home runs, knocked in more runs, and amassed more total bases than any other player in the game from 1937 to 1947, although he did so largely because a bad knee kept him out of the service during World War II. York hit more than 30 home runs four times for the Tigers, setting a new major league record in August 1937, when he reached the seats 18 times over the course of the month. The 6'1", 210-pound York also drove in more than 100 runs five times and batted over .300 three times in his nine years with the Tigers, helping them capture two A.L. pennants and one world championship. Nevertheless, York often found himself being booed by the fans at Briggs Stadium, who voiced their displeasure over his defensive deficiencies, occasional batting slumps, and Native American ancestry.

Born in Ragland, Alabama, on August 17, 1913, Preston Rudolph York moved with his family to a small mill town outside Cartersville, Georgia, at a very early age. After leaving school in the third grade to help support his family, young Rudy, who was part Cherokee and part Irish, soon took a job at the American Textile Company (ATCO). While still employed at ATCO a few years later, York began playing for the company's baseball team, more than holding his own against much older players.

Having excelled against older competition as a young teenager, York eventually signed to play professionally with Knoxville of the Southern Association shortly after he turned 17 years of age. Two years later, he became a member of the Tigers organization, after which he spent the next few years in the minor leagues playing several different positions in an effort to determine which spot best suited him. Too slow-footed and clumsy to play either third base or second, York received brief trials in the outfield and behind the plate, before he finally found his niche at first base. Through all his trials and tribulations, though, York remained an imposing figure in the batter's box, eventually winning Texas League MVP honors in 1935 and American Association MVP accolades in 1936. Prior to that, he made one brief appearance with the Tigers, getting one hit for them in six trips to the plate late in 1934.

His path to the majors blocked by Detroit's incumbent first baseman, Hank Greenberg, York spent the first few weeks of the 1937 campaign in the minor leagues before finally being promoted by the Tigers in early May. However, with Greenberg firmly entrenched at first, Marv Owen manning third, and Mickey Cochrane and Birdie Tebbetts sharing the catching duties, York spent much of May riding the Detroit bench, seeing only occasional action at the hot corner. Still, it appeared to be only a matter of time before Cochrane inserted him into the starting lineup, as the team's player/manager suggested when he said, "I don't see how I can afford to keep York on the bench. He has shown me so much batting power, which we certainly can use, that it looks like the proper thing to do is to have him in our lineup . . . his defensive play has not been so bad either. He's made a couple of wrong moves because of inexperience at that [third] base, but I think he'll get over that shortly. All he seemingly has to do is tap the ball to hit it out of the park."

An injury to Owen presented York with his first opportunity to gather significant playing time, although the latter failed to make much of an impression in his limited trial at the hot corner. Displaying a lack of range and an inability to properly field bunts, York began to incur the wrath of Tiger fans, who jeered his defensive lapses. Taking his fielding woes with him to the plate, York failed to deliver the offensive firepower the team expected from him, resulting in another period of inactivity when Owen returned to the lineup.

However, Cochrane, whose playing career ended in late May as the result of a beaning, soon turned to York once more, this time asking him to replace the struggling Tebbetts behind home plate. Although the happy-go-lucky York initially balked at the idea of assuming the catching duties, claiming that it required "too much thinking to get any fun out of baseball," he agreed to do so if Cochrane promised to leave him there. Inserted into the lineup as the team's starting catcher for the first time on August 4, York subsequently went on a tear, establishing a new record for the most home runs hit in one month by driving 18 balls out of the park over the course of the next 28 games. York's 18 homers surpassed the previous mark of 17 set by Babe Ruth in September 1927. The young slugger's tremendous feat prompted noted sportswriter Shirley Povich to write in the *Washington Post*, "The booming bat of 24-year-old Rudy York, Detroit's late entry into the home run race, spoke in tones heard 'round the baseball world this afternoon as one of Babe Ruth's proudest and supposedly invincible records went crashing into discard."

York also established a new record (since broken) by knocking in 49 runs during the month, breaking in the process Lou Gehrig's existing mark. Although York cooled off somewhat during the month of September, even spending a few days in the hospital with an infected arm, he finished the season with 35 homers, 103 RBIs, 72 runs scored, and a .307 batting average, despite playing in only 104 games and accumulating just 375 official at-bats.

York subsequently spent most of 1938 serving as Detroit's starting catcher, but he also saw some action in the outfield. Yet, even though he batted .298 and placed among the league leaders with 33 home runs, 127 RBIs, and a .579 slugging percentage, his lack of mobility behind the plate relegated him to a part-time role the following year. Appearing in 102 games and accumulating a total of just 329 official at-bats, York concluded the 1939 campaign with 20 homers, 68 RBIs, and a .307 batting average.

Convinced that they needed to get York's powerful bat in the lineup every day, the Tigers persuaded Hank Greenberg to move to left field prior to the start of the 1940 season, creating a spot at first for the right-handed slugger. The experiment reaped huge benefits for the Tigers, who went on to capture the A.L. pennant, with Greenberg earning MVP honors by hitting 41 home runs, driving in 150 runs, and batting .340, while York earned an eighth-place finish in the balloting by batting .316, scoring 105 runs, and placing among the league leaders with 33 homers, 134 RBIs, 46 doubles, 343 total bases, and a .583 slugging percentage.

Despite spending most of the second half of the campaign playing with a broken bone in his left wrist, York posted solid numbers again in 1941, hitting 27 home runs, driving in 111 runs, and scoring 91 times, but his batting average slipped to .259. However, with Greenberg serving in the military, the absence of another power threat in Detroit's lineup began to take its toll on York in 1942, causing him to finish the season with only 21 homers, 90 RBIs, and a .260 batting average.

Unable to serve his country during World War II due to a "loose knee," York struggled during the first half of the 1943 campaign, hitting just 13 home runs through July. With fans expecting York to pick up much of the slack in Greenberg's absence, the former's offensive woes did not sit well with the Tiger faithful, who subsequently took to booing him incessantly. Before long, York became the object of scorn at Briggs Stadium, prompting H. G. Salinger, who covered the team for the *Detroit News*, to write in September 1943:

> York got away to a bad start and soon found himself in a severe slump. He went from bad to worse. . . . His fielding became as bad as his batting, and he appeared to be on the verge of a nervous breakdown. . . . The crowds at Briggs Stadium were 'riding' Rudy. Few players in history have ever been "ridden" harder. They booed him from the time his name was announced in the starting lineup until the last man was out. They booed him every time he came to bat, every time he went after a batted ball, every time he took a throw. The razzing didn't start this year. The fans were "aboard" York last season. He took an unmerciful booing all through 1942, and the booing increased with the start of the present season.

Fortunately, Salinger came to York's defense earlier in the summer, reminding Tiger fans that York had always done whatever was asked of him since he joined the team several years earlier. Salinger's reproach helped alleviate the pressure on York, who proceeded to go on another August rampage that saw him hit 17 home runs, en route to hitting a league-leading 34 round-trippers. He also topped the circuit with 118 RBIs, 301 total bases, and a .527 slugging percentage, earning in the process a third-place finish in the A.L. MVP balloting.

York spent two more years with the Tigers, combining for 36 home runs and 185 RBIs in 1944 and 1945, before being traded to Boston for infielder Eddie Lake following Hank Greenberg's return from the military. He ended his time in Detroit with 239 home runs, 936 runs batted in, 738 runs scored, 1,317 hits, 236 doubles, a .282 batting average, a .369 on-base percentage, and a .503 slugging percentage. In spite of his reputation as a defensive liability, York led all A.L. first basemen in assists twice, putouts once, and double plays turned once while playing for the Tigers.

York played well for the Red Sox during their 1946 pennant-winning campaign, hitting 17 home runs, driving in 119 runs, batting .276, and homering twice during their seven-game World Series loss to St. Louis. However, they elected to trade him to the Chicago White Sox the following year after he posted a batting average of just .212 for them through mid-June. Prior to his departure, though, York nearly lost his life when a fire, believed to have been started by a cigarette, swept through his hotel room.

After putting up decent numbers in Chicago the rest of the year, York assumed a backup role with the Philadelphia Athletics in 1948, compiling a batting average of just .157 in only 51 at-bats for them before being released at season's end. Unable to catch on with any other major league team, York spent the next few years performing at the minor league level, finally retiring as an active player at the conclusion of the 1952 campaign. He ended his 13-year major league career with 277 home runs, 1,152 RBIs, 876 runs scored, 1,621 hits, 291 doubles, a .275 batting average, a .362 on-base percentage, and a .483 slugging percentage.

York remained in baseball for another decade following his retirement, serving briefly as a manager in the low minor leagues, scouting for the Yankees and Houston Colt .45s/Astros, and coaching first base for the Red Sox from 1959 to 1962. After leaving baseball, he returned to Cartersville, where he worked as a self-employed house painter until lung cancer forced him to have part of a lung removed in November 1969. After an initial recovery, York developed pneumonia and died in the hospital in Rome, Georgia, on February 5, 1970. He was only 56 years old at the time of his passing.

TIGERS CAREER HIGHLIGHTS

Best Season

York compiled a career-high 1.026 OPS in 1937, when his fabulous month of August enabled him to bat .307, hit 35 home runs, and drive in 103 runs, in only 104 games and 375 official at-bats. However, he had his three most productive seasons in 1938, 1940, and 1943. York led the league in a major statistical category for the only time in his career in the last of those campaigns, topping the circuit with 34 homers, 118 RBIs, 301 total bases, and a .527 slugging percentage. However, he did so with most of the game's finest players serving in the military. Furthermore, his .271 batting average and .893 OPS failed to approach the marks he posted the other two years. In addition to hitting 33 home runs, knocking in 127 runs, batting .298, and compiling an OPS of .995 in 1938, York hit 4 grand slams. Nevertheless, he had his finest all-around season in 1940, when he hit 33 homers, posted a .993 OPS, and established career highs with 134 RBIs, 105 runs scored, 186 hits, 46 doubles, 343 total bases, and a .316 batting average, en route to earning an eighth-place finish in the A.L. MVP voting. York ranked among the league leaders in 10 different offensive categories, placing second in RBIs, doubles, and total bases, and finishing third in home runs.

Memorable Moments/Greatest Performances

York began his memorable month of August 1937 by going 2-for-5, with a homer, double, and 4 RBIs in an 11–7 Tigers win over Philadelphia on August 4. York's extraordinary month included a number of other notable performances, the first of which took place on August 17, when he celebrated his 24th birthday by going 4-for-5, with a homer, triple, and 3 RBIs during another 11–7 Detroit victory, this time over the Chicago White Sox. Just two days later, York again tormented Chicago's pitching staff, collecting 3 hits, 2 home runs, and 6 RBIs during a 12–4 Tigers win. On August 22, he began a streak of five consecutive games in which he hit at least one home run, going deep three times in a double header split with the A's on the 24th. York closed out the month by going 4-for-4 on the 31st, with 2 homers and 7 RBIs during a 12–3 win over Washington. His 2 home runs enabled him to eclipse Babe Ruth's previous mark of 17 set in September 1927.

York got one of the biggest hits of his career on September 27, 1940, when his two-run homer off Cleveland ace Bob Feller gave the Tigers the only two runs they needed to clinch the pennant with a 2–0 win over the Indians.

York, though, played his greatest game on September 1, 1941, leading the Tigers to a 9–5 win over St. Louis in the first game of a double header sweep by going 4-for-5, with 3 home runs, 5 RBIs, and 3 runs scored.

NOTABLE ACHIEVEMENTS

- Hit more than 30 home runs four times, topping 20 homers on three other occasions.
- Knocked in more than 100 runs five times, surpassing 120 RBIs twice.
- Scored more than 100 runs once (105 in 1940).
- Batted over .300 three times.
- Finished in double digits in triples once (11 in 1943).
- Surpassed 40 doubles once (46 in 1940).
- Compiled on-base percentage in excess of .400 twice.
- Posted slugging percentage in excess of .500 five times, topping .600 once (.651 in 1937).
- Compiled OPS in excess of 1.000 once (1.026 in 1937).
- Led the American League in home runs once; RBIs once; slugging percentage once; and total bases once.
- Led A.L. first basemen in assists twice; putouts once; and double plays once.
- Ranks among Tigers career leaders in: home runs (8th); slugging percentage (6th); and OPS (7th).
- Holds A.L. record for most home runs in one month (18 in August of 1937).
- Hit 3 home runs in one game on September 1, 1941.
- Finished third in 1943 A.L. MVP voting.
- 1943 *Sporting News* All-Star selection.
- Five-time A.L. All-Star (1938, 1941–1944).
- Two-time A.L. champion (1940, 1945).
- 1945 world champion.

18

Bill Freehan

Courtesy of T. Scott Brandon

T he American League's premier catcher for much of the 1960s, Bill Freehan established himself as the Tigers' unquestioned on-field leader during his time in Detroit, doing a superb job of handling a pitching staff that included star hurlers Denny McLain and Mickey Lolich. Described by sportswriter Arnold Hano as "a thinking man's catcher" and "an elemental ballplayer" who possessed "an unusual blend of brawn and brains," the 6'3", 210-pound Freehan proved to be a pillar of strength behind home plate, catching well in excess of 100 games eight straight times at one point, despite playing his position with reckless abandon. Arguably the finest defensive receiver of his time, Freehan won five consecutive Gold Gloves, retiring in 1976 as Major League Baseball's all-time leader among catchers in putouts (9,941), total chances (10,734), and career fielding percentage (.9933). A solid hitter, Freehan batted .300 once, surpassed 20 home runs three times, and knocked in more than 80 runs twice, en route to earning 11 All-Star nominations, two top-five finishes in the A.L. MVP voting, and recognition by Detroit fans in 1999 as the greatest catcher in Tigers history.

Born in Detroit, Michigan, on November 29, 1941, William Ashley Freehan grew up in nearby Royal Oak, where he got his start in baseball by competing on the Michigan sandlots. After moving with his family to St. Petersburg, Florida, at the age of 14, Freehan attended Bishop Barry High School, but he returned to Detroit each summer to play sandlot baseball. Having established himself as a multisport star at Bishop Barry, Freehan accepted a scholarship offer to play football and baseball at the University of Michigan. However, before earning his degree, Freehan signed with his hometown Tigers as an amateur free agent in 1961 when they offered him a $100,000 signing bonus. The 19-year-old Freehan did not see any of the money for another five years, though, since his father retained the bonus until young Bill finally obtained his degree in 1966 by studying during the offseason.

Freehan advanced rapidly through the Tigers' farm system, appearing in a total of only 77 games before earning a late-season call-up to Detroit in September 1961. Still only 19 years of age, Freehan handled himself quite well during the season's final week, going 4-for-10 in his initial trial period. He subsequently spent the entire 1962 campaign with Denver in the American Association, before returning to the Tigers for good the following year.

Freehan experienced a moderate amount of success in his first full season, hitting 9 home runs, driving in 36 runs, and batting .243, while splitting time behind the plate with veteran receiver Gus Triandos. Convinced that Freehan had all the tools necessary to become a top-flight receiver, the Tigers dealt Triandos to Philadelphia during the subsequent offseason, leaving the starting catching duties to the 22-year-old Michigan native. Freehan rewarded the Tigers for the faith they placed in him by hitting 18 home runs, driving in 80 runs, and batting .300, en route to earning his first All-Star selection and a seventh-place finish in the league MVP balloting. By batting .300, the right-hand-hitting Freehan became the first Detroit receiver to top .300 since Mickey Cochrane hit .319 in 1935. Equally important, Freehan quickly earned the trust of his pitchers and coaching staff, with Tigers manager Charlie Dressen noting that even the team's veteran hurlers such as Dave Wickersham entrusted him with calling the game for them. Expressing his admiration for Freehan, Dressen told *Baseball Digest's* Jim Sargent, "He suddenly grew up, and his pitchers have confidence in him now. So do the other players. Quick-like, the Tigers had a leader."

General Manager Jim Campbell also praised the young receiver, stating, "We put the full load on Freehan's shoulders and he didn't stumble."

Although Freehan posted less impressive offensive numbers in 1965, concluding the campaign with just 10 homers, 43 RBIs, and a .234 batting average, he earned the first of his five consecutive Gold Gloves by leading all A.L. catchers in putouts for the first of six times. He compiled similar numbers on offense the following year, but still managed to earn a top-20 finish in the league MVP voting by once again excelling behind the plate, topping all A.L. receivers in putouts and fielding percentage

Advised by new manager Mayo Smith and batting coach Wally Moses prior to the start of the 1967 season to move closer to the plate, Freehan dramatically improved his offensive performance, finishing the year with 20 home runs, 74 RBIs, and a .282 batting average. He also broke Elston Howard's 1964 A.L. single-season records for catchers by amassing 950 putouts and 1,021 total chances, en route to helping the Tigers finish just one game behind first-place Boston in the A.L. pennant race. For his efforts, Freehan placed third in the MVP balloting.

Freehan followed that up with another outstanding all-around season in 1968, helping the Tigers capture their first pennant in 23 years by placing among the league leaders with 25 home runs, 84 RBIs, a .366 on-base percentage, and a .454 slugging percentage, while also breaking his own records by accumulating 971 putouts and 1,050 total chances behind the plate. The baseball writers acknowledged the many contributions Freehan made to the Tigers over the course of the season by placing him second to teammate Denny McLain in the league MVP voting.

Although Freehan had arguably his most productive offensive season for the Tigers in 1968, he perhaps made his greatest contribution to the eventual world champions with the deft manner with which he handled their pitching staff. Despite playing in hitter-friendly Tiger Stadium, Detroit pitchers posted the third-lowest team ERA (2.71) in the league, with McLain winning 31 games and Mickey Lolich posting another 17 victories. Freehan also continued to play brilliant defense, drawing praise from several quarters for the manner in which he sacrificed his body for the betterment of his team. Milton Richman of the *Los Angeles Herald* wrote, "What makes

Freehan so extraordinary is that he plants his two big feet firmly in the ground, doesn't bother giving the base runner barreling down on him from third base so much as a sidelong glance, and plain refuses to budge, even when said base runner hits him at mid-ship like a torpedo. For that, he has the respect of ballplayers everywhere. They know they don't make catchers like Freehan anymore."

Meanwhile, Chicago White Sox manager Eddie Stanky suggested, "On any close play at the plate, it's like running into a freight train."

Bothered by an old back injury sustained a few years earlier, Freehan experienced diminished offensive production in both 1969 and 1970, totaling 32 home runs and 101 RBIs those two seasons, while posting batting averages of .262 and .241. Yet, he continued to take his position behind home plate whenever possible, although he also occasionally filled in at first base for Norm Cash. Looking back at the physical problems he suffered during that time, Freehan recalled, "Some days were good and some days were bad. It got so my legs would be numb on certain days when I stepped out of my car at the ballpark." To ease his discomfort, Freehan consented to spinal surgery, which he underwent on September 2, 1970.

Healthy again in 1971, Freehan started 142 games behind the plate and had a solid offensive season, hitting 21 home runs, driving in 71 runs, and batting .277, en route to earning his eighth straight All-Star selection. Although Freehan made the All-Star team in three of the next four years, he caught more than 100 games only two more times and accumulated more than 500 plate appearances just once more, having his best season during that time in 1974, when he hit 18 homers, knocked in 60 runs, and batted .297. After Freehan appeared in only 71 games for them in 1976, the Tigers elected to release him, bringing the career of the 35-year-old receiver to an end. Freehan subsequently retired with career totals of 200 home runs, 758 RBIs, 706 runs scored, 1,591 hits, 35 triples, and 241 doubles, a batting average of .262, a .340 on-base percentage, and a .412 slugging percentage. His 1,581 games behind home plate remain the most by any catcher in Tigers history.

Following his retirement, Freehan served the Tigers for a while as a special coach, tutoring young receiver Lance Parrish on the finer points of playing his position. He also spent two years doing color commentary for Seattle Mariners broadcasts, before taking on a similar role on PASS Sports television for his beloved Tigers. Freehan later returned to the University of Michigan, where he served as head baseball coach from 1989 to 1995. After leaving his post there, he rejoined the Tigers, for whom he spent the 2002–2005 campaigns serving as the organizational catching instructor. Now retired, Freehan lives in the Detroit suburb of Bloomfield Hills.

Looking back at his playing career, Freehan says, "I wanted to hit well. I just never put that ahead of my primary responsibility. The catcher has to be the captain of the field. I felt if I did my job behind the plate, I was contributing to the team in the best way I could."

CAREER HIGHLIGHTS

Best Season

Freehan clearly had his three best seasons in 1964, 1967, and 1968, earning a top-10 finish in the A.L. MVP voting in each of those years. In addition to hitting 18 home runs and driving in 80 runs in the first of those campaigns, Freehan established career highs with 69 runs scored, 156 hits, 8 triples, and a .300 batting average. Three years later, he hit 20 homers, knocked in 74 runs, scored 66 times, and batted .282. Although Freehan batted just .263 in 1968, he placed among the league leaders in five different offensive categories, including home runs (25), runs batted in (84), on-base percentage (.366), slugging percentage (.454), and OPS (.819). Freehan also established new A.L. records for most putouts and total chances by a catcher, earning in the process a second-place finish in the league MVP voting. Factoring into the equation that Freehan posted the numbers he did in the "Year of the Pitcher," the 1968 campaign would have to be considered his finest all-around season.

Memorable Moments/Greatest Performances

Due in large part to Denny McLain's 14 strikeouts over 6⅔ innings, Freehan tied a major league record by recording 19 putouts at catcher on June 15, 1965.

Freehan also had a number of big days at the plate for the Tigers, with one of those coming on July 5, 1968, when he homered twice and drove in 6 runs in an 8–5 home win over Oakland. He had a similarly productive day on April 10, 1969, leading the Tigers to a 12–3 victory over Cleveland by going 3-for-5, with 2 homers and 5 RBIs, knocking in 4 of those runs with a grand slam homer off Indians fire-baller Sam McDowell. Freehan had another huge game on September 8, 1974, when he went 4-for-5, with a homer and 7 RBIs, in an 11–3 win over the Yankees in New York. However, Freehan had his greatest day on August 9, 1971, when he hit 3 home runs in a wild 12–11 loss to the Red Sox at Fenway Park. Freehan lofted two of his homers over the Green Monster in left and another into the centerfield bleachers.

Nevertheless, Freehan will always be remembered most fondly by Tigers fans for his involvement in two plays that occurred during the 1968 World Series. The first of those took place in the fifth inning of Game Five, when, with the Cardinals in front by a score of 3–2 and holding a 3-games-to-1 lead in the Series, Freehan tagged out at the plate speedster Lou Brock, who attempted to score from second on Julian Javier's single to left field. Willie Horton's throw from the outfield barely nipped Brock, who attempted to score standing up. The play helped shift the momentum of the Series, enabling the Tigers to mount a memorable comeback. Freehan achieved another measure of immortality in Game Seven, recording the final out of the Series by catching Tim McCarver's foul pop-up near the first base line. Tigers hurler Mickey Lolich subsequently leaped into Freehan's arms, creating one of the most indelible images in Detroit baseball history. Freehan later said, "When Lolich jumps on you, well, he's not a small man. But it was a great feeling!"

NOTABLE ACHIEVEMENTS

- Hit more than 20 home runs three times.
- Batted .300 in 1964.
- Led A.L. catchers in putouts six times; fielding percentage three times; caught stealing percentage once; and double plays turned once.
- Holds Tigers career records for most games caught (1,581) and most times hit by pitch (114).
- Ranks among Tigers career leaders in home runs (10th); games played (10th); plate appearances (10th); and at-bats (10th).
- Ranks 13th all-time among major league catchers in putouts (9,941).
- Retired with major league records for most putouts (9,941) and chances (10,714), and highest fielding percentage (.993) by a catcher.
- In 1968, set A.L. single-season records for most putouts (971) and chances (1,050).
- Hit 3 home runs in one game on August 9, 1971.
- Finished third in 1967 A.L. MVP voting and second in 1968 balloting.
- Five-time Gold Glove winner (1965–1969).
- Four-time *Sporting News* All-Star selection (1967, 1968, 1969, 1971).
- Eleven-time A.L. All-Star (1964–1973, 1975).
- 1968 A.L. champion.
- 1968 world champion.

19

Lance Parrish

Courtesy of James Hering

Immediately following in these rankings the man who helped develop his catching skills early in his career, Lance Parrish spent parts of 10 seasons in Detroit, serving as the Tigers' primary receiver in nine of those. An eight-time A.L. All-Star, Parrish also won three Gold Gloves and five Silver Sluggers while playing for the Tigers, hitting 212 home runs and driving in 700 runs along the way. A powerful right-handed batter who flouted convention by working out feverishly with weights, the 6'3", 220-pound

Parrish hit more than 20 home runs in six of seven seasons at one point, surpassing 30 four-baggers on two separate occasions. Spending most of his peak seasons batting cleanup for the Tigers, Parrish also topped 100 RBIs once, driving in 98 runs two other times. Meanwhile, despite annually placing near the top of the league rankings in passed balls, Parrish's strong throwing arm and ability to handle a pitching staff made him an above-average defensive receiver who most people considered to be the junior circuit's finest all-around catcher of his time.

Born in Clairton, Pennsylvania, on June 15, 1956, Lance Michael Parrish moved with his family to California at the age of six. After starring in baseball and football at Walnut High School, during which time he also briefly served as a bodyguard for pop-music icon Tina Turner, Parrish received a scholarship offer to play football at UCLA. However, he instead chose to pursue a career in baseball when the Tigers selected him in the first round of the 1974 amateur draft with the 16th overall pick. Despite being drafted as a third baseman, Parrish gradually transitioned to the position of catcher over the course of his first two minor league seasons, during which time he failed to distinguish himself as a hitter. But, after continuing to struggle at the plate in his third year of pro ball, Parrish improved dramatically while playing for AAA Evansville in 1977, raising his batting average to .279 and leading the team with 25 home runs and 90 RBIs. Parrish's strong performance earned him a late-season call-up to Detroit, after which he batted just .196 in fewer than 50 official at-bats, although he also hit 3 homers and drove in 7 runs.

Platooned behind the plate with the left-hand-swinging Milt May by Tigers manager Ralph Houk for most of 1978, Parrish batted .219, hit 14 homers, and knocked in 41 runs, in just under 300 official plate appearances. Parrish became Detroit's full-time starter at the position the following year when Les Moss replaced Houk at the helm. Moss, who earlier managed Parrish in the minor leagues, praised his young receiver, claiming he was "going to be the next superstar in the American League. He will be one of the best in the business. He has tremendous power and throws as well as anybody. When I had him at Evansville, he was the best player in the league. I think he's ready to be an outstanding player."

Parrish took a major step toward living up to the big buildup Moss gave him by hitting 19 home runs, driving in 65 runs, and batting .276 in his first year as a regular member of Detroit's starting lineup. However, he also led all A.L. catchers with 21 passed balls, prompting the Tigers to summon former defensive standout Bill Freehan to work with him behind the plate prior to the start of the ensuing campaign.

Although Parrish continued to rank among the league leaders in passed balls in subsequent seasons, he improved considerably under Freehan's tutelage, eventually evolving into one of the junior circuit's top defensive receivers. Blessed with a powerful throwing arm, Parrish finished second among A.L. catchers in assists four times. He also placed among the league leaders in caught-stealing percentage three times, typically throwing out somewhere in the vicinity of 45 percent of attempted base-stealers. But, Parrish's greatest skill as a receiver proved to be his handling of Detroit's pitching staff. Former catcher and manager Bob Melvin, who spent his first season in the majors backing up Parrish in Detroit, said, "I learned a lot from him coming up. Lance was supposedly an offensive guy, but they called him the 'Big Wheel' because he drove that train. He was very in tune with the pitchers and was very serious about what he did behind the plate. He was as good an all-around catcher as anyone that I have been around."

Although quiet by nature, Parrish had the ability to speak his mind whenever he felt he needed to do so. When Jack Morris lost his composure on the mound one day, Parrish took it upon himself to chastise the Tigers ace, telling him, "Nobody likes to play behind you when you act this way." Crushed by Parrish's harsh words, Morris said following the contest, "Lance saved me. I try, but sometimes I can't control myself. I needed something. Lance has so much more class than I have. I'm not going to cross Lance. He's like a big brother to me, and he knows just what to say to me."

Still, Parrish made his greatest impact in the batter's box, having his breakout season in 1980, when he earned All-Star and Silver Slugger honors for the first time by hitting 24 home runs, driving in 82 runs, scoring 79 times, and batting .286. After posting subpar numbers during the strike-shortened 1981 campaign, he began an extremely successful four-year run during which he averaged 30 homers and 99 RBIs. Parrish earned a spot on *The Sporting News* All-Star team for the first of two times in 1982 by hitting 32 home runs, knocking in 87 runs, scoring 75 times, and batting .284. He followed that up by batting .269, scoring 80 runs, and placing among the league leaders with 27 homers, 114 RBIs, and 42 doubles in 1983, while also winning the first of his three straight Gold Gloves. Although Parrish subsequently batted just .237 for Detroit's 1984 world championship ball club, he drove in 98 runs and hit a career-high 33 homers. He again knocked in 98 runs in 1985, while also hitting 28 home runs and batting .273.

Plagued by back problems throughout the 1986 campaign, Parrish appeared in only 91 games for the Tigers. Nevertheless, he managed to make the A.L. All-Star team and win his fifth Silver Slugger by hitting 22 home runs, driving in 62 runs, and batting .257.

A free agent at season's end, Parrish looked forward to continuing his career with the Tigers, stating, "I'd like to play in Detroit my entire career. I haven't had any problems with the Tigers in the past about contracts. I really don't anticipate any now. When the time comes, I think we can work something out—at least I hope we can." However, when concerns over Parrish's ailing back prompted team president Jim Campbell to offer him the same $850,000 salary he earned the previous season, Parrish elected to sign as a free agent with the Philadelphia Phillies. He left Detroit with career totals of 212 home runs, 700 RBIs, 577 runs scored, 1,123 hits, and 201 doubles, a .263 batting average, a .317 on-base percentage, and a .469 slugging percentage.

Parrish had a difficult time adjusting to the National League, posting batting averages of just .245 and .215, while compiling totals of only 32 home runs and 127 RBIs in his two years with the Phillies, before returning to the American League as a member of the California Angels in 1989. He spent the next 3½ years with the Angels, earning his final All-Star selection and Silver Slugger in 1990, when he hit 24 homers, knocked in 70 runs, and batted .268. Released by the Angels midway through the 1992 campaign, Parrish subsequently spent the remainder of his career serving as a backup in Seattle, Cleveland, Pittsburgh, and Toronto, before announcing his retirement after he failed to make Pittsburgh's roster prior to the start of the 1996 season. He ended his career with 324 home runs, 1,070 RBIs, 856 runs scored, 1,782 hits, 305 doubles, a .252 batting average, a .313 on-base percentage, and a .440 slugging percentage. Parrish's total of 299 home runs as a catcher places him sixth all-time among major league receivers. He also ranks 11th in games caught (1,818) and 15th in putouts (9,647).

Following his playing career, Parrish became a coach, first for the Kansas City Royals (1996), then for the minor league San Antonio Missions (1997–1998), and finally for the Tigers (1999–2001). He moved up to the broadcast booth in 2002, serving as the color commentator for Tigers games on Detroit's WKBD station. He returned to the Detroit dugout the following year when former teammate Alan Trammell became the team's manager. Parrish remained on Trammell's coaching staff until the Tigers relieved both men of their duties at the end of the 2005 season. He later managed two different minor league teams, before the Erie Sea-Wolves, Detroit's AA affiliate, hired him to direct them from the dugout beginning in 2014.

TIGERS CAREER HIGHLIGHTS

Best Season

Parrish had a productive 1984 campaign, knocking in 98 runs and hitting a career-high 33 homers. However, he also batted just .237, compiled an on-base percentage of only .287, and posted an OPS of .730 that fell far short of the .786 mark he averaged during his time in Detroit. Parrish actually compiled better overall numbers for the Tigers in 1980, 1982, 1983, and 1985. In addition to hitting 24 home runs, driving in 82 runs, scoring 79 times, and posting an OPS of .825 in the first of those years, he batted a career-high .286. In the last of those seasons, Parrish homered 28 times, knocked in 98 runs, batted .273, and compiled an OPS of .802. Parrish had a big year in 1982, when he hit 32 homers, drove in 87 runs, scored 75 times, batted .284, and posted a career-high .867 OPS. But he had his finest all-around season in 1983, earning his only top-10 finish in the A.L MVP voting (he finished ninth) by hitting 27 home runs, batting .269, posting an OPS of .796, and establishing career highs with 114 RBIs, 80 runs scored, 163 hits, 42 doubles, and 292 total bases. He also earned Gold Glove honors for the first of three straight times by leading all A.L. receivers in caught-stealing percentage (48.6), and placing second in fielding percentage (.995), putouts (695), and assists (73).

Memorable Moments/Greatest Performances

After appearing in his first major league game just two days earlier, Parrish made his second start in the big leagues a memorable one, going 3-for-4, hitting his first home run, knocking in 4 runs, and scoring 4 times in a 12–5 home win over Baltimore in the second game of a doubleheader split with the Orioles on September 7, 1977.

Parrish hit one of the most dramatic home runs of his career on May 16, 1978, when he ended a 4-hour, 30-minute marathon with the Mariners by taking Seattle left-hander Shane Rawley deep with one man aboard in the bottom of the 16th inning to give the Tigers a 4–2 walk-off win. He hit another memorable homer on August 7, 1984, giving the Tigers a 7–5 victory over the Red Sox in the second game of a doubleheader split by homering with one man on base in the top of the 11th inning.

Parrish experienced his greatest moment behind the plate on April 7, 1984, when he caught Jack Morris's no-hitter.

Even though Tiger fans recall far more vividly Kirk Gibson's dramatic three-run homer off Goose Gossage in the bottom of the eighth inning of Game Five of the 1984 World Series, Parrish hit a huge solo home run off Gossage in the previous frame, giving the Tigers an insurance run that proved to be the winning score in an 8–4 Detroit victory.

NOTABLE ACHIEVEMENTS

- Hit more than 20 home runs six times, topping 30 homers twice.
- Knocked in more than 100 runs once (114 in 1983).
- Surpassed 30 doubles twice, topping 40 two-baggers once (42 in 1983).
- Posted slugging percentage in excess of .500 once (.529 in 1982).
- Led A.L. catchers with 48.6 caught-stealing percentage in 1983.
- Ranks ninth all-time on Tigers with 212 home runs.
- Three-time Gold Glove winner (1983–1985).
- Five-time Silver Slugger winner.
- Two-time *Sporting News* All-Star selection (1982, 1984).
- Six-time A.L. All-Star (1980, 1982–1986).
- 1984 A.L. champion.
- 1984 world champion.

20

Willie Horton

Courtesy of LegendaryAuctions.com

powerful right-handed batter who eventually became one of the most popular players in Tigers history, Willie Horton spent parts of 15 seasons in Detroit, establishing himself during that time as one of the American League's top sluggers. Horton hit 262 home runs while playing for the Tigers, topping 20 round-trippers six times as a member of the team, despite missing a significant amount of playing time virtually every year due to an assortment of injuries. He also knocked in nearly 900 runs during his time in the Motor City, surpassing 100 RBIs on two separate occasions. Yet Horton came to represent something more than just a baseball star to the people of Detroit, who learned to admire him even more for the manner in which he helped bridge relations between the Tigers and the African American community through the years. The first black star to play for his hometown Tigers, Horton emerged as a peacemaker during one of the most turbulent times in U.S. history, using his inner strength and quiet leadership to improve race relations in one of the most ethnically mixed cities in the nation.

Born in Arno, Virginia, on October 18, 1942, William Wattison Horton moved with his family to Detroit, Michigan, at the age of five. After starring in baseball at Northwestern High School, the 18-year-old Horton signed with the Tigers as an amateur free agent following his graduation in 1961. Subsequently assigned to Duluth-Superior in the Northern League, the 5'10", 210-pound Horton soon found himself being compared to a young Roy Campanella due to his stocky build and powerful right-handed bat. Horton's slugging at each minor league level enabled him to advance rapidly through Detroit's farm system, earning him a late-season call-up to Motown in September 1963. Appearing in 15 games with the Tigers over the final three weeks of the campaign, Horton acquitted himself extremely well, batting .326 and hitting his first major league home run.

Horton's strong performance in spring training of 1964 greatly impressed Tigers manager Charlie Dressen, who commented, "He looks like a natural hitter to me. Willie throws well, and he can run." However, after initially earning a spot on the major league roster, Horton struggled during the early stages of the campaign, prompting the Tigers to return him to the minors for more seasoning in mid-May. Although Horton rejoined the Tigers later in the year, he spent most of the season at AAA Syracuse, hitting 28 homers, driving in 99 runs, and batting .288 for the Chiefs. In 25 games and 80 official at-bats with the Tigers, Horton batted just .163, with 1 home run and 10 RBIs.

Overcoming the loss of both his parents in a New Year's Day car accident during the subsequent offseason, Horton returned to the Tigers in 1965, stating prior to the start of the campaign, "Whatever I do this year, I'm doing for my dad and mother." Following up on his promise, Horton posted big numbers in his first full season, placing among the league leaders with 29 home runs and 104 RBIs, batting .273, and being named to the All-Star team for the first of four times after earning the Tigers' starting left-field job early in the year. He followed that up with a similarly productive 1966 campaign in which he once again placed near the top of the league rankings with 27 homers and 100 RBIs. Despite being hampered by a bad ankle that limited him to just 122 games in 1967, Horton still managed to hit 19 home runs and drive in 67 runs. However, the 24-year-old outfielder made his biggest impact on the city of Detroit off the field that year.

With the civil rights movement already in full swing, racial tensions in Detroit reached an all-time high in the summer of 1967 after police officers raided a west-side speakeasy and arrested several African American patrons in attendance to help celebrate the return of two Vietnam War veterans. A subsequent confrontation between policemen and angry protestors resulted in five days of riots, culminating with President Johnson's decision to summon the National Guard. In the end, 43 people lost their lives, more than 450 people suffered injuries, 7,200 individuals were arrested, and 2,000 buildings were burned down.

During the early stages of the rioting, Horton, who, as the Tigers' first black star, had already established himself as a hero within the city's African American community, left Tiger Stadium in full uniform in an effort to quell the uprising. Standing on top of a car in the middle of the burning streets, Horton addressed the irate crowd, issuing a plea for restraint. Although his appeal went unanswered, Horton's willingness to put himself in harm's way gained him the admiration and respect of whites and blacks alike, making him a civil rights hero of sorts within the city of Detroit. The Tigers' World Series victory over St. Louis the following year helped to further heal the city, with Horton suggesting 30 years later, "1968 was a win for the entire city of Detroit. It came a year after riots had torn up our streets, our people, and our relationships. I remember walking down Livernois Avenue during the summer of '67 and seeing all the destruction, all the terror. . . . It was a completely helpless feeling. So, '68 brought people together at a time that was so very important."

Horton proved to be the Tigers' most consistent hitter over the course of the 1968 campaign, placing among the league leaders with 36 home runs, 85 RBIs, and a .285 batting average, en route to earning All-Star honors for the second time and a fourth-place finish in the A.L. MVP voting. He subsequently homered once, drove in 3 runs, batted .304, and compiled an OPS of 1.013 against St. Louis in the World Series, with his Game Five throw to the plate that nailed Cardinals speedster Lou Brock attempting to score helping to shift the momentum of the Fall Classic in Detroit's favor.

Injuries and "personal pressures" forced Horton to miss three weeks of the 1969 season, limiting him to 141 games and 134 starts. Nevertheless, he finished the year with 28 homers and 91 RBIs, before deciding during the subsequent offseason to employ a new training regimen that helped him keep his weight down, leaving him in the best shape of his career. Having shed some 15 pounds prior to reporting to spring training, Horton got off to a fast start in 1970, hitting 17 home runs, driving in 69 runs, and batting .305, before suffering an ankle injury that ended his season prematurely on July 24. More misfortune came Horton's way in 1971, when a pitch from Chicago's Rich Hinton struck him in the left eye, keeping him out of the lineup for a month. Yet, he still managed to finish the season with 22 homers, 72 RBIs, and a .289 batting average.

After reporting to spring training the following year overweight and out of shape, Horton suffered through his worst season, concluding the 1972 campaign with only 11 homers, 36 RBIs, and a .231 batting average. Horton rebounded in 1973, though, finishing the season with 17 home runs, 53 RBIs, and a career-high .316 batting average, even though leg and wrist problems limited him to just 111 games. Forced to undergo knee surgery midway through the ensuing campaign, Horton assumed the role of full-time DH when he returned to the Tigers in 1975. Appearing in more than 120 games for the first time in six years, Horton hit 25 homers, knocked in 92 runs, and batted .275, en route to earning a spot on *The Sporting News* A.L. All-Star team as the league's top designated hitter. Although Horton initially balked at the idea of not playing the field, he came to embrace his new role, later commenting, "The only reason I thought I might not like it was because I thought it might feel like I wasn't doing enough for the club. It's not that way though. Now I have to keep up with what's going on all the time."

Unfortunately, injuries plagued Horton again in 1976, limiting him to 114 games, 14 homers, and 56 RBIs. With Rusty Staub slated to serve as Detroit's primary DH in 1977, and with the 34-year-old Horton no longer capable of playing the outfield, the Tigers traded arguably their most popular player to the Texas Rangers shortly after the regular season got underway. Serving almost exclusively as a DH, Horton posted decent numbers in each of the next two seasons, which he split between Texas, Cleveland, Oakland, and Toronto. However, he had one more big year left in him, hitting 29 home runs, driving in 106 runs, and batting .279 for Seattle in 1979, en route to earning A.L. Comeback Player of the Year honors after signing with the Mariners as a free agent during the previous offseason. After one more year in Seattle, Horton failed to catch on with either the Texas Rangers or Pittsburgh Pirates, forcing him to spend two years in the minor leagues, before ending his playing career in the Mexican League in 1983. Horton retired with career totals of 325 home runs, 1,163 RBIs, 873 runs scored, 1,993 hits, 40 triples, and 284 doubles, a .273 batting average, a .332 on-base percentage, and a .457 slugging percentage. During his time in Detroit, he hit 262 home runs, knocked in 886 runs, scored 671 times, amassed 1,490 hits, 211 doubles, and 31 triples, batted .276, compiled a .337 on-base percentage, and posted a .472 slugging percentage.

Following his retirement, Horton served briefly as a coach with the Yankees and White Sox, before eventually rejoining the Tigers in 2000 as a special adviser. He continues to serve in the team's front office today. The Tigers retired Horton's uniform number 23 in 2000 and constructed a bronze statue of him beyond the left-field stands at Comerica Park. Horton is the only former Detroit player not in the Hall of Fame to be so honored. Although Horton compiled solid numbers in his years with the Tigers, the statue serves more as a testament to the crucial role he played in restoring peace and harmony to the city of Detroit.

After declaring October 18, 2004, "Willie Horton Day" in Michigan, in honor of the former slugger's 62nd birthday, Michigan governor Jennifer Granholm stated, "Willie Horton is one of those rare baseball players who doesn't need a diamond to truly sparkle and shine—he's a star on and off the field. This fitting recognition will continue to inform future generations of his accomplishments."

TIGERS CAREER HIGHLIGHTS

Best Season

Horton compiled impressive numbers for the Tigers in both 1965 and 1966, hitting 29 home runs, driving in 104 runs, and batting .273 in the first of those campaigns, before homering 27 times, knocking in 100 runs, and batting .262 the following year. However, he had his finest all-around season for the Tigers in 1968, when he helped lead them to the A.L. pennant by finishing second in the league with 36 home runs, 278 total bases, a .543 slugging percentage, and an .895 OPS, and placing fourth in the circuit with 85 RBIs and a .285 batting average. Horton's 36 homers, .543 slugging percentage, and .895 OPS all represented career-high marks.

Memorable Moments/Greatest Performances

Horton broke into the big leagues in memorable fashion, singling in his first at-bat on September 10, 1963, before hitting a pinch-hit 2-run homer off Hall of Fame right-hander Robin Roberts in just his second trip to the plate four days later.

Horton went on a home run binge in mid-May 1965, homering six times over the course of four games, in leading the Tigers to three straight wins over Washington, and another over Boston. Each of Horton's blasts traveled more than 400 feet, with the slugger going a combined 12-for-18 during that stretch of games, with 15 RBIs and 10 runs scored. Although Horton failed to reach the seats in Detroit's next win over the Red Sox, he continued his hot hitting, going 3-for-4, with 1 RBI and 1 run scored.

Horton hit one of the most dramatic home runs of his career on September 21, 1966, when he gave the Tigers a 2–1 victory over the California Angels by hitting a 2-out, 2-run homer off Dean Chance in the bottom of the ninth inning.

Horton had a huge game against Boston on April 17, 1971, going 5-for-6, with 2 homers and 6 RBIs, in a 10–9, 10-inning home win over the Red Sox. After knocking in 5 runs earlier in the contest with a grand slam and solo homer, Horton drove in the winning run with a bases loaded single in the bottom of the tenth.

Horton, though, had the greatest day of his career on June 9, 1970, when he led the Tigers to an 8–3 home win over the Milwaukee Brewers by hitting 3 home runs and driving in 7 runs.

Yet, even though Horton rarely received credit for his defense, he made the most memorable play of his career in the outfield during the 1968 World Series. With the Cardinals ahead in the Fall Classic 3-games-to-1 and holding a 3–2 lead in the fifth inning of Game Five, Lou Brock attempted to extend the St. Louis lead by scoring from second base on a line-drive single to left field by Julian Javier. However, Horton got to the ball quickly and fired a one-hop strike to Bill Freehan, who caught the ball, blocked home plate with his foot, and tagged out Brock, who curiously chose not to slide. The Tigers came back to win the contest by a score of 5–3, and then defeated the Cardinals in the next two games, to capture their first world championship in 23 years. Tigers center fielder Jim Northrup later said, "If Willie doesn't throw him out, and if Brock slides, we probably lose that ballgame. But Brock didn't slide, and Freehan had the plate covered. They gave us a chance to come back, and we did."

NOTABLE ACHIEVEMENTS

- Hit more than 20 home runs six times, topping 30 homers once (36 in 1968).

- Knocked in more than 100 runs twice.
- Batted over .300 twice.
- Posted slugging percentage in excess of .500 four times.
- Led A.L. left fielders with .991 fielding percentage in 1965.
- Ranks fourth all-time on Tigers with 262 home runs.
- Finished fourth in 1968 A.L. MVP voting.
- Two-time *Sporting News* All-Star selection (1968, 1975).
- Four-time A.L. All-Star (1965, 1968, 1970, 1973).
- 1968 A.L. champion.
- 1968 world champion.

21

Mickey Lolich

Courtesy of LegendaryAuctions.com

A durable left-hander who threw more than 300 innings four straight times for the Tigers, Mickey Lolich spent his first few seasons in the Motor City playing second fiddle to Denny McLain in Detroit's starting rotation. Lolich, though, eventually went on to establish himself as the ace of the Tigers' pitching staff, posting more than 20 victories twice, while also winning in excess of 16 games on six other occasions. Featuring an outstanding curveball, a low-to-mid 90s fastball, and, in later years, a cut fastball,

Lolich proved to be one of the most difficult pitchers in the American League for opposing hitters to solve, fanning more than 200 batters seven times, and topping the magical 300-mark once. Blessed with what is commonly referred to as a "rubber arm," Lolich consistently ranked among the league's top hurlers in starts, complete games, and innings pitched, starting more than 40 games four times, tossing more than 20 complete games on three occasions, and throwing more than 200 innings 12 straight times. By the time Lolich left the Tigers at the conclusion of the 1975 campaign, he had started more games, amassed more strikeouts, and tossed more shutouts than any other pitcher in franchise history. He also ranked among the club's all-time leaders in wins, innings pitched, complete games, and pitching appearances. The portly southpaw accomplished all he did despite possessing a physique that prompted him to describe himself as "the beer-drinker's idol."

Born in Portland, Oregon, on September 12, 1940, Michael Stephen Lolich initially favored his right arm until he broke his left arm and shoulder as a toddler by tipping over a motorcycle onto himself. Forced to do exercises to strengthen his torn muscles once his cast came off, Mickey subsequently learned to throw left-handed, but he continued to bat from the right side and write with his right hand.

After starring on the mound for local Lincoln High School, Lolich signed with the Tigers as an amateur free agent on June 30, 1958. He spent the next five years in the minor leagues, nearly seeing his aspirations of reaching the majors come to an end after being struck below the right eye by a line drive while pitching for AAA Denver. Working somewhat tentatively thereafter, Lolich struggled the next two seasons, prompting him to briefly consider leaving the game altogether. However, after being loaned out to the Portland Beavers, Lolich received pivotal advice from pitching coach Jerry Staley, who advised the young southpaw to focus more on his control, rather than attempting to strike out every batter he faced.

After changing his approach on the mound, Lolich advanced to AAA Syracuse, where he pitched well enough to earn a call-up to Detroit in May 1963. Working as a spot-starter/long reliever the rest of the year, the 22-year-old Lolich compiled a record of 5–9 and an ERA of 3.55 for the Tigers, in 144⅓ innings of work. In discussing the rookie left-hander, Tigers vice president Rick Ferrell observed, "That young Lolich is all business out there. I like his breaking stuff."

Lolich developed into arguably Detroit's most reliable starter the following season, concluding the 1964 campaign with a record of 18–9, a 3.26 ERA, 192 strikeouts, and 6 shutouts. Commenting on Lolich's quick maturation, new Detroit manager Charlie Dressen noted, "Lolich's fastball is so good that he can get away with a mistake once in a while. But the big difference is that he comes in with the curve when he's behind the hitter."

Lolich had another solid season in 1965, going 15–9 with a 3.44 ERA, throwing 243⅔ innings, and finishing second in the league to Cleveland fire-baller Sam McDowell with 226 strikeouts. However, he pitched less effectively in 1966, compiling a record of 14–14 and a career-high 4.77 ERA. Despite suffering through a 10-game losing streak midway through the ensuing campaign, Lolich eventually righted himself, finishing 1967 with a record of 14–13, a 3.04 ERA, 174 strikeouts, and a league-leading 6 shutouts. After Lolich fanned 13 Red Sox batters during a late-season contest at Tiger Stadium, Boston's slugging first baseman George Scott proclaimed, "That's the best left-hander I've seen all year."

As he continued to develop a reputation as one of the Junior Circuit's top southpaws over the course of his first few seasons, Lolich grew increasingly large around the middle, adding several inches to his waistline. Listed at 6'1" and 170 pounds when he first arrived in Detroit nearly five years earlier, Lolich tipped the scales at well in excess of 200 pounds by the end of 1967. In addressing his physical condition, Lolich commented, "I do have a big tummy, I'll admit. There's nothing I can do about it. It's my posture. When I'm going good, nobody says anything about it. If I lose a few games, they start saying I'm out of shape."

Few people had anything negative to say about Lolich in 1968. Despite being overshadowed by fellow Tigers hurler Denny McLain, who posted 31 victories for the A.L. champions, Lolich had a very good year himself, going 17–9, with a 3.19 ERA and 197 strikeouts. He then pitched magnificently against St. Louis in the World Series, leading the Tigers to a stirring comeback by winning all three of his starts, including a victory over Bob Gibson in the Series finale on only two days' rest.

Lolich continued to pitch well in 1969, compiling a 3.14 ERA, finishing second in the league with 271 strikeouts, and also placing among the leaders with 19 wins, 15 complete games, and 280⅔ innings pitched. He experienced something of a setback the following season, though, going just 14–19 with a 3.80 ERA.

Having added to his repertoire of pitches a cut fastball he learned from pitching coach Johnny Sain, Lolich subsequently put together back-to-back 20-win seasons. Pitching for a Detroit team that finished second in the A.L. East with 91 victories in 1971, Lolich compiled an ERA of 2.92 and led all league hurlers with 25 wins, 45 starts, 308 strikeouts, 29 complete games, and 376 innings pitched, en route to earning a fifth-place finish in the MVP voting. He also finished second to league MVP Vida Blue in the Cy

Young balloting. Lolich followed that up by going 22–14 in 1972, with a 2.50 ERA, 250 strikeouts, 23 complete games, and 327⅓ innings pitched, earning in the process a top-10 finish in the MVP voting and a third-place finish in the Cy Young balloting.

Although Lolich failed to reach the same lofty level in either of the next two campaigns, posting a combined record of just 32–36, he remained one of baseball's most durable pitchers, continuing his string of four consecutive seasons in which he worked at least 300 innings. He also struck out more than 200 batters for the fifth and sixth straight times. Revealing the unusual method he used to keep his arm strong, Lolich explained, "I never used ice. I would stand in the shower after a game and soak my pitching arm under hot water for 30 minutes. The water was scalding hot. After 30 minutes, my arm would be red, but it would feel fine and I'd be throwing on the sidelines in two days. I never had a sore arm."

Even though Lolich had a good fastball, he didn't consider himself to be a particularly hard thrower, stating at one point early in his career, "I can't throw as hard as [Sam] McDowell and a lot of guys. [Tigers pitcher] Dave Wickersham showed me something two years ago. He doesn't throw hard at all. He's got control, and he makes the hitter go after his pitch. That's what I have to do."

Employing a philosophy that emphasized staying ahead in the count, Lolich preferred to let the opposing hitter get himself out, later stating, "I tried to throw two of my first three pitches to a batter for strikes. I was like, 'Here, hit it.'" His approach worked well since Lolich ended up striking out more batters (2,679) than any other left-handed pitcher in A.L. history.

In discussing his former teammate, longtime Tigers outfielder Jim Northrup said, "Mickey Lolich had great stuff. If you didn't get him in the first inning, you could forget it. He had a wicked curveball and a great fastball."

Receiving poor run support from a weak-hitting Tigers team that scored just 570 runs and won only 57 games in 1975, Lolich finished the season with a record of just 12–18. With the 35-year-old southpaw clearly on the downside of his career, the Tigers elected to trade him to the New York Mets for veteran outfielder Rusty Staub on December 12, 1975, bringing to an end Lolich's 13-year stay in Detroit. In addition to amassing 2,679 strikeouts, Lolich left the Tigers having compiled a career record of 207–175, an ERA of 3.45, 190 complete games, and 39 shutouts, in 3,361⅔ total innings of work. He continues to rank among the Tigers' all-time leaders in virtually every major statistical category for pitchers.

Lolich later described the events that transpired his final days in Detroit, recalling, "(General manager) Jim Campbell called me at home and said they had made a deal with New York, and that the deal couldn't be completed unless I agreed to the trade because I was a 10-year veteran. I said no. I didn't have any desire to go to New York. And then he started coming on a little bit strong, saying that if I don't go I will take a cut in salary and he will not give me what I want (in Detroit)."

Lolich continued, "They didn't want me in Detroit anymore. He wanted Rusty Staub and said that things weren't going to be very comfortable for me around Detroit, and that the New York Mets had offered me a very good raise. . . . It was an emotional experience and an emotional time in my life. I was sort of upset with Jim and the way he handled everything. And I said yes. A week later, I said no. I wish I hadn't made the deal. He caught me at a weak moment and away I went."

Lolich added, "I would have loved to have been like an Al Kaline and play my entire major league career with Detroit. I was the all-time winning left-handed pitcher with the Tigers. I needed another 12 victories to be the all-time winning pitcher for the Tigers. I really would have liked to have stayed with Detroit. But when you're in baseball and when you're in sports, there's really no sentiment when it comes to the front office."

Lolich ended up spending just one unhappy season in New York, often finding himself at odds with the team's trainer and pitching coach, both of whom suggested he alter his training regimen and treat his arm with ice. After posting a record of just 8–13 for the Mets in 1976, Lolich announced his retirement in order to get out of the last year of his two-year contract. He subsequently sat out the entire 1977 campaign and opened a doughnut shop in suburban Detroit. A free agent prior to the start of the 1978 season, Lolich approached Jim Campbell about returning to the Tigers but ended up signing with the Padres instead after Campbell showed no interest. Lolich spent two seasons in San Diego working mostly out of the bullpen, before retiring at the conclusion of the 1979 campaign with a career record of 217–191, an ERA of 3.44, 2,832 strikeouts, 41 shutouts, 195 complete games, and 3,638⅓ innings pitched. He currently ranks 18th on Major League Baseball's all-time strikeout list.

Following his retirement, Lolich returned to his doughnut business, continuing to operate shops in the Detroit suburbs of Rochester and Lake Orion for several years until finally electing to sell the business and retire to his homes in Oregon and Michigan. Lolich remains active in charitable work and serves as a coach at the Tigers' Fantasy Camp in Lakeland, Florida, nearly every year. Some 40 years after he threw his last pitch for the Tigers, Lolich continues to be celebrated as one of the most popular sports figures in a workingman's city. As the *Detroit News* put it, "He didn't act like a big shot superstar, he was one of us."

TIGERS CAREER HIGHLIGHTS

Best Season

Lolich had his two most dominant seasons in 1971 and 1972, winning more than 20 games for the only two times in his career. In comparing the numbers he compiled those two seasons, Lolich finished with a better WHIP (1.088) and ERA (2.50) in 1972 than he did in 1971 (1.138 and 2.92). He also placed in the league's top three in wins (22), strikeouts (250), complete games (23), and innings pitched (327⅓) in the second of those campaigns. However, Lolich led all A.L. hurlers in five different pitching categories in 1971, when he established career highs with 25 wins (25–14), 308 strikeouts, 45 starts, 29 complete games, and 376 innings pitched. And, even though Lolich compiled a higher ERA in 1971, he finished 10th in the league rankings both years. Furthermore, he posted his best showings in the A.L. MVP and Cy Young voting in the first of those years, coming in fifth and second, respectively. All things considered, Lolich had his best season in 1971.

Memorable Moments/Greatest Performances

Lolich turned in the first truly dominant performance of his career on April 24, 1964, when he tossed a 3-hit shutout in defeating the hard-hitting Minnesota Twins by a score of 5–0. Lolich matched his earlier effort nearly four months later, on August 18, when he blanked the Angels 1–0, surrendering just 3 hits and striking out 10 during the contest. He subsequently pitched extraordinarily well during the first two weeks of September, throwing 3 straight shutouts and 30⅔ consecutive scoreless innings at one point. His exceptional run culminated with a September 9, 4–0 shutout of the Yankees—a game in which he defeated his boyhood idol Whitey Ford.

Lolich went on another extremely impressive run late in 1967, winning 9 of his final 10 decisions, and concluding the campaign by tossing 3 straight shutouts and 28⅔ consecutive scoreless innings.

Lolich pitched one of his most memorable games on May 29, 1965, when he threw a 10-inning, complete game 2-hitter in defeating the Indians by a score of 1-0.

Lolich struck out 16 batters in a game twice in 1969, accomplishing the feat for the first time on May 23 during a 6–3 victory over the California Angels. He duplicated his earlier effort less than three weeks later, on June 9, tying his own franchise record by fanning 16 Seattle Pilots during a contest the Tigers eventually lost 3–2 in 10 innings. In addition to striking out 16 batters in his 9 innings of work, Lolich allowed the Pilots just 1 run on 4 hits.

Lolich nearly matched his career-high mark in his final start of the 1972 campaign, striking out 15 batters during a 4–1 win over the Boston Red Sox. He subsequently pitched brilliantly in his two starts against Oakland in the ALCS, surrendering just 3 earned runs and 14 hits in 19 total innings of work, despite losing his lone decision.

Still, there is little doubt that Lolich reached the apex of his career in the 1968 World Series. After evening the Fall Classic at a game apiece by defeating the Cardinals by a score of 8–1 in Game 2, Lolich kept the Tigers' hopes alive by posting a 5–3 win in Game 5. After the Tigers evened the Series with a 13–1 win in Game Six, Lolich returned to the mound on only two days' rest to face Bob Gibson in the Series finale. Both hurlers worked six scoreless frames, until Detroit finally broke through against Gibson for three runs in the top of the seventh. The Tigers went on to win the game by a score of 4–1, capturing in the process their first world championship in 23 years. Reflecting back on his Game Seven performance, Lolich said, "I didn't know how long I could go. After the fifth inning, Mayo (Tigers manager Mayo Smith) looked at me every inning, and I would tell him I was okay. Then, when they got me some runs in the seventh, I told Mayo I would finish it." Lolich ended up winning Series MVP honors by going 3–0, with a 1.67 ERA, 21 strikeouts, and 3 complete games.

NOTABLE ACHIEVEMENTS

- Won more than 20 games twice, surpassing 15 victories six other times.
- Compiled ERA below 3.00 twice.
- Struck out more than 200 batters seven times, topping 300 strikeouts once (308 in 1971).
- Completed more than 20 games three times.
- Threw more than 200 innings 12 straight seasons, surpassing 300 innings pitched four times.
- Led all A.L. pitchers in wins once; strikeouts once; innings pitched once; complete games once; shutouts once; and games started once.

- Holds Tigers career records for most strikeouts (2,679); shutouts (39); and starts (459).
- Ranks among Tigers career leaders in wins (3rd); innings pitched (3rd); complete games (6th); and pitching appearances (3rd).
- Holds Tigers single-season records for most strikeouts (308) and most starts (45), both in 1971.
- Ranks first all-time among A.L. left-handed pitchers with 2,679 strikeouts.
- Ranks third all-time among MLB left-handed pitchers with 2,832 career strikeouts.
- Won 3 games in 1968 World Series.
- 1968 World Series MVP.
- Finished fifth in 1971 A.L. MVP balloting.
- Finished second in 1971 A.L. Cy Young voting.
- Finished third in 1972 A.L. Cy Young voting.
- Three-time A.L. All-Star (1969, 1971, 1972).
- 1968 A.L. champion.
- 1968 world champion.

22

Tommy Bridges

Courtesy of MearsOnlineAuctions.com

A smallish right-hander once referred to by Tigers Hall of Fame manager and catcher Mickey Cochrane as "a hundred and fifty pounds of courage," Tommy Bridges anchored Detroit's pitching staff for nearly a decade, establishing himself over the course of his 16 seasons in the Motor City as one of the top hurlers in franchise history. A three-time 20-game winner, the 5'10", 155-pound Bridges posted a total of 194 victories for the Tigers, en route to joining Hank Greenberg as the only players to appear in four World Series for the team. Particularly effective from 1934 to 1936, Bridges compiled an overall mark of 66–32 during that time, winning more than 20 games each season and leading the American League in strikeouts twice. In all, Bridges posted double-digit wins 10 times, doing so in nine consecutive seasons at one point. Upon his retirement in 1946, he ranked third in franchise history in wins and first in strikeouts, with his 1,674 strikeouts representing the eighth-highest total in A.L. history at the time. Nearly 70 years after he threw his last pitch for the Tigers, Bridges continues to rank among the team's all-time leaders in virtually every major statistical category for pitchers.

Born in Gordonsville, Tennessee, on December 28, 1906, Thomas Jefferson Davis Bridges was expected to follow in the footsteps of his father, a country doctor in Smith County. However, after graduating from the University of Tennessee, the younger Bridges instead chose to pursue a career in baseball, getting his start in pro ball with the Wheeling Stogies of the Class C Middle Atlantic League in 1929. Although Bridges compiled a record of just 7–8 with Evansville of the Three-I League during the first few months of the ensuing campaign, his earlier 20-strikeout performance at Wheeling prompted the Tigers to bring him up at midseason. Bridges made his major league debut with the Tigers on August 13, 1930, coming out of the bullpen to retire the first two batters he faced—Babe Ruth on a ground out, and Lou Gehrig on a strikeout. He subsequently appeared in seven more games with the Tigers over the final few weeks of the season, winning 3 of his 5 decisions and posting an ERA of 4.06.

Despite displaying a considerable amount of wildness on the mound at times (he walked 108 batters in 173 innings), Bridges gradually worked his way into Detroit's starting rotation in 1931, concluding the campaign with an unimpressive 8–16 record and 4.99 ERA for a team that won only 61 games during the regular season. Although Bridges continued to struggle with his control somewhat the following year, he improved upon his overall performance dramatically, finishing the season with a record of 14–12 and an ERA of 3.36, and topping the circuit with 4 shutouts. After finishing 14–12 again in 1933, tossing 17 complete games, and placing second in the league with a 3.09 ERA, Bridges developed into an elite pitcher during Detroit's 1934 pennant-winning campaign, earning the first of his six All-Star selections by going 22–11 with a 3.67 ERA, and finishing second in the league with 151 strikeouts, 23 complete games, and 275 innings pitched. He followed that up with two more exceptional seasons, posting a record of 21–10, tossing 23 complete games and 274⅓ innings, and leading the league with 163 strikeouts in 1935, before going 23–11, with 26 complete games, 294⅔ innings pitched, and an A.L.-leading 175 strikeouts in 1936. Bridges also helped the Tigers capture their first world championship by posting two victories in the 1935 World Series.

Blessed with an outstanding fastball, Bridges nevertheless depended heavily on his curveball, which Hall of Fame catchers Mickey Cochrane and Rick Ferrell both identified as the best they ever saw. Longtime Tigers teammate Virgil Trucks concurred, stating in an article entitled "He Tossed No-Hitters Twice in a Season" that appeared in the February 1995 edition of *Baseball Digest*, "Primarily, I was a fastball pitcher, and nobody could teach me to throw a fastball because nobody on that ball club could throw any harder than I could. But, I did watch Tommy Bridges to learn how to throw a curveball; I think he had the greatest curveball I've ever seen."

Although small and frail-looking, Bridges had long, slender fingers that enabled him to master his signature pitch, which he used to set up his fastball. Still, Bridges refused to credit one pitch more than the other when it came to his success, stating, "A curve isn't worth a hoot unless they respect your fastball." Meanwhile, Cochrane maintained that Bridges won more games with his fastball than with his curve.

Even though the 1934–1936 campaigns proved to be the finest of Bridges's career, he remained an extremely effective pitcher for the Tigers until he entered the Army in 1943. After finishing a combined 28–21 in 1937 and 1938, Bridges had one of his finest seasons in 1939, posting a record of 17–7, for a career-best .708 winning percentage, while ranking among the league leaders with a 3.50 ERA and 16 complete games. He also pitched well for Detroit's 1940 pennant-winning club, going 12–9, with a 3.37 ERA. No longer able to assume the heavy workload he shouldered earlier in his career, Bridges started only 22 games in each of the next three seasons, posting a combined record of 30–26 from 1941 to 1943.

Called into the military late in 1943, Bridges missed virtually all of the next two seasons before he returned to the Tigers toward the tail end of the 1945 campaign to participate in their march to the world championship. He subsequently appeared in only 9 games for the Tigers in 1946 before the club elected to release him. Bridges ended his career in Detroit with a record of 194–138, for an excellent .584 winning percentage. He also compiled a 3.57 ERA, amassed 1,674 strikeouts in 2,826 innings of work, threw 200 complete games and 33 shutouts, and posted a career WHIP of 1.368.

After being released by the Tigers, Bridges spent most of the next four years pitching for Portland in the Pacific Coast League, then retired after spending the 1950 season with the San Francisco Seals in that same league. Following his retirement as an active player, Bridges became a combination coach and scout for the Cincinnati Reds in 1951, then later scouted for the Tigers from 1958 to 1960, and for the New York Mets from 1963 to 1968.

Unfortunately, another side of Bridges emerged after he initially returned to the Tigers late in 1945. Raised by his parents to live his life in a God-fearing manner, Bridges developed a reputation among his teammates as a sober, sensitive, and intelligent man during his glory years in Detroit. However, he began drinking sometime after he entered the service, with his problem only worsening after he found himself relegated to pitching in the Pacific Coast League. Bridges subsequently left his wife for another woman in 1950, after which he returned to the Detroit area. Upon his return to the Motor City, Bridges ran into former teammates Eldon Auker and Billy Rogell, who were shocked to see him in such a dissolute state. Nevertheless, Rogell, who had become a city councilman in Detroit, used his influence to line up a job for Bridges, but the latter never showed up for work. After spending the better part of the next 18 years working as a scout for three different major league teams, Bridges died in Nashville, Tennessee, on April 19, 1968. He was 61 years old at the time of his passing.

CAREER HIGHLIGHTS

Best Season

Bridges clearly pitched his best ball for the Tigers from 1934 to 1936, and any one of those three seasons would have made a good choice. I ultimately elected to go with the last of those campaigns due to the slightly greater level of dominance he displayed over the course of that 1936 season. In addition to leading all A.L. hurlers with a career-high 23 wins and 175 strikeouts, Bridges finished second in the league with 26 complete games, 294⅔ innings pitched, and 5 shutouts, establishing in the process career-high marks in each of those categories as well. Although Bridges compiled a slightly lower ERA in 1935 (3.51 to 3.60) and posted a better WHIP in 1934 (1.284 to 1.371), his overall numbers adjusted to the league average were somewhat better in 1936. Bridges also earned his only top-10 finish in the A.L. MVP voting in 1936, coming in ninth in the balloting. All things considered, he had the best season of his career in 1936.

Memorable Moments/Greatest Performances

Bridges nearly achieved baseball immortality on August 5, 1932, when he retired the first 26 Washington Senators he faced before finally surrendering a single to pinch hitter Dave Harris with two men out in the top of the ninth inning. After closing out Detroit's 13–0 victory by inducing the next batter to ground out, Bridges responded to reporters that criticized Washington manager Walter Johnson's decision to send up a pinch hitter for the opposing pitcher by stating, "I would rather earn it (a perfect game) the competitive way than have it handed to me."

Bridges pitched another memorable game against the Senators on May 24, 1933, allowing them just one hit during a 3–1 Tigers win. Joe Kuhel delivered Washington's lone safety, an eighth-inning homer, marking the first time in A.L. history that a pitcher allowed a home run in a one-hitter. Bridges also struck out eight and walked just one during the contest. Exactly four months later, on September 24, Bridges again came tantalizingly close to tossing a no-hitter, allowing just a pair of ninth-inning singles during a 2–1 win over the St. Louis Browns.

Bridges also took center stage on August 11, 1942, when he hooked up with Cleveland's Al Milnar in one of the great pitching duels of all time. Milnar allowed the Tigers no runs and just 2 hits over 15 innings, while Bridges held the Indians scoreless through 14 frames. With Cleveland scheduled to bat in the bottom of the fifteenth, the game ended in a 0–0 tie when umpires suspended play since the rules in place at the time did not permit the contest to be continued under the lights.

However, the most famous moment of Bridges's career took place in the 1935 World Series, when he helped the Tigers clinch their first world championship by defeating the Cubs for the second time in as many starts, going the distance in a 4–3 Detroit victory in Game Six. The pivotal moment of the contest occurred in the top of the ninth inning, when, leading off the frame with the score tied at 3–3, Chicago's Stan Hack tripled against Bridges. The little right-hander subsequently retired the next three batters in order, on a strikeout, a weak grounder back to the mound, and a harmless fly to left field, to prevent the go-ahead run from scoring. The Tigers then closed out the Series in the bottom of the inning when Goose Goslin delivered the winning run with an RBI single. Tigers catcher and manager Mickey Cochrane, who scored the winning run on Goslin's single, praised his pitcher following the contest, proclaiming, "A hundred and fifty pounds of courage. If there ever is a payoff on courage, this little 150-pound pitcher is the greatest World Series hero."

NOTABLE ACHIEVEMENTS

- Won more than 20 games three times, surpassing 15 victories on two other occasions.
- Finished in double digits in wins nine straight times.
- Posted winning percentage in excess of .700 once (.708 in 1939).
- Compiled ERA below 3.00 twice.
- Threw more than 200 innings six times.
- Completed more than 20 games three times.
- Led A.L. pitchers in wins once; strikeouts twice; and shutouts once.
- Led A.L. pitchers in putouts once and fielding percentage once.
- Ranks among Tigers career leaders in wins (6th); strikeouts (5th); shutouts (3rd); complete games (5th); innings pitched (6th); games started (6th); and pitching appearances (10th).
- Six-time A.L. All-Star.
- Four-time A.L. champion (1934, 1935, 1940, 1945).
- Two-time world champion (1935, 1945).

Hooks Dauss

Courtesy of the Library of Congress, Harris & Ewing Collection

The vast majority of Tiger fans from recent generations likely have never even heard of Hooks Dauss. At the very least, they are far more famil- iar with the names of the other hurlers that preceded him on this list. Dauss, who pitched for mostly mediocre Tiger teams from 1912 to 1926, never posted three victories in one World Series, as did Mickey Lolich. In fact, he never even had an opportunity to pitch in the Fall Classic. Nor did Dauss capture A.L. MVP honors, as did Hal Newhouser (twice) and Justin

Verlander. Nevertheless, Dauss, who often found himself being overshadowed by Detroit's star-studded outfield during his career, won more games than any other pitcher in Tigers history, compiling a total of 223 victories in his 15 years with the club. A three-time 20-game winner, Dauss also posted 19 victories on two other occasions, despite pitching for teams that seriously contended for the A.L. pennant just three times. Gradually emerging as the workhorse of Detroit's pitching staff during the latter stages of the dead-ball era, Dauss also threw more than 300 innings three times and tossed more than 20 complete games on seven occasions, en route to earning a second-place ranking in franchise history in each of those categories. Yet, in spite of his many accomplishments, Dauss remained a modest man following his playing days, often telling other retired ballplayers in the St. Louis area that he never considered himself to be a great pitcher, and that he never pitched in any memorable games.

Born in Indianapolis, Indiana, on September 22, 1889, George August Dauss attended the local elementary school with his two brothers, before spending a year studying at the Manual Training High School in Indianapolis. While in high school, Dauss developed a reputation as a talented right-handed pitcher with an outstanding curve ball. Subsequently nicknamed "Hooks" or "Hookie" for the sharp break on his signature pitch, Dauss began his professional career at the age of 19, when he joined the South Bend team in the Central League. Released shortly thereafter by South Bend's manager, who considered the 5'10", 168-pound right-hander to be too small to succeed at the professional level, Dauss signed on with the Northern League's Duluth club, with whom he spent the 1909 and 1910 campaigns. After two years at Duluth and another at Winona in the same league, Dauss joined St. Paul, a member of the Pittsburgh Pirates' farm system. While pitching at St. Paul, Dauss drew the attention of Tigers scout "Deacon" Jim McGuire, who purchased his rights in late August of 1912. Dauss made his major league debut with the Tigers one month later, posting a 6–2 win over Cleveland on September 28, just six days after celebrating his 23rd birthday.

Inserted into Detroit's starting rotation by manager Hughie Jennings at the start of the ensuing campaign, Dauss finished 13–12, with a 2.48 ERA, 22 complete games, and 225 innings pitched, marking the first of 11 consecutive times he tossed more than 200 frames. After being courted by the rival Federal League during the subsequent offseason, Dauss elected to stay in Detroit, rewarding team management for re-signing him by compiling an ERA of 2.86 and placing among the league leaders with 19 wins, 22 complete games, and 302 innings pitched.

Pitching for a Tigers team that finished a close second to Boston in the A.L. pennant race in 1915 with a record of 100–54, Dauss teamed up with Harry Coveleski and Jean Dubuc to give the club a formidable three-some at the top of its rotation. With the trio combining for 63 victories, Dauss compiled the most impressive numbers of his career, concluding the campaign with a record of 24–13, an ERA of 2.50, 27 complete games, and 310 innings pitched. Although neither he nor the Tigers ever quite made it back to that same level in his 11 remaining years in Detroit, Dauss remained an extremely reliable and durable pitcher, averaging 15 wins during that time, while consistently tossing close to 20 complete games and 250 innings. He performed particularly well in 1916, 1917, 1919, and 1923. In the first of those campaigns, Dauss posted 19 wins and an ERA of 3.21. Despite finishing just 17–14 the following season, Dauss compiled a career-best 2.43 ERA. He finished 21–9 in 1919, with 22 complete games and 256 innings pitched. He also won 21 games in 1923, while tossing a career-high 316 innings.

In addition to establishing himself as one of the American League's most durable pitchers during his time in Detroit, Dauss developed a rep-utation for being one of the circuit's top fielders at his position. Dauss led all A.L. hurlers in assists three times, en route to amassing a career total of 1,128 assists that places him 14th on the all-time list. His career range factor and fielding percentage also far exceed the figures compiled by the average pitcher of his era.

Although Dauss remained an effective pitcher for the Tigers until he retired at the conclusion of the 1926 campaign, he eventually developed a sore arm after being overused by manager Ty Cobb. Having little faith in the other members of his beleaguered pitching staff, Cobb constantly turned to Dauss, who made a total of 50 appearances in 1923 (39 as a starter, and 11 more as a reliever). Fulfilling both roles in each of the next two seasons as well finally took its toll on Dauss, who developed a sore arm in the spring of 1926. Yet, he still managed to post a record of 12–6 and finish second in the league with 9 saves, before announcing his retirement at season's end after being diagnosed with an irregular heartbeat. He concluded his career with a record of 223–182, for a winning percentage of .551. Dauss also compiled an ERA of 3.30, struck out 1,201 batters, threw 3,391 innings, tossed 245 complete games and 22 shutouts, amassed 41 saves, and posted a career WHIP of 1.320. He continues to rank among the Tigers' all-time leaders in most statistical categories for pitchers.

Following his playing career, Dauss retired to his 320-acre farm near his wife's hometown of St. Louis. However, severely limited by his physical malady in terms of how much manual labor he had the ability to perform, Dauss eventually took a job at Pinkerton's National Detective Agency in St. Louis. As Dauss grew older, his heart condition gradually worsened, causing him to die on July 27, 1963, at the age of 73, from a ruptured aorta. More than half a century after his passing, Dauss remains one of the best players ever to perform for the Tigers that few people know anything about.

CAREER HIGHLIGHTS

Best Season

Dauss pitched extremely well for the Tigers in 1923, concluding the campaign with a record of 21–13 and an ERA of 3.62—a respectable mark for the "live-ball era" that began three seasons earlier. He also ranked among the league leaders with 22 complete games, 316 innings pitched, 4 shutouts, 5 saves, and 50 appearances. But Dauss had the finest season of his career in 1915, when he compiled an ERA of 2.50, finished second among A.L. hurlers with 24 victories, and also placed near the top of the league rankings with 27 complete games, 310 innings pitched, and 132 strikeouts. In addition to establishing career highs in wins and complete games, he threw the second most innings and compiled the third lowest ERA and WHIP (1.214) of his 15-year career.

Memorable Moments/Greatest Performances

Dauss made his wedding day a memorable one, following a morning double-ring ceremony with a 7–1 victory over the Browns on the afternoon of May 29, 1915.

Although Dauss developed a reputation as a weak hitter over the course of his career, he gave the Tigers a 4–3 win over Washington on June 4, 1916, by delivering a walk-off triple in the bottom of the ninth inning. Dauss's game-winning hit came against a young pitcher named Sam Rice, who eventually gained induction into the Hall of Fame as an outfielder. Disheartened by the fact that he lost the game to "probably the worst hitting pitcher in baseball," Rice decided to give up pitching altogether.

Dauss pitched one of his best games on June 18, 1917, shutting out the Senators 1–0 on just 3 hits. Washington advanced only one man as far as second base the entire contest.

After working 8 innings just two days earlier, Dauss turned in a heroic effort on August 4, 1918, enabling the Tigers to earn a split of their doubleheader with the Senators by throwing 10 scoreless innings of relief in Detroit's 7–6, 18-inning victory in Game Two. Dauss worked the final 10 frames, allowing Washington just 5 hits and 3 walks, while striking out 6.

NOTABLE ACHIEVEMENTS

- Won more than 20 games three times, surpassing 16 victories on four other occasions.
- Posted winning percentage in excess of .700 once (.700 in 1919).
- Compiled ERA below 3.00 five times, posting mark below 2.50 twice.
- Threw more than 200 innings 12 times, tossing more than 300 frames on three occasions.
- Completed more than 20 games seven times.
- Finished second among A.L. pitchers in wins twice.
- Led A.L. pitchers in assists three times.
- Holds Tigers career record for most wins (223).
- Ranks among Tigers career leaders in strikeouts (8th); shutouts (9th); complete games (2nd); innings pitched (2nd); games started (4th); and pitching appearances (2nd).

24

Harvey Kuenn

Courtesy of LegendaryAuctions.com

An outstanding line-drive hitter who regularly placed near the top of the league rankings in batting average, hits, and doubles during his time with the Tigers, Harvey Kuenn spent seven full seasons in Detroit, posting a batting average well in excess of .300 in all but one of those years. In addition to leading the American League with a career-high .353 batting average in 1959, the right-handed-hitting Kuenn topped the junior circuit in hits four times and doubles three times. A member of the A.L. All-Star team in each of his seven full years with the Tigers, Kuenn also earned three top-10 finishes in the league MVP balloting, after placing 15th in the voting in his maiden season of 1953, when he also won Rookie of the Year honors. Yet, Kuenn is perhaps remembered most by Tiger fans for his inclusion in one of the most unusual trades in baseball history—one that saw Detroit deal the league's leading hitter the previous season for the circuit's defending home run champion.

Born in the Milwaukee suburb of West Allis, Wisconsin, on December 4, 1930, Harvey Edward Kuenn lived a baseball-obsessed childhood while growing up on Milwaukee's south side. Trained by his father, a talented third baseman on some of the area's top semipro teams, young Harvey developed a passion for the game at an early age, hoping to one day play in the major leagues. After graduating from Milwaukee Lutheran High School, where he starred in baseball, football, and basketball, Kuenn briefly attended Luther College in Decorah, Iowa, before he elected to accept a scholarship offer from the University of Wisconsin to play baseball for the Badgers. Kuenn established himself as one of the nation's top prospects at Wisconsin, becoming the first Badger in the school's history to earn first-team All-America honors by posting a batting average of .436 as a junior. Subsequently offered $55,000 to sign with the Tigers, Kuenn decided to forgo his final year of collegiate eligibility, inking a deal with Detroit on June 9, 1952.

After being assigned to Class B Davenport in the old Three-I League, the 21-year-old Kuenn made an immediate impression on Detroit's front office by posting a batting average of .340 in his first 63 minor league games. Called up by the Tigers on September 6, Kuenn spent the final month of the 1952 campaign being mentored by veteran shortstop Johnny Pesky, who helped the youngster adjust to life in the majors. Starting 19 games at shortstop for the Tigers, Kuenn collected 26 hits in 80 official at-bats, en route to compiling a .325 batting average in his first big-league season.

Named Detroit's starting shortstop and leadoff hitter prior to the start of the ensuing campaign, Kuenn performed brilliantly, posting a batting average of .308, scoring 94 runs, and leading the league with 209 hits, 731 plate appearances, and 679 at-bats. Kuenn's outstanding play earned him A.L. Rookie of the Year honors and the first of eight consecutive selections to the All-Star team. Kuenn displayed remarkable consistency in each of the next two seasons, as he continued to establish himself as one of the junior circuit's top batsmen. As a sophomore in 1954, he batted .306, scored 81 runs, again led the league in at-bats (656) and hits

(201), and amazingly struck out only 13 times. Kuenn followed that up by hitting .306 again in 1955, finishing third in the league with 190 hits, and establishing new career highs with 8 home runs, 62 RBIs, 101 runs scored, and a league-leading 38 doubles.

Although Kuenn lacked home run power, he possessed an exceptional line-drive stroke that enabled him to hit just about any pitch to any part of the field that he wanted. He also rarely struck out, as can be evidenced by his total of just 404 whiffs in more than 7,600 career plate appearances. And, even though the 6'2", 190-pound Kuenn never hit more than 12 home runs in any season, many people felt he had the ability to reach the seats more than he did. However, he once said that he did not like to hit home runs because they tended to throw off his rhythm at the plate. Kuenn also did a creditable job in the field, even though he lacked outstanding foot speed, annually placing among the league's leading shortstops in assists, putouts, and fielding percentage. In fact, after leading all players at his position in putouts as a rookie, he topped the circuit in both putouts and assists the following year.

Kuenn had one of his finest seasons in 1956, when he placed among the league leaders with a .332 batting average, 96 runs scored, 7 triples, and 32 doubles, topped the circuit with 196 hits, and established career highs with 12 home runs and 88 runs batted in, while also leading all A.L. shortstops in fielding percentage for the only time. His exceptional all-around play earned him a fourth-place finish in the league MVP voting. However, Kuenn saw his offensive numbers plummet the following year—a season in which he batted just .277, knocked in only 44 runs, and scored just 74 times. Furthermore, Kuenn, who never possessed great quickness to begin with, displayed less range in the field than ever before as his frame grew increasingly large.

After initially toying with the idea of moving Kuenn to third base, the Tigers finally decided to shift him to centerfield prior to the start of the 1958 campaign. Kuenn responded well to his change in positions, leading all A.L. outfielders with 358 putouts, while rebounding at the plate by finishing third in the league with a .319 batting average and topping the circuit with 39 doubles. Kuenn again switched positions in 1959, this time trading places with Al Kaline, who moved to center field, while Kuenn took over for him in right. Once again displaying his versatility, Kuenn did a solid job at his new post, leading all A.L. right fielders with a .990 fielding percentage. It was at the bat, though, that he truly excelled, finishing the year with 9 home runs, 71 RBIs, 99 runs scored, and a league-leading .353

batting average, 198 hits, and 42 doubles, en route to earning an eighth-place finish in the A.L. MVP balloting.

Ironically, the 1959 campaign turned out to be Kuenn's last in Detroit. In a trade often referred to by Cleveland fans as "the curse of Rocky Colavito," the Tigers dealt Kuenn to the Indians just two days before the opening of the 1960 season for Colavito, who had topped the junior circuit with 42 home runs the previous year. The trade marked the only time in baseball history that a defending league batting champion was dealt for a defending home run champion. Kuenn left Detroit with career totals of 53 home runs, 423 RBIs, 620 runs scored, 1,372 hits, 43 triples, and 244 doubles, a batting average of .314, a .360 on-base percentage, and a .426 slugging percentage.

Jeered by Cleveland fans, who blamed him for the popular Colavito's departure, Kuenn nevertheless posted a batting average of .308 for the Indians in 1960, even though he missed nearly a month of the campaign with a pulled muscle. Traded to the Giants for veteran pitcher Johnny Antonelli and promising young outfielder Willie Kirkland at season's end, Kuenn spent the next four years in San Francisco. Although he never regained his earlier form, he compiled decent numbers for the Giants, having his best year for them in 1962, when he batted .304, knocked in 68 runs, and scored 73 times. The Giants traded Kuenn to the Chicago Cubs early in 1965, after which the veteran outfielder split his final two seasons between the Cubs and Phillies, before announcing his retirement at the conclusion of the 1966 campaign. Kuenn ended his playing career with 87 home runs, 671 runs batted in, 951 runs scored, 2,092 hits, 56 triples, 356 doubles, a .303 batting average, a .357 on-base percentage, and a .408 slugging percentage.

Following his retirement, Kuenn briefly worked at a Milwaukee television station, before accepting a job as a sales representative with a local printing company. However, he returned to baseball in 1971 when the Milwaukee Brewers named him their new batting coach. Kuenn remained in that position for the next 12 years, mentoring during that time some of the game's best young hitters, including future Hall of Famers Robin Yount and Paul Molitor.

Kuenn also overcame a series of life-threatening illnesses while serving as Brewers batting coach, undergoing open-heart surgery in 1976 and stomach surgery in 1977, before having his right leg amputated below the knee in 1980. Through all his trials and tribulations, though, Kuenn remained loyal to the Brewers, who rewarded him on June 2, 1982 by naming him their new manager. Kuenn subsequently piloted a team that began the season just 23–24 to an overall record of 95–67, earning in the process A.L. Manager of the Year honors. The hard-hitting Brewers, who subsequently became known as "Harvey's Wall-Bangers," eventually came within one game of winning the World Series.

Relieved of his managerial duties after the Brewers finished just 87–75 the following year, Kuenn accepted an offer to remain with the organization as a scout and minor league hitting instructor. He continued to fulfill that role until the poor circulation that plagued him for much of the previous 12 years caused him to suffer a heart attack that took his life on February 28, 1988. Kuenn was only 57 years of age at the time of his passing.

TIGERS CAREER HIGHLIGHTS

Best Season

It could be argued that Kuenn had his best season for the Tigers in 1956, when, in addition to finishing third in the league with a .332 batting average, he scored 96 runs, topped the circuit with 196 hits, and established career highs with 12 home runs and 88 RBIs, en route to earning a fourth-place finish in the A.L. MVP voting. Kuenn's 85 RBIs from the leadoff position in Detroit's batting order remained a major league record until Boston's Nomar Garciaparra knocked in 98 runs out of the leadoff spot in 1997.

Nevertheless, it would be difficult to go against Kuenn's exceptional 1959 campaign. Although he hit fewer home runs (9) and drove in fewer runs (71) than he did three years earlier, Kuenn compiled better numbers in virtually every other statistical category, finishing the season with 99 runs scored, a career-high .402 on-base percentage, .501 slugging percentage, and .903 OPS, and a league-leading 198 hits, 42 doubles, and .353 batting average. Kuenn's 42 doubles and .353 batting average also represented career-high marks, clearly making the 1959 season the finest of his career.

Memorable Moments/Greatest Performances

Kuenn experienced one of his most memorable moments as a member of the Tigers on July 5, 1954, when his walk-off homer in the bottom of the eleventh inning gave the Tigers a 1–0 victory in Game Two of their doubleheader split with Cleveland.

Kuenn also had a number of big days at the plate for the Tigers, with one of those coming on April 30, 1955, when he led Detroit to an 11–7 win over Washington by going 5-for-5, with 3 runs scored. He had another huge game against the Senators on July 23, 1959, leading his team to an 11–2 romp by going 4-for-4, with 3 RBIs, 4 runs scored, and 2 stolen bases.

NOTABLE ACHIEVEMENTS

- Batted over .300 seven times, surpassing .330 twice and hitting over .350 once (.353 in 1959).
- Scored more than 100 runs once (101 in 1955).
- Surpassed 200 hits twice.
- Topped 30 doubles six times, accumulating more than 40 two-baggers once (42 in 1959).
- Compiled on-base percentage in excess of .400 once (.402 in 1959).
- Posted slugging percentage in excess of .500 once (.501 in 1959).
- Led the American League in batting average once; hits four times; and doubles three times.
- Led A.L. shortstops in assists once; putouts twice; and fielding percentage once.
- Led A.L. outfielders in putouts once.
- Led A.L. right-fielders in fielding percentage once.
- Holds Tigers single-season record for most at-bats (679 in 1953).
- 1953 A.L. Rookie of the Year.
- Finished fourth in 1956 A.L. MVP voting.
- 1956 *Sporting News* All-Star selection.
- Seven-time A.L. All-Star.

25

Denny McLain

Courtesy of Denny McClain

After winning his second consecutive A.L. Cy Young Award at only 25 years of age in 1969, Denny McLain seemed destined for Cooperstown. In addition to capturing Cy Young honors twice in just five full seasons and parts of two others with the Tigers, the hard-throwing right-hander had already posted 114 victories, earned three All-Star nominations, and been named A.L. MVP once, accomplishing the last feat in 1968, when he became the first pitcher in 34 years to reach the 30-win plateau.

It appeared as if nothing could stand in the way of McLain, who lived by his own set of rules, showing up late for games, coming and going as he pleased in his own airplane, and criticizing teammates, management, Tiger fans, and the city of Detroit whenever he felt so inclined. Bill Freehan, McLain's primary catcher with the Tigers, once wrote, "The rules for Denny just don't seem to be the same as for the rest of us." McLain expressed his feelings on the matter by saying, "When you can do it out there between the white lines, you can live any way you want."

McLain did indeed excel between the white lines from 1965 to 1969, averaging nearly 22 wins and just over 200 strikeouts over the course of those five seasons, en route to establishing himself as one of the game's most prominent figures. However, the success he experienced on the mound convinced the brash and cocky McLain that he needed to answer to no one, making him a walking time bomb. Revealing the reckless attitude with which he went through life, McLain likened himself to his idol Frank Sinatra, whom he admired as much for his brazen behavior as for his legendary singing voice, stating on one occasion, "Sinatra doesn't give a damn about anything, and neither do I."

Unfortunately, McLain's irresponsible behavior ended up sabotaging his career, bringing his period of dominance to an early end, and forcing him into premature retirement. McLain's association with organized crime and subsequent conviction on charges of embezzlement led to a life in which he spent a significant amount of time in prison, leaving us all to wonder what might have been had he followed a different path.

Born in Markham, Illinois, on March 29, 1944, Dennis Dale McLain suffered through a difficult childhood, frequently incurring the wrath of his chain-smoking, beer-guzzling father, and failing to receive sufficient nurturing from a mother he later depicted as a cold and heartless woman. Displaying an aversion for authority at an early age due to his unhappy upbringing, McLain developed a reputation as an indifferent student while attending Catholic schools, with one teacher later recalling, "He had a lot of trouble keeping his mouth shut." Following his graduation from Chicago's Mount Carmel High School, where he starred in baseball as a pitcher and shortstop, McLain signed with the Chicago White Sox as an amateur free agent in 1962. The 18-year-old right-hander subsequently spent just one year in Chicago's farm system before the Tigers claimed him off waivers when the White Sox left him unprotected in a special draft of minor league players. McLain advanced rapidly through Detroit's farm system after becoming a member of the organization in April 1963, earning his first call-up to the big leagues shortly before the conclusion of the regular season. Making the

first three starts of his career over the final two weeks of the campaign, Mc-
Lain won 2 of his 3 decisions, compiled an ERA of 4.29, tossed 2 complete
games, and struck out 22 batters in 21 innings of work. After spending the
first two months of the ensuing campaign at Syracuse in the International
League, McLain rejoined the Tigers in early June, after which he proceeded
to go 4–5 the rest of the year, with a 4.05 ERA in 100 innings of work.

McLain emerged as Detroit's top pitcher in 1965, finishing his first full
season with a record of 16–6, and placing among the league leaders with a
2.61 ERA, 4 shutouts, and 192 strikeouts. Although his ERA rose to 3.92
the following year, McLain earned the first of his three All-Star selections by
going 20–14, with 192 strikeouts, 264⅔ innings pitched, and 14 complete
games. The 1967 campaign proved to be something of a struggle for Mc-
Lain, who went 17–16 with a 3.79 ERA for a Tigers team that finished just
one game behind Boston in the A.L. pennant race. Particularly ineffective
during the month of September, McLain went winless after August 29, attributing his lack of success to a pair of severely injured toes on his left foot.
While McLain claimed he sustained the injury during a household mishap,
several of his teammates doubted his words, with one going so far as to say,
"A lot of guys think he did it kicking a water cooler when he was knocked
out of the game the day before. He can still be damn irresponsible." Some
three years later, in an article that appeared in the February 1970 edition of
Sports Illustrated, the magazine cited sources who alleged that an organized
crime figure had injured McLain's foot by stomping on it as a means of
exacting revenge on him for failing to pay off on a bet.

After irritating his teammates with his poor performance during the
final month of the 1967 campaign, McLain drew the ire of Tiger fans in
early May of the following season when he accused them in the local newspapers of being "the biggest front-running fans in the world." Nevertheless,
McLain's extraordinary performance over the course of the regular season
eventually forced the fans of Detroit to overlook his comments. In arguably the greatest season ever turned in by a Tigers hurler, McLain became
the first major league pitcher since Dizzy Dean in 1934 to win 30 games,
finishing the year with a mark of 31–6. He also led the league with 28
complete games and 336 innings pitched, while placing among the leaders
with a 1.96 ERA and 280 strikeouts, en route to earning A.L. MVP and
Cy Young honors. Although McLain faltered somewhat in the World Series,
losing Games One and Four to Cardinals ace Bob Gibson, he redeemed
himself to some degree in Game Six, going the distance in a 13–1 drub-
bing of the National League champions. However, once again displaying
his penchant for speaking his mind without considering the consequences,

McLain drew a considerable amount of criticism during the subsequent offseason for comments he made about teammate Mickey Lolich, who won Series MVP honors by defeating the Cardinals three times. Instead of praising Lolich when asked about his performance in the World Series, McLain created more controversy by saying, "I wouldn't trade one Bob Gibson for 12 Mickey Loliches."

After initially harboring some resentment toward McLain for his ill-advised remark, Tiger fans found it difficult to remain upset with him when he again performed brilliantly in 1969, winning his second straight Cy Young Award (he shared the honor with Baltimore's Mike Cuellar) by going 24–9, with a 2.80 ERA, 181 strikeouts, 23 complete games, and a league-leading 9 shutouts and 325 innings pitched.

One of the most impressive things about the success McLain experienced over the course of his two Cy Young seasons is that he relied essentially on one pitch—a letter-high fastball with movement (an offering that was considered to be a strike during the 1960s). Although he also mixed in a hard slider, changeup, and overhand curve from time to time, McLain depended mostly on the high fastball, which he generally threw in the strike zone, even when ahead in the count. Gladly accepting the inherent challenge of the pitcher-hitter confrontation, McLain conducted himself very much like a gunfighter on the mound, pulling his hat brim down so low that he found it necessary to tilt his head backward to see the signs from his catcher. He worked quickly and rarely tried to deceive the hitter, challenging him with every pitch. If a batter made solid contact with his fastball during one trip to the plate, McLain typically gave him the same pitch in the same location his next time up, as if saying to him, "Here you go. Let's see you hit it again."

Apparently on top of the world heading into the 1970 campaign, McLain unfortunately experienced a swift and dramatic fall from grace. His troubles began when *Sports Illustrated* and *Penthouse* magazines both published articles in February that detailed McLain's involvement in bookmaking activities. After developing a fondness for betting on horses early in his career, McLain allegedly later expanded his gambling interests to a bookmaking operation in which he became a hands-off, silent partner. Although McLain denied many of the accusations that appeared in the story, he admitted to investing in the bookmaking business before eventually withdrawing his support when his partners reneged on him. After learning of the allegations, Baseball Commissioner Bowie Kuhn suspended McLain indefinitely while he investigated the charges made against him. Kuhn announced the results of his findings on April 1, 1970, when he chose to continue McLain's suspension until July1. In making his announcement, Kuhn stated, "While McLain believed he had become a partner in this operation and has so admitted to me, it would appear that he was the victim of a confidence scheme. I would thus conclude that McLain was never a partner and had no proprietary interest in the bookmaking operation." Kuhn also absolved McLain from any charges that suggested his actions impacted in any way the 1967 pennant race.

Subsequently asked by a reporter to explain the difference between McLain attempting to become a bookmaker and actually becoming one, Kuhn responded: "I think you have to consider the difference is the same as between murder and attempted murder."

Although McLain's punishment could have been considerably worse, his inability to earn an income during the first three months of the 1970 season proved to be a substantial hardship to him since his lawyer had absconded with all his funds before fleeing to Japan. With no other source of income, McLain suddenly found himself forced to file for bankruptcy.

Unfortunately, McLain never again experienced much success on the playing field after he returned to the Tigers on July 1. In addition to going just 3–5 with a 4.63 ERA the remainder of the year, the enigmatic right-hander found it difficult to stay out of trouble, suffering a pair of suspensions in September—one for dousing two Detroit writers with buckets of ice water following a contest on August 28, and the other for carrying a gun on a team flight. Furthermore, McLain's waistline continued to expand, as his practice of consuming a case of Pepsi each day finally began to catch up with him.

Eager to rid themselves of what they now considered to be a huge headache, the Tigers included McLain in an eight-player trade they completed with the Washington Senators on October 9, 1970, that netted them shortstop Ed Brinkman, third baseman Aurelio Rodriguez, and pitchers Joe Coleman and Jim Hannan in return. While Rodriguez, Brinkman, and Coleman all made significant contributions to the Tigers over the course of the next few seasons, McLain's career continued to spiral downward. Plagued by philosophical differences with Washington manager Ted Williams and arm problems worsened by numerous cortisone injections he took for his ailing shoulder, McLain suffered through a horrendous 1971 campaign that saw him go just 10–22, with a 4.28 ERA. Traded to Oakland at the end of the year, McLain subsequently split the 1972 season between the A's and Atlanta Braves, appearing in a total of only 20 games, and finishing a combined 4–7 with a 6.37 ERA. After being released by the Braves prior to the start of the 1973 campaign, McLain spent part of the year in the minor leagues before announcing his retirement from baseball at only 29 years of age. He ended his career with a record of 131–91, an ERA of 3.39, 1,282 strikeouts in 1,886 innings of work, 105 complete games, and 29 shutouts. During his time in Detroit, McLain compiled a record of 117–62 and an ERA of 3.13, struck out 1,150 batters in 1,593 innings of work, threw 94 complete games, and tossed 26 shutouts. He continues to rank among the franchise's all-time leaders in shutouts, strikeouts, and winning percentage (.654). Meanwhile, McLain's WHIP of 1.112 remains the best in Tigers history.

Following his retirement, McLain pursued various avenues as a means of earning income, including running a bar, investing in a big-screen television business, opening a line of walk-in medical clinics, and writing a book. However, none of those business ventures proved to be particularly successful, forcing him to once again file for bankruptcy in 1977. McLain subsequently discovered that he had the ability to earn a comfortable living by engaging in such dubious activities as hustling golf, loan sharking, and bookmaking. He even reportedly once accepted $160,000 to fly a wanted felon out of the country.

McLain's illicit lifestyle eventually caught up to him in 1984, when the U.S. Justice Department indicted him on charges of racketeering, extortion, and cocaine trafficking. After initially being sentenced to 23 years in prison, McLain ended up serving only 30 months when an appeals court threw out the verdict on procedural grounds.

McLain spent the next several years getting his life back in order, writing another book, appearing at card shows, working for a minor league hockey team, and hosting his own radio show. However, after his oldest daughter, Kristen, died at the age of 26 on March 20, 1992, in a car accident caused by a drunk driver, McLain lapsed into a deep depression that prompted him to return to his larcenous ways. After purchasing the Peet Packing Company, a struggling 100-year-old meatpacking firm in Chesaning, Michigan, McLain and his partner allegedly stole $3 million from the company's pension fund, causing the business to go bankrupt less than two years later. Convicted on charges of embezzlement, mail fraud, money laundering, and conspiracy, McLain subsequently spent seven more years in prison, before being released in 2003. He has since remained on the straight and narrow, writing a monthly editorial column, releasing his autobiography, *I Told You I Wasn't Perfect*, and blogging regularly for *In Play! Magazine*, a Detroit sports magazine.

In discussing a happier time in McLain's life, good friend and former teammate Jim Northrup recalled in February 2003, "Denny McLain won

31 games in 1968 and came back with 24–9 the next year. That's absolutely amazing. For two years, he was the best pitcher I ever saw. Mickey Lolich had better stuff, but Denny McLain was just a magician on the mound. His mental attitude was superior. Denny was one of a kind. He had a little larceny in him, but that's another story."

TIGERS CAREER HIGHLIGHTS

Best Season

Even though McLain had an exceptional season in 1969 , he clearly pitched his best ball for the Tigers one year earlier. In the "Year of the Pitcher," McLain proved to be the American League's top hurler, establishing career-best marks with a record of 31–6, an ERA of 1.96, 280 strikeouts, a 0.905 WHIP, and a league-leading .838 winning percentage, 41 starts, 28 complete games, and 336 innings pitched.

Memorable Moments/Greatest Performances

McLain made an extremely successful major league debut on September 21, 1963, going the distance and allowing just one earned run during a 4–3 win over the Chicago White Sox, while also hitting the only home run of his career. After coming on in relief in the top of the first inning of a June 15, 1965, game against Boston, McLain set a major league record for relievers by striking out the first 7 batters he faced. He went on to fan 14 batters over 6⅔ innings in a game the Tigers eventually won by a score of 6–5.

McLain turned in two of his finest performances in May 1966, tossing a pair of one-hitters. After allowing just one safety during a 1–0 victory over the White Sox on May 6, McLain surrendered just a two-run, fifth-inning double to A's catcher Phil Roof during a 5–2 Tigers win on May 30.

McLain experienced arguably the most memorable moment of his career on September 14, 1968, when the Tigers scored 2 runs in the bottom of the ninth inning to defeat the Athletics by a score of 5–4, giving the talented right-hander his 30th win of the year.

McLain also achieved a measure of immortality in his very next start, when he allowed his boyhood idol, Mickey Mantle, to surpass Jimmie Foxx on the all-time home run list by grooving a pitch to him right down the middle. With the Tigers comfortably ahead of the Yankees by a score of 6–1 in the top of the eighth inning, McLain called his catcher out to the mound and told him to inform Mantle that he intended to throw him nothing but "batting practice" fastballs. After Mantle skeptically took one offering and fouled off another, he deposited McLain's next pitch deep into the right-field seats, for the 535th homer of his storied career. Then, as Mantle rounded third base, he looked over at McLain, who coyly winked at him. Although a possible rebuke from the league office forced McLain to deny assisting Mantle in any way following the contest, he later admitted to having complicity in the events that took place.

NOTABLE ACHIEVEMENTS

- Won more than 20 games three times, surpassing 30 victories once (31 in 1968).
- Compiled winning percentage in excess of .700 three times, topping .800 once (.838 in 1968).
- Compiled ERA below 3.00 three times, posting mark under 2.00 once (1.96 in 1968).
- Struck out more than 200 batters once (280 in 1968).
- Completed more than 20 games twice.
- Threw more than 200 innings five times, tossing more than 300 frames twice.
- Posted WHIP under 1.000 once (0.905 in 1968).
- Led all A.L. pitchers in wins twice; winning percentage once; innings pitched twice; complete games once; and shutouts once.
- Ranks first all-time among Tigers pitchers with a career WHIP of 1.112.
- Ranks among Tigers career leaders in winning percentage (2nd); shutouts (7th); and strikeouts (10th).
- Holds Tigers single-season records for most wins (31 in 1968) and shutouts (9 in 1969).
- 1968 A.L. MVP.
- Two-time A.L. Cy Young Award winner (1968, 1969).
- 1968 MLB Player of the Year.
- Two-time *Sporting News* A.L. Pitcher of the Year (1968, 1969).
- Two-time *Sporting News* All-Star selection (1968, 1969).
- Three-time A.L. All-Star (1966, 1968, 1969).
- 1968 A.L. champion.
- 1968 world champion.

Kirk Gibson

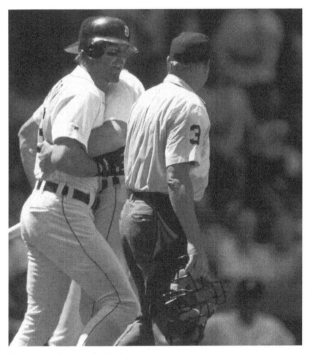

Courtesy of MearsOnlineAuctions.com

B lessed with exceptional running speed and tremendous power at the plate, Kirk Gibson found himself being referred to as "the next Mickey Mantle" by Tigers manager Sparky Anderson shortly after both men arrived in Detroit in 1980. Although the 6'3", 220-pound Gibson never lived up to the hype created by Anderson, he had several outstanding seasons for the Tigers, becoming in 1984 the first player in franchise history to surpass 20 home runs and 20 stolen bases in the same year—a feat he accomplished in each of the next three seasons as well. An extremely passionate and demonstrative player, Gibson shared a love–hate relationship with the fans of Detroit, who admired him for his fiery temperament, physical gifts, and ability to perform well under pressure, but also resented him at times for his arrogance, self-absorbed nature, and gruff demeanor. By the time Gibson left Detroit at the conclusion of the 1987 campaign, though, he had established himself as one of the team's most popular players, so much so that Tiger fans selected him in 1999 to the team's all-time outfield, along with legendary Hall of Famers Ty Cobb and Al Kaline.

Born in Pontiac, Michigan, on May 28, 1957, Kirk Harold Gibson attended Kettering High School in nearby Waterford, where he starred in baseball, football, basketball, and track. After accepting a football scholarship from Michigan State University following his graduation, Gibson spent the next three years concentrating solely on football, before taking up baseball as a senior in order to give him more leverage in the NFL draft. Excelling in both sports in his final year at MSU, Gibson earned All-American honors as a flanker in football, and as an outfielder in baseball, establishing school records for most home runs and RBIs in his one season of college ball. Subsequently selected by the Tigers in the first round of the 1978 amateur draft with the 12th overall pick, and by the St. Louis Cardinals in the seventh round of the 1979 NFL Draft, Gibson elected to pursue a career in baseball due to the greater longevity it offered him as a professional athlete.

Gibson spent the next season and a half in the minor leagues, before earning his first big-league call-up in September 1979. Appearing in 12 games with the Tigers over the final three weeks of the campaign, the 22-year-old outfielder batted .237 in 38 official trips to the plate, knocked in 4 runs, and hit his first major league homer. Gibson earned a spot on the Tigers' roster in spring training the following year, putting on display for all to see his rare combination of speed and power. Making a particularly strong impression on new Detroit manager Sparky Anderson, who, in his typically impetuous manner, dubbed him "the next Mickey Mantle," Gibson found himself starting in the Tigers' outfield before long. However, after injuring his wrist while batting against Milwaukee on June 16, Gibson saw his rookie campaign come to a premature end, finishing the season with 9 home runs, 16 RBIs, and a .263 batting average, in 185 official at-bats. He subsequently underwent surgery in August that required the insertion of a steel plate in his arm to correct an abnormal bone development.

Gibson regained his starting job in the outfield when he returned to the Tigers in 1981, seeing a significant amount of playing time in both right field and center. But, even though he performed well when healthy, Gibson continued to be plagued by injuries in each of the next two seasons. After batting .328, hitting 9 home runs, knocking in 40 runs, and stealing 17 bases in 83 games in 1981, Gibson batted .278, hit 8 home runs, and drove in 35 runs the following year, when wrist, knee, and calf problems limited him to only 69 games.

Although Gibson remained relatively healthy in 1983, he experienced the most difficult campaign of his career. Criticized in the local newspapers by Sparky Anderson for conducting himself in an unprofessional manner both on and off the field, Gibson found himself demoted to the role of part-time designated hitter early in the year, angering him to such an extent that he closed the door to his manager's office one day and proceeded to vent his frustration. Following Gibson's rant, Anderson asked him if he was done and told him to "open the door and get your ass outta here."

Gibson also began to incur the wrath of Tiger fans for the rudeness he often displayed toward them that reflected his narcissistic nature. Hardly a favorite of the local media either for the condescending manner with which he treated them, Gibson received a considerable amount of negative press, with one writer describing him as "hostile and menacing." Looking back years later at the difficulties he experienced at that particular point in his career, a more mature Gibson said, "I lost my focus. I wasn't a good player. I had poor work habits." Booed mercilessly by the fans at Tiger Stadium throughout the 1983 season, Gibson ended up hitting 15 home runs, driving in 51 runs, and batting just .227, in 128 games and 401 official at-bats.

Despondent over his poor performance and the harsh treatment he received the previous year, Gibson approached the 1984 season with a new attitude after seeing a therapist at the Pacific Institute during the offseason. Having employed a strenuous workout regimen before arriving at spring training, Gibson entered the 1984 campaign in the best shape of his young career. The 26-year-old outfielder also worked tirelessly for the first time on improving his outfield defense, putting in countless hours with Al Kaline, who the Tigers brought in to work with him.

Gibson's dedication and newfound attitude ended up paying huge dividends, as, playing right field full-time for the first time in his career, he helped lead the Tigers to the pennant by hitting 27 home runs, knocking in 91 runs, scoring 92 times, stealing 29 bases, batting .282, and placing among the league leaders with a .516 slugging percentage and an OPS of .879, en route to earning a sixth-place finish in the MVP balloting. In addition to becoming the first player in franchise history to surpass 20 homers and 20 steals in the same season, Gibson's 10 triples and 23 doubles made him the first Tiger to finish in double digits in all four categories since

Charlie Gehringer accomplished the feat in 1930. Gibson subsequently came up big for the Tigers in the postseason, earning ALCS MVP honors by hitting a homer, driving in 2 runs, and batting .417 during Detroit's three-game sweep of Kansas City, before homering twice, knocking in 7 runs, and batting .333 against San Diego in the World Series.

Sparky Anderson, who later apologized for putting too much pressure on Gibson early in his career by comparing him to Mickey Mantle, acknowledged the amazing transformation the young outfielder underwent by stating, "I've never seen a player change his direction so completely. His personality, his drive, his dedication are unsurpassed. He knew how to make things happen. Gibby gets the highest rating as a player from me."

Gibson continued to excel for the Tigers in each of the next three seasons, averaging 27 home runs, 87 RBIs, 92 runs scored, and 30 stolen bases from 1985 to 1987, despite missing a significant amount of playing time in both 1986 and 1987. After batting .287, scoring 96 runs, and reaching career-high marks with 29 homers and 97 RBIs in 1985, he batted .268, homered 28 times, knocked in 86 runs, and stole a career-best 34 bases the following year, even though a severely twisted ankle forced him to sit out 33 games. Gibson subsequently began the 1987 campaign on the disabled list with a torn rib muscle, before returning to the Tigers in early May to hit 24 home runs, drive in 79 runs, score 95 times, steal 26 bases, and bat .277.

After becoming a free agent at the end of 1987, Gibson signed a three-year, $4.5 million deal with the Dodgers, prompting new Tigers owner Tom Monaghan to call him "a disgrace to the Tiger uniform with his half-beard, half-stubble." Monaghan added that he believed the Tigers would be better off without him.

Having been sufficiently reproached by his former ball club's owner, Gibson set about establishing his presence with his new team, doing so in spring training by admonishing his teammates for playing a childish prank on him. Demanding that his Dodger mates display a greater level of professionalism since he joined them with the intent of winning a championship, Gibson soon became the emotional and spiritual leader of a club that surprised everyone by capturing the N.L. pennant. He also performed well on the field, earning league MVP honors by hitting 25 homers, driving in 76 runs, scoring 106 times, stealing 31 bases, and batting .290. A hobbling Gibson subsequently gave the Dodgers all the momentum they needed to defeat heavily favored Oakland in the World Series by hitting one of the most memorable home runs in the history of the Fall Classic—a 2-out, 2-run blast in the bottom of the ninth inning of Game One against A's closer Dennis Eckersley that turned an apparent 4–3 loss into a 5–4 victory.

Unfortunately, Gibson accomplished little else in his other two seasons in Los Angeles, with the torn hamstring that kept him out of virtually the entire 1988 World Series eventually requiring surgery to repair. After appearing in a total of only 160 games for the Dodgers in 1989 and 1990, Gibson signed with the Kansas City Royals when he once again became a free agent. He spent one year in Kansas City, hitting 16 homers, driving in 55 runs, and batting just .236, before being dealt to the Pirates prior to the start of the 1992 campaign. Gibson struggled terribly in Pittsburgh, compiling a batting average of just .196 in his 16 games with the Pirates, before the club elected to release him on May 5. After spending the remainder of 1992 enjoying time with his family in Michigan, Gibson chose to return to the Tigers as a free agent the following year, inking a deal with new owner Mike Ilitch. Gibson spent the remainder of his career back in Detroit, posting solid numbers in 1993 and 1994, before assuming a part-time role with the club in 1995. Having lost much of the fire that burned inside him earlier in his playing days, the 38-year-old Gibson decided to call it quits at the conclusion of the 1995 campaign, ending his career with 255 home runs, 870 RBIs, 985 runs scored, 1,553 hits, 54 triples, 260 doubles, 284 stolen bases, a .268 batting average, a .352 on-base percentage, and a .463 slugging percentage. Over parts of 12 seasons in Detroit, Gibson hit 195 homers, knocked in 668 runs, scored 698 times, amassed 1,140 hits, 45 triples, 187 doubles, and 194 stolen bases, batted .273, compiled a .354 on-base percentage, and posted a .480 slugging percentage.

Following his retirement as a player, Gibson spent five seasons as a television analyst in Detroit, before becoming a coach for the Tigers in 2003. He subsequently joined the Arizona Diamondbacks, for whom he served as bench coach until mid-2010, when the team promoted him to manager. Gibson piloted the Diamondbacks for the next 4½ seasons, earning N.L. Manager of the Year honors in 2011, when he led them to the N.L. West title. However, after Arizona finished a major league worst 64–98 in 2014, team ownership decided to relieve Gibson of his duties.

Kirk Gibson never quite lived up to his enormous potential as a player. In spite of his prodigious power at the plate, he never hit more than 29 home runs in a season. Despite his tremendous running speed, he also never developed into anything more than a marginal defensive outfielder with a weak throwing arm. Nevertheless, Gibson brought certain intangible qualities to the teams for which he played, inspiring his teammates with his intensity and aggressive style of play. Longtime Toronto Blue Jays manager Cito Gaston stated in *Out by a Step: The 100 Best Players Not in the Baseball Hall of Fame*, "Kirk Gibson was quite a player. I don't think people really knew how hard he played, and how intense he was playing. And his speed—he had great running speed; he could beat you with a home run, beat you with his speed."

TIGERS CAREER HIGHLIGHTS

Best Season

Gibson had his first big year for the Tigers in 1984, when he earned his only top-10 finish in the A.L. MVP voting by hitting 27 home runs, driving in 91 runs, scoring 92 times, stealing 29 bases, batting .282, and compiling an OPS of .879. However, he had his finest all-around season one year later, concluding the 1985 campaign with a career-high 29 homers, 97 RBIs, 167 hits, 37 doubles, and 301 total bases, while also scoring 96 times, stealing 30 bases, batting .287, and posting an OPS of .882.

Memorable Moments/Greatest Performances

Gibson's great power enabled him to hit several tape measure home runs, with the longest of those coming during a 6–2 loss to Boston on June 14, 1983. Connecting against Red Sox right-hander Mike Brown, Gibson drove a ball an estimated 523 feet over the right-field roof at Tiger Stadium.

Gibson hit a pair of game-winning homers during the 1984 championship campaign, giving the Tigers a 2–1 victory over the A's on May 30 by connecting against Oakland starter Steve McCatty for a solo shot in the top of the ninth inning. Almost exactly one month later, on June 29, Gibson hit a 2-run homer in the bottom of the ninth inning that gave the Tigers a 7–5 win in the second game of their doubleheader split with the Twins. He hit another 2-run blast earlier in the contest, giving him 2 homers and 4 RBIs on the day. Gibson, though, had his biggest day of the year on June 10, when he led the Tigers to a doubleheader sweep of the Orioles by collecting 6 hits and 6 RBIs.

Gibson began the 1986 season in style, leading the Tigers to a 6–5 win over the Red Sox on Opening Day by going 4-for-4, with a pair of homers, 5 RBIs, 2 runs scored, and a stolen base. Later in the year, he set a major league record by driving in the winning run in five consecutive games.

However, Gibson unquestionably experienced his most memorable moment as a member of the Tigers in the final game of the 1984 World Series, when he cemented Detroit's five-game victory over San Diego by driving a Rich Gossage offering into the upper right-field deck at Tiger Stadium for a three-run homer that gave the Tigers a commanding 8–4 lead they protected in the ensuing frame. Gibson's blast off Gossage, who insisted on facing the Detroit slugger even though he had first base open, was his second of the game, giving him 3 hits, 5 RBIs, and 3 runs scored on the day.

NOTABLE ACHIEVEMENTS

- Hit more than 20 home runs five times.
- Batted over .300 once (.328 in 1981).
- Finished in double digits in triples once (10 in 1984).
- Surpassed 30 doubles once (37 in 1985).
- Stole more than 20 bases four times, topping 30 steals twice.
- Posted slugging percentage in excess of .500 three times.
- First Tigers player to surpass 20 home runs and 20 steals in the same season (1984–1987).
- Ranks sixth in Tigers history with 194 stolen bases.
- 1984 ALCS MVP.
- 1984 A.L. champion.
- 1984 world champion.

Travis Fryman

Travis Fryman (right) with Wade Boggs at the 1996 All-Star Game.
Courtesy of Adam Okurowski

The fact that Travis Fryman invariably came out second-best in the in-evitable comparisons made between himself and Alan Trammell—the man who immediately preceded him at shortstop in Detroit—often caused him to be overlooked by Tiger fans. Nevertheless, Fryman estab-lished himself as one of the finest all-around infielders in franchise history over the course of his eight seasons in Detroit, surpassing 20 homers five times, topping 100 RBIs twice, batting .300 once, and leading all players at his position in assists three times, putouts once, fielding percentage twice, and double plays turned once. Although the Tigers finished with a winning record in just two of Fryman's eight years with them, the shortstop/third baseman's hitting and fielding skills earned him four All-Star nominations and one Silver Slugger. Fryman continued his outstanding play after he left Detroit at the conclusion of the 1997 campaign, helping Cleveland capture three A.L. Central titles, earning his final All-Star selection, and winning the only Gold Glove of his career.

Born in Lexington, Kentucky, on March 25, 1969, David Travis Fryman grew up during the 1970s rooting for Cincinnati's Big Red Machine, before moving with his family to Florida as a teenager. After the young infielder made a name for himself at Gonzalez Tate High School in Pensacola, Florida, the Tigers selected him in the first round of the 1987 amateur draft, with the 30th overall pick. Fryman spent the next three years in the minor leagues, before earning his first call-up to Detroit in July 1990, when he suddenly found himself playing for Sparky Anderson, who had earlier managed the Reds team Fryman followed as a youngster. Playing mostly third base for the Tigers over the final three months of the campaign, Fryman struggled somewhat with the glove, committing a total of 14 errors in his 66 games in the field. However, he handled himself quite well at the plate, batting .297, hitting 9 home runs, and driving in 27 runs, in only 232 official at-bats.

Inserted into Detroit's starting lineup at the start of the ensuing campaign, Fryman spent the first few months of the season at third base, before an injury to Alan Trammell prompted Anderson to move him to shortstop. While Fryman improved somewhat in the field, committing a total of 23 errors in his 156 games on the left side of the infield, he continued to impress on offense, hitting 21 homers, knocking in 91 runs, and batting .259.

With Trammell out for virtually all of 1992, Fryman inherited the starting shortstop job from the Tigers legend. Doing an extremely creditable job in his first full season at short, Fryman committed 22 errors in the field and led all A.L. players with 489 assists. He also posted big numbers on offense, winning a Silver Slugger and earning the first of his three consecutive All-Star nominations by hitting 20 home runs, driving in 96 runs, scoring 87 times, and batting .266.

Initially considered to be the heir apparent to Trammell at shortstop, Fryman found a permanent home at third base shortly after the veteran infielder returned to the Detroit lineup in 1993. Although Fryman had good range and a strong throwing arm, he lacked the dexterity of Trammell, who appeared far more fluid and graceful in the field. Shifted back to third midway through the campaign, Fryman spent the remainder of his career at the hot corner, where he went on to lead all players at his position in putouts once, fielding percentage twice, and assists three straight times as a member of the Tigers. Meanwhile, he had one of his finest offensive seasons in 1993, finishing the year with 22 home runs, 97 RBIs, 98 runs scored, and a .300 batting average.

Fryman performed well during the strike-shortened 1994 campaign, hitting 18 homers and driving in 85 runs, in only 114 games. After hitting just 15 home runs and knocking in only 81 runs the following year, Fryman returned to top form in 1996, concluding the campaign with 22 round-trippers and 100 runs batted in. He posted almost identical numbers the following year, when he hit 22 homers, drove in 102 runs, and scored 90 times.

Still only 28 years old heading into the 1998 season, Fryman expected to spend many more years in Detroit, later stating, "The veterans on the club and Sparky Anderson told me, when certain guys were gone, it was going to be my team. And that's what happened when Alan Trammell retired [at the end of 1996]." However, new Tigers general manager Randy Smith decided to trade Fryman and his $6.5 million salary to the expansion Arizona Diamondbacks for fellow third baseman Joe Randa and two minor leaguers, doing so without even telephoning him to inform him of the deal. Fryman left Detroit with career totals of 149 home runs, 679 RBIs, 607 runs scored, 1,176 hits, 229 doubles, 29 triples, and 58 stolen bases, a .274 batting average, a .334 on-base percentage, and a .444 slugging percentage.

Not yet fully recovered from the shock of leaving the only organization he had ever known, Fryman found himself traded to Cleveland for veteran third sacker Matt Williams less than two weeks later. In discussing his team's latest acquisition, Indians manager Mike Hargrove said, "We always liked him. He's always been a dangerous and productive hitter, and he's done it in some weak lineups."

Fryman eventually came to enjoy his time in Cleveland, where he joined a team that finished first in the A.L. Central in each of the three previous seasons, advancing to the World Series in two of those years. The Indians continued their winning ways with Fryman manning the hot corner for them, capturing three of the next four division titles. Fryman contributed significantly to the Cleveland effort in 1998, hitting 28 home runs, driving in 96 runs, and batting .287 in his first year with his new club. Following an injury-marred 1999 campaign, he had another big year in 2000, earning A.L. All-Star and Gold Glove honors by hitting 22 homers, scoring 93 times, establishing career highs with 106 RBIs, 184 hits, 38 doubles, a .321

batting average, and a .908 OPS, and leading all league third basemen with a .978 fielding percentage.

Hampered by injuries throughout the 2001 season, Fryman appeared in only 98 games for the A.L. Central champs, batting .263, hitting just 3 homers, and driving in only 38 runs. After battling numerous injuries again in 2002, he elected to announce his retirement at only 34 years of age. Fryman ended his career with 223 home runs, 1,022 RBIs, 895 runs scored, 1,776 hits, 345 doubles, 40 triples, 72 stolen bases, a .274 batting average, a .336 on-base percentage, and a .443 slugging percentage.

Following his retirement, Fryman spent three seasons managing in Cleveland's farm system, before eventually accepting a position as a roving minor league batting instructor within the organization.

TIGERS CAREER HIGHLIGHTS

Best Season

Although Fryman reached the 100-RBI mark for his only two times as a member of the Tigers in 1996 and 1997, he had his finest all-around season for the club in 1993. In addition to hitting 22 home runs and driving in 97 runs, Fryman posted the best numbers of his eight-year Tigers career in hits (182), doubles (37), total bases (295), runs scored (98), batting average (.300), on-base percentage (.379), and slugging percentage (.486), placing among the league leaders in each of the first three categories.

Memorable Moments/Greatest Performances

During a 20–3 pounding of the Seattle Mariners on April 17, 1993, Fryman tied a franchise record by scoring 5 times. He went 4-for-5 on the day, with a walk and a stolen base.

Later in the year, on July 28, 1993, Fryman became the first Detroit player in 43 years to hit for the cycle when he accomplished the feat during a 12–7 home loss to the Yankees. Fryman finished the day 5-for-5, with 4 RBIs and 2 runs scored.

Fryman again collected 5 hits in 5 trips to the plate on June 1, 1994, doing so during an 11–3 win over the Orioles in Baltimore.

NOTABLE ACHIEVEMENTS

- Hit more than 20 home runs five times.
- Knocked in more than 100 runs twice.
- Batted .300 once (1993).
- Topped 30 doubles five times.
- Led the American League with 13 sacrifice flies in 1994.
- Led the American League with 489 assists in 1992.
- Led A.L. third basemen in assists three times; putouts once; double plays once; and fielding percentage twice.
- Hit for cycle on July 28, 1993 (vs. Yankees).
- 1992 Silver Slugger winner.
- Two-time *Sporting News* All-Star selection (1992, 1993).
- Four-time A.L. All-Star.

Jim Bunning

Courtesy of LegendaryAuctions.com

lthough he perhaps gained even greater fame following his playing career as a member of the U.S. House of Representatives and U.S. Senate, Jim Bunning initially made a name for himself as one of Major League Baseball's most consistent and durable pitchers. During a 17-year career spent primarily with the Tigers and Phillies, Bunning won a total of 224 games, posting double-digit wins in 11 consecutive seasons at one point. In addition to surpassing 17 victories in eight of those campaigns, the hard-throwing right-hander made at least 30 starts and threw well in excess of 200 innings each year, topping 40 starts and 300 innings twice each. Over parts of nine seasons in Detroit, Bunning posted 118 victories and 1,406 strikeouts. By also winning 106 games and striking out 1,449 batters after leaving the Tigers, Bunning became just the second pitcher in baseball history to record more than 100 victories and 1,000 strikeouts in both the American and National Leagues.

Born in Southgate, Kentucky, on October 23, 1931, James Paul David Bunning attended St. Xavier High School in Cincinnati, Ohio, before enrolling in Xavier University, where he earned a bachelor's degree in economics. Bunning began his career in pro ball while still in school, signing with the Tigers as an amateur free agent in 1950. He subsequently spent nearly six long years toiling in the minor leagues, before finally being called up to Detroit during the second half of the 1955 campaign. After making his big-league debut with the club on July 20, the 6'3", 195-pound Bunning failed to impress, finishing the year with a record of 3–5 and an ERA of 6.35. Yet, the Tigers remained convinced that Bunning had a bright future ahead of him, describing the 24-year-old right-hander as having "an excellent curveball, a confusing delivery, and a sneaky fastball."

Unhappy with his poor performance, Bunning spent the ensuing offseason playing in the Cuban Winter League, where he learned how to throw the slider, which eventually became his signature pitch. Working on his new offering while splitting the 1956 campaign between the Tigers and their top farm club, Bunning arrived in Detroit in 1957 ready to assume a regular spot in the starting rotation. Employing his full arsenal of pitches and a sweeping sidearm delivery that caused his knuckles to nearly scrape the ground on his follow-through, Bunning quickly developed into one of the Junior Circuit's top hurlers, leading the league with 20 wins and 267⅓ innings pitched, while also placing among the leaders with a 2.69 ERA, 182 strikeouts, and 14 complete games. Bunning's exceptional performance earned him All-Star honors for the first of seven times and a ninth-place finish in the A.L. MVP voting. Though not nearly as effective in any of the next three seasons, Bunning still managed to compile an overall mark of 42–39, finish second in the league in ERA once, place near the top of the league rankings in innings pitched twice, and lead all A.L. hurlers in strikeouts twice.

Particularly difficult for opposing right-handed batters to face due to his exaggerated sidearm motion, Bunning annually ranked among the A.L. leaders in strikeouts, placing no lower than third in any season from 1957 to 1963. Meanwhile, Bunning caused problems for left-handed hitters as well, with the lefty-swinging Jesse Gonder, who later faced him in the National League, stating, "He would get two strikes on you, and you didn't want to be caught looking, so you swung."

After finishing just 11–14 despite compiling an outstanding ERA of 2.79 for a Tigers team that finished 12 games under .500 in 1960, Bunning went 17–11, with a 3.19 ERA, 194 strikeouts, and 268 innings pitched the following year, ranking among the league leaders in all four categories. Although Bunning's ERA jumped to 3.59 in 1962, he again placed near the top of the league rankings in wins (19), strikeouts (184), and innings pitched (258). However, even though Bunning finished second in the league with 196 strikeouts in 1963, the Tigers elected to part ways with him after he compiled a record of just 12–13 and an ERA of 3.88. Dealt to the Phillies, along with veteran catcher Gus Triandos, for outfielder Don Demeter and pitcher Jack Hamilton on December 5, 1963, Bunning left Detroit with a career record of 118–87, an ERA of 3.45, 1,406 strikeouts, 78 complete games, 16 shutouts, and 1,692 hits allowed in 1,867⅓ total innings of work. His 1,406 strikeouts and WHIP of 1.208 continue to place him in the Tigers' all-time top 10.

Bunning subsequently began an extremely successful run in Philadelphia—one in which he established himself as one of the National League's finest pitchers. Bunning won 19 games three straight times for the Phillies, posting an overall mark of 57–31 for them from 1964 to 1966. He also tossed well in excess of 250 innings, compiled an ERA below 3.00, and struck out well in excess of 200 batters in each of those seasons, ranking among the N.L. leaders in all three categories all three times. Bunning also pitched exceptionally well in 1967, when, despite finishing just 17–15, he earned a second-place finish in the Cy Young voting by compiling a 2.29 ERA and topping the circuit with 253 strikeouts, 6 shutouts, and 302⅓ innings pitched.

Traded to Pittsburgh at the conclusion of that 1967 campaign, Bunning never again reached such heights, compiling an overall record of just 32–51 over the course of his final four seasons, which he split between the Pirates, Dodgers, and Phillies. Bunning ended his career back in Philadelphia in 1971, retiring at the end of the year with a composite record of 106–97 in National League play. He finished his career with an overall mark of 224–184, an ERA of 3.27, 2,855 strikeouts, 151 complete games, 40 shutouts, 3,760⅓ innings pitched, and a WHIP of 1.179. Bunning's 2,855 strikeouts placed him second only to Walter Johnson among major league pitchers at the time of his retirement. During his time in the senior circuit, Bunning also joined the legendary Cy Young as the only pitchers in history to that point to post more than 100 victories and strike out more than 1,000 batters in each league. He also became one of a select few to throw a no-hitter in each league, tossing a perfect game for the Phillies against the New York Mets on Father's Day 1964, after pitching a no-hitter for the Tigers six years earlier.

After retiring as a player, Bunning spent five years managing in the minor leagues, before returning to his home state of Kentucky. He subsequently chose to enter the world of politics, beginning his political career as a Kentucky state representative, before eventually being elected in 1986 to the U.S. House of Representatives as a Republican from a heavily Democratic district. After serving in the House for 12 years, Bunning was elected to the U.S. Senate, where he served two terms before announcing his decision not to run for reelection. During his years of service in the House of Representatives, Bunning gained induction into the Baseball Hall of Fame, being elected by the members of the Veterans Committee in 1996.

TIGERS CAREER HIGHLIGHTS

Best Season

Bunning had big years for the Tigers in 1959, 1961, and 1962, posting 17, 17, and 19 wins, respectively, while also placing among the league leaders in strikeouts, innings pitched, and complete games each season. However, he pitched his best ball for the Tigers in 1957, compiling a record of 20–8 that made him the league's top winner. Bunning also led all A.L. hurlers with 267⅓ innings pitched, finished third in the league with a .714 winning percentage and a 2.69 ERA, and placed second with 182 strikeouts and a WHIP of 1.070, which represented his best mark as a member of the Tigers.

Memorable Moments/Greatest Performances

Teammate Frank Lary built his reputation largely on the success he experienced against the Yankees, but Bunning also fared pretty well against the Bronx Bombers, particularly in June 1958, when he defeated the eventual world champions twice in less than a week. After allowing the Yankees just 3 hits during a 3–0 shutout on June 15, Bunning returned to the mound five days later to beat them by a score 7–1, striking out 14 batters in the process.

Exactly one month later, on July 20, 1958, Bunning pitched his most memorable game as a member of the Tigers, hurling a 3–0 no-hitter against the Boston Red Sox. Bunning struck out 12 during the contest, with only 2 walks and a hit batsman marring his performance.

Bunning threw another gem on August 25, 1961, allowing the Senators just 2 hits during a 6–0 Tigers win.

Bunning also attained a level of immortality on August 2, 1959, when he became the first pitcher in more than 30 years to pitch a "perfect" inning by striking out three Red Sox batters on only 9 pitches. Relieving Detroit starter Paul Foytack at the start of the top of the ninth inning with Boston holding a 5–4 lead, Bunning made short work of Sammy White, Jim Mahoney, and Ike Delock, becoming in the process the first A.L. hurler to strike out the side on 9 pitches since Philadelphia's Lefty Grove accomplished the feat in 1928.

NOTABLE ACHIEVEMENTS

- Won 20 games in 1957.
- Posted at least 17 victories three other times.
- Posted winning percentage in excess of .700 once (.714 in 1957).
- Compiled ERA under 3.00 twice.
- Struck out more than 200 batters twice.
- Threw more than 200 innings seven times, tossing more than 250 frames on four occasions.
- Led A.L. pitchers in wins once; strikeouts twice; innings pitched once; and fielding percentage four times.
- Ranks among Tigers career leaders in strikeouts (6th) and WHIP (8th).
- 1957 *Sporting News* All-Star selection.
- Five-time A.L. All-Star (1957, 1959, 1961–1963).
- Elected to Baseball Hall of Fame by members of Veterans Committee in 1996.

Bobby Higginson

victim of bad timing, Bobby Higginson proved to be one of the few bright spots on a Tigers team that regularly finished with one of the American League's worst records during his time in Detroit. Arriving in the Motor City in 1995, Higginson played for Tiger clubs that compiled an overall mark of just 712–1,050 over the course of the next 11 seasons. After the hard-hitting outfielder announced his retirement in 2005, the Tigers laid claim to their first A.L. Central title the very next year. Nevertheless,

Higginson played gallantly his entire time in Detroit, surpassing 25 home runs four times, topping 100 RBIs twice, scoring more than 100 runs once, and batting over .300 twice. A solid outfielder with a very strong throwing arm, Higginson also led all players at his position in putouts twice, while posting double-digit assists seven times, en route to leading all A.L. outfielders in assists on four separate occasions.

Born in Philadelphia, Pennsylvania, on August 18, 1970, Robert Leigh Higginson starred in baseball at local Frankford High School, before attending Philadelphia's Temple University. After being selected by the Tigers in the 12th round of the 1992 amateur draft, Higginson spent the next three years advancing through their farm system, finally arriving in Detroit in 1995, when he earned a spot on the major league roster with his outstanding play during spring training.

The Tigers team that the 24-year-old Higginson joined in April 1995 was one in transition. After winning more games during the 1980s than any other team with the exception of the Yankees, Detroit had an aging roster, with veteran holdovers Kirk Gibson, Alan Trammell, and Lou Whitaker all nearing retirement. The 1995 campaign would also prove to be the last in Motown for longtime manager Sparky Anderson, who would be followed, in fairly rapid succession, by Buddy Bell, Lance Parrish, Phil Garner, and Trammell. With no top prospects coming up through the organization, the Tigers subsequently entered into the darkest period of their history, posting more than 70 victories in only four of the next 11 seasons.

Yet, after hitting 14 home runs, driving in 43 runs, and batting just .224 as a rookie, Higginson developed into the Tigers' top offensive threat in 1996, concluding the campaign with 26 homers, 81 RBIs, 75 runs scored, and a .320 batting average. He followed that up by hitting 27 homers, knocking in 101 runs, scoring 94 times, and batting .299 in 1997. Splitting his time between left field and right, Higginson also led all A.L. outfielders with a career-high 20 assists. His outstanding all-around performance prompted the Detroit chapter of the BBWAA to name him "Tiger of the Year" for the first of two times (he also earned the honor in 2000).

The left-hand-swinging Higginson, who stood 5'11" tall and weighed 180 pounds, found Tiger Stadium very much to his liking, often using his compact swing to deposit balls into the ballpark's short porch in right field's upper deck. He also made good use of his strong right throwing arm, annually placing near the top of the league rankings in outfield assists.

Higginson had another solid year for the Tigers in 1998, hitting 25 home runs, driving in 85 runs, scoring 92 times, and batting .284, before suffering through an injury-marred 1999 campaign that saw him finish with just 12 homers, 46 RBIs, 51 runs scored, and a .239 batting average.

Even though the Tigers moved into spacious Comerica Park in 2000, Higginson rebounded from his poor performance the previous season by hitting 30 home runs, driving in 102 runs, scoring 104 times, and batting an even .300. He also led all A.L. outfielders with 19 assists, after moving over to left field from right, where he spent most of the previous two seasons.

However, the combination of Comerica's far-reaching fences and a poor supporting cast adversely affected Higginson's offensive production in subsequent seasons, preventing him from ever again posting big numbers. After surpassing 25 home runs in four of the five previous seasons, Higginson totaled just 53 homers from 2001 to 2004. He also averaged only 63 RBIs and 65 runs scored during that time, while posting batting averages of .277, .282, .235, and .246. After missing all but 10 games in 2005 following his second knee surgery in less than 14 months, Higginson chose to announce his retirement, thanking Tiger fans for their support over the years by taking out a two-page ad in both Detroit newspapers. He ended his career with 187 home runs, 709 RBIs, 736 runs scored, 1,336 hits, 33 triples, 270 doubles, 91 stolen bases, a .272 batting average, a .358 on-base percentage, and a .455 slugging percentage. Ironically, the Tigers, who failed to compile a winning record in any of Higginson's 11 years with them, won the American League pennant the very next year.

CAREER HIGHLIGHTS

Best Season

It could be argued that Higginson played his best ball for the Tigers in 1996, when he hit 26 home runs, knocked in 81 runs, scored 75 times, and established career highs in batting average (.320), on-base percentage (.404), slugging percentage (.577), and OPS (.982). However, he appeared in only 130 games for a Tigers team that finished the regular season with a dismal record of 53–109. That being the case, Higginson made his greatest overall impact in 2000, when, despite playing in spacious Comerica Park, he batted .300, compiled an OPS of .915, and reached career-high marks in homers (30), RBIs (102), runs scored (104), hits (179), doubles (44), and total bases (321). Higginson also collected a league-leading 19 outfield assists and finished first among A.L. left fielders with 305 putouts.

Memorable Moments/Greatest Performances

Higginson had several exceptional days at the plate for the Tigers, with the first of those coming on June 25, 1996, when he led his team to a 10–8 win over Oakland by going 3-for-5, with a home run, 2 doubles, and 5 runs batted in. He had another huge game on August 22, 1997, collecting 5 hits during a 16–1 pounding of the Brewers in Milwaukee. Higginson drove in a career-high 7 runs against Toronto on June 13, 2000, leading the Tigers to a 16–3 home win over the Blue Jays by going 4-for-4, with a pair of 3-run homers.

Higginson also had the distinction of breaking up Roy Halladay's bid for a no-hitter with two men out in the top of the ninth inning in a game against the Blue Jays on September 27, 1998. With Halladay having tossed 8⅔ hitless innings against the Tigers in just his second major league start, Higginson hit the rookie right-hander's first pitch over the left-field wall for an opposite-field home run. Halladay subsequently retired the next batter he faced, giving him a 2–1, one-hit victory over the Tigers.

Nevertheless, the two most memorable games of Higginson's career turned out to be a pair of three-home-run performances he turned in almost exactly three years apart. On June 30, 1997, Higginson went deep three times during a 14–0 win over the Mets in interleague play, finishing the game with 7 RBIs and 4 runs scored. He also homered in his first trip to the plate the following day, tying in the process a major league record by reaching the seats in four consecutive official at-bats (he also drew two bases on balls during the streak). Nearly three years later, on June 24, 2000, Higginson duplicated his earlier feat by hitting three home runs during a 14–8 victory over Cleveland in the second game of a doubleheader split with the Indians. He also drove in 6 runs during the contest.

NOTABLE ACHIEVEMENTS

- Hit more than 20 home runs four times, topping 30 homers once (30 in 2000).
- Knocked in more than 100 runs twice.
- Scored more than 100 runs once (104 in 2000).
- Batted over .300 twice, reaching .320 once (.320 in 1996).
- Surpassed 30 doubles four times, topping 40 two-baggers once (44 in 2000).
- Stole 20 bases once (20 in 2001).

- Compiled on-base percentage in excess of .400 once (.404 in 1996).
- Posted slugging percentage in excess of .500 three times.
- Led A.L. outfielders in assists four times and double plays turned once.
- Led A.L. left fielders in putouts twice and double plays turned three times.
- Hit 3 home runs in one game twice (6/30/97 vs. New York Mets; 6/24/2000 vs. Cleveland).

30

Frank Lary

Courtesy of MearsOnlineAuctions.com

The anchor of Detroit's pitching staff from 1955 to 1961, Frank Lary earned the nickname the "Yankee Killer" due to the inordinate amount of success he experienced against the American League's dominant team. En route to compiling a lifetime record of 28–13 against the Yankees, Lary posted an overall mark of 27–10 against them during that seven-year period. Although the hard-throwing right-hander saved many of his finest performances for New York, he proved to be an extremely effective pitcher against the rest of the league, winning more than 20 games twice and leading all A.L. hurlers in wins once, complete games three times, and innings pitched three times. A true workhorse, Lary won more games (117), threw more innings (1,799⅔), tossed more complete games (115), and faced more batters (7,569) than any other A.L. pitcher between 1955 and 1961. Unfortunately, the heavy workload he assumed eventually took its toll on him, causing him to develop a sore arm in 1962 that relegated him to a much lesser role in his four remaining big-league seasons.

Born in Northport, Alabama, on April 10, 1930, Frank Strong Lary starred in baseball and football at Northport High School before enrolling at the University of Alabama, where he led the Crimson Tide into the College World Series as a sophomore. Impressed with Lary's 10–1 record in his second season at Alabama, the Tigers offered him a $6,000 contract in 1950 that prompted the 20-year-old right-hander to forgo his final two years of college eligibility. After splitting the remainder of the 1950 campaign between Thomasville, in the Georgia-Florida League, and Jamestown in the PONY League, Lary missed all of the next two seasons while serving in the U.S. Army during the Korean War. Upon his return to organized ball, Lary spent the 1953 and 1954 seasons with the International League's Buffalo Bisons, compiling an overall mark of 32–22 that earned him a late-season call-up to Detroit in September 1954.

Lary became a regular member of the Tigers' starting rotation the following year, concluding the 1955 campaign with a somewhat disappointing record of 14–15, even though he ranked among the league leaders with a 3.10 ERA, 16 complete games, and 235 innings pitched. However, after incorporating the knuckleball into his repertoire of pitches that previously included a hard fastball, quick curve, and deceptive slider, Lary developed into a top-flight starter in 1956. In fact, once Lary began using the new pitch on a regular basis, he became practically unbeatable, winning 17 of his final 20 decisions, en route to posting an overall record of 21–13 that made him the league's top winner. He also ranked among the leaders with a 3.15 ERA, 165 strikeouts, and 20 complete games, while topping all A.L. hurlers with 38 starts and 294 innings pitched.

Detroit catcher Red Wilson believed that Lary's use of the knuckleball made him a more effective pitcher because it allowed him to get ahead in the count. Speaking of Lary's new pitch, Wilson told Hal Middlesworth in *The Sporting News*, "They [hitters] don't want any part of it, so they start taking their cuts earlier now. Of course, that works to Frank's advantage another way. He can put a little more on the fast one and still have the knuckler as a threat in reserve."

Lary proved to be much less effective in 1957, finishing the year with a record of just 11–16 and an ERA of 3.98. Although pitching for a mediocre Tigers team caused Lary to finish just one game over .500 the following year, with a record of 16–15, he rebounded in a big way, compiling an ERA of 2.90 and leading the league with 19 complete games and 260⅓ innings pitched. Lary followed that up by posting a mark of 17–10 in 1959, before going 15–15, with a league-leading 15 complete games and 274⅓ innings pitched in 1960.

Throughout the period, Lary continued to build on his reputation as a "Yankee Killer," compiling a record of 5–1 against a Yankees team that finished 97–57 and won the World Series in 1956. He also went 7–1 against the eventual world champions in 1958, becoming in the process the first pitcher to win seven games against New York in one year since Chicago's Ed Cicotte accomplished the feat in 1916. When asked by reporters on numerous occasions to explain his uncanny ability to defeat the Bronx Bombers, Lary typically replied, "I just throw them that breaking stuff of mine."

However, Red Wilson, who collaborated with Lary on 19 of his victories over the Yankees, suggested many years later, "Playing New York, Frank had a real desire to beat the Yankees, like we all did, because they were the best team in the league."

Joe Falls of *The Sporting News* took things one step further, writing in the March 18, 1959 edition of that magazine, "As far as Frank Lary is concerned, the War Between the States never did end. There merely was an 89-year interlude between Lee's surrender at Appomattox in 1865 and Lary's arrival in the Major Leagues in 1954. The objective has remained the same: rout the Yankees."

Falls also discussed the manner in which Lary tended to bear down more with men on base, claiming that, with runners aboard, Lary "becomes a mean, scowling competitor who looks like he'd throw the ball through a batter's heart if it meant getting him out. But, with the bases empty, Lary has as much trouble as a lady driver backing into a garage."

Meanwhile, reflecting back on the somewhat mediocre 128–116 record Lary ended up compiling over the course of his career, Red Wilson claimed during a 2007 interview that his former teammate could have won more games if he had better control. Wilson noted, "Frank didn't cut the corners very well. He wasn't what I would call a 'control pitcher.' Most big leaguers can hit a good fastball, so you have to get it over the corners."

After failing to win more than 17 games in any of the previous four seasons, Lary turned in a stellar performance in 1961, posting a record of 23–9 for a Tigers team that finished the year with 101 victories. In addition to finishing runner-up in the league in wins, Lary placed second with 275⅓ innings pitched, topped the circuit with 22 complete games, and led all A.L. hurlers with 32 putouts, en route to earning Gold Glove honors, a third-place finish in the Cy Young voting, and a seventh-place finish in the league MVP balloting.

As fate would have it, the 1961 campaign turned out to be Lary's last big year. Already experiencing soreness in his pitching arm prior to the start of the 1962 season, Lary exacerbated his situation when he altered his pitching motion to offset a leg injury he incurred while running the bases against the Yankees on Opening Day. Looking back at the events that subsequently transpired, Lary suggested, "As a pitcher, when you have an injury like that, it's possible that you favor it and do something to your delivery."

In his attempt to compensate for his injury, Lary ended up doing irrevocable damage to his pitching shoulder. Subsequently forced to spend much of 1962 on the disabled list, Lary made only 14 starts, winning just 2 of his 8 decisions and posting an inordinately high 5.74 ERA. After beginning the ensuing campaign in the minor leagues, Lary made an unsuccessful attempt to return to the Tigers' starting rotation, once again making only 14 starts and compiling a record of just 2–6. He appeared in just six games over the course of the first two months of the 1964 campaign before the Tigers elected to sell him to the New York Mets. The veteran right-hander split the remainder of his final two seasons between the Mets, Braves, and Chicago White Sox, compiling an overall record of just 5–6, before announcing his retirement after being released by the White Sox at the end of 1965. Lary ended his career with a record of 128–116, an ERA of 3.49, 1,099 strikeouts in 2,162⅓ innings of work, 126 complete games, and 21 shutouts. Having compiled virtually all those numbers while pitching for the Tigers, Lary remains among the franchise's all-time leaders in shutouts, starts, and innings pitched.

Following his playing career, Lary became a roving pitching coach for the Mets. He also spent a couple of seasons scouting for other teams. After retiring from baseball, he returned to his home in Alabama, where he opened a construction business.

While Lary was still at the peak of his career in 1961, *Sports Illustrated* profiled the veteran right-hander, writing:

> Frank Lary is a classic kind of ballplayer—the type, alas, you don't see much of these days. He is a throwback to the Cardinals of the 30's; a cotton pickin', gee-tar strummin', red clay Alabama farm boy, unspoiled by a little college or a lot of success. He is mean on the mound and a joker off

it. To strangers he is quiet, but to the Tigers he is the Jonathan Winters of the dugout, keeping them loose and laughing. Sometimes he is a Casey Stengel, his legs bowed, his pants rolled above his knees. Then he is the trainer, complete in white shirt, white trousers, and with a Turkish towel wrapped around his head.

TIGERS CAREER HIGHLIGHTS

Best Season

Lary pitched exceptionally well for the Tigers in 1956, when his league-leading 21 wins made him the first Detroit pitcher to surpass 20 victories since Hal Newhouser reached the 20-win plateau in 1948. Lary also established career highs with 294 innings pitched and 165 strikeouts. Nevertheless, 1961 would have to be considered his signature season. In addition to finishing second in the league with 23 wins and 275⅓ innings pitched, he compiled a 3.24 ERA, tossed a career-high 4 shutouts, topped the circuit with 22 complete games, and finished fifth in the league with a WHIP of 1.155, which represented the lowest mark of his outstanding seven-year run.

Memorable Moments/Greatest Performances

Lary pitched a number of memorable games for the Tigers, with the first of those coming on August 3, 1955, when he tossed a 2-hit shutout at Washington, defeating the Senators by a score of 3–0.

One of Lary's finest all-around performances went to waste, as he opened the 1956 campaign by allowing just 2 runs and 6 hits during a 2–1 loss to the A's. Lary accounted for Detroit's only run of the game with an inside-the-park home run off Kansas City starter Alex Kellner.

Lary, who won 17 of his final 20 decisions in 1956, turned in arguably the best effort of his sensational run on September 23, when he allowed just 2 hits during an 11–1 win over Cleveland. Lary didn't allow the Indians a hit until Bobby Avila singled with one man out in the top of the eighth inning.

Lary pitched extraordinarily well during one stretch in June 1958, tossing three straight shutouts and 29 consecutive scoreless innings before finally faltering against Boston on June 27. After blanking the Red Sox 7–0 on June 11, Lary shut out the Yankees 2–0 on the 15th. He followed that up by defeating the Yankees again on the 21st, this time by a score of 1–0. Lary allowed a total of just 16 hits during the longest scoreless streak of his career.

Lary pitched his best game of the 1960 campaign on May 11, when he tossed 11 scoreless innings, in defeating Pedro Ramos and the Washington Senators by a score of 1–0.

Lary also pitched a number of memorable games in 1961, throwing a one-hit shutout in his first start, in defeating the White Sox by a score of 7–0. On July 9, he allowed just 3 hits during a 1–0 victory over the Angels. And Lary, a pretty fair hitter over the course of his career, won his own game on May 12 by hitting a leadoff homer in the top of the ninth inning during a 4–3 victory over the Yankees.

NOTABLE ACHIEVEMENTS

- Won more than 20 games twice, surpassing 15 victories three other times.
- Posted winning percentage in excess of .700 once (.719 in 1961).
- Compiled ERA below 3.00 once (2.90 in 1958).
- Completed at least 20 games twice.
- Threw more than 200 innings seven times, tossing more than 250 frames on four occasions.
- Led A.L. pitchers in wins once; complete games three times; innings pitched three times; games started twice; and putouts twice.
- Ranks among Tigers career leaders in shutouts (10th); innings pitched (10th); and games started (10th).
- Finished third in 1961 Cy Young voting.
- Finished seventh in 1961 A.L. MVP voting.
- 1961 *Sporting News* All-Star Selection.
- Two-time A.L. All-Star (1960, 1961).

31

Magglio Ordonez

Courtesy of Keith Allison

onsidered by most baseball people to be on the downside of his career at only 30 years of age following two surgeries on his badly injured left knee, Magglio Ordonez drew little interest from most major league ball clubs when he became a free agent at the conclusion of the 2004 campaign. With most teams believing that the slugging outfielder was not likely to return to the earlier form that enabled him to hit more than 30 home runs, drive in well over 100 runs, and bat in excess of .300 four straight times for the Chicago White Sox, Ordonez received only a handful of of-fers, with the most generous of those coming from the Detroit Tigers, who ended up signing him to a five-year, $85 million deal. Yet, even though the Tigers took a huge gamble when they offered Ordonez the second largest contract they had ever given a player at the time, they never regretted mak-ing the move. After seeing limited duty his first year in Detroit, Ordonez put together three consecutive outstanding seasons for the Tigers, surpass-ing 20 homers and 100 RBIs each year, batting well over .300 twice, placing second in the A.L. MVP voting once, and helping his new team advance to the World Series for the first time in 22 years in 2006. Unfortunately, in-juries and advancing age limited Ordonez's period of dominance in Detroit to just those three seasons. Nevertheless, "Maggs," as he came to be known, ended up spending seven productive years in Detroit, establishing himself during that time as one of the team's most reliable hitters.

Born in Caracas, Distrito Federal, Venezuela, on January 28, 1974, Magglio Delgado Ordonez attended Coro Falcon High School, before signing with the Chicago White Sox as a 17-year-old amateur free agent in 1991. Ordonez spent most of the next six years in Chicago's farm system refining his baseball skills, maturing mentally and physically, and learning a new culture. After finally making his big-league debut with the White Sox in late August 1997, Ordonez displayed his exceptional hitting ability over the course of the season's final month by hitting 4 home runs, driving in 11 runs, and batting .319, in 21 games and 69 official plate appearances. Ordonez established himself as Chicago's starting right fielder the following year, earning a fifth-place finish in the A.L. Rookie of the Year balloting by hitting 14 homers, knocking in 65 runs, scoring 70 times, and batting .282.

The right-handed-hitting Ordonez subsequently emerged as a top of-fensive threat in 1999, beginning a string of four straight seasons in which he surpassed 30 home runs and 100 RBIs. He also batted over .300 each year, scored in excess of 100 runs three times, and earned All-Star honors three times. Ordonez had his two best seasons for the White Sox in 2000 and 2002, winning a Silver Slugger each year. After hitting 32 homers, driving in 126 runs, scoring 102 times, and batting .315 in the first of those campaigns, Ordonez earned an eighth-place finish in the league MVP voting in 2002 by establishing new career highs in home runs (38), RBIs (135), runs scored (116), doubles (47), and batting average (.320). He followed that up with another solid performance in 2003, earning his fourth All-Star selection in five years by hitting 29 homers, driving in 99 runs, scoring 95 times, and batting .317. Although the 6-foot, 215-pound Ordonez lacked outstanding running speed, he also did a creditable job in the outfield, annually placing near the top of the league rankings among right fielders in putouts, assists, and fielding percentage.

After nearly being traded to Boston for star shortstop Nomar Garciaparra during the 2003 offseason, Ordonez saw his career take a sudden downturn on May 19, 2004, when he collided with second baseman Willie Harris while chasing Omar Vizquel's pop-up to short right field during a contest against the Cleveland Indians. Two trips to the disabled list and two surgeries on his left knee followed, very much putting in doubt Ordonez's ability to ever again be a significant contributor to any major league team.

A free agent at the conclusion of the 2004 campaign, Ordonez found himself being courted by just a handful of teams before ultimately deciding to accept a five-year, $85 million offer from the Tigers. Yet, due to their concerns over Ordonez's surgically repaired knee, the Tigers inserted a clause in the contract that gave them the option to buy out the deal for $3 million if he ended up spending more than 25 days on the disabled list due to a recurrence of the injury.

Ordonez's tenure in Detroit began somewhat ominously when he missed virtually the entire first half of the 2005 campaign after undergoing corrective surgery to repair a hernia he incurred during the season's first week. However, after rejoining the Tigers in early July, Ordonez finished the season strong, hitting 8 home runs, driving in 46 runs, and batting .302 in 82 games and just over 300 official at-bats. Ordonez subsequently returned to top form in 2006, helping the Tigers advance to the playoffs and earning All-Star honors for the fifth time in his career by hitting 24 homers, knocking in 104 runs, and batting .298. He followed that up with an exceptional 2007 campaign in which he hit 28 home runs, scored 117 runs, placed second in the league with 139 RBIs, 216 hits, 354 total bases, and a .434 on-base percentage, and topped the circuit with a .363 batting average and 54 doubles. Ordonez's extraordinary performance earned him a second-place finish to Alex Rodriguez in the A.L. MVP voting.

Ordonez had one more extremely productive year for the Tigers, hitting 21 homers, driving in 103 runs, and batting .317 in 2008, before Father Time finally began to catch up with him. Although Ordonez batted .310 in 2009, he hit just 9 home runs and drove in only 50 runs, in 131 games and nearly 500 official plate appearances. He then missed the final two months of the ensuing campaign after fracturing his ankle sliding into home plate in late July. Subsequently re-signed by the Tigers to a one-year, $10 million contract, Ordonez spent one more year in Detroit, hitting 5 homers, knocking in 32 runs, and batting .255 in a part-time role, before announcing his retirement early in 2012 after the Tigers chose not to bring

him back for another season. He officially retired from Major League Baseball in a special ceremony held at Comerica Park on June 3, 2012. Ordonez
ended his playing career with 294 home runs, 1,236 runs batted in, 1,076
runs scored, 2,156 hits, 426 doubles, 21 triples, a .309 batting average,
a .369 on-base percentage, and a .502 slugging percentage. In his years
with the Tigers, he hit 107 homers, drove in 533 runs, scored 452 times,
amassed 989 hits, 186 doubles, and 6 triples, batted .312, compiled a .373
on-base percentage, and posted a .476 slugging percentage. In addition
to being named to a total of six A.L. All-Star teams over the course of his
career, Ordonez earned three Silver Sluggers and two top-10 finishes in the
league MVP voting.

Following his retirement, Ordonez chose to enter the world of politics,
being elected mayor of the Juan Antonio Sotillo municipality in his native
country of Venezuela on December 8, 2013.

TIGERS CAREER HIGHLIGHTS

Best Season

Although Ordonez also performed well for the Tigers in 2006 and 2008,
there is little doubt that he had his finest season for them in 2007. In addition to hitting 28 home runs, Ordonez established career-high marks in
RBIs (139), runs scored (117), hits (216), on-base percentage (.434), OPS
(1.029), batting average (.363), and doubles (54), leading the American
League in each of the last two categories. Ordonez's .363 batting average
represented the highest figure compiled by a Tigers batsman since Charlie
Gehringer topped the junior circuit with a mark of .371 in 1937. Meanwhile, George Kell (56 in 1950) was the last Detroit player to compile as
many doubles in a season, and Rocky Colavito (140 in 1961) was the only
Tigers player in the past 60 years to accumulate more RBIs in a season.

Memorable Moments/Greatest Performances

Ordonez turned in a number of memorable performances over the course
of his fabulous 2007 campaign, with the first of those coming on April 24,
when he helped the Tigers overcome an early 7–0 deficit to the Angels by
going 3-for-3, with 3 RBIs and 3 runs scored, including a two-run homer
in the top of the ninth inning that put Detroit out in front by a score of
8–7. Unfortunately, the Angels tied the game with a run in the bottom of
the inning, before pushing across the winning run in the ensuing frame.

Later in the year, on August 12, Ordonez became just the second player in Tigers history to hit two home runs in one inning when he homered twice and knocked in 4 runs during an eight-run second inning outburst against the A's. Ordonez, who raised his batting average to .357 during the 11–6 victory over Oakland, joined Al Kaline as the only Tigers to reach the seats twice in the same frame. Kaline accomplished the feat 52 years earlier, during a 16–0 win over the then-Kansas City Athletics on April 17, 1955.

Ordonez, though, saved perhaps his finest performance for September 10, 2007, when he led the Tigers to a come-from-behind 5–4 win over the Toronto Blue Jays by going 4-for-5, with 2 RBIs and a run scored. Detroit's cleanup hitter delivered the game's decisive blow in the bottom of the ninth inning when he culminated a 4-run Tiger rally with a two-out, bases loaded single to right field that brought home the tying and winning runs.

Yet, Ordonez will always be remembered most fondly by Tiger fans for a pair of outstanding games he turned in during the 2006 postseason. After being held in check by New York's pitching staff in the first three games of the ALDS, Ordonez helped the Tigers advance to the ALCS by collecting 2 hits, including a home run, driving in 2 runs, and scoring 3 times during an 8–3 series-clinching win over the Yankees. He subsequently delivered the most memorable hit of his career in Game Four of Detroit's ALCS sweep of Oakland, sending the Tigers to the World Series by hitting a walk-off, three-run home run with two men out in the bottom of the ninth inning. The blast, Ordonez's second of the contest, gave the Tigers a 6–3 victory.

NOTABLE ACHIEVEMENTS

- Hit more than 20 home runs three times.
- Knocked in more than 100 runs three times, topping 130 RBIs once (139 in 2007).
- Scored more than 100 runs once (117 in 2007).
- Batted over .300 five times, topping .360 once (.363 in 2007).
- Surpassed 200 hits once (216 in 2007).
- Surpassed 30 doubles three times, topping 50 two-baggers once (54 in 2007).
- Compiled on-base percentage in excess of .400 once (.434 in 2007).
- Posted slugging percentage in excess of .500 once (.595 in 2007).
- Compiled OPS in excess of 1.000 once (1.029 in 2007).
- Led the American League in batting average once and doubles once.

- Led A.L. right fielders with .996 fielding percentage in 2007.
- August 2007 A.L. Player of the Month.
- Finished second in 2007 A.L. MVP voting.
- 2007 Silver Slugger winner.
- Two-time A.L. All-Star (2006, 2007).
- 2006 A.L. champion.

Tony Clark

Courtesy of Charles Thurmond

The Tigers' most productive hitter for much of the dark period that extended from 1994 to 2005, Tony Clark spent seven seasons in Detroit, establishing himself during that time as one of the American League's most formidable batsmen. Although the Tigers finished near the bottom of their division each year Clark remained with the club, the switch-hitting first baseman continued to give them a powerful presence in the middle of their batting order, slugging more than 30 home runs three times and knocking in more than 100 runs twice. An outstanding team leader, Clark played for two division-winning ball clubs after he left Detroit, providing veteran leadership to a Yankees team that advanced to the ALCS in 2004, and an Arizona Diamondbacks squad that advanced to the NLCS in 2007.

Born in Newton, Kansas, on June 15, 1972, Anthony Christopher Clark attended Christian High School in El Cajon, California, where he earned All-American honors in baseball and basketball. Particularly dominant on the hardwood, the 6'8" Clark scored a San Diego–area record 2,549 points over the course of his high school career, while also breaking Bill Walton's single-season record of 1,337 points scored by averaging 43.7 points per game as a senior. After graduating from Christian High, Clark enrolled at San Diego State University, where he continued to play basketball until injuring his back as a freshman. Clark, who had previously been selected by the Tigers with the second overall pick of the 1990 amateur draft (the Braves selected Chipper Jones with the first pick), subsequently decided to concentrate solely on baseball, continuing his ascension through Detroit's farm system, which he began in 1990. The towering first baseman finally arrived in Detroit in September 1995, beginning his major league career by hitting 3 home runs, driving in 11 runs, and batting .238 over the final month of the campaign.

After spending the first four months of the 1996 season serving primarily as Cecil Fielder's backup, Clark took over as Detroit's starting first baseman when the Tigers dealt Fielder to the Yankees just prior to the trade deadline. Playing regularly for the first time in his young career, Clark finished the season strong, concluding the campaign with a .250 batting average, 27 homers, and 72 RBIs, in only 100 games and 376 official at-bats, en route to earning a third-place finish in the A.L. Rookie of the Year voting. Clark emerged as a top offensive threat the following year, when, despite striking out 144 times, he batted .276, scored 105 runs, and led the team with 32 home runs, 117 runs batted in, and 93 bases on balls. Although still only 25 years of age, Clark also assumed the role of team leader, establishing his voice as the most powerful in the Detroit clubhouse. With the Tigers improving their record by 26 games, posting an overall mark of 79–83, Clark earned MVP consideration, placing 18th in the balloting.

Clark compiled big numbers for the Tigers in each of the next two seasons, hitting 34 home runs, driving in 103 runs, and batting .291 in 1998, before hitting 31 homers, knocking in 99 runs, and batting .280 the following year. However, injuries to his rib cage and lower back limited Clark to only 60 games in 2000, enabling him to hit just 13 home runs and knock in only 37 runs, in just over 200 official at-bats. Despite missing close to a month of the ensuing campaign with various injuries, Clark had a solid season, earning the only All-Star nomination of his career by hitting 16 homers, driving in 75 runs, and batting .287. Yet, concerns over Clark's impending free agency prompted the Tigers to release him at the end of the year, bringing his time in Detroit to an end. Clark left the Tigers with career totals of 156 home runs, 514 RBIs, 428 runs scored, 783 hits, 156 doubles, and 7 triples, a .277 batting average, a .355 on-base percentage, and a .502 slugging percentage, with the last figure placing him seventh on the club's all-time list.

Following his release by the Tigers, Clark led a somewhat nomadic existence the next three years, before finally finding a home in Arizona in 2005. After spending the 2002 season serving as a part-time player with the Red Sox, Clark assumed a similar role in New York, first for the Mets in 2003, and then for the Yankees in 2004, helping the latter advance to the playoffs by hitting 16 homers and driving in 49 runs, in only 253 official at-bats. A free agent again at the end of the 2004 campaign, Clark signed with the Arizona Diamondbacks, with whom he spent the next three seasons. After experiencing an offensive resurgence in his first year in Arizona, hitting 30 home runs, knocking in 87 runs, and batting a career-high .304, Clark spent the next two seasons serving as a backup, totaling just 23 homers and 67 RBIs. He subsequently spent most of 2008 with the San Diego Padres, before returning to Arizona late in the year to finish out his playing career with the Diamondbacks. Clark announced his retirement shortly after being released by Arizona on July 13, 2009, ending his career with 251 home runs, 824 RBIs, 629 runs scored, 1,188 hits, 233 doubles, 11 triples, a .262 batting average, a .339 on-base percentage, and a .485 slugging percentage.

After initially becoming a studio analyst with the MLB Network following his retirement, Clark became active in the Major League Baseball Players Association, where he served as director of player relations from 2010 until July 2013, when he was named deputy to executive director Michael Weiner. Upon Weiner's passing on November 21, 2013, Clark assumed his post, after which he named Hall of Famer Dave Winfield as his deputy.

Although Clark has since moved on to bigger, more important things, he fondly remembers his days in Detroit, stating, "That was where I grew up. That was the first organization that gave me an opportunity to play in the big leagues, so I'll always be appreciative of that."

TIGERS CAREER HIGHLIGHTS

Best Season

Clark had a big year for the Tigers in 1998, when he knocked in 103 runs, scored 84 times, batted .291, compiled an OPS of .880, and established career highs with 34 home runs, 175 hits, 37 doubles, and 314 total bases. However, Detroit finished last in the A.L. Central with a dismal record of 65–97. Clark actually made more of an overall impact the previous season, when he helped the Tigers finish within 4 games of .500 by hitting 32 homers, driving in 117 runs, scoring 105 times, amassing 160 hits, 28 doubles, and 290 total bases, batting .276, and posting an OPS of .876. He also led all A.L. first basemen in putouts, accumulating a total of 1,423 that represented easily the highest mark of his career.

Memorable Moments/Greatest Performances

Clark had a big day at the plate on August 22, 1997, helping the Tigers defeat Milwaukee 16–1 by going 3-for-5, with a pair of doubles, 4 RBIs, and 2 runs scored.

On April 6, 2001, Clark hit safely twice in the sixth inning of a 10–9, 10-inning victory over the White Sox, driving in 4 runs that frame with a grand slam home run. The switch-hitting Clark, who homered from both sides of the plate in the same game seven times over the course of his career, did so six times as a member of the Tigers. In 1998, he became the first player in MLB history to switch-hit home runs three times in one season, doing so on June 17 vs. Minnesota, July 26 vs. Cleveland, and August 1 vs. Tampa Bay. Only two other players (Nick Swisher and Mark Teixeira) have since been able to accomplish the feat.

NOTABLE ACHIEVEMENTS

- Hit more than 30 home runs three times.
- Knocked in more than 100 runs twice.
- Scored more than 100 runs once (105 in 1997).
- Surpassed 30 doubles once (37 in 1998).
- Compiled slugging percentage in excess of .500 five times.

- Led A.L. first basemen with 1,423 putouts in 1997.
- Ranks seventh all-time on Tigers with .502 career slugging percentage.
- First player in MLB history to switch-hit homers from both sides of plate in same game three times in one season.
- 2001 A.L. All-Star.

33

Max Scherzer

Courtesy of Keith Allison

One of the premier pitchers in baseball the past few seasons, Max Scherzer has proven to be nothing short of sensational since being acquired by the Tigers from the Arizona Diamondbacks as part of a three-team deal prior to the start of the 2010 campaign. After going a combined 27–20 his first two seasons in Motown, Scherzer developed into a truly dominant pitcher in 2012, joining Justin Verlander at the top of Detroit's starting rotation to give the Tigers arguably the most formidable pitching duo in all of baseball. Over the course of the past three seasons, Scherzer has compiled an overall record of 55–15, en route to posting a career winning percentage of .701 during his time in Detroit that ranks as the best in franchise history. Scherzer has led the American League in wins in two of the last three seasons, struck out well in excess of 200 batters each year, and earned two top-five finishes in the Cy Young voting, winning the award in 2013, when his 21–3 record gave him a winning percentage of .875 that ranks as the second-best single-season mark in team history. Only a departure from Detroit via free agency is likely to prevent the hard-throwing right-hander from going down as one of the greatest Tiger pitchers ever.

Born in St. Louis, Missouri, on July 27, 1984, Maxwell M. Scherzer grew up in nearby Chesterfield, where he attended Parkway Central High School. Drafted by the St. Louis Cardinals in the 43rd round of the 2003 Major League Baseball Draft following his graduation from Parkway Central, Scherzer instead chose to enroll at the University of Missouri in the city of Columbia, where he earned Big 12 Pitcher of the Year honors in 2005. Having improved his draft stock considerably while in college, Scherzer elected to sign with the Arizona Diamondbacks after they selected him in the first round of the 2006 amateur draft, with the 11th overall pick.

Scherzer spent just one full season in the minor leagues before being called up by the Diamondbacks on April 27, 2008. Making his major league debut with the club two days later, the 23-year-old right-hander worked 4⅓ perfect innings of relief against the Houston Astros, striking out seven and establishing a new MLB record for the most consecutive batters retired (13) by a pitcher making his first appearance in a major league game as a reliever. Subsequently inserted into Arizona's starting rotation, Scherzer struggled in his seven starts, prompting the Diamondbacks to move him back to the bullpen. Working a total of 56 innings over the course of the campaign, Scherzer finished the year with a record of 0–4, a 3.05 ERA, 66 strikeouts, and 74 base runners allowed.

After participating in the Arizona Fall League during the offseason, Scherzer earned a regular spot in the Diamondbacks' starting rotation in 2009, finishing the year 9–11 with an ERA of 4.12. Yet, in spite of his rather pedestrian record, Scherzer showed a considerable amount of promise, striking out 174 batters in 170⅓ innings of work.

Seeking to become younger and strengthen themselves after finishing just one game behind first-place Minnesota in the A.L. Central the previous season, the Tigers completed a three-team trade with the Yankees and Diamondbacks on December 9, 2009, that netted them Scherzer, pitchers Daniel Schlereth and Phil Coke, and outfielder Austin Jackson—one of the top prospects in the Yankee organization. In addition to receiving Edwin Jackson from the Tigers in the deal, Arizona acquired pitcher Ian Kennedy from the Yankees. New York, in turn, received centerfielder Curtis Granderson from the Tigers.

Although Kennedy developed into an effective pitcher in Arizona and Granderson had a couple of big years in New York, the Tigers benefited from the trade more than anyone. Not only did Jackson do an outstanding job of patrolling centerfield for them the next 4½ seasons, but Scherzer gradually emerged as the ace of their pitching staff. The 6'3", 220-pound right-hander had a solid first year in Detroit, compiling a record of 12–11 and an ERA of 3.50, and striking out 184 batters in 195⅔ innings of work. Despite posting a mark of 15–9 the following season, he pitched somewhat less effectively, finishing the year with an ERA of 4.43, striking out 174 batters, and allowing more hits than innings pitched (207 to 195) for the only time in his career.

Scherzer took a major step forward in 2012, even though he lost his only brother to suicide early that summer, concluding the campaign with a record of 16–7 and an ERA of 3.74, and finishing second in the league to teammate Justin Verlander with 231 strikeouts. With Verlander suffering through a slightly subpar 2013 season, Scherzer supplanted him as the ace of the Tigers' starting rotation, leading all A.L. hurlers with a record of 21–3, a winning percentage of .875, and a WHIP of 0.970, while also placing second in the league with 240 strikeouts. Scherzer's exceptional performance earned him A.L. Cy Young and *Sporting News* A.L. Pitcher of the Year honors, a 12th-place finish in the league MVP voting, and the first of two straight All-Star selections.

Over the course of his Cy Young campaign, Scherzer put on display for all to see his wide assortment of pitches that he throws from a low three-quarters delivery. Although a 94–95 mph fastball with good movement and an 85–86 mph slider remain his primary offerings, he also has in his arsenal a 78–79 mph curveball that he uses sparingly and an 82–85 mph changeup that he employs mostly against left-handed hitters.

Scherzer's brilliant 2013 performance gave him the confidence to turn down a multiyear offer from the Tigers at season's end, prompting him instead to reach agreement with them on a one-year deal worth $15.525 million. His gamble ended up paying off since he had another huge year in 2014, compiling an ERA of 3.15 and a record of 18–5 that tied him for the league lead in wins. Scherzer also placed near the top of the league rankings with 252 strikeouts and 220⅓ innings pitched. His 18 wins against only 5 losses gave him an overall mark of 82–35 with the Tigers that translates to a franchise-best .701 career winning percentage. During his time in Detroit, Scherzer has also compiled an ERA of 3.52, struck out 1,081 batters in 1,013 innings of work, and posted a WHIP of 1.197 that places him in the team's all-time top 10. Meanwhile, his average of 9.604 strikeouts per nine innings is the best in franchise history.

Unfortunately, Scherzer's chances of returning to Detroit in 2015 do not appear to be particularly good at this juncture, even though he stated at one point during the previous season, "I do hope I'm back. I love this clubhouse, love the players in here. I've gone to battle with these guys for five years."

Tigers General Manager Dave Dombrowski paints a less-promising picture, though, telling *Detroit.cbslocal.com* on October 14, 2014, "We had thorough conversations before the season, and I don't know that that's (Scherzer's returning) all dictated by us at this point. I think we made ourselves pretty well-known at that time, where we stood, and he's a quality pitcher, and we know that. He's done a lot for our organization, but it's apparent that his representative wanted him to test free agency, so that comes up in a couple weeks."

Dombrowski continued, "I think we probably made more of an effort to sign Max earlier in the year at that time, so I don't think your odds improve over what they were earlier because why would they improve if we have one-on-one ability to speak with you compared to him and 29 other clubs? But only time will tell."

Since the Tigers reportedly offered Scherzer a six-year deal worth $144 million at the conclusion of the 2013 campaign, it will likely take a king's ransom to sign him to a long-term contract at this point. As Dombrowski suggested, only time will tell where he eventually winds up.

TIGERS CAREER HIGHLIGHTS

Best Season

Scherzer pitched exceptionally well in 2014, posting a league-leading 18 wins against only 5 losses, compiling an ERA of 3.15, and establishing career highs with 252 strikeouts and 220⅓ innings pitched. Nevertheless, the 2013 campaign would have to be considered his finest. In addition to finishing fifth in the league with a 2.90 ERA and leading all A.L. hurlers with 21 wins and an .875 winning percentage, Scherzer struck out 240 batters and led the league with a WHIP of 0.970 that represents easily the best mark of his career. En route to earning A.L. Cy Young honors, Scherzer established a new Tigers record by becoming the first pitcher in franchise history to win his first 13 decisions.

Memorable Moments/Greatest Performances

Although he worked just 5⅔ innings during the contest, Scherzer turned in his first dominant performance for the Tigers on May 30, 2010, when he allowed just 2 hits and struck out 14 batters during a 10–2 victory over the Oakland A's. The 14 strikeouts tied Scherzer for the second-highest single-game total ever compiled by a Tigers hurler, placing him behind only Mickey Lolich, who once fanned 16 batters in a game.

Scherzer topped his earlier effort on May 20, 2012, when he struck out 15 batters over 7 innings during a 4–3 interleague win over Pittsburgh. Scherzer surrendered 4 hits and 2 runs to the Pirates during the contest.

Scherzer pitched exceptionally well for the Tigers in the 2012 postseason, compiling a record of 1–0 and an ERA of 2.08 in his three starts, while striking out 26 batters in 17⅓ innings of work. He came up big again in the 2013 playoffs, turning in a dominant performance in Game 1 of the ALDS, when he recorded 11 strikeouts and allowed just one hit through the first six innings, before surrendering a two-run homer to Yoenis Céspedes in the bottom of the seventh. Scherzer ended up winning the game 3–2, allowing just three hits and two runs in his seven innings of work. He also came out of the bullpen to get the win in Game 4, allowing three hits and one run over two innings.

Scherzer, though, saved his most overpowering performance for the Boston Red Sox in Game Two of the ALCS, striking out 13 and allowing just two hits and one run to the eventual world champions, before being relieved prior to the start of the eighth inning with the Tigers holding a 5–1 lead. Unfortunately, a quartet of Detroit relievers subsequently surrendered five runs to the Red Sox over the course of the next two innings, enabling Boston to come out on top by a score of 6–5.

NOTABLE ACHIEVEMENTS

- Has surpassed 20 victories once (21 in 2013).
- Has won at least 15 games three other times.
- Has compiled an ERA under 3.00 once (2.90 in 2013).
- Has posted a winning percentage in excess of .700 twice, surpassing .800 once (.875 in 2013).
- Has struck out more than 200 batters three times.
- Has thrown more than 200 innings twice.

- Has compiled WHIP below 1.000 once (0.970 in 2013).
- Has led A.L. pitchers in wins twice; winning percentage once; and WHIP once.
- Holds Tigers career records for highest winning percentage (.701) and most strikeouts per nine innings pitched (9.604).
- Ranks seventh in Tigers history with career WHIP of 1.197.
- Holds two best single-season strikeouts per nine innings pitched marks in Tigers history (11.078 in 2012; and 10.293 in 2014).
- Compiled second-best single-season winning percentage in Tigers history with mark of .875 in 2013.
- 2013 A.L. Cy Young Award winner.
- 2013 *Sporting News* A.L. Pitcher of the Year.
- Two-time A.L. All-Star (2013, 2014).
- 2012 A.L. champion.

34

Pete Fox

Pete Fox (left) with Jimmie Foxx.
Courtesy of Boston Public Library, Leslie Jones Collection

An excellent line-drive hitter with outstanding speed and occasional home run power, Pete Fox spent eight seasons in Detroit, helping the Tigers win three A.L. pennants and one world championship during that time. Capable of hitting virtually anywhere in the batting order, Fox generally manned either the leadoff, second or sixth spot in Detroit's lineup, providing ample support for the team's other top offensive threats, Charlie Gehringer, Hank Greenberg, and Rudy York. Fox hit over .300 three straight times for the Tigers, never posting a mark below .285 as a member of the club. The right-handed-hitting outfielder also scored more than 100 runs three times, stole more than 20 bases twice, amassed more than 200 hits once, and compiled an on-base percentage in excess of .400 once. Playing primarily right field for the Tigers, Fox established himself as one of the top defensive players at his position as well, leading all A.L. right fielders in fielding percentage four times, assists once, and double plays once, while annually ranking among the leaders in putouts.

Born in Evansville, Indiana, on March 8, 1909, Ervin Fox attended local Bosse High School, during which time he also pitched in various sandlot leagues. After signing with the local Three-I League club in 1929, Fox began focusing on his hitting and outfield play at the suggestion of his coaches. Developing rapidly into an excellent offensive player, Fox led the Texas League with a .357 batting average while playing for Beaumont in 1932. During his time there, Fox also earned the nickname "Pete," which would remain his moniker the rest of his career. Initially called "Rabbit" by Texas League fans because of his running speed, Fox saw his nickname gradually evolve into "Peter Rabbit" and, finally, just "Pete."

Fox's exceptional 1932 campaign prompted the Tigers to promote him to the big club the following year. Earning the starting centerfield job early in 1933, Fox had a solid rookie season, batting .288, hitting 7 homers, driving in 57 runs, scoring 82 times, and placing among the league leaders with 13 triples. Shifted to right field at the start of the ensuing campaign, Fox contributed to Detroit's successful run to the pennant by batting .285, scoring 101 runs, and finishing fourth in the league with 25 stolen bases. He also led all A.L. outfielders with 4 double plays turned.

Fox developed into a top offensive performer in 1935, when he helped the Tigers return to the World Series by hitting a career-high 15 home runs, knocking in 73 runs, and placing among the league leaders with 116 runs scored, 38 doubles, and a .321 batting average. He punctuated his outstanding season by knocking in 4 runs, collecting 10 hits, and batting .385 during Detroit's six-game victory over Chicago in the World Series.

After being limited by injuries to only 73 games in 1936, Fox returned with a vengeance in 1937, posting a career-high .331 batting average, hitting 12 home runs, driving in 82 runs, scoring 116 times, and accumulating 208 hits and 39 doubles. He followed that up with two more solid seasons before he began to see his playing time diminish. Fox compiled excellent numbers in 1938, concluding the campaign with a .293 batting average, 91 runs scored, and a career-best 96 RBIs. Although his production fell off somewhat the following year (66 RBIs and 69 runs scored), he stole 23 bases and compiled a batting average of .295.

The shifting of Hank Greenberg to left field and the emergence of young center fielder Barney McCosky created something of a logjam in the Detroit outfield in 1940, relegating Fox to a part-time role. Nevertheless, he still managed to bat .289, before being sold to the Boston Red Sox at season's end. Fox spent the next five years in Boston, serving the Red Sox primarily as a part-time player, although the absence of Ted Williams and Dom DiMaggio during World War II enabled him to regain his starting job for two seasons. Fox remained a solid hitter during that time, batting over .300 twice for the Red Sox, and even earning his lone All-Star selection in 1944. However, Boston released Fox after he appeared in only 66 games and batted just .245 for them in 1945. Fox subsequently announced his retirement, ending his career with 65 home runs, 694 RBIs, 895 runs scored, 1,678 hits, 75 triples, 314 doubles, 158 stolen bases, a .298 batting average, a .347 on-base percentage, and a .415 slugging percentage. In his eight seasons with the Tigers, Fox hit 59 homers, drove in 493 runs, scored 670 times, accumulated 1,182 hits, 52 triples, and 222 doubles, stole 107 bases, batted .302, compiled a .351 on-base percentage, and posted a .430 slugging percentage.

After retiring as an active player, Fox became a minor league manager, piloting Pawtucket in the New England League, Waterloo in the Three-I League, and Hot Springs in the Cottons States League. He later scouted for the Tigers and the Chicago White Sox until cataracts forced him to take a job in the early 1950s with a Detroit firm owned by a boyhood friend from Evansville. Fox died of cancer at his home in Detroit on July 5, 1966, at 57 years of age. The Indiana Baseball Hall of Fame opened its doors to him 14 years later.

TIGERS CAREER HIGHLIGHTS

Best Season

It could be argued that Fox had his finest season in 1935, when, appearing in 131 games, he hit 15 home runs, drove in 73 runs, scored 116 times, amassed 38 doubles, batted .321, and compiled a career-high .895 OPS. Nevertheless, the fact that Fox played in 17 more games in 1937 enabled him to make his greatest overall impact that year. In addition to hitting 12 homers, knocking in 82 runs, scoring 116 times, and posting an OPS of .848, he established career highs with 208 hits, 39 doubles, 299 total bases, and a batting average of .331.

Memorable Moments/Greatest Performances

Fox had the greatest day of his career on June 30, 1935, when he led the Tigers to a doubleheader sweep of the St. Louis Browns by collecting 8 hits, scoring 8 runs, and driving in 9 more. After going 3-for-5, with a grand slam, 6 RBIs, and 4 runs scored in Detroit's 18–1 victory in the opener, Fox collected 5 hits in the team's 11–6 win in Game 2, including a homer and a double. He also knocked in 3 runs and scored four more times in the night-cap, finishing the day 8-for-11, with 2 home runs and 15 total bases. Fox's brilliant performance came in the midst of a career-long 29-game hitting streak that finally ended in Washington nearly two weeks later, on July 11.

Fox had another memorable day on August 14, 1937, when he went 7-for-11, with a homer, double, 2 RBIs, and 5 runs scored during another doubleheader sweep of St. Louis, this one by scores of 16–1 and 20–7.

An outstanding postseason performer throughout his career, Fox compiled a lifetime batting average of .327 for the Tigers in World Series play. After batting .286 and amassing a Series-record six doubles in 1934, Fox led all players with 10 hits and a .385 batting average in the 1935 Fall Classic.

NOTABLE ACHIEVEMENTS

- Batted over .300 three times, topping .320 twice.
- Scored more than 100 runs three times.
- Topped 200 hits once (208 in 1937).
- Finished in double digits in triples twice.
- Surpassed 30 doubles four times.
- Stole more than 20 bases twice.
- Compiled on-base percentage in excess of .400 once (.405 in 1936).
- Posted slugging percentage in excess of .500 once (.513 in 1935).
- Led A.L. outfielders with .994 fielding percentage in 1938.
- Led A.L. right fielders in: fielding percentage four times; assists once; and double plays once.
- Three-time A.L. champion (1934, 1935, 1940).
- 1935 world champion.

35

Barney McCosky

Courtesy of Richard Albersheim, AlbersheimStore.com

A speedy outfielder with a sweet left-handed swing, Barney McCosky spent four productive years in Detroit before his induction into the military during World War II and a subsequent back injury brought his time with the Tigers to a premature end. The first graduate of Detroit's sandlots and high schools to play for the Tigers, McCosky proved to be an instant success after he joined his hometown team in 1939, batting over .300 for the first of three straight times, placing among the league leaders in runs scored, hits, doubles, triples, and stolen bases, and topping all A.L. center fielders in putouts and fielding percentage. McCosky continued to excel in his three remaining years in Detroit, annually finishing near the top of the league rankings in batting average, hits, and triples, while also displaying exceptional range in the outfield.

Born to Lithuanian-Polish parents in the mining town of Coal Run, Pennsylvania, on April 11, 1917, William Barney McCosky moved with his family to the city of Detroit at the age of five. Already playing sandlot ball by the time the Great Depression began in 1930, McCosky dreamed of one day playing alongside his hero Charlie Gehringer for the hometown Tigers. Patterning his batting stance and grip after his favorite player, McCoskey starred at Southwestern High School, batting .457 as a junior and .727 as a senior. Nevertheless, the aspiring outfielder initially turned down an offer made by Detroit scout Aloysius "Wish" Egan, instead expressing an interest in attending college. However, Egan and the Tigers eventually persuaded McCosky to sign on the dotted line by offering him a contract that allowed him to play one year of minor league ball before making a final decision. If McCosky failed to perform well in the minors, Detroit agreed to pay for his college education.

The Tigers' gamble on McCosky ended up paying off, since the young outfielder advanced rapidly through their farm system. After three short years in the minors, McCosky arrived in Detroit, earning the team's starting centerfield job on Opening Day in 1939. Displaying a smooth left-handed swing, a keen batting eye, and outstanding speed in the outfield and on the base paths, the 6'1", 184-pound McCosky had an exceptional rookie season, batting .311, driving in 58 runs out of his leadoff spot in the batting order, scoring 120 times, collecting 190 hits, 14 triples, and 33 doubles, stealing 20 bases, and compiling an on-base percentage of .384. A right-handed thrower, McCosky also played the outfield with grace and skill, leading all A.L. outfielders with 428 putouts and topping all league center-fielders with a .986 fielding percentage. McCosky shattered the "sophomore jinx" the following year, when he batted .340, scored 123 runs, amassed 39 doubles, and topped the junior circuit with 200 hits and 19 triples, helping the Tigers capture the A.L. pennant in the process.

Already a fan favorite by the end of his second season, McCosky consistently heard cheers emanating from the stands at Briggs Stadium since the hometown fans enjoyed rooting for one of their own. McCosky's modest and self-effacing nature also made him popular with his teammates and the local newspaper writers, who, according to columnist Jerry Green, began comparing the 23-year-old outfielder to Tiger legend Ty Cobb in terms of his "style, speed, and ability." Meanwhile, shortly after Hank Greenberg enlisted in the service early in 1941, Associated Press cartoonist Thomas (Pap) Paprocki wrote, "In the fuss and fanfare of the induction of Hank Greenberg into the Army, Barney McCosky's fine work for the Detroit Tigers in the outfield and at the plate has been almost completely overlooked."

McCosky, who lacked home run power but accumulated many doubles and triples by driving balls to both gaps, attributed his early success to his batting stance and bat control, stating, "I would just try to meet the ball, not swing hard . . . just like a pepper game."

McCosky often sought out his childhood hero, Charlie Gehringer, for advice. The star second baseman, who took McCosky under his wing after the latter joined the club in 1939, watched the young outfielder carefully as he assumed his normal batting stance, which saw him plant his front foot up in the batter's box as a means of limiting his stride and preventing him from lifting the foot too soon. Gehringer, though, rarely found fault with his protégé's hitting style, more often than not responding to McCosky's queries with a simple, "Keep going."

McCosky had another good season for the Tigers in 1941, although he experienced adversity for the first time in his young career when he wrenched his back while rounding second base during a game against the White Sox at Chicago's Comiskey Park on May 11. Forced to be carried off the field by his teammates, McCosky ended up missing nearly a month of the campaign. Nevertheless, he resumed his hot hitting after he returned to action a few weeks later, finishing the season with a .324 batting average, 80 runs scored, 8 triples, 25 doubles, and a .401 on-base percentage. McCosky spent one more year in Detroit before being pressed into military duty. With Hank Greenberg already in the service and Charlie Gehringer reduced to the role of pinch hitter in his final major league season, McCosky and Rudy York represented the Tigers' primary offensive threats in 1942. For his part, McCosky hit a career-high 7 home runs, knocked in 50 runs, scored 75 times, and led the team with 176 hits, 11 triples, and a .293 batting average.

After being inducted into the U.S. Navy following the conclusion of the 1942 campaign, McCosky spent the next three years serving in the military, failing to return home in time to help his teammates defeat the Chicago Cubs in the 1945 World Series. During the early stages of his enlistment period, McCosky spent time at the Great Lakes Naval Training Center, north of Chicago, and the Bainbridge, Maryland, naval base for advanced training. He also later served in Hawaii and elsewhere in the Pacific, spending virtually all his time as a recreation specialist. In discussing his role, McCosky said, "We had to give exercises, umpire ballgames, set up basketball tournaments, be instructors . . . all this stuff. Everybody played hard, and we really enjoyed playing out there [in the Pacific Theater]."

Even though McCosky's position kept him away from the battle lines much of the time, his three years away from the game significantly impacted his performance when he returned to the Tigers at the start of the 1946 season. Furthermore, his back problems worsened, and he soon injured his leg, robbing him of much of the outstanding running speed he had during the early stages of his career. After McCoskey compiled a batting average of just .198 over the first few weeks of the 1946 campaign, the Tigers traded him to the Philadelphia Athletics for young third baseman George Kell. In analyzing the May 18 deal, New York sportswriter Dan Daniel suggested, "As a prewar baseball name, McCosky stands out. As an actual asset, he is of doubtful worth. Barney is suffering from a leg injury which is said to be chronic. His Detroit batting average this season is under .200."

On the other hand, Kell later recalled in his autobiography, *Hello Everybody, I'm George Kell*, how shocked he was to learn of Detroit's decision to trade a "legitimate star" and "hometown boy" like McCosky for an "unknown third baseman." The future Hall of Fame third sacker and Tigers broadcasting legend also revealed that McCosky told him at the time of the trade, "You'll be better off here in Detroit. You're going to love it here. I hate to leave because this is home. I've had good years here."

In spite of his sadness over leaving Detroit, McCosky rebounded in a big way once he arrived in Philadelphia, compiling a batting average of .354 in 92 games with the Athletics over the final four months of the campaign. McCosky continued to provide the Athletics with solid hitting in 1947 and 1948, posting marks of .328 and .326, respectively, before suffering a serious back injury in the second of those years that brought an end to his time as a full-time player.

The unfortunate incident took place against his former team on June 15, 1948, when McCosky injured himself while attempting to rob Detroit outfielder Dick Wakefield of a home run during the first night game ever played at Briggs Stadium. Backpedaling in an effort to snare Wakefield's long drive to left field, McCosky hit the concrete wall and fell awkwardly on the wooden frame holding the tarpaulin, twisting his back in the process. After passing out and being carried from the field on a stretcher, McCosky amazingly missed only two weeks of action. Yet, he ended up needing spinal fusion surgery, missed the entire 1949 campaign, and never returned to his earlier form after he rejoined the Athletics in 1950. McCosky split his final three seasons between Philadelphia, Cincinnati, and Cleveland, failing to appear in more than 54 games in any one of those years, and announcing his retirement after the Indians released him on July 14, 1953. McCosky ended his career with 24 home runs, 397 RBIs, 664 runs scored, 1,301 hits, 71 triples, 214 doubles, a .312 batting average, a .386 on-base percentage, and a .414 slugging percentage. Over parts of five seasons with the Tigers, he hit 19 homers, knocked in 231 runs, scored 409 times, collected 744 hits, 52 triples, and 130 doubles, batted .312, compiled a .386 on-base percentage, and posted a .434 slugging percentage.

Although former Tigers teammate Hank Greenberg offered McCosky a coaching job in Cleveland's farm system following the latter's retirement, McCosky instead chose to return to Detroit, where he operated a party store on Joy Road, between Greenfield and Southfield, and also worked as a car salesman. He eventually moved to Venice, Florida, where he passed away at the age of 79, on September 6, 1996.

TIGERS CAREER HIGHLIGHTS

Best Season

McCosky had an outstanding rookie season in 1939, batting .311 and placing among the league leaders in runs scored (120), hits (190), triples (14), doubles (33), and stolen bases (20). However, he compiled the best numbers of his career one year later, concluding the 1940 campaign with a batting average of .340, a .408 on-base percentage, a .491 slugging percentage, 123 runs scored, 39 doubles, and a league-leading 200 hits and 19 triples, en route to earning one of his three top-20 finishes in the A.L. MVP voting.

Memorable Moments/Greatest Performances

McCosky helped make history on June 22, 1939, when he led off Detroit's game against Philadelphia with a home run. When Earl Averill followed with another solo blast, the duo became just the second pair of teammates in A.L. history to open a contest with a pair of homers.

Although the Tigers ended up losing the 1940 World Series to Cincinnati in seven games, McCosky turned in a memorable performance, posting a batting average of .304 by collecting 7 hits in 23 official trips to the plate, scoring 5 runs, and drawing 7 bases on balls. In addition to finishing the Series with an on-base percentage of .467, McCosky ran the bases and played the outfield exceptionally well, prompting John Kieran of the *New York Times* to call him "a great all-around player."

McCosky made significant contributions to a number of Detroit wins the following season, leading the Tigers to a 4–3 victory over Bob Feller and the Cleveland Indians on August 7, 1941, by going 3-for-5 with a stolen base, and scoring the game-winning run in the thirteenth inning. On August 20, McCosky made a winner out of Tommy Bridges by driving in the game's only run with an RBI single in the bottom of the 10th inning of a 1–0 win over the Yankees. Just two days later, he hit a three-run homer in the bottom of the ninth inning that enabled the Tigers to defeat Washington by a score of 5-4.

NOTABLE ACHIEVEMENTS

- Batted over .300 three times, topping .320 twice.
- Scored more than 120 runs twice.
- Surpassed 200 hits once (200 in 1940).
- Finished in double digits in triples three times, topping 15 three-baggers once (19 in 1940).
- Surpassed 30 doubles twice.
- Stole more than 20 bases once (20 in 1939).
- Compiled on-base percentage in excess of .400 twice.
- Led the American League in hits once and triples once.
- Led A.L. outfielders with 428 putouts in 1939.
- Led A.L. center fielders in putouts once and fielding percentage once.
- Led A.L. left fielders with 336 putouts in 1942.
- 1940 A.L. champion.

Dick McAuliffe

Courtesy of MearsOnlineAuctions.com

versatile infielder known for his unorthodox batting stance, Dick McAuliffe earned All-Star honors at two different positions for the Tigers during the 1960s, making the A.L. squad three straight times—twice as a shortstop and once as a second baseman. Serving as the Tigers' leadoff hitter for most of his 14 seasons in Detroit, McAuliffe displayed a keen batting eye and unusual power at the plate for a middle infielder of his day, drawing more than 100 bases on balls twice, and hitting more than 20 home runs on three separate occasions. A key contributor to Detroit's 1968 world championship team, McAuliffe led the American League with 95 runs scored, while simultaneously tying a major league record by going the entire season without grounding into a double play. By the time McAuliffe left the Tigers at the conclusion of the 1973 campaign, he ranked among the franchise's all-time leaders in five different offensive categories. More than 40 years later, he remains eighth in team history in both triples and walks.

Born in Hartford, Connecticut, on November 29, 1939, Richard John McAuliffe grew up in the tiny town of Unionville. After starring in baseball, football, and basketball at Farmington High School, McAuliffe signed with the Tigers as an amateur free agent in 1957. He spent the next three years advancing through Detroit's farm system, developing during that time the unusual batting stance for which he later became so well noted. The left-hand-hitting McAuliffe explained years later: "In the minors, I had a hard time adjusting to the velocity, and I hit everything to left field, so they were flooding me on the left side. My coach Wayne Blackburn had me open up my hips and lean back so I could hit the ball where it was pitched and not over-stride. At first, it was difficult to balance but, once I got used to sitting back and then pivoting, it was no problem."

Featuring a batting stance that many likened to that of former New York Giants star Mel Ott, McAuliffe held his hands very high while facing the pitcher almost directly. Then, as the pitcher began his delivery to home plate, McAuliffe closed his stance somewhat, moved his front (right) foot to a more conventional position, and lifted it slightly prior to starting his swing.

McAuliffe's new approach at the plate enabled him to lead the Sally League in runs scored and triples in 1960, earning him his first call-up to the big leagues in September 1960. Appearing in 8 games for the Tigers over the final two weeks of the season, McAuliffe collected 7 hits in 27 trips to the plate, compiling in the process a .259 batting average. After beginning the ensuing campaign at AAA Denver, McAuliffe returned to the Tigers for good in June 1961. Splitting his time between shortstop and third base, the 20-year-old infielder ended up appearing in 80 games and amassing 285 official at-bats for the Tigers, hitting 6 home runs, driving in 33 runs, scoring 36 times, and batting .256. However, while McAuliffe did a creditable job at the plate, he struggled in the field, committing a total of 19 errors. Playing mostly second and third base in 1962, McAuliffe remained erratic in the field, committing 30 miscues in 139 games. Nevertheless, he continued to display promise as a hitter, hitting 12 homers, knocking in 63 runs, batting .263, and compiling a .349 on-base percentage.

McAuliffe took over at shortstop full time in 1963, improving his defense somewhat by making 22 errors in his 133 games at his new post. After spending the previous two seasons hitting out of either the sixth or seventh spot, McAuliffe also assumed a more prominent position in Detroit's batting order, gradually working his way up to the number 2 spot, before eventually moving into the leadoff position two years later. Garnering more than 500 official at-bats for the first time in his young career, McAuliffe hit 13 home runs, knocked in 61 runs, scored 77 times, and batted .262. Although his batting average slipped to .241 the following year, McAuliffe established new career highs with 24 home runs, 66 RBIs, 85 runs scored, and 77 bases on balls, with the last figure enabling him to compile a respectable .334 on-base percentage.

Despite being limited by a broken hand to just 113 games in 1965, McAuliffe earned A.L. All-Star honors for the first of three straight times by hitting 15 homers, driving in 54 runs, scoring 61 times, and batting .260. He followed that up with one of his finest seasons in 1966, hitting 23 home runs, knocking in 56 runs, scoring 83 times, batting a career-high .274, and placing among the league leaders with 8 triples, a .373 on-base percentage, and a .509 slugging percentage. After moving over to second base to make room at short for the slick-fielding Ray Oyler prior to the start of the 1967 campaign, McAuliffe earned his third consecutive All-Star selection by hitting 22 homers, driving in 65 runs, and finishing near the top of the league rankings with 92 runs scored, 7 triples, 105 bases on balls, and a .364 on-base percentage.

McAuliffe subsequently proved to be the offensive catalyst for the Tigers when they captured the A.L. pennant in 1968, earning a seventh-place finish in the league MVP voting by hitting 16 home runs, knocking in 56 runs, topping the circuit with 95 runs scored, placing among the leaders with 10 triples and 82 bases on balls, and going the entire season without grounding into a double play. He also committed only 9 errors in the field.

In discussing his role as leadoff hitter for the world champion Tigers, McAuliffe stated, "I was the type of guy who had a pretty good eye at the plate and got a fair amount of walks. My on-base percentage was always good, so, therefore, if I'm on base quite often, it gives a chance for the number two, three and four hitters to drive me in."

McAuliffe also managed to jump-start Detroit's offense on a number of occasions himself, homering to lead off a game a total of 19 times over the course of his career.

As for his ability to stay out of the double play, McAuliffe told interviewer Peter Zanardi in the early 1990s, "I wasn't quick . . . I wasn't fast. I could get down to first base, being left-handed, and having a quick start at home plate. But, one thing that helped me was leading off so many times with nobody on base."

Known for his aggressive style of play, McAuliffe helped instill in his Tiger teammates a level of intensity that all successful teams need. In discussing that particular aspect of his game, McAuliffe noted, "I always played hard and was very determined, something I learned from my high school coach Leo Pinsky, who was very tough and a hustle, hustle coach. Through my father I was a Yankee fan at an early age, and Phil Rizzuto was my idol—a scrappy little player and a damned good one. What carried me through my long career was having determination and desire."

A knee injury and subsequent surgery limited McAuliffe to only 74 games in 1969. Although the 30-year-old infielder returned to the Tigers the following year to play in 146 games and place among the league leaders with 101 walks, he batted just .234 and scored only 73 times, beginning in the process a downward spiral that continued the next few seasons. After hitting 18 homers but batting just .208 in 1971, McAuliffe assumed a part-time role with the club the next two years, before being traded to Boston for outfielder Ben Oglivie at the conclusion of the 1973 campaign. McAuliffe left Detroit with career totals of 192 home runs, 672 RBIs, 856 runs scored, 1,471 hits, 70 triples, and 218 doubles, a batting average of .249, a .345 on-base percentage, and a .408 slugging percentage.

Looking back at his final days in Detroit, McAuliffe revealed:

> Towards the end of the (1973) season I had it out with Jim Campbell and told him, "You guys never treated me fair financially." I was halfway down the payroll and there were guys making more money who hadn't been there as long as I had. I knew I didn't have too much left but I wanted to get a little bit of a reward. He said, "no, that's not our policy." I told Campbell I wouldn't be back next year. I wanted to finish my career in Detroit and would have if Campbell had come through. He later called me and asked if I wanted to go to Boston, which was closer to my home, and I said fine. I just wish I had finished my career with the Tigers.

McAuliffe assumed a part-time role in Boston in 1974, batting just .210 in 100 games, before retiring at season's end. Although he spent most of 1975 managing in Boston's farm system, McAuliffe ended up returning to the playing field for 7 games when an injury to Red Sox starting third baseman Rico Petrocelli left the team shorthanded. After choosing not to resume his managerial duties the following year, McAuliffe went into the private sector, running a couple of baseball schools in his native Connecticut, before opening a highly successful coin-operated washing machine business that he sold after 10 years. Looking back at the legacy he left behind, McAuliffe says, "The game was very important to me. I took it to heart. I played as hard as I could. I always thought I gave 100 percent, and was proud of the feats I'd done. I thought overall . . . I should have done better. That's just my personal feeling. I think I've been successful."

TIGERS CAREER HIGHLIGHTS

Best Season

Although McAuliffe committed 32 errors at shortstop in 1964, he posted solid offensive numbers for the Tigers, hitting a career-high 24 home runs, driving in 66 runs, and scoring 85 others, despite batting just .241. McAuliffe earned All-Star honors for the third straight time in 1967 by hitting 22 homers, knocking in 65 runs, scoring 92 times, and finishing third in the league with 105 bases on balls. Yet, his .239 batting average and 28 fielding miscues both left something to be desired, even though he compiled a very respectable .364 on-base percentage. McAuliffe earned MVP consideration for the only time in his career in 1968, when he batted .249, hit 16 home runs, drove in 56 runs, and led the league with 95 runs scored. Nevertheless, McAuliffe had his best all-around year in 1966, when, despite appearing in only 124 games, he hit 23 homers, knocked in 56 runs, scored 83 times, and established career highs with a .274 batting average, a .373 on-base percentage, and a .509 slugging percentage. McAuliffe's .882 OPS surpassed by nearly 60 points the second-highest mark he ever posted in that category.

Memorable Moments/Greatest Performances

McAuliffe began his major league career in grand fashion, hitting safely in his first three trips to the plate against Cleveland's Jim Perry during a 9–1 Tigers win over the Indians on September 20, 1960. The 20-year-old infielder finished the day 3-for-5, with 2 singles, a triple, 1 RBI, and 1 run scored.

McAuliffe had the first four-hit game of his career two years later, going 4-for-4 during a 5–1 home win over Boston on May 11, 1962.

McAuliffe went on a power surge in late April 1969, leading off consecutive games against Washington with home runs. Unfortunately for the Tigers, they lost both contests, falling to the Senators by scores of 7–1 and 5–4. He flexed his muscles again on September 17, 1972, when he led the

Tigers to a 6–2 victory over the Brewers by homering twice and driving in 4 runs against Milwaukee starter Jim Colborn.

Yet, McAuliffe is perhaps remembered most for his involvement in a brawl that took place on August 22, 1968, that earned him the nickname "Mad Dog." After singling in his first trip to the plate against Chicago's Tommy John, McAuliffe suffered the indignity of having two pitches thrown in the direction of his head. An irate McAuliffe charged the mound after the second offering, driving his knee into John's shoulder in the process, and sidelining the left-hander for the remainder of the year with a broken collarbone. Subsequently suspended for five games, McAuliffe remains convinced to this day that John threw both pitches with ill intent, stating during an interview conducted 30 years later, "The first pitch at me was right at my head, and I mean right at my head. The catcher never laid any leather on it, and it hit the backstop. The next pitch, he spun me down, threw it behind me."

NOTABLE ACHIEVEMENTS

- Hit more than 20 home runs three times.
- Finished in double digits in triples once (10 in 1968).
- Drew more than 100 bases on balls twice.
- Posted slugging percentage in excess of .500 once (.509 in 1966).
- Led the American League with 95 runs scored in 1968.
- Ranks among Tigers career leaders in triples (8th) and bases on balls (8th).
- Tied major league record in 1968 by going entire season without grounding into a double play.
- Finished seventh in 1968 A.L. MVP voting.
- Three-time A.L. All-Star (1965, 1966, 1967).
- 1968 A.L. champion.
- 1968 world champion.

37

Ray Boone

Courtesy of LegendaryAuctions.com

The patriarch of the first three-generation family to play in the major leagues, Ray Boone spent parts of six seasons in Detroit, establishing himself during that time as one of the Tigers' top offensive threats. In addition to surpassing 20 home runs in four of his five full years with the Tigers, the hard-hitting third baseman batted over .300 twice and knocked in more than 80 runs four times, leading the American League with a career-high 116 RBIs in 1955. Teaming up with Al Kaline and Harvey

Kuenn, Boone helped give the Tigers arguably the junior circuit's most formidable threesome during the mid-1950s, although they failed to seriously contend for the A.L. pennant during his tour of duty with them. A solid fielder, Boone annually placed among the leaders at his position in putouts, assists, double plays, and fielding percentage, leading all A.L. third sackers with 170 putouts in 1954. Nevertheless, Boone is perhaps best remembered for the manner in which his son, Bob, and his two grandsons, Aaron and Bret, carried on his baseball legacy.

Born in San Diego, California, on July 27, 1923, Raymond Otis Boone attended San Diego's Herbert Hoover High School, the alma mater of his boyhood idol, Ted Williams. After earning All-Southern California honors as a catcher his last two years at Herbert Hoover, Boone signed with the Cleveland Indians as an amateur free agent in 1942. Boone subsequently batted .306 in 89 games with Wausau of the Class C Northern League, before he elected to put his playing career on hold for the next three years by enlisting in the navy to serve his country during World War II. Following his discharge in 1946, Boone returned to Cleveland's farm system, continuing to develop his catching skills at Wilkes-Barre of the Class A Eastern League in 1946, before eventually being converted into a shortstop while playing for Oklahoma City of the AA Texas League the following year. After Boone posted a batting average of .355 in his 87 games with Oklahoma City in 1948, the Indians summoned him to the big leagues for the first time on August 27. The 25-year-old shortstop appeared in just six games for Cleveland during the season's final month, mostly as a late-inning defensive replacement, collecting 2 hits in his 5 official trips to the plate.

With starting third baseman Ken Keltner slumping badly and Cleveland's 32-year-old player/manager Lou Boudreau slowing up a bit at shortstop, Boudreau moved himself to third base and named Boone the Indians' new starting shortstop midway through the 1949 campaign. Although Boone subsequently struggled somewhat in the field, committing 21 errors in only 76 games at short, he posted decent offensive numbers, hitting 4 homers, driving in 26 runs, and compiling a batting average of .252. Boone's performance in each of the next three seasons followed a similar script, with him annually ranking among the league leaders in fielding miscues while simultaneously failing to distinguish himself at the plate. Nevertheless, Cleveland general manager Hank Greenberg continued to support his starting shortstop, proclaiming late in 1952, "I will tell you something about Boone. Many people in Cleveland think we ought to get rid of him. If we do, I know of at least four American League clubs that would be happy to have him. It's easy for someone to see that a player has had a bad season. It isn't so easy to find a fellow who is certain to do better. If Boone is not a big-league shortstop, why are those four other clubs anxious to get him?"

One of the four A.L. clubs interested in obtaining Boone's services, the Tigers, ended up acquiring him in an eight-player trade they completed with the Indians on June 15, 1953, that also sent Al Aber, Steve Gromek, and Dick Welk to Detroit in exchange for Owen Friend, Joe Ginsberg, Art Houtteman, and Bill Wight. The Tigers reaped huge benefits from the deal since Boone turned out to be easily the most prominent figure included in the trade. Blessed with a powerful throwing arm, but limited in range somewhat by bad knees and ankles, Boone was actually better suited to play third base than shortstop. Inserted at the hot corner immediately upon his arrival in Detroit by second-year manager Fred Hutchinson, Boone thrived at his new position, improving his defense while also developing into a far more productive hitter. After hitting 4 home runs, driving in 21 runs, and batting .241 in his 31 games with Cleveland, the right-handed swinging Boone hit 22 homers, knocked in 93 runs, and batted .312 in 101 games with the Tigers over the final 3½ months of the campaign. Boone's 26 home runs and 114 RBIs on the year both placed him among the league leaders, as did his 94 runs scored, 8 triples, .390 on-base percentage, and .519 slugging percentage. Boone's strong performance so impressed Hutchinson that the Tiger skipper said at season's end, "With Boone and (rookie shortstop Harvey) Kuenn, I believe we can figure that the left side of the infield is in good hands for at least five years."

Tigers general manager Charlie Gehringer also expressed his satisfaction with Boone when he stated, "He found himself at third at Detroit and gained confidence in the field. That helped his batting. I always considered him a sound hitter. He isn't fooled often. Have you noticed how he guards the plate and tries to hit to right field when the count is two strikes? Other hitters would profit if they did this instead of taking that last wild swing."

Boone followed up his solid 1953 campaign by hitting 20 homers, driving in 85 runs, and batting .295 in 1954, en route to earning his first of two All-Star selections. He also excelled in the field, leading all A.L. third basemen in putouts, while also finishing second in assists, fourth in double plays, and fourth in fielding percentage. Despite being plagued by aching knees throughout the ensuing campaign, Boone again contributed significantly to the Detroit offense, hitting 20 home runs, batting .284, and tying Boston outfielder Jackie Jensen for the league lead with 116 RBIs. He also placed second among players at his position in putouts, assists, and double plays.

In addition to establishing himself as a fan favorite in Detroit with his outstanding all-around play, Boone left a lasting impression on New York Yankees manager Casey Stengel, who said, "In my book, that Ray Boone of the Tigers is the best clutch hitter we face in the course of the season. There's a guy who makes you give him good pitches. Then, when you give them to him, he's apt to belt 'em a mile."

Boone had his last big year for the Tigers in 1956, earning All-Star honors by hitting 25 homers, driving in 81 runs, and batting a career-high .308. Shifted to first base prior to the start of the following season to minimize the wear and tear on his knees, which required regular cortisone injections, Boone experienced a major drop-off in offensive production, finishing the year with only 12 home runs, 65 RBIs, and a .273 batting average. With Boone off to a slow start in 1958, the Tigers elected to part ways with the veteran infielder, including him in a four-player trade they completed with the Chicago White Sox on June 15. Boone remained in Chicago for less than one full year, after which he spent most of his final two big-league seasons serving as a utility player for the Kansas City Athletics, Milwaukee Brewers, and Boston Red Sox. After being released by the Red Sox late in 1960, Boone announced his retirement, ending his career with 151 home runs, 737 RBIs, 645 runs scored, 1,260 hits, 46 triples, 162 doubles, a .275 batting average, a .361 on-base percentage, and a .429 slugging percentage. While playing for the Tigers, he hit 105 homers, knocked in 460 runs, scored 351 times, accumulated 723 hits, 30 triples, and 100 doubles, batted .291, compiled a .372 on-base percentage, and posted a .482 slugging percentage.

Following his playing career, Boone spent more than 30 years working as a scout for the Red Sox, also serving them as an extra coach at spring training. In his role as scout, Boone signed several notable players for Boston, including Curt Schilling, Gary Allenson, and Marty Barrett. During that time, his son Bob established himself as one of the top catchers in the game, earning All-Star honors on four separate occasions. Several years later, Ray's two grandsons, Aaron and Bret, also appeared in the All-Star game, making the Boones the only family to have all members in each generation participate in the Midsummer Classic.

After leaving baseball, Boone spent his final years suffering from diabetes, before passing away from a heart attack at the age of 81 on October 17, 2004. At his memorial service held one week later, grandson Bret told those in attendance, "All the stories I saw referred to (Ray) as the patriarch of the Boone family. I looked up the word 'patriarch' to see exactly what that meant. It said a patriarch was the father and ruler of the family. That's what Gramps was."

TIGERS CAREER HIGHLIGHTS

Best Season

Boone compiled his best overall numbers as a member of the Tigers in 1955 and 1956, concluding the first of those campaigns with 20 homers, a league-leading 116 RBIs, and a .284 batting average, before hitting 25 home runs, driving in 81 runs, scoring 77 times, and batting .308 the following year. However, he actually played his best ball for the Tigers after he joined them in mid-June 1953. Although Boone appeared in just 101 of Detroit's games that year, he hit 22 home runs, knocked in 93 runs, scored 73 others, batted .312, compiled a .395 on-base percentage, and posted a .556 slugging percentage over the season's final 3½ months. Boone's .951 OPS surpassed the marks he posted in each of the other two seasons (.822 in 1955; .920 in 1956) by a considerable margin, making his first year in Detroit his most productive.

Memorable Moments/Greatest Performances

Boone made his Tigers debut a memorable one, going 3-for-3, with a homer, double, 2 walks, and 2 runs scored during a 5–3 win over the Red Sox at Fenway Park on June 16, 1953. Less than two months later, on August 12, 1953, Boone tied a major league record (since broken) by hitting his fourth grand slam of the year during a 7–3 Tigers win over the Browns in St. Louis.

Boone helped the American League put an end to the senior circuit's 4-game winning streak in the annual All-Star Game by following one of Al Rosen's 2 homers with a blast of his own during the American's 11–9 victory over the Nationals in the 1954 All-Star tilt.

Boone had arguably his greatest day at the plate for the Tigers on September 24, 1956, when he went 5-for-5, with 2 home runs and 3 RBIs during a 14–11 loss to the Chicago White Sox. Boone's performance nearly enabled the Tigers to overcome an early 11–0 deficit.

NOTABLE ACHIEVEMENTS

- Hit more than 20 home runs four times.
- Knocked in more than 100 runs once (116 in 1955).
- Batted over .300 twice.
- Compiled on-base percentage in excess of .400 once (.403 in 1956).
- Posted slugging percentage in excess of .500 twice.
- Led the American League with 116 RBIs in 1955.
- Led A.L. third basemen with 170 putouts in 1954.
- Two-time A.L. All-Star (1954, 1956).

38

Billy Rogell

Courtesy of T. Scott Brandon

lthough largely overlooked in favor of Hank Greenberg, Charlie Gehringer, and some of the other more prominent members of Detroit's
starting lineup, Billy Rogell contributed significantly to the success the
Tigers experienced during the mid-1930s. An outstanding fielder and solid
hitter, Rogell led all A.L. shortstops in fielding percentage three straight
years, while also topping all players at his position in double plays twice,
putouts once, and assists once. Paired with Gehringer for more than 1,000

games, Rogell helped give the Tigers one of the longest tenured double play combinations in the history of the sport, trailing only Lou Whitaker and Alan Trammell in Detroit annals. An effective offensive player, Rogell proved to be an excellent leadoff hitter, batting over .290 three times, driving in more than 100 runs once, scoring more than 85 runs five times, and striking out a total of only 316 times in more than 5,000 plate appearances over the course of his 10 seasons in Detroit.

Born in Springfield, Illinois, on November 24, 1904, William George Rogell attended Fenger High School in Chicago, after which he spent two seasons playing in the Southwestern League. Signed to a contract by the Red Sox prior to the start of the 1925 campaign, the switch-hitting Rogell did not find Boston very much to his liking, struggling in particular with the team's insistence that he become strictly a right-handed batter. Reflecting back on his time in Beantown, Rogell later said, "They just screwed me up for a couple of years."

After compiling a batting average of just .195 in 58 games with the Red Sox in 1925, mostly as a second baseman, Rogell spent the entire 1926 campaign in the minors. Recalled by Boston in 1927, Rogell spent the next two seasons serving the Red Sox primarily as a utility infielder, appearing in a total of 184 games and posting batting averages of .266 and .233. After being released by Boston at the end of 1928, Rogell spent the ensuing campaign with St. Paul of the American Association, batting .336 and driving in 90 runs for the Saints. Impressed by the young infielder's performance, the Tigers signed Rogell prior to the start of the 1930 season in the hope that he might become their shortstop of the future. However, Rogell's early-season struggles soon forced him to the bench, where he spent the remainder of the year. Appearing in a total of only 54 games, Rogell concluded his first season in Detroit with just 9 RBIs, 20 runs scored, and a batting average of .167. Not one to give up easily, Rogell rebounded the following year to bat .303 in a part-time role, earning himself in the process a more prominent position in the team's future plans.

After being named Detroit's starting shortstop prior to the start of the 1932 season, Rogell ended up posting solid numbers, finishing the year with 9 home runs, 61 RBIs, 88 runs scored, 14 stolen bases, and a .271 batting average. He followed that up with another good year in 1933, when, appearing in every game for the first of two straight times, he batted .295, compiled a .381 on-base percentage, and ranked among the A.L. leaders with 42 doubles. Rogell also led all league shortstops with 326 putouts and 116 double plays turned. The 29-year-old shortstop subsequently had the finest season of his career in 1934, helping the Tigers capture their first pennant in 25 years by batting .296, knocking in 100 runs, and scoring 114 times. Rogell's 100 RBIs contributed greatly to the major league record 462 runs batted in Detroit's starting infield amassed over the course of the campaign.

Although teammates Hank Greenberg, Charlie Gehringer, Mickey Cochrane, and Schoolboy Rowe garnered most of the newspaper headlines during the Tigers' successful run to the A.L. championship, Rogell proved to be absolutely indispensable to the team over the course of the regular season. In addition to providing outstanding offense from his leadoff position in the batting order, he ranked among the league's top defensive shortstops, leading all players at his position with 518 assists, while also finishing third in double plays and fielding percentage. Third baseman Marv Owen, who manned the left side of Detroit's infield with Rogell for five years, later marveled at his teammate's defensive prowess, stating, "He's the only player I ever knew who could catch a bad hop . . . I don't know how he did it."

An outstanding base runner as well, Rogell swiped 13 bags in 1934, even though he probably could have stolen many more had he elected to do so. But, as he said years later, "They (the Tigers) didn't want me to steal. I had Gehringer and Cochrane and Greenberg hitting behind me."

Rogell also believed that batting leadoff significantly reduced his batting average since he had to take a lot of pitches in order to let his teammates get a good look at the opposing pitcher's "stuff." Steve Steinberg revealed in his Internet column *SteveSteinberg.net* that Rogell once told him, "It (batting leadoff) cost me 20 points in average, but that was my job."

A fierce competitor who played the game with an edge, Rogell proved to be a study in contrast to his double play partner Charlie Gehringer, who became known as the "Mechanical Man," due in large part to his placid demeanor. As told in *The New Bill James Historical Baseball Abstract*, Detroit catcher and manager Mickey Cochrane once reproached his shortstop and second baseman for failing to cover second base on an attempted steal. After Cochrane charged out from behind home plate and screamed at both men, an astonished Rogell looked at Gehringer to see if the latter had anything to say. Seeing that the second baseman had no intention of responding, Rogell yelled to Cochrane, "Goddamn you! Don't you come charging out here telling me how to play shortstop! You go back there and do the catching, and I'll play shortstop! If I'm not good enough, you can find someone else!" Sufficiently chided, the team's player/manager went back behind the plate and assumed his normal position.

Rogell again made major contributions when the Tigers won their second consecutive pennant in 1935, batting .275, driving in 71 runs, scoring

89 times, placing among the league leaders with 11 triples, and leading all A.L. shortstops in fielding percentage for the first of three straight times. He also finished second in assists and topped all players at his position in double plays turned for the second time. Rogell had two more solid seasons before his offensive production began to diminish somewhat, averaging 66 RBIs and 85 runs scored in 1936 and 1937. However, after batting .259, knocking in 55 runs, and scoring 76 times in 1938, he injured his arm playing handball during the subsequent offseason and ended up losing his starting job to 24-year-old Frank Croucher. After Rogell appeared in only 74 games in 1939, the Tigers traded him to the Chicago Cubs for Dick Bartell in a deal the newspapers described as a trade of "one worn-out shortstop for another."

By going to Chicago, Rogell joined a club whose members still resented him and his former Tiger teammates for defeating them in the 1935 World Series. Treated coldly upon his arrival, Rogell often found himself defending his former team, at one point nearly coming to blows with Cubs manager/catcher Gabby Hartnett, who finally shouted to the team's new infielder, "You don't belong here!" After spending virtually all of 1940 riding the Chicago bench, Rogell announced his retirement, ending his career with 42 home runs, 609 RBIs, 756 runs scored, 1,375 hits, 75 triples, 256 doubles, a .267 batting average, a .351 on-base percentage, and a .370 slugging percentage. In his 10 seasons with the Tigers, Rogell hit 39 homers, knocked in 532 runs, scored 669 times, collected 1,210 hits, 64 triples, and 227 doubles, batted .274, compiled a .362 on-base percentage, and posted a 381 slugging percentage.

Although he also had brief stints in the minor leagues as a player and coach, Rogell spent the bulk of his retirement serving as a member of the Detroit City Council, where, among other issues, he fought to get the Southfield Freeway and Metro Airport built. During his 38 years on the council, Rogell also used his position to provide assistance to old ballplayers living in the Detroit area. Years after retiring from public life, Rogell told the *Detroit News*, "All I ever wanted was Detroit to be a better place to live."

After leaving the council, Rogell spent the rest of his retirement in Detroit, where, at age 94, he threw out the first pitch at the final game ever played at Tiger Stadium on September 27, 1999, nearly 70 years after he made his first appearance in a Tigers uniform in the same park. Rogell lived another four years, passing away from pneumonia on August 9, 2003, at the ripe old age of 98. Following his passing, legendary Tigers broadcaster Ernie Harwell said of Rogell, "He was a feisty maverick. He was a good guy in baseball and politics."

TIGERS CAREER HIGHLIGHTS

Best Season

Although Rogell posted solid numbers for the Tigers each year from 1932 to 1938, he clearly had his finest season in 1934, when he batted .296, compiled a .374 on-base percentage, stole 13 bases, accumulated 8 triples and 32 doubles, and established career highs with 100 RBIs, 114 runs scored, and 175 hits. Rogell also led all A.L. shortstops with 518 assists—the second-highest total of his career.

Memorable Moments/Greatest Performances

Despite playing the 1934 World Series on a broken ankle, Rogell performed admirably for the Tigers, collecting 8 hits and driving in 4 runs during Detroit's seven-game loss to St. Louis. The Tiger shortstop turned in his finest effort of the Series in Game Four, leading his team to a 10–4 victory by getting 2 hits and knocking in 4 runs. Rogell also played well in the following year's Fall Classic, collecting 7 hits in 24 official trips to the plate against Chicago's pitching staff, en route to compiling a .292 batting average.

Rogell set a new A.L. record on August 19, 1938, when he walked for the seventh consecutive time. He accomplished the feat over a three-game span.

Yet, the most memorable moment of Rogell's career took place in the fourth inning of Game Four of the 1934 World Series, when, in an effort to complete a double play, the Tigers shortstop hit base runner Dizzy Dean squarely in the forehead with his return throw to first base. Dean, who had been bearing down on Rogell in an effort to break up the twin-killing, subsequently had to be helped off the field after the ball ricocheted off his head and landed more than 100 feet away in the outfield. After being taken to the hospital for tests following the game, Dean quipped, "The doctors X-rayed my head and found nothing." Meanwhile, Rogell later said of the play, "If I'd have known his head was there, I would have thrown the ball harder."

NOTABLE ACHIEVEMENTS

- Knocked in 100 runs once (100 in 1934).
- Scored more than 100 runs once (114 in 1934).

- Batted over .300 once (.303 in 1931).
- Finished in double digits in triples twice.
- Surpassed 30 doubles three times, topping 40 two-baggers once (42 in 1933).
- Led the American League in games played twice.
- Led A.L. shortstops in fielding percentage three times; double plays twice; assists once; and putouts once.
- Two-time A.L. champion (1934, 1935).
- 1935 world champion.

39

Donie Bush

Courtesy of the Library of Congress, Bain
Collection

One of the finest all-around shortstops of the dead-ball era, Donie Bush made significant contributions to the Tigers on both offense and defense over the course of his 14 seasons in Detroit. A diminutive switch-hitter with a keen batting eye, superb bunting skills, and excellent base-running ability, Bush spent most of his time batting leadoff for the Tigers, helping to set the table for middle-of-the order run-producers Ty Cobb, Sam Crawford, and Bobby Veach. Taking full advantage of his

5'6", 140-pound frame, Bush annually placed among the A.L. leaders in bases on balls, topping the Junior Circuit in that category on five separate occasions. He also led the league in sacrifice bunts twice, compiling a total of 337 over the course of his career that ranks as the fifth highest figure in major league history. Bush stole more than 30 bases eight times as well, en route to amassing a career total of 406 thefts. Meanwhile, Bush used his quickness in the field to lead all A.L. shortstops in putouts three times and assists five times, with his 425 putouts in 1914 tying a major league mark that still stands. Bush also participated in nine triple plays during his 16-year career—the most of any player in baseball history.

Born in Indianapolis, Indiana, on October 8, 1887, Owen Joseph Bush grew up on the east side of Indianapolis, where his mother raised him alone following the death of his father at an early age. Bush began his career in baseball shortly after he left his hometown for the woodlands of Canada, first displaying his skills with Sault Ste. Marie, Ontario, in the Class D Cooper Country League in 1905. After splitting the ensuing campaign between three different teams in the lower minor leagues, Bush spent 1907 with the South Bend Greens, where he earned the reputation as the fastest, best all-around shortstop the Central League had ever seen. Sold to the Indianapolis Indians of the American Association prior to the start of the 1908 season, Bush subsequently joined the Tigers late in the year after Detroit owner Frank Navin purchased him for the then-considerable sum of $6,000 to replace the injured Charley O'Leary at shortstop.

Making an immediate impact upon his arrival in the Motor City, Bush helped the Tigers edge out Cleveland for the American League pennant by batting .294 and scoring 13 runs in his 20 games with the club, while also exhibiting outstanding range in the field. The 20-year-old shortstop's exceptional play down the stretch prompted *Baseball Magazine* to write at season's end: "This diminutive and youthful shortstop came to the rescue of the Detroit club and made it possible for them to win the American League pennant. . . . He helped to win the American Association pennant for the Hoosiers with his wonderful all-around work, and then came on to Detroit in time to save Jennings' (Hughie) team from defeat. He is about as fast as Cobb on the bases, a great fielding shortstop and a good batsman—a man who hits right or left-handed with equal efficiency."

Bush claimed the Tigers' starting shortstop job the following year, helping them capture their third consecutive A.L. pennant by batting .273, compiling a .380 on-base percentage, stealing 53 bases, finishing second in the league to teammate Cobb with 114 runs scored, and topping the circuit with 88 bases on balls, 52 sacrifice hits, 157 games played, and 676 plate appearances. His 52 sacrifices remains the fourth highest total in major league history. Despite committing a league-leading 71 errors in the field, Bush also managed to compile the fourth-best fielding percentage among A.L. shortstops, while leading all players at his position with 567 assists. Noted baseball writer Alfred Spink, who founded *The Sporting News* in 1886, subsequently described Bush, "the midget shortstop," as "one of the best players that ever filled that position . . . Bush, the grand little Detroit shortstop, has in a single year won a reputation that other stars well may envy. No member of the Tiger nine is more respected by opposing teams."

It was also during that 1909 season that Bush acquired the nickname "Donie," which teammate Ed Killian bestowed upon him. Bush explained years later, "One day, after I had struck out, I asked Eddie Killian what kind of ball I swung at and missed. Killian said it was a donie ball. I never learned what a donie ball was, but the Tigers started calling me Donie and the name just stuck."

Although the Tigers failed to repeat as A.L. champions in 1910, Bush had another solid season, batting .262, placing among the league leaders with 90 runs scored, 49 stolen bases, and a .365 on-base percentage, and topping the circuit with 78 bases on balls. He also finished second among A.L. shortstops in assists and putouts, while reducing his error total to 51, en route to leading all players at his position in fielding percentage for the only time in his career.

Even though Bush failed to reach .260 in batting in any of the next six campaigns, four times finishing somewhere between .225 and .232, he remained an integral part of Detroit's offense, using his outstanding quickness and ability to reach base via the walk to set the table for the men who followed him in the Tigers' batting order. Bush drew more than 100 bases on balls three times between 1911 and 1916, leading the league in that category on three separate occasions. He also stole at least 35 bases five times and scored more than 100 runs twice, scoring at least 97 times on three other occasions. Meanwhile, Bush led all A.L. shortstops in assists in four of those six seasons, while also topping all players at his position in putouts twice. Bush's 97 runs scored, 35 stolen bases, .252 batting average, .373 on-base percentage, league-leading 112 walks and 544 assists, and major league record 425 putouts in 1914 enabled him to earn a tie for third place in the A.L. MVP voting.

All the while, Bush continued to draw praise for all the "little things" he did on the ball field to help his team win. In 1912, *The Sporting Life* noted, "Bush is one of the hardest men in the game to pitch to. He is so small that a pitcher has to have absolute control to get the ball over for him, and it makes him a most valuable lead-off man for a team, because there is hardly a day that he does not reach the bases one or more times."

Baseball Magazine praised Bush for his range, stating, "In the field, Bush sometimes appears ragged, but this is not owing to lack of finish in handling stinging grounders. It is rather a direct result of his eagerness to spear everything within his reach, and just a little beyond. No chance is too hard for him to try, and more than most fielders can say he pulls down the drive and relays it to first."

Bush had one of his finest offensive seasons in 1917, when he batted .281, stole 34 bases, and led the league with 112 runs scored. However, his offensive production dropped precipitously the next two years, as he batted just .234 and .244, scored a total of only 156 runs, and stole just 31 total bases. Bush rebounded somewhat in 1920, batting .263, scoring 85 times, and leading the league with 48 sacrifice bunts. But, convinced that the 33-year-old Bush had already seen his best days, the Tigers placed him on waivers in August 1921, ending his 13-year association with the ball club. Reporting on Bush's departure from Detroit, an article in the August 25, 1921 edition of *The Sporting News* noted:

> The passing of Bush removes one of the spectacular figures of Detroit baseball history. . . . Built low to the ground and extremely aggressive, Bush presented a spectacle that appealed to the heart of the gallery. He always did things in a sensational manner. His style made the hard ones look harder and the easy chances look hard. . . . Of Bush's fielding, the outstanding feature always was his throwing. In that, more than in anything else, Bush stood apart. He had an uncanny ability to judge the speed of a runner on his way to first. He never seemed to hurry a throw, and he seemed never to throw with speed. Most of the time he apparently lobbed the ball, but he always got his man, sometimes by a fraction of a step—but he got him. This ability of Bush's was always a matter of amazement to spectators, and they could never solve the riddle of it.

Bush left the Tigers with career totals of 9 home runs, 427 RBIs, 1,242 runs scored, 1,745 hits, 73 triples, 181 doubles, 402 stolen bases, and 1,125 walks, a batting average of .250, a .357 on-base percentage, and a .301 slugging percentage. He continues to rank among the franchise's all-time leaders in runs scored, hits, triples, stolen bases, and walks.

After leaving Detroit, Bush joined the Washington Senators, with whom he spent the rest of 1921 and all of 1922 serving as a backup infielder, before retiring as an active player shortly after Senators owner Clark Griffith named him manager of his ball club early in 1923. At the time of his retirement, Bush's 1,158 bases on balls placed him second only to Eddie Collins on Major League Baseball's all-time list. During the decade that extended from 1910 to 1919, Bush walked more times than any other player in the game. He also scored more runs over the course of those 10 seasons than anyone else, with the exception of Ty Cobb, Eddie Collins, and Tris Speaker.

Following his retirement as a player, Bush remained active in professional baseball for another 50 years, serving at different times as a manager, team owner, and scout. His managerial career included stints with the Senators (1923), Indianapolis Indians (1924–1926, 1943–1944), Pittsburgh Pirates (1927–1929), Chicago White Sox (1930–1931), Cincinnati Reds (1933), Minneapolis Millers (1932, 1934–1938), and Louisville Colonels (1939), with his most notable effort coming in 1927, when he piloted the Pirates to the N.L. flag. Bush also co-owned the Louisville Colonels from 1938 to 1940 and the Indianapolis Indians from 1941 to 1952, also serving as president of the Indians during his tenure there. After scouting for the Boston Red Sox from 1953 to 1955, Bush returned to Indianapolis, where he once again served as president from 1956 to 1969. Given the title of "King of Baseball" during MLB's 1963 winter meetings, Bush ended his 65-year association with the national pastime in 1972, when he fell ill during spring training while working as a scout for the Chicago White Sox. Bush passed away three weeks later, at the age of 84, after returning to his home in Indianapolis.

The inordinate amount of significance placed on batting averages during the dead-ball era often caused Bush's offensive contributions to be largely overlooked. Nevertheless, the diminutive shortstop had his supporters, with *Baseball Magazine*'s J. C. Kofoed commenting in 1915, "Just why fans have relegated Bush to the 'poor-hitting class' is beyond me. Donie gets on base and scores more often than any of his slugging mates on the Detroit club."

TIGERS CAREER HIGHLIGHTS

Best Season

Although Bush earned a third-place finish in the 1914 A.L. MVP voting by scoring 97 runs, stealing 35 bases, batting .252, topping the junior circuit with 112 walks, and leading all players at his position in putouts and assists, it could be argued that he had better all-around years in 1909 and 1917. In addition to batting .281 in the second of those campaigns, Bush stole 34 bases, walked 80 times, amassed a career-high 163 hits, and led the league with 112 runs scored.

Meanwhile, Bush led all A.L. players with 88 walks, 52 sacrifice hits, 157 games played, and 676 plate appearances in 1909. He also batted .273, scored 114 runs, and established career highs with 53 stolen bases, a .380 on-base percentage, a .694 OPS, and a league-leading 567 assists at shortstop. Bush's 53 steals set an A.L. rookie record that stood for 83 years, until Cleveland's Kenny Lofton swiped 66 bags in 1992. All things considered, Bush had his finest season for the Tigers in 1909.

Memorable Moments/Greatest Performances

Bush got one of the most notable hits of his career on July 11, 1917, when his infield single in the bottom of the eighth inning broke up a potential no-hitter by Boston's Babe Ruth, who went on to defeat the Tigers by a score of 1–0. Long after he retired, Ruth called the one-hit victory the greatest thrill of his career.

Bush also gained a measure of notoriety by being involved in a record 9 triple plays over the course of his career, with 8 of those coming as a member of the Tigers.

Bush truly stepped to the forefront, though, during the 1909 World Series. While Tiger stars Ty Cobb and Sam Crawford posted batting averages of just .231 and .250, respectively, in Detroit's seven-game loss to Pittsburgh, Bush excelled at the plate in his lone appearance in the Fall Classic, batting .318, drawing 5 bases on balls, scoring 5 runs, compiling a .483 on-base percentage, and posting an OPS of .846.

NOTABLE ACHIEVEMENTS

- Scored more than 100 runs four times.
- Stole more than 30 bases eight times, surpassing 40 steals on four occasions.
- Drew more than 100 bases on balls three times.
- Finished in double digits in triples once (10 in 1913).
- Led the American League in runs scored once; bases on balls five times; sacrifice hits twice; games played once; and plate appearances five times.
- Led A.L. shortstops in assists five times; putouts three times; and fielding percentage once.

- Holds A.L. record for shortstops with 969 chances in 1914.
- Holds major league record for shortstops with 425 putouts in 1914.
- Holds share of major league record for most triple plays (9; tied with Bid McPhee).
- Ranks among Tigers career leaders in: stolen bases (2nd); runs scored (5th); hits (10th); triples (7th); walks (5th); games played (9th); plate appearances (7th); and at-bats (8th).
- Finished third in 1914 A.L. MVP voting.
- Two-time A.L. champion (1908, 1909).

40

Ron LeFlore

Courtesy of CollectAuctions.com

irst discovered playing baseball at Jackson State Penitentiary by then-Tigers manager Billy Martin, Ron LeFlore traveled a long and arduous road to the major leagues. Sentenced at the age of 21 to a term of between 5 and 15 years in state prison for armed robbery, the Detroit native spent most of his youth running afoul of the law, before learning a legitimate profession while behind bars. Signed to a contract by the Tigers in 1973, LeFlore joined the club one year later, earning the starting

center-field job shortly thereafter with his solid line-drive stroke and blazing speed that made him one of the league's top base-stealers. Over the
course of six seasons with the Tigers, LeFlore batted over .300, stole more
than 50 bases, and scored more than 100 runs three times each, earning
All-Star honors once and two top-20 finishes in the A.L. MVP voting.
LeFlore's 78 steals in 1979 remain the third-highest single-season total in
franchise history. Meanwhile, even though he appeared in a total of only
787 games with the Tigers, LeFlore continues to rank fourth on the club's
all-time stolen base list.

Born in Detroit, Michigan, on June 16, 1948, Ronald LeFlore received
a great deal of exposure to the darker side of life while growing up in a
crime-ridden section of the Motor City. The son of an unemployed alco-
holic father and a hard-working mother, whose compassion and resolve
kept the family together, LeFlore spent his early teenage years as a heroin
addict and small-time drug dealer who amused himself many evenings by
breaking into the Stroh's Brewery on Gratiot Avenue, stealing beer, and
getting drunk with his friends. After dropping out of school, LeFlore was
arrested for the first time at the age of 15, before eventually being sentenced
to 5–15 years in state prison for armed robbery.

Never having played in any kind of organized baseball league before,
LeFlore picked up the game quickly while serving his sentence at Jackson
State Penitentiary, prompting fellow inmate Jimmy Karalla to contact Billy
Martin in the hope that the Tigers' manager might be willing to observe
the young outfielder in action. After getting permission for day-parole and
a tryout at Tiger Stadium, LeFlore made such a strong impression on those
in attendance that the Tigers signed him to a contract that enabled him to
meet the conditions for parole. Subsequently assigned to the Clinton Pilots
of the Class A Midwest League for the remainder of the 1973 season, Le-
Flore batted .277, before spending much of the ensuing campaign starring
for the Lakeland Tigers of the Class A Florida State League. Following a
short stay at AAA Evansville, LeFlore joined the Tigers on August 1, 1974,
compiling a batting average of .260, stealing 23 bases, and scoring 37 runs
over the course of the season's final 59 games.

Awarded the starting centerfield job by new Detroit manager Ralph
Houk early in 1975, LeFlore posted solid numbers in his first full season,
batting .258, hitting 8 home runs, driving in 37 runs, scoring 66 times,
and stealing 28 bases out of the leadoff spot in the batting order. Asked
about his sordid past on numerous occasions during the early stages of the
campaign, LeFlore stated in the June 1975 edition of *Baseball Digest*, "I can
handle it. You get yourself into the kind of situation I did, and you've got

to answer some tough questions. Everybody asks about the prison thing, but next year maybe they won't."

In addition to answering questions about his past, LeFlore had to overcome his relative lack of experience on the playing field. Although the 27-year-old outfielder had all the physical tools necessary to succeed at the major league level, he frequently displayed a lack of instincts, particularly on the base paths and in the outfield. In spite of his exceptional running speed, the 6-foot, 200-pound LeFlore proved to be successful on only 64 percent of his stolen base attempts over the course of his first two seasons. He also committed a total of 20 errors during that time, often exhibiting an inability to get a proper jump on the ball from his post in center field. Furthermore, LeFlore compiled an inordinate amount of strikeouts for a leadoff hitter, fanning 139 times in 1975.

Although LeFlore never developed into anything more than a marginal outfielder during his time in Detroit, he worked hard to improve his defense, eventually leading all A.L. outfielders with 440 putouts in 1978. He also gradually developed into a top base-stealer, an outstanding run-scorer, and a solid line-drive hitter. In 1976, LeFlore began an exceptional four-year run during which he batted at least .297, scored at least 93 runs, and stole no fewer than 39 bases each season. He earned the only All-Star selection of his career in the first of those campaigns by placing among the league leaders with 58 stolen bases, 93 runs scored, 172 hits, a .316 batting average, and a .376 on-base percentage. LeFlore followed that up in 1977 by stealing 39 bases, scoring 100 runs, and establishing career highs with 16 homers, 212 hits, and a .325 batting average. He subsequently batted .297, amassed 198 hits, and led the league with 126 runs scored and 68 steals in 1978, before batting an even .300, scoring 110 runs, and stealing 78 bases the following year.

In spite of LeFlore's strong on-field performance the previous few seasons, the Tigers elected to part ways with him prior to the start of the 1980 campaign following a salary dispute, trading him to the Montreal Expos for pitcher Dan Schatzeder. Before LeFlore left Detroit, though, the amazing details of his life were recounted in a book entitled *Breakout* and a made-for-TV movie called *One in a Million*. LeFlore left the Tigers with career totals of 51 home runs, 265 RBIs, 532 runs scored, 970 hits, 38 triples, 126 doubles, and 294 stolen bases, a .297 batting average, a .348 on-base percentage, and a .406 slugging percentage.

LeFlore spent only one season in Montreal, batting .257, scoring 95 runs, and topping the senior circuit with 97 stolen bases in 1980, making him the first player to lead both leagues in that category. After signing with the Chicago White Sox as a free agent at the end of the year, LeFlore assumed a part-time role in Chicago's outfield the next two seasons, experiencing a limited amount of success before being released by the club just prior to the start of the 1983 campaign. Having been accused by the White Sox of being out of shape, missing workouts, and sleeping in the clubhouse in his final year with the club, LeFlore chose to announce his retirement at only 34 years of age, although he had earlier led the teams for which he played to believe that he was 4 years younger than his actual age. LeFlore ended his career with 59 home runs, 353 RBIs, 731 runs scored, 1,283 hits, 57 triples, 172 doubles, 455 stolen bases, a .288 batting average, a .342 on-base percentage, and a .392 slugging percentage.

Unable to land a coaching position with some major league club following his retirement, LeFlore assumed various odd jobs, including working as an airport baggage handler, working as an instructor at a baseball school, and playing in the now-defunct professional Senior League. Along the way, he experienced a considerable amount of adversity, losing a 49-day-old child to Sudden Infant Death Syndrome, facing felony charges of possession of a controlled substance, and being arrested twice for nonpayment of child support. However, LeFlore encountered his greatest hardship in the summer of 2011, when he lost his right leg to arterial vascular disease—a result of his having smoked cigarettes since his teenage years. In addressing his situation, LeFlore, who now lives from month to month on Social Security and his baseball pension, admitted, "I've had some ups and downs." The man who once terrorized opposing teams on the base paths and used his blinding speed to track down balls in the outfield added, "Sometimes I want to jump up and take off—but I can't do that anymore. . . . I've got to worry about my balance all the time. I've got to watch where I walk. I can't look off because I've got no feeling in my leg. I've got to be careful where I step."

TIGERS CAREER HIGHLIGHTS

Best Season

LeFlore had his two best years for the Tigers in 1977 and 1978, placing among the league leaders in numerous statistical categories both seasons. In the first of those campaigns, he knocked in 57 runs, stole 39 bases, scored 100 times, and established career highs with 212 hits, 16 homers, 30 doubles, 310 total bases, a .325 batting average, and an OPS of .838. Although LeFlore posted slightly less impressive overall numbers in 1978, concluding the campaign with 12 homers, 62 RBIs, 30 doubles, 198 hits, 270 total bases, a .297 batting average, and an OPS of .766, he led the American League with 126 runs scored and 68 stolen bases – two very important figures for a leadoff hitter. And, even though he batted 28 points lower than he did the previous season, he walked almost twice as many times (65 to 37), giving him virtually the same on-base percentage (.361 to .363). With the offensive numbers being too close to call, it ended up coming down to the superior defensive play that LeFlore exhibited in 1978, when he led all A.L. outfielders with 400 putouts—75 more than he accumulated one year earlier. Factoring everything into the equation, LeFlore had his best all-around season in 1978.

Memorable Moments/Greatest Performances

LeFlore fashioned a pair of impressive hitting streaks during his time in Detroit, batting safely in 30 straight games in 1976, before hitting in 27 consecutive games two years later. LeFlore's 30-game streak, which ranked as the longest in the American League in 27 years, remains the third-longest in Tigers history. Highlights of the streak, which began on April 17 and ended on May 28, include a 2-hit, 4-stolen-base performance during a 10–1 win over the White Sox on May 1, a 3-hit game against Chicago on May 9, and a 3-hit game against Cleveland on May 14. However, LeFlore had his biggest day on May 23, when he led the Tigers to a 10–6 victory over the Orioles by going 4-for-5, with 3 RBIs and 2 runs scored. Over the course of those 30 games, LeFlore batted .392, with 15 extra base hits, 13 stolen bases, and 22 runs scored.

NOTABLE ACHIEVEMENTS

- Batted over .300 three times, topping .320 once (.325 in 1977).
- Scored more than 100 runs three times, surpassing 120 runs scored once (126 in 1978).
- Topped 200 hits once (212 in 1977).
- Finished in double digits in triples twice.
- Surpassed 30 doubles twice.
- Stole more than 20 bases 6 times, topping 50 steals 3 times, 60 steals twice, and 70 thefts once.
- Led the American League in runs scored once and stolen bases once.

- Led A.L. outfielders in putouts once.
- Led A.L. center fielders in assists twice and double plays turned once.
- Ranks fourth all-time on Tigers with 294 career stolen bases.
- Holds Tigers single-season record for most plate appearances (741 in 1978).
- 1976 A.L. All-Star.

41

Bill Donovan

Courtesy of LegendaryAuctions.com

D ubbed "Wild Bill" for his erratic control and volatile temperament, Bill Donovan spent parts of 11 seasons in Detroit, serving as a key member of Tigers clubs that captured consecutive pennants in 1907, 1908, and 1909. A consistent winner during his time in Detroit, Donovan posted at least 16 victories six times, compiling a record of 25–4 in 1907 that helped the Tigers edge out Philadelphia for the A.L. pennant by just 1½ games. Employing a good fastball and lively curveball, Donovan also consistently ranked among the league leaders in strikeouts, shutouts, complete games, and innings pitched, combining with George Mullin to give the Tigers a formidable twosome at the top of their starting rotation. Donovan became a success at the major league level even though he began his career inauspiciously, posting a total of only 3 victories in his first three seasons with the Washington Senators and Brooklyn Superbas in the National League.

Born in Lawrence, Massachusetts, on October 13, 1876, William Edward Donovan spent his earliest years in baseball playing locally in Lawrence, before moving on to Waverly, New York. After being signed by the original Washington Senators of the National League, the 21-year-old Donovan made his major league debut with the club early in 1898, spending the remainder of the year serving as a part-time pitcher and backup outfielder. By walking 69 batters in only 88 innings of work, Donovan acquired the nickname Wild Bill, a moniker that remained with him the rest of his career. Failing to impress the Senators as either a pitcher or a hitter, Donovan found himself optioned to Richmond in the Atlantic League at season's end. However, the Brooklyn Superbas elected to purchase his contract from Richmond in July 1899, enabling the young right-hander to return to the majors. Although Brooklyn captured the N.L. pennant in each of the next two seasons, Donovan contributed very little, posting an overall record of just 2–4 in only 10 total appearances.

With his career apparently headed nowhere, Donovan suddenly emerged as an elite pitcher in 1901, topping the senior circuit with 25 wins and 3 saves, while also ranking among the league leaders with 36 complete games, 351 innings pitched, 226 strikeouts, and a 2.77 ERA. He followed that up with a solid 1902 campaign during which he posted 17 victories, struck out 170 batters, and threw 30 complete games and 298 innings.

Approached by the Tigers during the subsequent offseason, Donovan decided to switch leagues, taking his sharp-breaking curveball to the newly formed junior circuit. The 5'11", 190-pound Donovan fared well in his first year in Detroit, concluding the 1903 campaign with a record of 17–16 for a team that finished 6 games below .500. He also compiled a 2.29 ERA, threw 307 innings, led the league with 34 complete games, and finished second among A.L. hurlers with 187 strikeouts. Donovan continued to pitch effectively for a Tigers team that finished just 62–90 the following year, compiling a record of 16–16 and an ERA of 2.46, while also tossing 30 complete games and 293 innings. With the Tigers improving their record to 79–74 in 1905, Donovan increased his win total to 18. However, a sore arm the following year relegated him to a record of just 9–15. Donovan also angered A.L. president Ban Johnson in 1906 by leading a player revolt against Tigers manager Bill Armour.

The arrival of Hughie Jennings as Detroit's new manager and the development of Ty Cobb into a truly great player enabled the Tigers to begin a three-year run as A.L. champions in 1907. Donovan also proved to be a huge contributor, compiling a record of 25–4, despite missing the first few weeks of the season due to a lack of conditioning. He also posted a 2.19 ERA, threw 27 complete games, and tossed 271 innings. Donovan had another big year in 1908, concluding the campaign with a record of 18–7, a 2.08 ERA, and 25 complete games. A sore arm once again cut into his playing time significantly the following year, though, limiting him to just 21 appearances and 8 wins.

Donovan gradually became quite popular during his first several years in Detroit, charming sportswriters and fans alike with his engaging and affable personality. However, at the same time, he also developed a reputation as an "umpire baiter," frequently losing control of his temper and forcing officials to eject him from contests by vociferously questioning their calls. The owner of a very active social life as well, Donovan failed at times to take proper care of himself, as can be evidenced by a piece written by author Alfred H. Spink in *The National Game* in 1910 that stated, "Donovan is a giant and pitches, hits, and fields equally well. When in good shape, Donovan has fine speed, a wonderful break on his fastball, and is one of the best fielding pitchers in the country."

Healthy again in 1910, Donovan posted a record of 17–7, before slipping to just 10–9 the following year. Convinced that the 35-year-old pitcher had very little left, Tigers owner Frank Navin asked him early in 1912 to serve the team primarily as a scout. Later in the year, Navin sent Donovan down to Providence in the International League so that he might gain some managerial experience. Donovan ended up spending the better part of three years at Providence, during which time he became a part owner of the club, while also serving as a part-time pitcher. He returned to the major leagues to manage the Yankees in 1915, a position he held for the next three years, also appearing in a total of 10 games for them during that time. After being relieved of his duties in New York following the 1917 season, Donovan returned to Detroit, where he served as a coach in 1918. Donovan also made two appearances on the mound for the Tigers that year, making the final start of his career on the last day of the regular season. He officially announced his retirement at season's end, concluding his playing career with a record of 185–139, a 2.69 ERA, 35 shutouts, 289 complete games, 1,552 strikeouts in 2,965 innings of work, and a WHIP of 1.245. Over parts of 11 seasons in Detroit, Donovan posted a record of 140–96, compiled an ERA of 2.49, threw 29 shutouts and 213 complete games, struck out 1,079 batters in 2,137 innings of work, and compiled a WHIP of 1.192. He ranks among the Tigers career leaders in wins, ERA, shutouts, complete games, innings pitched, and WHIP.

Donovan left his coaching position with the Tigers at the conclusion of the 1918 campaign to manage Jersey City in the International League. After two years there, he became manager of the Philadelphia Phillies in 1921. However, after Donovan was summoned to Chicago in mid-July to testify at the "Black Sox" trial, Phillies management dismissed him just 87 games into the season amid concerns that his familiarity with many of the figures involved in the scandal compromised his integrity. Donovan subsequently returned to the minor leagues, where he spent the next two years managing his teams to championships. Set to be named the new manager of the Washington Senators late in 1923, Donovan boarded the 20th Century Limited train headed from New York to the winter baseball meetings in Chicago. However, a train wreck in Forsyth, New York, took Donovan's life on December 9, 1923. He was only 47 years old at the time of his passing.

TIGERS CAREER HIGHLIGHTS

Best Season

Even though pitching for a losing team caused Donovan to post a record of only 17–16 in 1903, he performed brilliantly his first year in Detroit, leading all A.L. hurlers with 34 complete games, and finishing among the leaders with 307 innings pitched, 187 strikeouts, and a 2.29 ERA. Donovan also pitched exceptionally well in 1908, compiling a record of 18–7, throwing 25 complete games and 243 innings, and establishing career-best marks in shutouts (6), ERA (2.08) and WHIP (1.084). He also walked only 53 batters and compiled a record of 8–1 against the other three pennant-contending ball clubs (Cleveland, Chicago, and St. Louis) in a race that went right down to the wire. Nevertheless, 1907 would have to be considered Donovan's signature season. In addition to posting a league-best .862 winning percentage with a record of 25–4, he compiled an ERA of 2.19, tossed 27 complete games and 271 innings, and finished with a WHIP of 1.122 that nearly equaled the mark he compiled one year later.

Memorable Moments/Greatest Performances

Donovan came up big during the latter stages of the 1907 campaign, following up a 5–4 win over second-place Philadelphia on the last Friday in

September with a 17-inning effort against the A's just three days later in a tie game that kept the Tigers in first place. Detroit clinched the pennant two days later with a doubleheader sweep of Washington. Donovan also turned in a strong performance in the opening game of the World Series, striking out 12 Chicago Cubs batters and working all 12 innings of a contest that ended in a 3–3 tie.

Donovan pitched arguably the biggest game of his career on the final day of the 1908 season, shutting out the Chicago White Sox by a score of 7–0 in a winner-take-all matchup that clinched the A.L. championship for the Tigers.

Donovan struggled somewhat in Detroit's three World Series losses, winning just one of his five decisions. Nevertheless, he compiled an extremely representative 2.88 ERA, earning his only victory in Game Two of the 1909 Fall Classic by going the distance in a 7–2 Tigers win.

A pretty fair hitter, Donovan compiled a lifetime batting average of .207, with perhaps his finest all-around effort coming on May 7, 1906, in an 8–3 win over Cleveland. In addition to banging out a triple during the contest, Donovan accomplished the rare feat of stealing second, third, and home in the same inning, swiping the last base on the front end of a double steal.

NOTABLE ACHIEVEMENTS

- Won more than 20 games once (25 in 1907), surpassing 16 victories five other times.
- Posted winning percentage in excess of .700 three times, topping .800 once (.862 in 1907).
- Compiled ERA below 2.50 seven times.
- Threw more than 200 innings seven times, tossing more than 300 frames once (307 in 1903).
- Completed at least 20 games seven times, topping 30 complete games twice.
- Led A.L. pitchers in winning percentage once and complete games once.
- Ranks among Tigers career leaders in wins (9th); ERA (4th); WHIP (7th); shutouts (5th); innings pitched (9th); and complete games (3rd).
- Three-time A.L. champion (1907–1909).

42

George Mullin

Courtesy of LegendaryAuctions.com

powerfully built right-hander with an intimidating fastball and a sharp-breaking curveball that Hall of Fame second baseman Johnny Evers once referred to as a "meteoric shoot," George Mullin proved to be one of baseball's most durable pitchers during his time in Detroit. A five-time 20-game winner for the Tigers, Mullin started at least 40 games in four consecutive seasons, while also tossing more than 30 complete games and throwing well in excess of 300 innings five straight times. More than a century after he threw his last pitch for the Tigers, Mullin continues to hold franchise records for most complete games and innings pitched—both in a career and in a single season. Although the stocky right-hander pitched in hard luck throughout much of his career, losing as many as 20 games twice, he won much more than he lost, serving as one of the most integral figures on Detroit's pennant-winning 1909 team by leading all A.L. hurlers with 29 victories and a .784 winning percentage. Mullin also contributed greatly to the Tigers' 1907 and 1908 A.L. championship clubs, emerging victorious a total of 37 times over the course of those two seasons.

Born in Toledo, Ohio, on July 4, 1880, George Joseph Mullin spent much of his youth working as a part-time messenger boy, while also attending Toledo's St. John's Jesuit Academy. Displaying an affinity for baseball at an early age, Mullin played in various semipro leagues as a teenager, before signing his first professional contract with Fort Wayne of the Western Association in 1901. After compiling a record of 21–20 and tossing 367 innings in his first year as a pro, the 21-year-old Mullin accepted an offer to join the Detroit Tigers at season's end.

Mullin wasted little time in establishing himself as a regular member of Detroit's starting rotation, throwing 25 complete games and 260 innings in his first A.L. season. Nevertheless, he pitched erratically for the Tigers in 1902, compiling an unimpressive 3.67 ERA and a record of just 13–16 for a team that finished next-to-last in the league with a mark of 52–83. Mullin also struggled with his control, walking 95 batters and leading all A.L. hurlers with 13 wild pitches. At the same time, though, he acquitted himself extremely well at the plate, compiling a batting average of .325.

Mullin improved upon his performance dramatically the following season, concluding the 1903 campaign with a record of 19–15, an ERA of 2.25, and 170 strikeouts. He also tossed 6 shutouts, 31 complete games, and 321 innings, beginning in the process a string of five consecutive seasons in which he surpassed 30 complete games and 300 innings. Yet Mullin continued to display a lack of control on the mound, also starting a streak of four straight seasons in which he led the league in walks.

Rapidly developing into a true workhorse, Mullin made 44 starts, threw 42 complete games, and tossed a career-high 382⅓ innings in 1904, ranking among the A.L. leaders in all three categories. His 42 complete games and 382⅓ innings pitched both remain single-season Tiger records. Mullin also compiled a very respectable 2.40 ERA. Nevertheless, he had little to show for his efforts, finishing the season with a record of only 17–23. Mullin continued to pitch in hard luck in each of the next four seasons, posting records of 21–21, 21–18, 20–20, and 17–13, despite compiling earned run averages that generally fell below the league average. He also annually placed near the top of the league rankings in complete games, innings pitched, and strikeouts, topping the circuit with 35 complete games and 348 innings pitched in 1905.

Over the course of his first seven seasons with the Tigers, Mullin developed a reputation as something of an eccentric, often attempting to gain a psychological advantage over opposing batters by employing such tactics as walking off the mound, loosening or tightening his belt, fixing his cap, tying his shoelaces, and removing imaginary dirt from his glove. He also talked to himself incessantly on the mound, even conversing with hitters and fans of opposing teams who heckled him when he engaged in his act.

Mullin also became known as an outstanding fielder and an unusually good hitting pitcher. Blessed with exceptional range and quickness, Mullin led all A.L. hurlers in putouts once and assists twice, concluding his career with a total of 1,244 assists that places him seventh on the all-time list for pitchers. Meanwhile, he batted over .300 twice, en route to compiling a lifetime batting average of .262.

Although listed as 5'11" and 188 pounds, Mullin experienced major fluctuations in weight during his career, with perhaps the greatest variation taking place prior to the start of the 1909 season. Trimming 40 pounds off his burly frame that had him tipping the scales at well in excess of 200 pounds at the end of the previous campaign, Mullin reported to spring training in the best shape of his career. The results became evident immediately as he opened the season with an 11-game winning streak that remained a club record until Max Scherzer posted 12 consecutive victories at the start of the 2013 campaign. Mullin went on to compile an overall mark of 29–8, along with a 2.22 ERA, 29 complete games, and 303⅔ innings pitched.

Mullin followed up his banner year with two more solid seasons, going 21–12 in 1910 and 18–10 in 1911, before the tremendous workload he assumed his first 10 years with the Tigers finally began to take its toll on him. After finishing just 12–17 with a 3.54 ERA in 1912, Mullin won just one of his first seven decisions at the start of the ensuing campaign, prompting the Tigers to sell him to Washington on May 16, 1913. Mullin's downward spiral continued with the Senators, who assigned him to Montreal of the International League after he posted a record of 3–5 and an ERA of 5.02 in his 11 appearances with them. After spending the remainder of 1913 in Montreal, Mullin jumped to the rival Federal League in 1914, where he posted a record of 14–10 for Indianapolis. He concluded his professional career the following year, going 2–2 for Newark in that same league. Over the course of 14 pro seasons, Mullin compiled a record of 228–196 and an ERA of 2.82, struck out 1,482 batters, threw 35 shutouts, 353 complete games, and 3,687 innings, and posted a career WHIP of 1.290. In his 12 years with the Tigers, he went 209–179, with a 2.76 ERA, 1,380 strikeouts, 34 shutouts, 336 complete games, and 3,394 innings pitched. In addition to holding franchise records for most complete games and innings pitched, Mullin ranks second in wins and shutouts.

After throwing his last pro pitch for Newark in 1915, Mullin continued to participate in semipro ball as a manager and pitcher for various clubs in Indiana and Ohio until 1919. He left baseball for good at the end of the 1921 season, after serving as assistant manager and coach of a club in Rockford, Illinois, of the Three-I League. Mullin subsequently returned to his home in Wabash, Indiana, where he lived and worked as a police officer until a lengthy illness that reduced his stout frame to a mere 100 pounds finally took his life on January 7, 1944. Mullin was 63 years old at the time of his passing.

Nearly 60 years later, author Warren Wilbert paid homage to Mullin in his book *What Makes an Elite Pitcher?* when he noted, "The pitching prowess and significant achievements of George Mullin seem to have faded away on the brittle pages of baseball history. Not even in the Motor City . . . is the name of George Mullin, the burly right-hander from Wabash, Indiana, mentioned."

TIGERS CAREER HIGHLIGHTS

Best Season

Mullin unquestionably had his finest season in 1909, when he established career-best marks in wins (29), winning percentage (.784), ERA (2.22), and WHIP (1.106). In addition to leading all A.L. hurlers in wins and winning percentage, he finished second in innings pitched (303⅔) and third in complete games (29). Mullin's 11 straight wins to open the season remained a club record for more than a century.

Memorable Moments/Greatest Performances

Mullin began his greatest season in style, tossing a one-hit shutout against Chicago on April 14, 1909, to give the Tigers a 2–0 victory on Opening Day.

Although Mullin compiled a record of just 3–3 in his three World Series with the Tigers, he pitched exceptionally well, completing all six games he started, and allowing just 45 hits and 12 earned runs in 58 total innings of work, en route to compiling an ERA of 1.86. Mullin posted Detroit's only victory in the 1908 Fall Classic, allowing the Chicago Cubs 7 hits and no earned runs during an 8–3 Tigers win in Game 3. The following year, he established a seven-game Series record by logging 32 innings against the Pittsburgh Pirates. Mullin posted two of Detroit's three victories against Pittsburgh, including a 5-hit, 10-strikeout performance during a 5–0 Tigers win in Game Four.

Even though Mullin concluded the 1912 campaign with a record of just 12–17, he pitched two of his most memorable games that year. After notching his 200th career victory on May 21 by out-dueling Washington's Walter Johnson 2–0, Mullin hurled the first no-hitter in franchise history during a 7–0 win over the St. Louis Browns on July 4, his 32nd birthday. Mullin punctuated his brilliant performance by delivering 3 hits and knocking in 2 runs.

NOTABLE ACHIEVEMENTS

- Won at least 20 games five times, topping 17 victories on four other occasions.
- Posted winning percentage in excess of .700 once (.784 in 1909).
- Compiled ERA below 2.50 three times.
- Threw more than 200 innings eleven times, tossing more than 300 frames six times.
- Completed more than 20 games eleven times, throwing more than 30 complete games five times, and tossing more than 40 once (42 in 1904).
- Led A.L. pitchers in wins once; winning percentage once; complete games once; and innings pitched once.
- Ranks seventh all-time among major league pitchers with 1,244 career assists.
- Holds Tigers career records for most complete games (336) and innings pitched (3,394).
- Ranks among Tigers career leaders in wins (2nd); ERA (6th); strikeouts (7th); shutouts (2nd); games started (3rd); and pitching appearances (8th).
- Holds Tigers single-season records for most complete games (42) and innings pitched (382⅓).
- Three-time A.L. champion (1907–1909).

43

John Hiller

Courtesy of MearsOnlineAuctions.com

The greatest relief pitcher in Tigers history, John Hiller spent his entire 15-year career in Detroit, working almost exclusively out of the bull-pen his final 9 seasons after earlier serving as a swingman. A study in courage and perseverance, Hiller established a new major league record by recording 38 saves in 1973, just two years after suffering a massive heart attack. The following season, the hard-throwing left-hander set an A.L. re-cord that still stands by winning 17 games in relief—one of three times he posted double-digit wins as a reliever. By the time Hiller retired in 1980, he ranked fourth in A.L. history in saves (125), trailing only Sparky Lyle, Hoyt Wilhelm, and Rollie Fingers. Meanwhile, his 545 pitching appearances placed him first on the Tigers' all-time list—a position he still maintains.

Born in Toronto, Ontario, Canada, on April 8, 1943, John Frederick Hiller grew up in nearby Scarborough, playing goaltender in various hockey youth leagues and rooting for the hometown Maple Leafs. A hockey fanatic during his formative years as an athlete, Hiller once joked that he would have given up a year of baseball just to spend one game tending goal in the National Hockey League. Nevertheless, after taking up baseball as a teenager in order to remain active between hockey seasons, Hiller gradually developed an affinity for the game, stating years later, "I just loved playing and got better and better."

After signing with the Tigers as an amateur free agent in 1962, Hiller spent the next three years advancing through Detroit's farm system, transitioning from a starter to a reliever while playing for Montgomery in the Southern League in 1965. Summoned to the big leagues for the first time in September 1965, the 22-year-old left-hander appeared in five games with the Tigers over the final three weeks of the season, tossing 6 scoreless innings of relief and earning his first major league save. Hiller subsequently spent virtually all of the ensuing campaign at AAA Syracuse, before being recalled by the Tigers early in 1967. Although he also made six starts following his return to Detroit, Hiller worked primarily out of the Tigers' bullpen, posting a record of 4–3 and a 2.63 ERA, while also saving 3 games, in 23 appearances and 65 total innings of work. Serving as a spot starter/middle-inning reliever in 1968, Hiller pitched well for the eventual world champions, finishing 9–6 with a 2.39 ERA, completing 4 of his 12 starts, picking up 2 saves, and surrendering only 92 hits in 128 innings of work.

Despite adding the slider to his repertoire of pitches, Hiller struggled somewhat in 1969, allowing 97 hits in 99⅓ innings of work, and posting a record of 4–4, with a 3.99 ERA and 4 saves, while continuing in his dual role of starter/reliever. He improved upon his performance somewhat the following season, though, going 6–6, with a 3.03 ERA and 3 saves, and surrendering just 82 hits to the opposition in 104 innings of work.

Only 27 years old at the conclusion of the 1970 campaign, Hiller experienced a life-threatening event on January 11, 1971, when he suffered three heart attacks. In truth, part of the blame for his health problems lay squarely on the shoulders of Hiller, who failed to take proper care of himself. Officially listed at 6'1" and 185 pounds in Detroit's yearbook, Hiller saw his weight balloon to nearly 225 pounds by the end of his fourth full season with the club. Hoping to improve his physical condition after recovering from his massive coronary, Hiller subsequently underwent experimental intestinal bypass surgery designed to help him lose weight. He then quit smoking, cut down on his drinking, and began eating healthier. After sitting out the entire 1971 campaign, Hiller worked out feverishly during the subsequent offseason, getting himself into the best shape of his young career. He also learned how to throw a changeup—an offering that eventually made him a more successful pitcher since it proved to be a perfect complement to his slider and 90–91 mph fastball.

Hiller pitched well after he rejoined the Tigers in July 1972, compiling a 2.03 ERA and saving 3 games. He completed his remarkable comeback the following year, turning in an extraordinary performance that saw him go 10–5, with a 1.44 ERA and a league-leading 38 saves in his first season as a full-time reliever. Hiller, who threw 125⅓ innings and led the league with 65 appearances, broke the single-season record of 37 saves established one year earlier by Cincinnati's Clay Carroll, en route to earning a fourth-place finish in the A.L. MVP voting and A.L. Fireman of the Year and Comeback Player of the Year honors. He also won Major League Baseball's Hutch Award, presented annually to the player who "best exemplifies the fighting spirit and competitive desire" of former Tigers manager Fred Hutchinson (who died of cancer) by persevering through adversity.

Hiller followed that up with another exceptional performance in 1974, throwing 150 innings, compiling a 2.64 ERA, saving 13 games, and compiling a record of 17–14 for a Detroit team that finished the regular season just 72–90. Hiller's 17 wins out of the bullpen established a new A.L. mark, earning him the only All-Star selection of his career.

Hiller again pitched well in 1975, saving 14 games and compiling a 2.17 ERA through July 25, before a pulled muscle brought his season to a premature end. Healthy again in 1976, Hiller had another big year, going 12–8, with 13 saves and a 2.38 ERA. After a subpar 1977 campaign in which he also started 8 games, Hiller returned to the bullpen full time in 1978, finishing the year with a record of 9–4, 15 saves, and a 2.34 ERA. However, he also injured his shoulder in late August, limiting his effectiveness the remainder of his career. After saving just 9 games and posting an inordinately high ERA of 5.22 in 1979, Hiller appeared in just 11 games in 1980 before he elected to announce his retirement on May 30. He ended his career with a record of 87–76, a 2.83 ERA, 125 saves, 1,036 strikeouts in 1,242 innings of work, and a WHIP of 1.268. He also threw 13 complete games and 6 shutouts. Hiller's 125 saves remained a club record until Mike Henneman surpassed it in 1993.

Looking back at his decision to retire early in 1980, Hiller says, "I was happy, my family was happy with my career. I was 37 years old—the oldest guy on the team and the last link to our '68 championship. We had a young club, with Sparky Anderson in as the new manager, and he wanted to clean house from the old establishment. I told Jim Campbell that it was time for me to go and the comment was, 'I respect your decision.'"

Following his retirement, Hiller initially planned to return to the Tigers as a roving pitching coach, before a circulatory blockage behind one of his knees necessitated the amputation of his leg. Hiller subsequently entered the insurance business and briefly owned a pet store in Duluth, Minnesota, before retiring to Michigan's Upper Peninsula, where he currently lives.

In discussing his legacy in *Baseball Men: The Comeback*, Hiller said, "Well, some people have told me I've been an inspiration. You don't know what it's meant to me. What can I say? I was just a ballplayer who wanted to make a living; I didn't set out to be a spokesman for anything, but I was happy for the opportunities to help when they came up. Every time I visited quite a few kids in the hospital or in cancer units, and every time I went there to help them, they helped me by showing their inner strength."

CAREER HIGHLIGHTS

Best Season

It could be argued that Hiller had his greatest season in 1974, when he broke Dick Radatz's A.L. record of 16 relief wins (set in 1964 with the Boston Red Sox) by amassing 17 victories coming out of the bullpen. Hiller also compiled a 2.64 ERA, saved 13 games, struck out 134 batters in 150 innings of work, and posted a WHIP of 1.260. By finishing with 17 wins and 13 saves, Hiller had a hand in 30 (or 42%) of Detroit's 72 victories. However, Hiller proved to be even more dominant in 1973, when he went 10–5 with a 1.44 ERA and established a new major league record by accumulating 38 saves. He also struck out 124 batters in 125⅓ innings of work, and allowed the opposition only 89 hits, en route to compiling a WHIP of 1.021. Hiller entered the game in the sixth inning or earlier a total of 13 times, working more than one inning in 40 of his 65 appearances. His 1.44 ERA remains a single-season record for Tigers hurlers. Hiller's fabulous performance earned him fourth-place finishes in both the A.L. Cy Young and A.L. MVP balloting.

Memorable Moments/Greatest Performances

Although Hiller ended up finding a home in the Tigers' bullpen, he displayed an ability to be an effective starter early in his career, tossing back-to-back shutouts in late August 1967. After hurling a complete-game 4-hitter in defeating Cleveland by a score of 4–0 on August 20, Hiller returned to the mound five days later to blank the Athletics on just 6 hits during a 3–0 victory.

Hiller also demonstrated a propensity for striking out batters in bunches during the early stages of his career, fanning the first 6 batters he faced during an August 6, 1968, start against the Indians. Hiller surpassed that figure two years later, when he struck out 7 consecutive Indians on the final day of the 1970 regular season. Making just his fifth start of the year, Hiller turned in arguably the finest performance of his career, defeating the Indians by a score of 1–0, on just 2 hits, while striking out 11. After fanning the side in both the third and fourth innings, Hiller struck out the first batter he faced in the fifth, tying in the process an A.L. record for the most consecutive batters retired on strikes.

Hiller also excelled during the 1972 postseason, throwing 3⅓ innings of scoreless, one-hit ball against Oakland in the ALCS, and picking up the win in Game Four after squelching an A's rally in the top of the tenth inning.

NOTABLE ACHIEVEMENTS

- Saved more than 30 games once (38 in 1973).
- Won more than 10 games three times.
- Compiled ERA below 3.00 eight times, posting under 2.00 once (1.44 in 1973).
- Threw more than 100 innings six times.
- Struck out more than 100 batters four times.
- Led A.L. pitchers with 38 saves and 65 appearances in 1973.
- Holds Tigers career record for most pitching appearances (545).
- Ranks among Tigers career leaders in saves (3rd) and ERA (7th).
- Holds Tigers single-season record for lowest ERA (1.44 in 1973).
- Holds A.L. record for most relief wins in a season (17 in 1974).
- Finished fourth in 1973 A.L. MVP voting.
- Finished fourth in 1973 A.L. Cy Young voting.

- 1973 Hutch Award winner.
- 1973 Comeback Player of the Year.
- 1973 Fireman of the Year.
- 1974 A.L. All-Star.
- 1968 A.L. champion.
- 1968 world champion.

Schoolboy Rowe

Courtesy of Boston Public Library, Leslie Jones Collection

ombining outstanding velocity with exceptional control, Lynwood "Schoolboy" Rowe established himself as one of the American League's premier pitchers his first few years with the Tigers, before chronic arm problems compromised his performance somewhat the rest of his career. After arriving in Detroit in 1933, Rowe helped lead the Tigers to their first A.L. pennant in 25 years the following season by compiling a record of 24–8. Along the way, the 6'4", 210-pound right-hander reeled off 16 consecutive victories, tying in the process a league mark previously shared by Walter Johnson, Lefty Grove, and Smokey Joe Wood. Rowe also posted 19 wins in each of the next two seasons, concluding his first four major league campaigns with a sparkling 69–35 record. Unfortunately, arm problems forced him to spend virtually all of the next two seasons in the minor leagues, robbing him of his once-blazing fastball and turning him into more of an off-speed pitcher. Yet, even though Rowe never fully regained his earlier form, he remained an effective pitcher for the Tigers his final few seasons with them, compiling an overall record of 36–27 between 1937 and 1942, including a league-leading mark of 16–3 in 1940. In all, Rowe helped the Tigers advance to the World Series three times, serving as a key member of their 1934 and 1940 A.L. pennant-winning pitching staffs, and their 1935 world championship staff.

Born in Waco, Texas, on January 11, 1910, Lynwood Thomas Rowe attended El Dorado High School after moving with his family to that Arkansas city as a young boy. Excelling in several sports as a teenager, including baseball, football, basketball, track, and tennis, Rowe earned the nickname "Schoolboy" at the age of 15 when he competed against fully grown men in a semiprofessional baseball league as a member of a team sponsored by his town's newspaper. Although Rowe attained All-State honors twice in football while in high school, he eventually decided to pursue a career in baseball. Discovered by a Detroit Tigers scout, whom he impressed with both his pitching and hitting skills, Rowe signed his first professional contract in 1932. He subsequently spent the entire campaign playing for the Beaumont Express in the Texas League, helping them capture the league championship by winning 19 games and finishing first in the circuit with a 2.30 earned run average.

Summoned to the big leagues, along with former Express teammate Hank Greenberg, at the start of the 1933 season, Rowe gradually earned a spot in Detroit's starting rotation, concluding the campaign with a 7–4 record and a 3.58 ERA. He developed into a star the following year, posting 16 straight wins at one point during the season, en route to compiling an overall mark of 24–8. Rowe finished the season second in the league with 24 wins and a .750 winning percentage, placed third in the circuit with 149 strikeouts and 266 innings pitched, and also ranked among the league leaders with 20 complete games and a 3.45 ERA. He also led all A.L. hurlers in strikeouts-to-walks ratio for the first of two straight times. Rowe's exceptional performance earned him a fourth-place finish in the A.L. MVP voting.

Rowe's overpowering fastball and excellent control both contributed greatly to the success he experienced on the mound at such an early stage in his career. He also excelled as a hitter, frequently helping his own cause by delivering key hits in games he started. After batting .303 and driving in 22 runs in only 109 at-bats in 1934, he hit .312 and knocked in 28 runs in the same number of at-bats the following year. Rowe's idiosyncratic nature also ably assisted him, with his tendency to talk to himself on the mound helping to keep opposing hitters off balance. After striking out against Rowe on one particular occasion, Lou Gehrig returned to the Yankee bench and muttered, "That's the strangest fella I've ever faced."

Before long, Rowe became a fan favorite in Detroit, with his Southern charm, outgoing personality, and eccentricities gaining him fame beyond the playing field. One of the most superstitious players in the history of the game, Rowe carried around amulets, talismans, rabbit's feet, four-leaf clovers, and lucky coins, always picked up his glove with his left hand, and even conversed with the ball from time to time. Particularly popular with female fans due to his good looks and public devotion to his high school sweetheart, Edna Mary Skinner, whom he married shortly after the 1934 World Series, Rowe increased his celebrity on September 13, 1934, when he asked his fiancée during a nationally broadcast radio interview, "How'm I doing, Edna honey?" Although Rowe's query further endeared him to women across the country, it set him up as a target for opposing players and fans, who subsequently enjoyed taunting him with his own words. When asked by a reporter that same season for the secret to his success, Rowe responded that he would "just eat a lot of vittles, climb on that mound, wrap my fingers around the ball, and say to it, 'Edna, honey, let's go.'"

Unfortunately, Rowe's period of dominance proved to be short-lived. After posting 19 victories in both 1935 and 1936, he developed a sore arm that allowed him to appear in a total of only 14 games for the Tigers over the course of the next two seasons. Rowe never again displayed the ability to dominate opposing hitters after he regained his regular spot in Detroit's starting rotation in 1939, concluding the campaign with a record of just 10–12 and an ERA of 4.99. However, he subsequently evolved into more of a complete pitcher, using a variety of off-speed pitches and his exceptional control to compensate for his loss in velocity. Although Rowe recorded only 61 strikeouts in 169 innings of work in 1940, he compiled a very respectable 3.46 ERA and posted a record of 16–3 that gave him a league-best .842 winning percentage.

No longer able to take the mound every fourth day by 1941, Rowe made only 14 starts and appeared in a total of only 27 games for the Tigers, compiling in the process a record of 8–6. Sold to Brooklyn early in 1942, Rowe remained with the Dodgers until they traded him to the Phillies prior to the start of the ensuing campaign. Experiencing something of a rebirth in Philadelphia in 1943, Rowe finished 14–8 with a 2.94 ERA and surrendered only 29 bases on balls in 199 innings of work.

Rowe missed all of 1944 and 1945 while serving in the U.S. Navy during World War II. However, he remained active in baseball, spending most of that time at the Great Lakes Naval Training Station, where he pitched and played the outfield for a Navy team composed of former professional players and managed by Mickey Cochrane.

Returning to the Phillies in 1946, the 36-year-old Rowe began a successful three-year run during which he compiled an overall record of 35–24 and earned the last of his three All-Star selections. Released by the Phillies after he finished just 3–7 with a 4.82 ERA in 1949, Rowe pitched in 16 games for San Diego in the Pacific Coast League in 1950 before retiring as an active player. He concluded his major league career with a record of 158–101, an ERA of 3.87, 137 complete games, 22 shutouts, a WHIP of 1.302, and 913 strikeouts in 2,219 innings of work. During his time in Detroit, Rowe posted a mark of 105–62, compiled an ERA of 4.01, threw 92 complete games and 16 shutouts, posted a WHIP of 1.331, and struck out 662 batters in 1,445 innings. His .629 winning percentage while pitching for the Tigers represents the fifth best mark in franchise history.

Following his playing career, Rowe served the Tigers in various capacities, spending time as a manager at Williamsport and as a roving scout assigned to cover Arkansas, Louisiana, Mississippi, and east Texas. He also spent the 1954 and 1955 campaigns working as the Tigers' pitching coach. Rowe passed away at his home in El Dorado, Arkansas, on January 8, 1961, just three days short of his 51st birthday, after suffering a heart attack.

TIGERS CAREER HIGHLIGHTS

Best Season

Although Rowe pitched extremely well for the Tigers in 1940, earning a seventh-place finish in the A.L. MVP voting by compiling a record of 16–3, he clearly had his best season in 1934. In addition to leading all A.L. hurlers with a strikeouts-to-walks ratio of nearly 2-to-1, Rowe finished second in the league with 24 wins and a .750 winning percentage. He also ranked among the leaders with 149 strikeouts, 20 complete games, 266 innings pitched, and a 3.45 ERA, en route to earning a fourth-place finish in the league MVP balloting.

Memorable Moments/Greatest Performances

Rowe turned in an exceptional performance in his first major league start, tossing a 6-hit shutout against the White Sox during a 3–0 Tigers win on April 15, 1933.

Rowe earned his 14th consecutive victory on August 17, 1934, when he defeated New York by a score of 2–0. Rowe surrendered just 3 hits to the hard-hitting Yankees, while striking out 11. A little over one week later, on August 25, Rowe tied the A.L. record for most consecutive wins by defeating the Senators 4–2 in Washington. Trailing in the contest by a score of 2–1 heading into the ninth inning, Rowe delivered the game-winning blow with an RBI single in the top of the frame.

Although the Tigers ended up losing the 1934 World Series to the Cardinals in seven games, Rowe performed brilliantly in Game Two, tying the Fall Classic at a game apiece by going the distance in a 12-inning, 3–2 Detroit win. Rowe shut out St. Louis over the final nine frames, retiring 22 straight batters at one point during the contest. He finished the Series with a record of 1–1 and a 2.95 ERA. Rowe again pitched well in the World Series the following year, tossing two complete games and compiling a 2.57 ERA, even though he won just one of his three decisions.

Rowe turned in one of his finest all-around performances on August 14, 1935, when he defeated the Senators by a score of 18–2 and went 5-for-5 at the plate, with a double, triple, 4 RBIs, and 3 runs scored.

NOTABLE ACHIEVEMENTS

- Won more than 20 games once, posting 19 victories on two other occasions.
- Posted winning percentage in excess of .700 twice, topping .800 once (.842 in 1940).
- Threw more than 200 innings three times.
- Completed more than 20 games twice.
- Led A.L. pitchers in winning percentage once and shutouts once.
- Led A.L. pitchers in fielding percentage twice.
- Ranks fifth in Tigers history with .629 career winning percentage.
- Holds share of A.L. record with 16 consecutive wins.
- Finished fourth in 1934 A.L. MVP voting.
- 1934 *Sporting News* All-Star selection.
- Two-time A.L. All-Star (1935, 1936).
- Three-time A.L. champion (1934, 1935, 1940).
- 1935 world champion.

Rocky Colavito

Courtesy of LegendaryAuctions.com

cquired by the Tigers in the stunning trade that sent Harvey Kuenn to the Indians, Rocky Colavito had already established himself as one of the American League's most popular players and feared sluggers by the time he arrived in Detroit in 1960. Although Tiger fans never treated Colavito with the same reverence he received in Cleveland, the hard-hitting outfielder proved to be an extremely productive player during his four years in Detroit, surpassing 30 home runs three times and 100 RBIs twice. Indeed, Colavito's performance over the course of the 1961 campaign remains one of the most prolific ever turned in by a Tigers player, with his 45 home runs and 140 RBIs continuing to rank among the top-five single-season totals ever compiled by a member of the team. Also a solid outfielder with a powerful throwing arm, Colavito led all players at his position in putouts three times, assists twice, and fielding percentage twice during his time in Detroit.

Born in the Bronx, New York, on August 10, 1933, Rocco Domenico Colavito, like most young Italian boys of the day, grew up idolizing Joe DiMaggio. Hoping to follow in his hero's footsteps, young Rocco dropped out of Theodore Roosevelt High School after his sophomore year to pursue his dream of playing in the major leagues. Looking back at his decision years later, Colavito admitted, "It was a big mistake. I didn't want kids to say, 'He dropped out of school and he made the big leagues.'"

A gifted athlete with outstanding power at the plate and an exceptional throwing arm, Colavito began playing semipro baseball immediately after leaving school. Eventually given a tryout at Yankee Stadium by the Indians, Colavito signed with Cleveland at the tender age of 17 in 1951, after appealing a ruling in place at the time that prohibited a player from signing a professional contract until his class graduated. Cleveland scout Mike McNally later recalled, "We had a tryout in the Bronx for about 8 or 10 kids. I saw Rocky make a throw from the outfield. That was enough for me. I don't think I have ever seen a stronger arm."

After initially being assigned to Daytona Beach of the Class D Florida State League, Colavito spent the next five years working his way up Cleveland's farm system, before finally earning a late-season call-up in September 1955. Appearing in just five games over the final three weeks of the campaign, the 22-year-old outfielder hit safely 4 times in 9 trips to the plate, compiling in the process a .444 batting average.

Colavito began the ensuing campaign in the Pacific Coast League but returned to Cleveland in June to begin a string of 11 consecutive seasons in which he hit more than 20 home runs. Starting in right field for the Indians, Colavito appeared in 101 games, hit 21 homers, knocked in 65 runs, and batted .276, en route to earning a second-place finish in the A.L. Rookie of the Year voting. He followed that up with another solid performance in 1957, finishing his first full season with 25 home runs, 84 RBIs, and a .252 batting average, and leading all players at his position in putouts for the first of five times.

After being convinced by Cleveland manager Joe Gordon to cut down on his swing the following year, Colavito emerged as one of baseball's top sluggers, concluding the 1958 campaign with 41 home runs, 113 RBIs, a career-high .303 batting average, and a league-leading .620 slugging percentage, while also placing third among A.L. outfielders with 14 assists and topping the circuit with 6 double plays turned from the outfield. Colavito's outstanding all-around performance enabled him to finish third in the A.L. MVP balloting. Although his batting average dropped precipitously to .257 in 1959, he knocked in 111 runs and led the league with 42 home runs and 301 total bases, en route to earning the first of his six All-Star selections and a fourth-place finish in the MVP voting. On June 10 of that year, Colavito became just the eighth player in major league history to hit 4 home runs in one game, accomplishing the feat in an 11–8 win over the Orioles in Baltimore.

Colavito's ability to hit home runs in huge bunches made him one of the American League's most feared sluggers. Despite being predominantly a pull hitter, the right-hand-swinging Colavito possessed power to all fields, as New York Yankees right-hander Bob Turley suggested when he said, "There isn't a park he can't drive 'em out of with his power. . . . Even if you fool him on a pitch, he can still hit the ball out of the park."

Although Colavito suffered from flat feet, limiting his speed on the base paths and range in the outfield, he caught nearly everything he reached, leading all players at his position in fielding percentage on three separate occasions. Meanwhile, base runners rarely challenged his powerful right arm, which opposing players compared favorably to that of Roberto Clemente.

Colavito's playing ability, muscular 6'3", 200-pound frame, matinee idol looks, and charisma turned him into an icon in the city of Cleveland before long. Boys emulated him on the sandlots, copying his batting stance and the manner in which he flexed his bat behind his back before stepping up to the plate to hit. Girls doted on him. And fans of all ages appreciated his work ethic and accommodating nature, which made him accessible to the many people who sought his autograph after each game.

The level of popularity Colavito reached during his time in Cleveland made it difficult for Indians fans to accept the announcement made on April 17, 1960—just two days before the opening of the regular season— that their favorite player had been dealt to the Tigers for defending A.L. batting champion Harvey Kuenn. Cleveland GM Frank "Trader" Lane attempted to quell the anger subsequently expressed by Indians fans by proclaiming to the press, "What's all the fuss about? All I did was trade hamburger for steak," but Tigers GM Bill DeWitt jokingly responded that he liked hamburger. The Detroit fans and media similarly rejoiced, with Edgar Hayes, sports editor of the *Detroit Times*, writing, "The Tigers lost 30 games by one run last season due to the lack of a long ball hitter. This deal strengthens the Tigers and weakens the Indians. Colavito hit 8 home runs in spring training this year, while the entire Detroit club has hit only 14."

The trade turned out to be a steal for the Tigers, who benefited greatly from Colavito's ability to hit the long ball. Colavito experienced something of an off-year in 1960, hitting 35 home runs, but driving in just 87 runs, scoring only 67 times, and batting just .249. However, he rebounded the following season, helping the Tigers post 101 victories by batting .290 and finishing among the league leaders with 45 home runs, 140 runs batted in, 129 runs scored, and 113 walks. After moving to left field in deference to Al Kaline, Colavito also led all players at his position in putouts and assists. Although his exceptional performance ended up being overshadowed somewhat by the fabulous campaigns turned in by teammate Norm Cash and New York's Roger Maris and Mickey Mantle, it nevertheless earned him an eighth-place finish in the A.L. MVP voting.

Still, Detroit fans never truly accepted Colavito, whose prolonged batting slumps infuriated them. Adding to the difficulties Colavito experienced after he arrived in Detroit was the hostile relationship he shared with sportswriter Joe Falls, who viewed the slugging outfielder as a "self-ordained deity." Falls, in fact, started a feature in which he chronicled the runs Colavito failed to drive in as a member of the Tigers, counting each stranded base runner as an RNBI (Run Not Batted In). Colavito also drew criticism for holding out for a higher salary than fan favorite Al Kaline at the conclusion of the 1961 campaign.

Even though Colavito failed to establish a good rapport with the local fans and media, he again posted big numbers in 1962, finishing the year with 37 homers, 112 RBIs, 90 runs scored, a .273 batting average, and a league-leading 309 total bases, while also topping all A.L. left-fielders with a career-high 359 putouts. Nevertheless, after Colavito experienced a slightly subpar 1963 season in which he hit 22 home runs, knocked in 91 runs, and batted .271, the Tigers elected to include him in a five-player trade they completed with Kansas City on November 18, 1963, that netted them second baseman Jerry Lumpe and pitchers Dave Wickersham and Ed Rakow in return. Colavito left Detroit having hit 139 home runs, driven in 430 runs, scored 377 times, collected 633 hits, batted .271, compiled a .364 on-base percentage, and posted a .501 slugging percentage in his four years with the Tigers.

Colavito ended up spending one productive season in Kansas City, hitting 34 homers and driving in 102 runs for the A's in 1964, before being reacquired by the Indians prior to the start of the 1965 campaign. He remained in Cleveland for the next 2½ years, leading the American League with 108 RBIs in 1965, before being dealt to the Chicago White Sox midway through the 1967 season. After seeing a limited amount of duty while splitting the 1968 campaign between the Dodgers and Yankees, Colavito retired at season's end, concluding his career with 374 home runs, 1,159 runs batted in, 971 runs scored, 1,730 hits, 21 triples, 283 doubles, a .266 batting average, a .359 on-base percentage, and a .489 slugging percentage. In addition to hitting more than 40 home runs three times, he knocked in more than 100 runs on six separate occasions. Colavito retired as the American League's third-leading right-handed home run hitter, trailing only Jimmie Foxx and Harmon Killebrew at the time.

Following his playing career, Colavito returned to Cleveland, where he spent three years working as a TV analyst for station WJW. He also served as a member of the Indians' coaching staff for three seasons, before later assuming a similar role for the Kansas City Royals during the early 1980s. Colavito currently resides in Berks County, Pennsylvania.

In 1994, Cleveland sportswriter Terry Pluto wrote a best-selling book entitled *The Curse of Rocky Colavito* in which he details the difficulties the Indians subsequently encountered after trading away the popular slugger to the Tigers in 1960. In describing the admiration the fans of Cleveland had for Colavito, Pluto wrote, "He was everything a ballplayer should be: dark, handsome eyes, and raw-boned build; and he hit home runs at a remarkable rate."

TIGERS CAREER HIGHLIGHTS

Best Season

Although Colavito also compiled impressive numbers the following year, concluding the 1962 campaign with 37 home runs, 112 RBIs, 90 runs scored, a .273 batting average, and a league-leading 309 total bases, he clearly had his best season for the Tigers in 1961. In addition to establishing career highs with 45 homers, 140 RBIs, 129 runs scored, 113 walks, and 338 total bases, Colavito amassed 169 hits and 30 doubles, batted .290, compiled a .402 on-base percentage, and posted a .580 slugging percentage, each of which represented his highest mark as a member of the Tigers. Colavito finished in the league's top five in five different offensive categories, placing third in RBIs, runs scored, and walks, finishing fourth in total bases, and ranking fifth in home runs.

Memorable Moments/Greatest Performances

After striking out four times and going hitless in six at bats in his first appearance against his former team in 1960's season opener, Colavito led the Tigers to a 6–4 win over the Indians in Cleveland the following day by hitting a home run and driving in 3 runs. Just two days later, on April 22, 1960, Colavito thrilled the fans of Detroit by homering in his first Briggs Stadium at-bat as a member of the Tigers during a 6–5 victory over the Chicago White Sox.

Colavito hit 3 home runs in a game twice for the Tigers, doing so for the first time in the second game of a doubleheader sweep of Washington on August 27, 1961. After hitting a solo blast during Detroit's 7–4 win in the opener, Colavito reached the seats three times in the Tigers' 10–1 victory in the nightcap, giving him a total of 4 homers and 7 RBIs on the day. His 4 home runs tied an A.L. record. Colavito again homered three times in the same contest on July 5, 1962, when he drove in all but one of his team's runs in a 7–6 loss to his former team, the Cleveland Indians.

On June 24, 1962, Colavito set a Tigers record by collecting 7 hits in one game, going 7-for-10, with 6 singles and a triple, during a 22-inning, 9–7 marathon loss to the Yankees in Detroit.

Colavito also received a considerable amount of notoriety on May 12, 1961, when he entered the stands at Yankee Stadium in the eighth inning to protect his wife and father from an inebriated fan. Colavito, who always had a large rooting section whenever he returned to the Bronx, later explained, "I always look up there, and, when I saw my father struggling with somebody, I went right over the rail. My father is 60, and nobody is going to hit him while I'm there." He added, "I found out that some drunken bum was bothering my wife." After being ejected from the contest, Colavito returned the next night to go 4-for-5, with 2 home runs, during an 8–3 Tigers win over the Yankees.

NOTABLE ACHIEVEMENTS

- Hit more than 20 home runs four times, topping 30 homers three times and 40 homers once (45 in 1961).
- Knocked in more than 100 runs twice, surpassing 140 RBIs once (140 in 1961).
- Scored more than 100 runs once (129 in 1961).
- Surpassed 30 doubles twice.

- Drew more than 100 walks once (113 in 1961).
- Compiled on-base percentage in excess of .400 once (.402 in 1961).
- Posted slugging percentage in excess of .500 twice.
- Led the American League with 309 total bases in 1962.
- Led A.L. outfielders in assists once and double plays turned once.
- Led A.L. left fielders in putouts twice; assists once; and fielding percentage twice.
- Led A.L. right fielders in putouts once; assists once; and double plays turned once.
- Ranks among Tigers career leaders in slugging percentage (8th) and OPS (10th).
- Hit 3 home runs in a game twice.
- 1961 *Sporting News* All-Star selection.
- Two-time A.L. All-Star (1961, 1962).

Goose Goslin

Courtesy of T. Scott Brandon

One of the American League's premier hitters of the 1920s and 1930s, Leon "Goose" Goslin had already batted over .300 nine times and knocked in more than 100 runs on eight separate occasions by the time he joined the Tigers in 1934. The hard-hitting left fielder continued his tremendous success in Detroit, batting over .300 twice and surpassing 100 RBIs in each of his first three seasons in the Motor City, in helping the Tigers capture two A.L. pennants and one world championship. Teaming up with Hank Greenberg and Charlie Gehringer to form what became known as Detroit's "G-Men," Goslin provided another powerful bat in the middle of the Tigers' lineup, giving them the most formidable threesome in all of baseball. One of the team's four representatives in the 1936 All-Star Game (Gehringer, Tommy Bridges, and Schoolboy Rowe also made the squad), Goslin compiled his best numbers as a member of the Tigers that year, hitting 24 homers, knocking in 125 runs, scoring 122 times, and batting .315. Yet, he is remembered most fondly by Detroit fans for the game-winning hit he delivered in Game Six of the 1935 World Series that gave the Tigers their first world championship.

Born in Salem, New Jersey, on October 16, 1900, Leon Allen Goslin attended local Salem High School, before leaving home at the age of 16 to join a semipro baseball team. After starting out as a pitcher, Goslin eventually moved to the outfield once he began playing minor league ball with Columbia in the Sally League. While at Columbia in 1919, Goslin was discovered by Washington scout Joe Engel, who recommended that Senators owner Clark Griffith sign him to a contract. After being inked to a deal by Griffith, the young outfielder spent two more years in the minors before being summoned to Washington during the latter stages of the 1921 campaign. Goslin appeared in 14 games with the Senators in September, batting .260, driving in 6 runs, and hitting his first major league home run.

Goslin's powerful left-handed swing eventually enabled him to break into Washington's starting lineup the following season, one in which he established himself as the team's everyday left fielder. Appearing in 101 games and accumulating fewer than 400 plate appearances, Goslin batted .324, hit 3 home runs, and knocked in 53 runs. However, while Goslin excelled at the plate from the very beginning, he represented something of a liability in the outfield. Plagued throughout his career by an inability to properly judge fly balls, Goslin seemed to stagger under balls hit in his direction, very much resembling a bird flapping its wings as he pursued the sphere with his arms waving. Goslin's erratic path and unseemly gestures soon gave birth to the nickname "Goose," a moniker that received further validation from his long neck and prominent proboscis.

Goslin posted solid numbers in 1923, finishing the season with 9 homers, 99 RBIs, a .300 batting average, and a league-leading 18 triples, before beginning an extraordinarily successful run during which he established himself as one of baseball's most potent batsmen. While playing for the Senators from 1924 to 1929, Goslin knocked in more than 100 runs five times, topping the circuit with 129 RBIs in the first of those campaigns. He also amassed more than 200 hits twice and batted well in excess of .300 five times, leading the league with a mark of .379 in 1928. And, even though Goslin played his home games in spacious Griffith Stadium, he hit more than 17 home runs four times.

The power emanating from Goslin's bat resulted from his strong wrists, broad shoulders, and ferocious swing. Featuring an exaggerated closed stance, from which he could almost see the catcher out of his left eye, the 5'11", 190-pound Goslin swung from his heels, his quick bat appearing as a blur of motion. In describing Goslin's hitting style, Shirley Povich of the *Washington Post* wrote, "Even when Goslin wasn't meeting the ball, he was an exciting hitter. He emulated the Ruthian custom of swinging himself off of his feet and depositing himself in the dust when he whiffed. He was the least plate shy guy who ever lived. Umpires used to threaten to banish him unless he stopped crowding the plate."

Even though playing in Griffith Stadium prevented Goslin from compiling huge home run totals during his time in Washington, he displayed his power by accumulating at least 15 triples five times and 30 doubles four times. Senators' manager Bucky Harris said of Goslin, "He dented that right-field wall in Griffith Stadium and knocked a lot of them over it. It didn't make any difference if the pitcher was left or right-handed, or threw a fastball or a changeup. If they tried to sneak one by Goose, he'd tag it."

Goslin remained in Washington until June 13, 1930, when the Senators traded him to the St. Louis Browns for pitcher General Crowder and fellow future Hall of Fame outfielder Heinie Manush. Away from Griffith Stadium's far-reaching fences, Goslin went on to establish career highs with 37 home runs and 138 RBIs. He followed that up with two more outstanding seasons for the Browns, before being dealt back to the Senators prior to the start of the 1933 campaign. Goslin's return to Washington proved to be short-lived, though, because the Tigers acquired him for outfielder John Stone during the subsequent offseason.

The 33-year-old Goslin posted solid, if unspectacular, numbers his first year in Detroit, concluding the campaign with 13 homers, 100 RBIs, 106 runs scored, 187 hits, a .305 batting average, a .373 on-base percentage, and a .453 slugging percentage. Providing ample protection for Hank Greenberg in the middle of Detroit's batting order, Goslin also helped lighten the mood in the Tiger clubhouse. Speaking of his former teammate, Tigers pitcher Elden Auker recalled, "He was some character . . . a really great guy. He was just happy-go-lucky, always laughing and joking and pulling pranks."

Auker also revealed that Goslin and Cincinnati Reds catcher Ernie Lombardi "waged an ongoing feud over who had the bigger nose." Goslin playfully suggested that Lombardi's nose was long enough to keep his cigar dry in the shower, and the Cincinnati catcher countered by remarking that Goslin "could get by on one breath a day." Auker related that the matter finally came to a head during an exhibition game waged between the two clubs, stating, "One spring, in our final exhibition in Cincinnati, Goose swung so hard, he turned himself completely around as a runner was stealing second. Lombardi went to throw the ball and his right hand hit Goose's nose. As Goose lay on the ground bleeding like a stuck hog, Lombardi said, 'That settles it; you've got the bigger nose. You've got such a big nose I can't even throw to second base. You can't get that nose out of the way.'"

After helping the Tigers win the pennant in 1934, Goslin contributed significantly to their second straight league championship the following year by hitting 9 homers, driving in 109 runs, scoring 87 times, and batting .292. He then gave the Tigers their first world championship by delivering an RBI single that drove in Mickey Cochrane with the winning run in the bottom of the ninth inning of Game Six of the World Series.

Goslin spent two more years in Detroit, putting up big numbers in 1936, before assuming a part-time role the following season. After being released by the Tigers immediately following the conclusion of the 1937 campaign, Goslin returned to Washington for one final tour of duty, serving the Senators primarily as a pinch hitter in 1938 before announcing his retirement at season's end. Goslin ended his career with 248 home runs, 1,610 RBIs, 1,482 runs scored, 2,735 hits, 173 triples, 500 doubles, a .316 batting average, a .387 on-base percentage, and a .500 slugging percentage. In addition to hitting more than 20 home runs three times, he knocked in more than 100 runs 11 times, scored more than 100 runs seven times, and batted over .300 on 11 different occasions. Goslin earned three top-10 finishes in the A.L. MVP voting while playing for the Senators, and he also placed 14th in the balloting as a member of the Tigers in 1934. In his four years in Detroit, Goslin hit 50 home runs, drove in 369 runs, scored 345 times, collected 582 hits, 22 triples, and 116 doubles, batted .297, compiled a .376 on-base percentage, and posted a .456 slugging percentage.

Goslin spent the first year of his retirement serving as player/manager of the Interstate League Trenton Senators, before proclaiming at the end of the 1939 season, "Next year, I want to be on the bench where I can see everything that goes on. A manager has no business being out in left field." He subsequently served the team strictly as a bench manager until August 1941, when the club's failures prompted him to hand in his resignation.

After leaving baseball, Goslin spent many years operating a boat rental company on Delaware Bay, until failing health caused him to close his business in 1969. Operated on for the removal of his larynx in 1970, Goslin lived one more year, passing away at his home in Bridgeton, New Jersey, at the age of 70 on May 15, 1971. The members of the Veterans Committee elected him to the Hall of Fame two years earlier, inducting him along with fellow outfielder Kiki Cuyler. Goslin broke down during his acceptance speech, stating, "I have been lucky. I want to thank God, who gave me the health and strength to compete with these great players. I will never forget this. I will take this to my grave."

TIGERS CAREER HIGHLIGHTS

Best Season

Although Goslin received more support in the A.L. MVP voting two years earlier, he clearly had his best season for the Tigers in 1936, earning his lone All-Star selection by batting .315, compiling a .403 on-base percentage and a .930 OPS, amassing 180 hits, and ranking in the league's top 10 with 24 home runs, 125 RBIs, 122 runs scored, 301 total bases, 14 stolen bases, and a .526 slugging percentage.

Memorable Moments/Greatest Performances

Goslin put together one of the longest hitting streaks in Tigers history in 1934, hitting safely in 30 consecutive games, before having his skein halted by Cleveland's Bob Weiland on June 6.

Goslin homered three times in one game on three separate occasions while playing for the Senators and Browns. Although he never accomplished that feat as a member of the Tigers, he went deep twice during a 9–4 loss to the Yankees on July 17, 1936. Goslin had another big game earlier in the year against the White Sox, driving in all 5 Tiger runs in a 6–5 loss to Chicago. Goslin delivered 4 of those runs with one swing of the bat—an eighth-inning grand slam that gave the Tigers a 5–2 lead they failed to hold in the ensuing frame.

Goslin also hit one of the more unusual home runs in baseball history on July 28, 1936, when his drive to deep right-center field caused New York center fielder Myril Hoag to collide with right fielder Joe DiMaggio. With both players lying on the field unconscious, Goslin rounded the bases with an inside-the-park home run.

However, Goslin got his most memorable hit for the Tigers on October 7, 1935, when his single in the bottom of the ninth inning of Game Six of the World Series delivered Mickey Cochrane with the Series clincher. Elden Auker recalled the decisive hit, which came with the scored tied 3–3 and the Tigers holding a 3–2 edge in games: "I was sitting on the dugout steps at the start of our half of the ninth, and Goose was sitting beside me. Goose hadn't had a hit all day and was the fourth hitter due up that inning. He turned to me and said something I'll never forget. 'I've got a hunch I'm going to be up there with the winning run on base, and we're going to win the ballgame.'" Mickey Cochrane got on to lead off the inning, then advanced to second on a Charlie Gehringer ground out. Facing left-hander Larry French, Goslin then lined the second pitch to right-center, driving in Cochrane with the winning run, and giving the Tigers their first world championship. As Auker and Goslin subsequently embraced, the pitcher recalled Goslin shouting to him, "What'd I tell ya? What'd I tell ya?"

NOTABLE ACHIEVEMENTS

- Hit more than 20 home runs once (24 in 1936).
- Knocked in more than 100 runs three times, topping 120 RBIs once (125 in 1936).
- Scored more than 100 runs twice, topping 120 runs scored once (122 in 1936).
- Batted over .300 twice.
- Surpassed 30 doubles three times.
- Compiled on-base percentage in excess of .400 once (.403 in 1936).
- Posted slugging percentage in excess of .500 once (.526 in 1936).
- 1936 A.L. All-Star.
- Number 89 on *The Sporting News* 1999 list of Baseball's 100 Greatest Players.
- Two-time A.L. champion (1934, 1935).
- 1935 world champion.
- Elected to Baseball Hall of Fame by members of Veterans Committee in 1968.

47

Jim Northrup

Courtesy of MearsOnlineAuctions.com

Nicknamed the "Silver Fox" due to his prematurely graying hair, Jim Northrup spent parts of 11 seasons in Detroit, playing all three outfield positions at different times for the Tigers. A solid defensive outfielder and productive hitter who excelled in the clutch, Northrup hit more than 20 home runs three times, batted over .290 twice, and knocked in more than 90 runs once, with his propensity for delivering big hits proving to be a key factor in Detroit's successful march to the 1968 A.L. pennant.

Northrup continued his timely hitting against the Cardinals in the World Series, homering twice, driving in 8 runs, and delivering the decisive blow in Game Seven, in helping the Tigers capture their first world championship in 23 years.

Born in the small farm town of Breckenridge, Michigan, on November 24, 1939, James Thomas Northrup grew up in nearby St. Louis, where he attended St. Louis High School. After excelling in all sports there, Northrup established himself as a multisport star at nearby Alma College, earning letters in baseball, football, basketball, track, and golf. Baseball, though, remained his first love, with Northrup stating years later, "I was born to play baseball."

Having rejected offers to play for the NFL's Chicago Bears and the AFL's New York Titans following his graduation in 1961, Northrup signed with the Tigers as an amateur free agent. He spent the next four years in the minor leagues, earning his first big-league call-up late in 1964 after winning International League Rookie of the Year honors by hitting 18 home runs, driving in 92 runs, and batting .312 for the Syracuse Chiefs. The 24-year-old outfielder appeared in five games for the Tigers during the season's final week, hitting safely just once in 12 trips to the plate, en route to compiling a batting average of .083.

After earning a roster spot the following spring, Northrup spent most of 1965 serving the Tigers as a fourth outfielder, backing up starters Al Kaline, Willie Horton, and Don Demeter. In just over 200 official at-bats, he homered twice, knocked in 16 runs, and batted .205. With Kaline spending a considerable amount of time in centerfield in 1966, Northrup took over as the team's primary right-fielder. Appearing in a total of 123 games and accumulating more than 400 official at-bats, Northrup posted solid offensive numbers, finishing the year with 16 homers, 58 RBIs, and a .265 batting average. Splitting his time between all three outfield positions in 1967, Northrup compiled similar numbers, concluding the campaign with 10 home runs, 61 RBIs, and a .271 batting average.

Although the left-hand-hitting Northrup failed to establish himself as a full-time starter his first few years with the Tigers, accumulating fewer than 500 official at-bats each season, he nevertheless proved to be one of the team's most reliable hitters. Employing a quick, compact inside-out swing, the 6'3", 195-pound Northrup drove the ball with power to all fields. He also did a solid job wherever the Tigers placed him in the outfield, displaying decent range and an accurate throwing arm.

With Al Kaline missing nearly two months of the 1968 campaign with a broken arm, Northrup assumed a more prominent role with the ball club. Appearing in 154 games and amassing nearly 650 total plate appearances, Northrup put up the best numbers of his young career, concluding the campaign with 21 home runs, 76 runs scored, a .264 batting average, and 90 RBIs, with the last figure placing him third in the league rankings. Displaying an ability to perform well under pressure, Northrup led all A.L. batsmen with 4 grand slams, delivering 3 of those over the course of one week in late June. Northrup's strong performance earned him a 13th-place finish in the league MVP voting at season's end. He continued to come up with big hits in the World Series, helping the Tigers overcome a three-games-to-one deficit to St. Louis in the Fall Classic by hitting a grand slam in Game Six and tripling in 2 runs during a 3-run, seventh-inning rally against Bob Gibson that ultimately gave the Tigers a 4–1 victory in the Series finale.

Commenting years later on Northrup's ability to perform well in the clutch, Hall of Fame reliever Rollie Fingers stated, "I usually didn't want to face him with the game on the line. He was pretty tough to strike out. Jim Northrup was a tough hitter."

Meanwhile, Al Kaline said of his former teammate during a 2009 interview, "He was a bear-down-type guy, and he was a better player than a lot of people give him credit for. Besides what he could do as a left-handed hitter, he had a good arm, and he ran well."

Northrup also had solid seasons for the Tigers in 1969 and 1970, hitting 25 home runs, driving in 66 runs, scoring 79 times, and batting .295 in the first of those campaigns, before hitting 24 homers, knocking in 80 runs, and scoring 71 times the following year. Although Northrup continued to play well over the course of the next three seasons, he clashed repeatedly with new Detroit manager Billy Martin, who the outfielder later claimed, "put most of us in a frame of mind where he took the fun out of the game."

Expounding upon that notion, Northrup suggested, "We got sick and tired of reading Martin say in the papers, 'I manage good, and they play bad.' 'I'd like to bunt, but my players can't do it' . . . It was all, 'I, I, I,' and 'me, me, me.' I did not respect him in any way."

Despite posting a career-high .307 batting average in 1973, Northrup found himself in Martin's doghouse much of the time, limiting him to a total of only 119 games over the course of the season. Although Detroit fired Martin during the latter stages of the campaign, the 34-year-old Northrup subsequently found himself unable to regain his starting job, posting a batting average of just .237 in 97 games with the Tigers in 1974, before being dealt to the Montreal Expos in early August. Northrup left

Detroit with career totals of 145 home runs, 570 RBIs, 571 runs scored, 1,184 hits, 42 triples, and 204 doubles, a .267 batting average, a .332 on-base percentage, and a .430 slugging percentage. After appearing in only 21 games with the Expos, Northrup was purchased by the Baltimore Orioles, with whom he ended his career in 1975. Choosing to announce his retirement at season's end, Northrup later suggested, "I'd had enough. I'd been away from home too much, and I wasn't with my kids enough. So that was the end of it." He finished his career with 153 home runs, 610 RBIs, 603 runs scored, 1,254 hits, a .267 batting average, a .333 on-base percentage, and a .429 slugging percentage.

After retiring from baseball, Northrup spent two years playing with the Detroit Caesars in the American Professional Slow Pitch Softball League. He later served as a color analyst for the Tigers on the PASS Sports cable television network, before founding Jim Northrup and Associates, a manufacturers' representative firm in Southfield, Michigan. Unfortunately, Northrup spent the latter stages of his life suffering from Alzheimer's disease and battling rheumatoid arthritis. He passed away at the age of 71, on June 8, 2011, after experiencing a seizure.

Upon learning of his former teammate's passing, Dick Tracewski told the *Detroit Free Press*, "Jim Northrup had the biggest hit that's ever been gotten for the Detroit Tigers. He won the World Series for us. He was big, tall and thin with a beautiful flowing swing, and he had real major power. . . . The thing I always remember, when he got to the ballpark and put on his uniform, he was ready to play. I never saw him take a shortcut, not run out a ball, not give a 100% effort at all times. He was a hell of a ballplayer, and he was a hell of a guy. I loved Jim Northrup."

Eight years before his passing, Northrup said during a 2003 interview, "You're born with talent, not made. I was born to play baseball, and I did. I grew up being a Tiger fan, and I'll always be a Tiger fan. But my hero was Ted Williams. I'm a left-hander, so I admired Ted. But I grew up knowing I would make the major leagues. I'm fortunate that I had that opportunity, and it worked out well for me."

TIGERS CAREER HIGHLIGHTS

Best Season

Northrup posted his best overall numbers for the Tigers in 1969, batting .295, compiling a .358 on-base percentage, and establishing career highs with 25 home runs, 79 runs scored, 160 hits, 31 doubles, and a .508 slugging percentage. Nevertheless, he had his finest all-around season in the "Year of the Pitcher," concluding the 1968 campaign with 21 homers, 29 doubles, 76 runs scored, 153 hits, a .264 batting average, a .324 on-base percentage, a .447 slugging percentage, and a career-best 90 RBIs and 7 triples. In addition to leading the Tigers in hits and RBIs, Northrup placed near the top of the league rankings in hits, home runs, doubles, triples, total bases, and RBIs, finishing third in the American League in the last category. Northrup's 4 grand slams topped the junior circuit, and he also broke up three no-hitters during the season.

Memorable Moments/Greatest Performances

Northrup had one of his biggest days at the plate on August 28, 1969, when he became the first Detroit player since Ty Cobb to go 6-for-6 in a game, doing so during a 5–3, 13-inning victory over the Oakland Athletics. Northrup homered twice and knocked in 3 runs during the contest, with his two-out, two-run blast in the bottom of the thirteenth giving the Tigers the win. He nearly matched his earlier effort on September 7, 1971, going 5-for-5, with 2 homers, 2 RBIs, and 3 runs scored, during a 3–2, 11-inning win over the Washington Senators.

Northrup had another huge game on July 11, 1973, when he led the Tigers to a 14–2 win over the Texas Rangers by going 3-for-4, with a pair of 3-run homers and a career-high 8 RBIs.

However, Northrup delivered many of his most memorable hits during Detroit's 1968 world championship campaign. On May 17 of that year, he gave the Tigers a 7–3 victory over the Washington Senators by hitting a walk-off grand slam in the bottom of the ninth inning. Five weeks later, Northrup began an extraordinary stretch during which he became the first player to hit three grand slams in one week. Northrup drove in 8 runs during a 14–3 mauling of the Indians on June 24, hitting grand slams in consecutive at-bats in the fifth and sixth innings. By doing so, he became one of only four players to hit a grand slam in consecutive innings. Northrup was at it again just five days later, leading the Tigers to a 5–2 win over the White Sox by hitting his fourth homer of the year with the bases loaded.

Northrup, though, saved the biggest hit of his career for the final game of the 1968 World Series. After hitting another grand slam home run during a 13–1 Detroit victory in Game Six, Northrup stepped up to the plate to face Bob Gibson in the top of the seventh inning of a scoreless tie, with two men out and two men on base. He subsequently drove a Gibson offering over the head of perennial Gold Glove winner Curt Flood in center field, knocking in Norm Cash and Willie Horton with the first two runs of the contest. Bill Freehan followed with a double that scored Northrup, giving Mickey Lolich added insurance in a 4–1 Tigers victory. Although Flood subsequently received a considerable amount of criticism for misplaying Northrup's drive, the Tiger center fielder defended his counterpart, stating years later, "We saw the film afterwards, and Curt Flood did slip on that ball I hit to center field, because it was wet out there. But that ball went 20 or 30 feet over his head. He wasn't going to catch it, no matter what." Northrup continued, "You can call that a misplay if you want. I call it a triple that won the World Series. I don't fault Flood, but he was playing me too much to pull. I wasn't a pull hitter, especially with Gibson on the mound. Flood probably didn't see the ball at first. It was a low stadium with a lot of white shirts behind home plate. I played out there, and you had to break where you thought the ball was going, because you could not see the ball for the first second or two. Flood broke the right way, and he slipped. But we got the opportunity to win the World Series, and we won it."

NOTABLE ACHIEVEMENTS

- Hit more than 20 home runs three times.
- Batted over .300 once (.307 in 1973).
- Surpassed 30 doubles once (31 in 1969).
- Posted slugging percentage in excess of .500 once (.508 in 1969).
- One of only four players in major league history to hit a grand slam in consecutive innings.
- One of only two players in major league history to hit 3 grand slams in one week.
- 1968 A.L. champion.
- 1968 world champion.

48

Chet Lemon

Courtesy of Tiger Stadium Ushers

Nicknamed "Chet the Jet" for his outstanding speed that enabled him to track down balls headed for the outfield gaps, Chet Lemon spent nine seasons in Detroit, after earlier establishing himself as one of the American League's finest all-around center fielders as a member of the Chicago White Sox. An exciting, hard-nosed player who always put forth a 100 percent effort on the playing field, Lemon earned All-Star honors three times over the course of his career, making the A.L. squad for the final time in 1984, when he helped the Tigers win the A.L. pennant by hitting 20 home runs, driving in 76 runs, scoring 77 times, batting .287, and doing an outstanding defensive job in centerfield. Lemon surpassed 20 homers and 75 runs scored two other times for the Tigers, en route to helping them post a winning record in each of his first seven seasons in Detroit.

Born in Jackson, Mississippi, on February 12, 1955, Chester Earl Lemon spent much of his youth in Southern California, where he attended Fremont High School in Los Angeles. After accepting a baseball scholarship offer from Pepperdine University in Malibu, Lemon temporarily put his education on hold when the Oakland Athletics selected him in the first round of the 1972 amateur draft, with the 22nd overall pick. Lemon spent the next three years advancing through Oakland's farm system as a third baseman, before being dealt to the Chicago White Sox for pitcher Stan Bahnsen in June 1975.

Lemon, who struggled terribly in the field throughout his minor league career, found his niche shortly after the White Sox called him up for the first time during the latter stages of the 1975 campaign. Recalling the events surrounding his successful transition to the outfield, Lemon said, "In late 1975, when I was with the Sox, I was at third base and a groundball was hit towards the middle. I started running and cut in front of the shortstop and actually wound up around Jorge Orta—at second base. The very next day, I was on the top step of the dugout; it was early in the day since I'd always be one of the first guys to show up. Chuck Tanner, the Sox manager, came up, put his arm around my shoulder, and said—and I can remember this like it was yesterday—'Son, I want you to start taking 100 fly balls a day because, if you stay an infielder, you're gonna kill somebody.'"

After appearing in 9 games with the White Sox late in 1975, Lemon earned the team's starting center field job the following year, concluding the campaign with modest offensive numbers. The 22-year-old outfielder subsequently blossomed into an outstanding all-around player in 1977, when he hit 19 home runs, drove in 67 runs, scored a career-high 99 times, collected 38 doubles, batted .273, and established a new A.L. record with 524 total chances and 512 putouts in the outfield. Lemon continued to perform well for the White Sox over the course of the next four seasons, batting over .300 three times, en route to compiling an overall mark of .304 during that time. He had his best season for the Sox in 1979, when he hit 17 homers, knocked in 86 runs, batted .318, and tied for the league lead with 44 doubles, earning in the process his second straight All-Star nomination.

In spite of the success Lemon experienced during his time in Chicago, concerns over his impending free agency prompted the White Sox to trade him to the Tigers for outfielder Steve Kemp prior to the start of the 1982 campaign. Commenting on the deal from Detroit's perspective, Tigers general manager Jim Campbell stated, "Lemon is a player we've had our eyes on for a long time. He hits for power and average and is one of the better defensive outfielders in our league."

Despite missing a significant amount of playing time due to injury, Lemon had a solid first season in Detroit, hitting 19 homers, driving in 52 runs, scoring 75 times, and batting .266. Opposing pitchers also plunked him more than any other A.L. batter for the third of four times in his career, with Lemon attributing his propensity for getting hit to the manner in which he crowded the plate. In discussing his batting style, Lemon explained, "I don't think I realized that I was that close to the plate. You know, I actually didn't mind being pitched inside; I wanted to be pitched inside. I felt I could always turn on pitches. If you look at my hits, like all those doubles, I think you'll find that I went down the left-field line in most of them. Larry Doby taught me a lot about hitting. He was my manager with the Sox for a while. He'd always say that I had one of the quickest bats through the strike zone he ever saw, so I didn't need to try to do too much."

After spending most of 1982 in right field, Lemon moved back over to center the following year, where he remained until 1988, when the Tigers acquired perennial Gold Glover Gary Pettis. Although Lemon failed to earn Gold Glove honors himself during his time in Detroit, the outstanding jump he got on balls enabled him to annually place among the league leaders in outfield putouts, with Tigers manager Sparky Anderson commenting in 1984, "Chet Lemon is the best center fielder in the game in either league today. He isn't the fastest, but he's the best at it because he works harder at it than anyone else."

Anderson later added, "After watching Chester the last several years, I have to say, without a doubt, he's the best center fielder I've seen in my 31 years in the game. Chester is a Pete Rose type. He never complains. He's always there, and he plays each game as if it were the seventh game of the World Series. Chester doesn't know any other way to play and that's his greatest asset. Combine all that with his little-boy desire to want to play every day, and it is no wonder Chester has all those fans who sit in the bleachers in the palm of his hand."

Although Lemon perhaps made his greatest contribution to the Tigers with his exceptional defensive play, he also gave them solid offensive production from the lower half of their batting order. After hitting 24 home runs, driving in 69 runs, scoring 78 times, batting .255, and getting hit a league-leading 20 times in 1983, he hit 20 homers, knocked in 76 runs, scored 77 times, and batted .287 for Detroit's world championship 1984 ball club. Lemon had four more good years for the Tigers, posting his best numbers in 1987, when he finished with 20 homers, 75 RBIs, 75 runs scored, and a .277 batting average. He subsequently received reduced playing time in 1989 and 1990, before the Tigers elected to give him his unconditional release just prior to the start of the 1991 season. Choosing to announce his retirement, Lemon ended his career with 215 home runs, 884 RBIs, 973 runs scored, 1,875 hits, 61 triples, 396 doubles, a .273 batting average, a .355 on-base percentage, and a .442 slugging percentage. During his time in Detroit, Lemon hit 142 homers, drove in 536 runs, scored 570 times, amassed 1,071 hits, 32 triples, and 218 doubles, batted .263, compiled a .349 on-base percentage, and posted a .437 slugging per-centage. Over the course of his career, Lemon established an A.L. record by recording more than 400 outfield putouts in five different seasons, doing so three times as a member of the Tigers.

Shortly after Lemon played his last game for the Tigers, he began ex-periencing serious health problems. Looking back at his life-threatening ordeal, Lemon said,

> In spring training 1991, the Tigers discovered that I had too many red blood cells in my body. The Tigers thought the numbers they got were wrong. My stomach was always hurting. I thought maybe I had an ulcer or it was just stress. The doctors couldn't find out what was causing it. They finally did an ultrasound and discovered that I had tiny little blood clots in my portal veins. My illness is usually found in older men of Jewish decent; it's practically never found in African American men, especially in the shape that I was in. About 30 minutes after they discovered that, I was rushed to intensive care, hooked up to machines and given blood thinners. Not only did I have blood clots, but I had too much blood and it was too thick, like a slush. The doctors were fearful that if one of those clots became loose . . . well, you know what happens when that takes place.

After undergoing nearly three months of intensive treatment in the hospital, Lemon overcame his illness and began coaching high school base-ball in the central Florida area. In 1993, he started the Chet Lemon School of Baseball and became the president of the Amateur Athletic Union district near Orlando. Some eight years later, he underwent successful surgery at the Mayo Clinic to have his spleen removed. Since that time, Lemon has remained active in coaching amateur baseball.

TIGERS CAREER HIGHLIGHTS

Best Season

Although Lemon also posted solid numbers for the Tigers in 1987, he had his finest all-around season in Detroit in 1984, when he hit 20 homers, knocked in 76 runs, scored 77 times, batted .287, collected 34 doubles, compiled an OPS of .852, accumulated 427 outfield putouts, and led all A.L. center fielders with a .995 fielding percentage, en route to earning the starting assignment in center for the junior circuit in the annual All-Star game.

Memorable Moments/Greatest Performances

Even though the Tigers lost the 1987 ALCS to Minnesota in 5 games, Lemon played extremely well, batting .278, hitting 2 homers, driving in 4 runs, and scoring 4 others.

Lemon hit one of his most memorable home runs on September 20, 1988, when his 2-run blast in the bottom of the ninth inning—the 200th of his career—gave the Tigers a 3–1 win over Cleveland.

Yet, it was with his glove that Lemon created two of his greatest moments as a member of the Tigers, making a pair of spectacular catches that enabled his team to secure critical wins. Lemon made the first of those grabs on July 24, 1983, when he helped the Tigers remain a half game behind Baltimore in the A.L. East standings by robbing Rod Carew of a game-winning homer in the bottom of the twelfth inning. With the Tigers holding a 4–3 lead over California, two men out, a runner at first, and Carew batting against Aurelio Lopez in the bottom of the 12th, the Angels' first baseman launched a long drive to the deepest part of Angels Stadium. Lemon turned, tracked the ball, and timed his leap perfectly, extending his glove beyond the centerfield wall and making the catch, to save the game for the Tigers.

Lemon made another memorable catch in Game Three of the 1984 World Series, helping the Tigers preserve their 5–2, eighth-inning lead over San Diego with an exceptional grab he turned in with two men out and Steve Garvey on third base. Facing closer Willie Hernandez, San Diego catcher Terry Kennedy drove the left-hander's full-count offering to deep center, chasing Lemon farther and farther back into Tiger Stadium's vast center-field expanse. As Tom Gage of the *Detroit News* described it, Lemon "backpedaled, turned, twisted, and made a fine catch." Commenting on the play following the contest, Lemon said, "When the ball was hit, I went back as far as I could. I had been playing shallow because we watched Kennedy in San Diego, and, with two strikes, he'd just be trying to make contact. After I got back on it, I just looked up, reached up, and it was there. The rest is history." Meanwhile, a despondent Garvey said after the game, "We still had a chance if Lemon doesn't make that catch."

NOTABLE ACHIEVEMENTS

- Surpassed 20 home runs three times.
- Topped 30 doubles twice.
- Led A.L. center fielders with .995 fielding percentage in 1984.
- 1984 A.L. All-Star.
- 1984 A.L. champion.
- 1984 world champion.

49

Dizzy Trout

Courtesy of MearsOnlineAuctions.com

Paul "Dizzy" Trout experienced little in the way of success over the course of his first four major league seasons, compiling an overall record of just 33–44 for the Tigers from 1939 to 1942. However, with many of the game's finest players absent for the next three years while serving in the military during World War II, Trout developed into an exceptional pitcher, teaming up with southpaw Hal Newhouser to give Detroit one of the most dominant righty/lefty tandems in baseball history. While

Newhouser earned the distinction of becoming the only pitcher ever to be named his league's MVP in back-to-back seasons, Trout posted consecutive 20-win campaigns in 1943 and 1944, en route to going a combined 82–54 from 1943 to 1946. In fact, Trout's brilliant performance in 1944 nearly prevented his teammate from winning the first of his MVP trophies, earning the former an extremely close second-place finish in the balloting. Unfortunately, the bespectacled right-hander posted a winning record for the Tigers just once more after 1946, preventing him from earning a higher place in these rankings.

Born in Sandcut, Indiana on June 29, 1915, Paul Howard Trout began his professional career in 1935 with the Terre Haute Tots, a local Three-I League team. After spending the next few years laboring in the minor leagues, the 6'2", 200-pound hard-throwing right-hander signed with the Tigers, with whom he earned a starting spot in spring training of 1939. At the same time, Trout adopted the nickname "Dizzy"—a moniker that stayed with him throughout the remainder of his playing days.

Hoping to gain attention during his first spring training, the 23-year-old rookie conducted himself in an extremely unconventional manner, spinning yarns to anyone willing to listen while sitting in the stands during exhibition games, once pitching out of a wheelbarrow, and wiping the sweat from his brow with a red bandanna he slowly removed from his hip pocket each time he found himself in trouble on the mound—all in an effort to justify the nickname he adopted before heading to camp. Trout, who greatly admired St. Louis Cardinals pitching ace Dizzy Dean, later explained, "I figured that if his name was worth $40,000 a year, then it was good enough for me. I thought that by acting a little screwy, I could draw extra customers for the club, furnish copy for the newspapers, and make more money for myself."

Trout's theatrics notwithstanding, he accomplished very little his first year in Detroit, compiling a record of 9–10 and an ERA of 3.61, while completing only 6 of his 22 starts. Trout fared no better in either of the next two campaigns after being removed from the Tigers' regular starting rotation. Spending most of his time working as a spot-starter/long reliever, Trout went a combined 12–16, walking nearly as many batters as he struck out, and completing just 7 of his 28 total starts. Inserted back into the rotation full time in 1942, Trout continued to struggle, going just 12–18 with a 3.43 ERA, and walking only two fewer men than he fanned, although he managed to complete nearly half his starts.

Lacking control on the mound, frequently allowing his fiery temperament to get the better of him, and scheduled to turn 28 years of age midway through the 1943 campaign, Trout appeared headed for a non-descript career. However, he suddenly began to show signs of maturity, learning to better control both his pitches and his emotions. Unable to enter the military after being classified 4-F due to a hearing impairment, Trout remained behind while the vast majority of the game's best players joined the service during World War II. Blossoming into one of the American League's top pitchers during their absence, Trout finished the 1943 season with a record of 20–12 and also established new career-bests with a 2.48 ERA, 111 strikeouts, 18 complete games, 246⅔ innings pitched, and a league-leading 5 shutouts. He improved upon those numbers dramatically in the ensuing campaign, going 27–14, with 144 strikeouts and a league-leading 2.12 ERA, 7 shutouts, 33 complete games, and 352⅓ innings pitched. Trout's fabulous performance earned him the first of his two All-Star selections, his lone nomination to *The Sporting News* All-Star team, and a close second-place finish in the A.L. MVP balloting to teammate Hal Newhouser, who edged him out by just four votes.

Although Trout never again reached such heights, he pitched extremely well for the Tigers in 1945 and 1946, placing among the league leaders in virtually every major statistical category for pitchers both years. After winning 18 games, compiling a 3.14 ERA, and tossing 18 complete games, 246⅓ innings, and 4 shutouts in the first of those seasons, he posted 17 victories, a 2.34 ERA, 23 complete games, 276⅓ innings, 5 shutouts, and a career-high 151 strikeouts in 1946. Particularly effective during the latter stages of the 1945 campaign, Trout proved to be a workhorse during Detroit's drive to the pennant, appearing in six games and winning four times over a nine-game stretch late in the year. He also excelled in the World Series, helping the Tigers defeat the Chicago Cubs in seven games by going 1–1 with a 0.66 ERA in the Fall Classic.

Trout remained with the Tigers until midway through the 1952 campaign, when they included him in a nine-player trade they completed with the Boston Red Sox that netted them shortstop Johnny Pesky and slugging first baseman Walt Dropo, among others. Trout compiled a winning record in just one of his final six years in Detroit, posting a mark of 13–5 in 1950. Over parts of 14 seasons with the Tigers, he compiled an overall record of 161–153 and an ERA of 3.20, struck out 1,199 batters in 2,591⅔ innings of work, threw 156 complete games and 28 shutouts, and posted a WHIP of 1.344. Trout continues to rank among the team's all-time leaders in several statistical categories. An outstanding hitter, Trout hit 19 home runs in 1,002 total plate appearances with the Tigers, reaching the seats more than any other pitcher in franchise history. He also knocked in 107 runs and compiled a batting average of .217 for the Tigers.

Trout spent the rest of 1952 in Boston, going 9–8 with a 3.64 ERA, before announcing his retirement at season's end. Reflecting back on his decision years later, Trout quipped, "One day I was pitching against Washington and the catcher called for a fastball. When it got to the plate, it was so slow that two pigeons were roosting on it. I decided to quit."

Trout turned to announcing after retiring from baseball, calling Tiger games with Van Patrick on radio WKMH and TV WJBK-TV from 1953 to 1955. As a broadcaster, Trout became known for his self-effacing humor, scrambled syntax, and folksy demeanor. After leaving the broadcast booth, Trout attempted a brief comeback with the Baltimore Orioles in 1957, making just two appearances before retiring for good. He subsequently joined the Chicago White Sox, serving them first as a pitching coach and, later, as a member of the front office. Trout remained in Chicago until 1972, when he passed away from stomach cancer at the age of 56.

TIGERS CAREER HIGHLIGHTS

Best Season

Trout had his first big year in 1943, when he tied A.L. MVP Spud Chandler for the league lead with 20 victories and 5 shutouts. He also ranked among the leaders with a 2.48 ERA, 18 complete games, and 246⅔ innings pitched. Nevertheless, Trout clearly had his greatest season in 1944, when he established career-best marks in virtually every statistical category, including wins (27), WHIP (1.127), ERA (2.12), shutouts (7), complete games (33), and innings pitched (352⅓), leading all A.L hurlers in each of the last four categories. He also had his best year at the plate, establishing career-highs with 5 home runs, 24 RBIs, and a .271 batting average.

Memorable Moments/Greatest Performances

Although Trout posted only 12 wins in 1942, he recorded one of those against the Yankees on June 17, handing the defending A.L. champions their first shutout of the year by tossing a 5-hit, 1–0 complete-game victory.

Trout had a number of memorable days in his banner year of 1944. On May 30, he defeated the Yankees by a score of 2–1, providing the winning margin with a leadoff homer in the bottom of the ninth inning. On August

25, Trout earned his 21st victory of the year by allowing just 4 hits during a 1–0 victory over the St. Louis Browns. Just four days later, he shut out the White Sox by a score of 7–0, helping his own cause by driving in 5 runs with a homer, double, and single.

However, Trout pitched the biggest game of his career on October 6, 1945, evening up the World Series at two games apiece by allowing the Cubs just 5 hits during a 4–1 Tigers win.

NOTABLE ACHIEVEMENTS

- Won at least 20 games twice, surpassing 17 victories on two other occasions.
- Posted winning percentage in excess of .700 once (.722 in 1950).
- Compiled ERA under 3.00 three times.
- Threw more than 200 innings four times, tossing more than 300 innings once (352⅓ in 1944).
- Threw more than 20 complete games twice, tossing more than 30 complete games once (33 in 1944).
- Led A.L. pitchers in wins once; ERA once; shutouts twice; complete games once; and innings pitched once.
- Led A.L. pitchers in assists three times and fielding percentage once.
- Ranks among Tigers career leaders in wins (7th); strikeouts (9th); shutouts (6th); complete games (7th); innings pitched (7th); games started (7th); and pitching appearances (4th).
- Holds Tigers career record for most home runs hit by a pitcher (19).
- Finished second in 1944 A.L. MVP voting.
- 1944 *Sporting News* All-Star selection.
- Two-time A.L. All-Star (1944, 1947).
- Two-time A.L. champion (1940, 1945).
- 1945 world champion.

50

Carlos Guillen

Courtesy of Keith Allison

An outstanding hitter and competent defensive shortstop who overcame life-threatening pulmonary tuberculosis in 2001 to carve out quite a career for himself, Carlos Guillen spent eight years in Detroit, establishing himself during that time as one of the Tigers' team leaders. A favorite of manager Jim Leyland, who often raved about his class and dignity, Guillen served as a mentor to his fellow Latin American players, proving to be particularly influential in the maturation process of a young Miguel

Cabrera. Meanwhile, Guillen excelled at the plate, batting over .300 three straight times for the Tigers, surpassing 20 home runs twice, and driving in more than 100 runs once, en route to earning three All-Star selections and one top-10 finish in the league MVP voting. Guillen accomplished all he did during his time in Detroit despite being beset by injuries that kept him out of the Tigers lineup much of the time.

Born in Maracay, Aragua, Venezuela, on September 30, 1975, Carlos Guillen signed with the Houston Astros as a 17-year-old amateur free agent shortly after he graduated from Aragua High School in 1992. Yet, even though he officially joined the Houston organization three years earlier, Guillen did not come stateside until 1995. After finally beginning his professional career, the 20-year-old Guillen earned a spot on *Baseball America*'s top-100 prospect list by batting .295 in the Gulf Coast Rookie League. He remained the property of Houston until the Astros included him in a July 31, 1998, trade that also sent pitchers Freddy Garcia and John Halama to the Seattle Mariners for star hurler Randy Johnson. Guillen made his major league debut a little over one month later, on September 6, batting .333 in his 10 games with the Mariners the remainder of the year.

After missing virtually all of 1999 with a torn right ACL, Guillen spent most of the ensuing campaign splitting time at third base with David Bell, while also serving as a backup to Alex Rodriguez at shortstop. Appearing in 90 games with the Mariners, Guillen hit 7 homers, drove in 42 runs, and batted .257, in just under 300 official plate appearances. Guillen, who played shortstop throughout his minor league career, moved to his more natural position the following year after Rodriguez signed a huge free-agent contract with the Texas Rangers at season's end.

Overcoming a serious bout with pulmonary tuberculosis, Guillen won Seattle's starting shortstop job in 2001, concluding the campaign with 5 home runs, 53 RBIs, 72 runs scored, and a .259 batting average, while also finishing fourth in the league among players at his position with a .980 fielding percentage. He remained a solid contributor on offense the next two seasons, totaling 16 home runs and 108 RBIs, and posting batting averages of .261 and .276. However, somewhat dissatisfied with Guillen's limited range and marginal hands (he committed a total of 32 errors in 2002 and 2003), the Mariners elected to trade their starting shortstop to the Detroit Tigers for a pair of minor leaguers prior to the start of the 2004 campaign.

Joining a young and reconfigured Tigers ball club that lost 119 games the previous season, Guillen, still only 28 years old himself, quickly developed into one of the team's leaders. Thriving in his new role, Guillen posted the best numbers of his young career, earning his first All-Star selection by hitting 20 home runs, driving in 97 runs, scoring 97 times, and finishing sixth in the league with a .318 batting average, despite missing most of the final month with a torn ACL. Commenting on his new home, Guillen told Gene Guidi of the *Detroit Free Press* in June of 2004, "I like it here. I like this team a lot. I like my teammates and the city. This is where I want to be."

Although Guillen recovered from his torn ACL during the subsequent offseason, he found himself being hampered throughout much of 2005 by an injured left hamstring. Effective whenever he played, Guillen ended up posting a batting average of .320. However, his inability to appear in more than 87 games limited him to just 5 homers and 23 RBIs.

Fully healthy by the start of 2006, Guillen proved to be one of the most prominent figures on a Detroit ball club that ended up advancing to the World Series. Appearing in more than 150 games for the first of two straight times, Guillen earned a 10th-place finish in the league MVP balloting by hitting 19 home runs, driving in 85 runs, scoring 100 times, and batting .320. He subsequently had an outstanding postseason, sandwiching a .571 batting average against New York in the ALDS and a .353 average against St. Louis in the World Series around a subpar .188 mark against Oakland in the ALCS. Guillen followed that up with another extremely productive year, hitting 21 homers, knocking in 102 runs, scoring 86 times, and batting .296, en route to earning All-Star honors for the second time in 2007.

After being shifted to third base prior to the start of the 2008 campaign to make room at short for the newly acquired Edgar Renteria, Guillen ended up appearing in only 113 games. Yet, even though he experienced a marked decrease in offensive production, finishing the year with a batting average of .286 and just 10 homers and 54 RBIs, Guillen made the All-Star team for the third time in his career. He spent three more injury-marred seasons in Detroit, never again appearing in more than 81 games, and spending most of his time alternating between left field, second base, and the DH spot. Limited by a left shoulder problem to 81 games and 322 plate appearances in 2009, Guillen batted just .242, with 11 home runs and 41 RBIs. An ailing left knee prevented Guillen from appearing in more than 68 games the following year, finally forcing him to undergo microfracture surgery in September. He subsequently struggled upon his return to the Tigers in July 2011, batting just .232, hitting only 3 homers, and driving in just 13 runs the remainder of the year in a backup role. After not being offered a contract by the Tigers at season's end, Guillen signed a minor league deal with the Seattle Mariners. However, he ultimately elected to retire instead, announcing his decision on March 6, 2012.

In making his announcement, Guillen told Geoff Baker of the *Seattle Times*, "It's a tough decision for me and for my family and everybody. Because I tried to come back, but I can't." Guillen added, "You have to keep your head up and be in the right position to keep going. But at this time, your body tells you, you know? . . . It's hard. It's funny, but I don't feel ready (to retire)."

Guillen ended his playing career with 124 home runs, 660 runs batted in, 733 runs scored, 1,331 hits, 266 doubles, 51 triples, a .285 batting average, a .355 on-base percentage, and a .443 slugging percentage. During his time in Detroit, he hit 95 homers, drove in 449 runs, scored 469 times, accumulated 892 hits, 186 doubles, and 35 triples, batted .297, compiled a .366 on-base percentage, and posted a .476 slugging percentage. More important, he helped bring leadership and stability to a young Tigers team that made the playoffs twice and advanced to the World Series once in his eight years in Motown.

TIGERS CAREER HIGHLIGHTS

Best Season

Guillen had one of his most productive seasons for the Tigers in 2007, when he batted .296, scored 86 runs, and established career highs with 21 home runs and 102 RBIs. However, he actually posted slightly better overall numbers in both 2004 and 2006. Guillen concluded the first of those campaigns with 20 homers, 97 RBIs, 97 runs scored, a .318 batting average, and a career-best 10 triples and .921 OPS. Two years later, he hit 19 home runs, knocked in 85 runs, posted an OPS of .920 that led all major league shortstops, and established career-high marks in runs scored (100), hits (174), doubles (41), stolen bases (20), and batting average (.320), en route to earning his only top-10 finish in the A.L. MVP voting. Either of those years would make an excellent choice. I ultimately settled on 2006, though, because Guillen appeared in 17 more games than he did in 2004 (153 to 136) and the Tigers ended up advancing to the World Series after winning 23 more games over the course of the regular season than they did two years earlier (95 to 72).

Memorable Moments/Greatest Performances

Guillen had one of his biggest days at the plate for the Tigers on April 29, 2006, when he helped lead them to an 18–1 mauling of the Minnesota Twins by going 3-for-4, with 2 homers, a double, 5 RBIs, and 3 runs scored. Three months later, on August 1, Guillen became the 10th player in Tigers history to hit for the cycle when he accomplished the feat during a 10–4 win over the Tampa Bay Devil Rays. He also stole a base, knocked in 2 runs, and scored 3 times during the contest. However, Guillen delivered arguably his most memorable hit of the year on September 12, when he greeted Texas reliever Ron Mahay with a leadoff home run in the bottom of the ninth inning, giving the Tigers a 3–2 walk-off win over the Rangers. Guillen also homered earlier in the contest.

Guillen came through in the clutch again on August 24, 2007, when he ended a 4-hour, 24-minute marathon against the Yankees by delivering a two-out, three-run homer off reliever Sean Henn in the bottom of the eleventh inning to give the Tigers a 9–6 walk-off win.

Although Guillen struggled against Oakland in the 2006 ALCS, he came up with a number of big hits against the Yankees in the ALDS and the Cardinals in the World Series. With New York holding a 1-0 lead over Detroit in the ALDS and ahead by a score of 3–2 in Game Two, Guillen delivered arguably the pivotal blow of the Series when he hit a game-tying home run off Mike Mussina in the top of the sixth inning. The Tigers scored again in the ensuing frame, en route to posting a 4–3 victory that evened the Series at a game apiece. They won the next two games, with Guillen finishing the Series with a homer, 2 RBIs, 3 runs scored, and 8 hits in 14 official at-bats, for a .571 batting average. Even though the Tigers subsequently lost the World Series to St. Louis in five games, Guillen's play proved to be one of the team's few bright spots. In addition to playing flawless defense, he batted .353, with 2 RBIs and 2 runs scored.

NOTABLE ACHIEVEMENTS

- Batted over .300 three times.
- Hit more than 20 home runs twice.
- Knocked in more than 100 runs once (102 in 2007).

- Scored 100 runs in 2006.
- Surpassed 200 hits once (212 in 2011).
- Finished in double digits in triples once (10 in 2004).
- Surpassed 30 doubles three times, topping 40 two-baggers once (41 in 2006).
- Stole 20 bases in 2006.
- Compiled on-base percentage of .400 in 2006.
- Posted slugging percentage in excess of .500 three times.
- Three-time A.L. All-Star (2004, 2007, 2008).
- 2006 A.L. champion.

Summary and Honorable Mentions: The Next 25

Having identified the 50 greatest players in Detroit Tigers history, the time has come to select the best of the best. Based on the rankings contained in this book, the members of the Tigers all-time team are listed below. Our squad includes the top player at each position, along with a pitching staff that features a five-man starting rotation and a closer. Our starting lineup also includes a designated hitter. Also listed are the members of the second team, whose closer was taken from the list of honorable mentions that will soon follow.

FIRST TEAM STARTING LINEUP

Player	Position
Ty Cobb	CF
Charlie Gehringer	2B
Miguel Cabrera	3B
Hank Greenberg	1B
Harry Heilmann	DH
Al Kaline	RF
Sam Crawford	LF
Alan Trammell	SS
Bill Freehan	C

FIRST TEAM PITCHING STAFF

Player	Position
Justin Verlander	SP
Hal Newhouser	SP

Player	Position
Jack Morris	SP
Mickey Lolich	SP
Tommy Bridges	SP
John Hiller	CL

SECOND TEAM STARTING LINEUP

Player	Position
Harvey Kuenn	CF
Lou Whitaker	2B
George Kell	3B
Bobby Veach	LF
Cecil Fielder	DH
Norm Cash	1B
Lance Parrish	C
Kirk Gibson	RF
Travis Fryman	SS

SECOND TEAM PITCHING STAFF

Player	Position
Hooks Dauss	SP
Denny McLain	SP
Jim Bunning	SP
Frank Lary	SP
Max Scherzer	SP
Willie Hernandez	CL

Although I limited my earlier rankings to the top 50 players in Tigers history, many other fine players have performed for the fans of the Motor City over the years, some of whom narrowly missed making the final cut. Following is a list of those players deserving of an honorable mention. These are the men I deemed worthy of being slotted into positions 51 to 75 in the overall rankings. The statistics they compiled during their time in Detroit and their most notable achievements as a member of the Tigers are also included.

Courtesy of RMYauctions.com

51. Heinie Manush (OF, 1923–1927)

Tigers Numbers: 38 HR, 345 RBIs, 385 Runs Scored, 674 Hits, 124 Doubles, 42 Triples, 48 SB, .321 AVG, .379 OBP, .475 SLG PCT.
Notable Achievements:
Batted over .300 three times, topping .370 once (.378 in 1926).
Scored more than 100 runs once (102 in 1927).
Finished in double digits in triples once (18 in 1927).
Surpassed 30 doubles twice.
Compiled on-base percentage in excess of .400 twice.
Posted slugging percentage in excess of .500 once (.564 in 1926).
Led the American League with .378 batting average in 1926.
Tied for seventh in Tigers history with .321 career batting average.
Finished fifth in 1926 A.L. MVP voting.
Elected to Baseball Hall of Fame by members of Veterans Committee in 1964.

52. Ivan Rodriguez (C, 2004–2008)

Tigers Numbers: 62 HR, 300 RBIs, 300 Runs Scored, 709 Hits, 140 Doubles, 17 Triples, 30 SB, .298 AVG, .328 OBP, .449 SLG PCT.
Notable Achievements:
Batted over .300 twice, topping .330 once (.334 in 2004).
Surpassed 30 doubles three times.
Posted slugging percentage in excess of .500 once (.510 in 2004).
Led A.L. catchers in fielding percentage once and caught-stealing percentage twice.
Three-time Gold Glove winner.
2004 Silver Slugger winner.
Two-time *Sporting News* All-Star selection (2004, 2005).
Four-time A.L. All-Star (2004–2007).
2006 A.L. champion.

53. Dan Petry (P, 1979–1987, 1990–1991)

Tigers Numbers: Record: 119–93, .561 Win Pct., 3.84 ERA, 48 CG, 10 Shutouts, 1,843 IP, 957 Strikeouts, 1.349 WHIP
Notable Achievements:
Surpassed 15 victories four times, topping 18 wins twice.
Threw more than 200 innings four times.
Led A.L. pitchers with 38 starts in 1983.
Led A.L. pitchers in putouts once and fielding percentage twice.
Tied for 10th in Tigers history with 274 games started.
Finished fifth in 1984 A.L. Cy Young voting.
1985 A.L. All-Star.
1984 A.L. champion.
1984 world champion.

54. Mickey Cochrane (C, 1934–1937)

Tigers Numbers: 11 HR, 152 RBIs, 218 Runs Scored, 335 Hits, 83 Doubles, 5 Triples, .313 AVG, .444 OBP, .430 SLG PCT.
Notable Achievements:
Batted over .300 three times.
Surpassed 30 doubles twice.

Courtesy of Boston Public Library,
Leslie Jones Collection

Compiled on-base percentage in excess of .400 four times.
1934 A.L. MVP.
Two-time *Sporting News* All-Star selection (1934, 1935).
Two-time A.L. All-Star (1934, 1935).
Two-time A.L. champion (1934, 1935).
1935 world champion.
Elected to Baseball Hall of Fame by members of BBWAA in 1947.

55. Willie Hernandez (P, 1984–1989)

Tigers Numbers: Record: 36–31, .537 Win Pct., 2.98 ERA, 120 Saves,
   1.121 WHIP
Notable Achievements:
Saved more than 30 games twice (1984, 1985).
Compiled ERA under 3.00 twice, posting mark below 2.00 once (1.92 in
   1984).

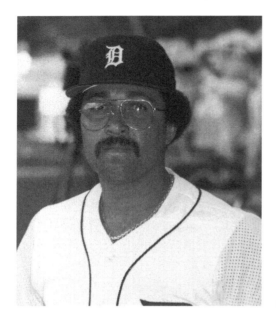

Courtesy of Tiger Stadium Ushers

Posted winning percentage in excess of .700 once (.750 in 1984).
Threw more than 100 innings twice (1984, 1985).
Compiled WHIP under 1.000 twice (1984, 1985).
Led A.L. pitchers with 80 appearances in 1984.
Ranks fourth in Tigers history with 120 career saves.
Holds Tigers single-season record for lowest WHIP (0.900 in 1985).
1984 A.L. Cy Young Award winner.
1984 A.L. MVP.
1984 *Sporting News* Pitcher of the Year.
1984 *Sporting News* All-Star selection.
Three-time A.L. All-Star (1984–86).
1984 A.L. champion.
1984 world champion.

56. Tony Phillips (2B, 3B, SS, OF, 1990–1994)

Tigers Numbers: 61 HR, 309 RBIs, 502 Runs Scored, 771 Hits, 129 Doubles, 15 Triples, 70 SB, .281 AVG, .395 OBP, .405 SLG PCT.
Notable Achievements:
Batted over .300 once (.313 in 1993).
Scored more than 100 runs twice.

Surpassed 30 doubles once (32 in 1992).
Walked more than 100 times twice.
Compiled on-base percentage in excess of .400 twice.
Led the American League in runs scored once and walks once.
Led A.L. left fielders in putouts once.

57. Placido Polanco (2B, 2005–2009)

Tigers Numbers: 37 HR, 285 RBIs, 393 Runs Scored, 806 Hits, 139 Doubles, 13 Triples, 26 SB, .311 AVG, .355 OBP, .418 SLG PCT.
Notable Achievements:
Batted over .300 three times, topping .330 twice.
Scored more than 100 runs once (105 in 2007).
Topped 200 hits once (200 in 2007).
Surpassed 30 doubles three times.
Led A.L. second basemen in putouts once and fielding percentage twice.
2006 ALCS MVP.
Two-time Gold Glove winner (2007, 2009).
2007 Silver Slugger winner.
2007 A.L. All-Star.
2006 A.L. champion.

58. Curtis Granderson (OF, 2004–2009)

Tigers Numbers: 102 HR, 299 RBIs, 435 Runs Scored, 702 Hits, 125 Doubles, 57 Triples, 67 SB, .272 AVG, .344 OBP, .484 SLG PCT.
Notable Achievements:
Hit more than 20 home runs three times, topping 30 homers once (30 in 2009).
Batted over .300 once (.302 in 2007).
Scored more than 100 runs twice (2007, 2008).
Finished in double digits in triples twice, topping 20 three-baggers once (23 in 2007).
Surpassed 30 doubles twice.
Stole more than 20 bases twice.
Posted slugging percentage in excess of .500 once (.552 in 2007).
Topped 20 homers, 20 triples, 20 doubles, 20 steals in 2007.
Led A.L. in triples twice.

Led A.L. outfielders in putouts once and fielding percentage once.
2009 A.L. All-Star.
2006 A.L. champion.

59. Virgil Trucks (P, 1941–1943, 1945–1952, 1956)

Tigers Numbers: Record: 114–96, .543 Win Pct., 3.50 ERA, 84 CG, 20
    Shutouts, 1,800⅔ IP, 1,046 Strikeouts, 1.305 WHIP
Notable Achievements:
Posted double-digit wins seven times, surpassing 16 victories twice.
Compiled ERA under 3.00 three times.
Threw more than 200 innings four times.
Led A.L. pitchers in shutouts once and strikeouts once.
Led A.L. pitchers in fielding percentage twice.
Ranks 10th in Tigers history with 20 career shutouts.
Threw two no-hitters in one year (5/15/52, 8/25/52).
1949 A.L. All-Star.
1945 A.L. champion.
1945 world champion.

Courtesy of MearsOnlineAuctions.com

60. Vic Wertz (OF, 1B, 1947–1952, 1961–1963)

Tigers Numbers: 109 HR, 531 RBIs, 443 Runs Scored, 798 Hits, 145 Doubles, 30 Triples, .286 AVG, .376 OBP, .476 SLG PCT.
Notable Achievements:
Hit more than 20 home runs three times.
Knocked in more than 100 runs twice, topping 120 RBIs both times.
Batted over .300 three times.
Surpassed 30 doubles once (37 in 1950).
Compiled on-base percentage in excess of .400 once (.408 in 1950).
Posted slugging percentage in excess of .500 twice.
Led A.L. with 155 games played in 1949.
Led A.L. right fielders in putouts twice.
Hit for cycle on 09/14/47.
Three-time A.L. All-Star (1949, 1951, 1952).

61. Gee Walker (OF, 1931–1937)

Tigers Numbers: 61 HR, 468 RBIs, 475 Runs Scored, 966 Hits, 216 Doubles, 32 Triples, 132 SB, .317 AVG, .351 OBP, .469 SLG PCT.

Gee Walker, Goose Goslin, and Jo-Jo White.
Courtesy of Boston Public Library, Leslie Jones Collection

Notable Achievements:
Batted over .300 five times, topping .320 three times.
Knocked in more than 100 runs once (113 in 1937).
Scored more than 100 runs twice.
Surpassed 200 hits once (213 in 1937).
Surpassed 30 doubles three times, topping 50 once (55 in 1936).
Stole more than 20 bases four times, swiping 30 bags in 1932.
Posted slugging percentage in excess of .500 once (.536 in 1936).
Led A.L. right fielders in assists once and double plays turned once.
Led A.L. left fielders in double plays turned once.
Ranks 11th in Tigers history with .317 career batting average.
Hit for cycle on 4/20/37.
1937 A.L. All-Star.
Two-time A.L. champion (1934, 1935).
1935 world champion.

62. Lu Blue (1B, 1921–1927)

Tigers Numbers: 19 HR, 407 RBIs, 669 Runs Scored, 1,002 Hits, 176 Doubles, 66 Triples, 85 SB, .295 AVG, .403 OBP, .403 SLG PCT.

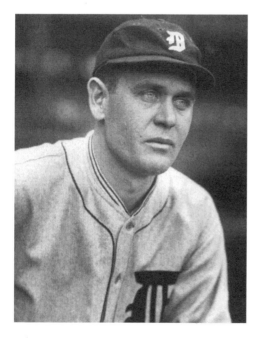

Courtesy of LegendaryAuctions.com

Notable Achievements:
Batted over .300 four times.
Scored more than 100 runs three times, topping 130 runs scored once (131 in 1922).
Finished in double digits in triples twice.
Surpassed 30 doubles twice.
Walked more than 100 times once (103 in 1921).
Compiled on-base percentage in excess of .400 five times.
Ranks among Tigers career leaders in on-base percentage (8th) and triples (10th).

63. Bob Fothergill (OF, 1922–1930)

Tigers Numbers: 26 HR, 447 RBIs, 381 Runs Scored, 823 Hits, 182 Doubles, 47 Triples, 36 SB, .337 AVG, .379 OBP, .482 SLG PCT.
Notable Achievements:
Batted over .300 eight times, topping .350 four times.
Knocked in more than 100 runs once (114 in 1927).
Finished in double digits in triples once (10 in 1928).

Courtesy of MearsOnlineAuctions.com

Surpassed 30 doubles twice.

Compiled on-base percentage in excess of .400 twice.

Posted slugging percentage in excess of .500 three times.

Ranks third in Tigers history with career batting average of .337.

Hit for cycle on 9/26/26.

64. Dale Alexander (1B, 1929–1932)

Tigers Numbers: 48 HR, 363 RBIs, 271 Runs Scored, 583 Hits, 123 Doubles, 26 Triples, .331 AVG, .391 OBP, .512 SLG PCT.

Notable Achievements:

Hit more than 20 home runs twice.

Knocked in more than 100 runs twice, topping 130 RBIs both times.

Batted over .300 three times, topping .320 all three times.

Scored more than 100 runs once (110 in 1929).

Surpassed 200 hits once (215 in 1929).

Finished in double digits in triples once (15 in 1929).

Surpassed 30 doubles three times, topping 40 two-baggers twice.

Compiled on-base percentage in excess of .400 twice.

Posted slugging percentage in excess of .500 twice.

Led the American League in hits once and games played twice.

Led A.L. first basemen in double plays turned once.

Ranks among Tigers career leaders in batting average (4th), slugging percentage (5th), and OPS (5th).

65. Victor Martinez (DH, 1B, C, 2011, 2013–14)

Tigers Numbers: 58 HR, 289 RBIs, 231 Runs Scored, 548 Hits, 109 Doubles, 0 Triples, .321 AVG, .381 OBP, .487 SLG PCT.

Notable Achievements:

Batted over .300 three times, topping .330 twice.

Hit more than 30 home runs once (32 in 2014).

Knocked in more than 100 runs twice.

Surpassed 30 doubles three times, reaching 40 once (2011).

Compiled on-base percentage in excess of .400 once (.409 in 2014).

Posted slugging percentage in excess of .500 once (.565 in 2014).

Led the American League with .409 on-base percentage and .974 OPS in 2014.

Courtesy of Keith Allison

Ranks among Tigers career leaders in batting average (7th) and OPS (8th). Finished second in 2014 A.L. MVP voting.

66. Steve Kemp (OF, 1977–1981)

Tigers Numbers: 89 HR, 422 RBIs, 378 Runs Scored, 711 Hits, 114 Doubles, 18 Triples, .284 AVG, .376 OBP, .450 SLG PCT.
Notable Achievements:
Hit more than 20 home runs twice.
Knocked in more than 100 runs twice.
Batted over .300 once (.318 in 1979).
Posted slugging percentage in excess of .500 once (.543 in 1979).
Led A.L. left fielders in: putouts once; assists once; and double plays turned twice.
1979 A.L. All-Star.

67. Mickey Stanley (OF, 1B, SS, 1964–1978)

Tigers Numbers: 117 HR, 500 RBIs, 641 Runs Scored, 1,243 Hits, 201 Doubles, 48 Triples, 44 SB, .248 AVG, .298 OBP, .377 SLG PCT.

Notable Achievements:
Finished in double digits in triples once (11 in 1970).
Led A.L. outfielders in fielding percentage twice.
Four-time Gold Glove winner (1968–1970, 1973).
1968 A.L. champion.
1968 world champion.

68. Todd Jones (P, 1997–2001, 2006–2008)

Tigers Numbers: Record: 23–32, .418 Win Pct., 4.07 ERA, 235 Saves, 1.456 WHIP
Notable Achievements:
Saved more than 30 games five times, topping 40 saves once (42 in 2000).
Posted winning percentage in excess of .800 once (.800 in 2008).
Led A.L. with 42 saves in 2000.
Holds Tigers career record with 235 saves.
Ranks sixth in Tigers history with 480 pitching appearances.
Finished fifth in 2000 A.L. Cy Young voting.
2000 A.L. All-Star.
2006 A.L. champion.

69. Mike Henneman (P, 1987–1995)

Tigers Numbers: Record: 57–34, .626 Win Pct., 3.05 ERA, 154 Saves, 1.305 WHIP
Notable Achievements:
Saved more than 20 games five times.
Won at least 10 games three times.
Compiled ERA under 3.00 four times, posting below 2.00 twice.
Posted winning percentage in excess of .700 three times.
Ranks among Tigers career leaders in: saves (2nd); winning percentage (6th); and pitching appearances (5th).
1989 A.L. All-Star.

70. Austin Jackson (OF, 2010–2014)

Tigers Numbers: 46 HR, 234 RBIs, 447 Runs Scored, 7430 Hits, 140 Doubles, 43 Triples, 78 SB, .277 AVG, .342 OBP, .413 SLG PCT.

Courtesy of Keith Allison

Notable Achievements:
Batted .300 in 2012.
Scored more than 100 runs twice.
Finished in double digits in triples three times.
Surpassed 30 doubles twice.
Stole more than 20 bases twice.
Led the American League in triples twice.
Finished second in 2010 A.L. Rookie of the Year voting.
2012 A.L. champion.

71. Rusty Staub (DH, OF, 1B, 1976–1979)

Tigers Numbers: 70 HR, 358 RBIs, 264 Runs Scored, 582 Hits, 104 Doubles, 8 Triples, .277 AVG, .353 OBP, .434 SLG PCT.
Notable Achievements:
Hit more than 20 home runs twice.
Knocked in more than 100 runs twice, topping 120 RBIs once (121 in 1978).
Surpassed 30 doubles twice.

Led A.L. with 161 games played in 1976.
Finished fifth in 1978 A.L. MVP voting.
1978 *Sporting News* All-Star selection.
1976 A.L. All-Star.

72. Darrell Evans (1B, 3B, DH, 1984–1988)

Tigers Numbers: 141 HR, 405 RBIs, 357 Runs Scored, 559 Hits, 72 Doubles, 1 Triple, .238 AVG, .357 OBP, .450 SLG PCT.
Notable Achievements:
Hit more than 20 home runs four times, topping 30 homers twice and 40 homers once (40 in 1985).
Walked 100 times in 1987.
Posted slugging percentage in excess of .500 twice.
Led A.L. with 40 home runs in 1985.
1984 A.L. champion.
1984 world champion.

Courtesy of MainlineAutographs.com

SUMMARY AND HONORABLE MENTIONS: THE NEXT 25 **345**

73. Damion Easley (2B, SS, 1996–2002)

Tigers Numbers: 104 HR, 400 RBIs, 456 Runs Scored, 803 Hits, 174 Doubles, 16 Triples, 81 SB, .260 AVG, .339 OBP, .428 SLG PCT.
Notable Achievements:
Hit more than 20 home runs three times.
Knocked in 100 runs in 1998.
Surpassed 30 doubles three times.
Stole more than 20 bases once (28 in 1997).
Led all A.L. players with 480 assists in 1998.
Led A.L. second basemen in: assists once; putouts once; fielding percentage twice; and double plays turned once.
Hit for cycle on 6/8/01.
1998 Silver Slugger winner.
1998 A.L. All-Star.

74. Jason Thompson (1B, 1976–1980)

Tigers Numbers: 98 HR, 354 RBIs, 279 Runs Scored, 565 Hits, 82 Doubles, 10 Triples, .256 AVG, .343 OBP, .436 SLG PCT.
Notable Achievements:
Hit more than 20 home runs three times, topping 30 homers once (31 in 1977).
Knocked in more than 100 runs once (105 in 1977).
Led A.L. first basemen in putouts once and double plays turned once.
Two-time A.L. All-Star (1977, 1978).

75. Joe Coleman (P, 1971–1976)

Tigers Numbers: Record: 88–73, .547 Win Pct., 3.82 ERA, 56 CG, 11 Shutouts, 1,407⅔ IP, 1,000 Strikeouts, 1.351 WHIP
Notable Achievements:
Won more than 20 games twice, posting 19 victories another time.
Compiled ERA under 3.00 once (2.80 in 1972).
Struck out more than 200 batters three times.
Threw more than 200 innings five straight times, surpassing 280 innings on four occasions.
1972 A.L. All-Star.

Glossary

ABBREVIATIONS AND STATISTICAL TERMS

AVG. Batting average. The number of hits divided by the number of at-bats.

CG. Complete games pitched.

CL. Closer.

ERA. Earned run average. The number of earned runs a pitcher gives up, per nine innings. This does not include runs that scored as a result of errors made in the field and is calculated by dividing the number of runs given up, by the number of innings pitched, and multiplying the result by 9.

HITS. Base hits. Awarded when a runner safely reaches at least first base upon a batted ball, if no error is recorded.

HR. Home runs. Fair ball hit over the fence, or one hit to a spot that allows the batter to circle the bases before the ball is returned to home plate.

IP. Innings pitched.

OBP. On-base percentage. Hits plus walks plus hit-by-pitches, divided by plate appearances.

OPS. On-base plus slugging. A hitter's on-base percentage added to his slugging percentage.

RBI. Runs batted in. Awarded to the batter when a runner scores upon a safely batted ball, a sacrifice, or a walk.

RUNS. Runs scored by a player.

SB. Stolen bases.

SLG PCT. Slugging percentage. The number of total bases earned by all singles, doubles, triples and home runs, divided by the total number of at-bats.

SO. Strikeouts.

SP. Starting pitcher.

WHIP. Walks plus hits per inning pitched. A pitcher's walks plus hits given up divided by innings pitched.

WIN PCT. Winning percentage. A pitcher's number of wins divided by his number of total decisions (i.e., wins plus losses).

Bibliography

BOOKS

DeMarco, Tony, et al. *The Sporting News Selects 50 Greatest Sluggers*. St. Louis: The Sporting News, 2000.

Shalin, Mike, and Neil Shalin. *Out by a Step: The 100 Best Players Not in the Baseball Hall of Fame*. Lanham, MD: Diamond Communications, 2002.

Thorn, John, and Palmer, Pete, eds., with Michael Gershman. *Total Baseball*. New York: HarperCollins, 1993.

Williams, Ted, with Jim Prime. *Ted Williams' Hit List*. Indianapolis, IN: Masters Press, 1996.

VIDEOS

The Glory of Their Times. Cappy Productions, 1985.

The Life and Times of Hank Greenberg. Twentieth-Century Fox, 2001.

The Sporting News' 100 Greatest Baseball Players. National Broadcasting Co., 1999.

Sports Century: Fifty Greatest Athletes—Ty Cobb. ESPN, 1999.

WEBSITES

The Ballplayers. BaseballLibrary.com (http://www.baseballlibrary.com/ballplayers).

Bio Project. SABR.org (http://www.sabr.org/bioproject).

Historical Stats. MLB.com (http://www.mlb.com/stats).

The Players. Baseball-Almanac.com (http://www.baseball-almanac.com/players).

The Players. Baseball-Reference.com (http://www.baseball-reference.com/players).

The Teams. Baseball-Reference.com (http://www.baseball-reference.com/teams).

The Sporting News All-Stars. BaseballChronology.com (http://www.baseballchronology .com/Baseball/Awards/TSN-AllStars.asp).

Index